SACRAMENTS, CEREMONIES AND THE STUART DIVINES

This book surveys developments in sacramental and liturgical discourse and discord, exploring the writings of English and Scottish divines, and focusing on baptism and the Lord's Supper. The reigns of James I and Charles I coincided with divergence and development in teaching on the sacraments in England and Scotland and with growing discord on liturgical texts and the ceremonial. Uniquely focusing on both nations in a single study, Bryan Spinks draws on theological treatises, sermons, catechisms, liturgical texts and writings by Scottish theologians hitherto neglected.

Exploring the European roots of the churches of England and Scotland and how they became entwined in developments culminating in the Solemn League and Covenant and Westminster Directory, this book presents an authoritative study of sacramental and liturgical debate, developments, and experiments during the Stuart period.

To
The Church of England
and
The Kirk of Scotland

ut unum sint

Sacraments, Ceremonies and the Stuart Divines

Sacramental theology and liturgy in England and Scotland
1603–1662

BRYAN D. SPINKS
Yale University Divinity School and Institute of Sacred Music, USA

Ashgate

Published by
Ashgate Publishing Limited
Gower House
Croft Road
Aldershot
Hants GU11 3HR
England

Ashgate Publishing Company
131 Main Street
Burlington, VT 05401-5600 USA

Ashgate website: http://www.ashgate.com

British Library Cataloguing in Publication Data
Spinks, Bryan D.
   Sacraments, ceremonies and the Stuart Divines : sacramental
   theology and liturgy in England and Scotland 1603–1662
   1.Sacraments - History of doctrines - 17th century
   2.Theology - Great Britain - History - 17th century
   3.Scotland - Church history - 17th century 4.England -
   Church history - 17th century
   I.Title
   274.1'06

Library of Congress Cataloging-in-Publication Data
Spinks, Bryan D.
   Sacraments, ceremonies and the Stuart Divines : sacramental theology and liturgy in
   England and Scotland 1603–1662 / Bryan D. Spinks.
      p. cm.
   Includes bibliographical references and index.
   ISBN 0-7546-1475-1
      1. Liturgics--Great Britain--History--17th century. 2. Great Britain--Church
   history--17th century. I. Title.

   BV193.G7 S75 2001
   264'.00941'09032—dc21

                                                                2001033586

ISBN 0 7546 1475 1

Typeset by Manton Typesetters, Louth, Lincolnshire, UK.
Printed in Great Britain by MPG Books Ltd, Bodmin, Cornwall.

Contents

List of Figures

Acknowledgements

This work had its origins in an invitation from the University of Oxford to deliver the Hensley Henson Lectures in the Trinity Term 2000. I am indebted to Professor Dairmaid MacCulloch and the Master and Fellows of St. Cross College, Oxford, for appointing me as a Visiting Fellow during May 2000, when the lectures were delivered, which gave me the opportunity to meet and talk with old friends and make new Oxford acquaintances. I am also grateful to Dairmaid for his encouragement to expand the lectures for publication. I was fortunate to be granted sabbatical leave by Yale University in the Fall semester 2000 which allowed me to undertake the additional research needed. I would also like to express gratitude for the award of a Lilly Theological Research grant through the Associated Theological Schools, which enabled me to visit the University of Aberdeen Special Collections, and Emmanuel College Library, Cambridge, to consult manuscripts, and allowed me to obtain photocopies of materials not accessible in New Haven. Dr Kenneth Fincham kindly read through the lectures, and saved me from a number of errors. He also kindly responded to a barrage of subsequent queries. Professor Iain Torrance supplied me with a number of texts, and drew my attention to the works of a number of Scottish divines, and has assisted in tracing portraits of some of them. The Revd Dr Gerry Gaeta balanced himself on a ladder on the balcony of the great hall in Magdalen College Oxford, to provide the photograph of the portrait of Henry Hammond.The staff of the Beinecke Library at Yale have been most helpful, and I must also thank Professor Paul Stuehrenberg and his staff at Yale Divinity Library for their assistance in acquiring books, microfilms and theses for consultation. My research assistants, Scott Howard and Kate Heichler, have helped track down portraits and engravings of some of the divines discussed in the book, checked quotations and read proofs.

Thanks are also due to a number of institutions for giving permission to reproduce photographs of the portraits: the University of Aberdeen; the University of St. Andrews; National Galleries, Scotland; the President and Fellows of Magdalen College Oxford, St. John's College, Oxford; Sidney Sussex College, Cambridge; Edinburgh University, and the Society of Antiquaries, London. Last but no means least, I wish to express thanks to Sarah Lloyd of Ashgate Publishing for help and encouragement with this project.

Bryan Spinks

Introduction

The subject matter of this book might well appear to be an instance of that category so aptly articulated by Qoheleth: 'Is there a thing of which it is said, "See this is new"? It has been already, in the ages before us' (Ecclesiastes 1:10 RSV). It is certainly the case that a number of excellent studies already exist relating to this subject. One may cite C.W. Dugmore's *Eucharistic Doctrine in England from Hooker to Waterland*, and E. Brookes Holifield's *The Covenant Sealed: The Development of Puritan Sacramental Theology in Old and New England 1570–1720*, as well as the more recent general treatments of select seventeenth century divines by Kenneth Stevenson.[1] Liturgical studies, too, have covered much of the terrain: the English material has been ably treated by Geoffrey Cuming, and some of the Scottish material by Gordon Donaldson.[2] I am indebted to all these endeavours, and I have indeed entered into their labour. Yet several interrelated reasons have prompted this fresh study.

First is the more recent evaluations of the policies and abilities of James VI and I. The older view of James as dull and inept has given way to one of a complex and clever politician, who deliberately played opposing factions against one another, and who was willing to change policies as his own interests and concerns changed. For example, W.B. Patterson's *King James VI and I and the Reunion of Christendom* investigates the remarkable ecumenical vision of this Stuart monarch.[3] Patterson comments:

> James was both a Protestant in the Calvinist tradition and an advocate of closer relations among all churches, including the Roman Catholic Church. His viewpoint was largely the result of his upbringing in Scotland during years of bitter sectarian conflict, but it also reflected his conviction that his was a religious faith based on scriptural revelation and consistent with the teachings of the ancient Church. Moreover, he believed that the liturgy, polity, and doctrinal standards of the Church of England were in the historic catholic tradition of Christianity. He therefore welcomed, even relished, religious discussions, and he worked towards the kind of organic unity which he believed the one, holy, catholic, and apostolic Church described in the Apostles' and Nicene Creed should exhibit. In the Europe of his day, moreover, he saw a resolution of differences between Protestants and Roman Catholics as imperative if a stable community of nations was to be created and sustained.[4]

Equally important are the studies of the Jacobean Court sermons by Peter McCollough and Lori Anne Ferrell; both provide an illuminating insight into the use made of preaching to promote royal policies and a particular view of monarchy.[5] Many of the published court sermons of James's reign addressed his problems as king of Scotland. Noting that a high proportion were by Lancelot Andrewes, and commenting upon the older view of Andrewes as the premier example of 'Anglicanism', Ferrell writes:

> In the context of the Jacobean court, Lancelot Andrewes more accurately functions as the representative voice of a small group of preachers whose styles of divinity challenged the predominant understanding of mainstream Church of England clergy at the turn of the seventeenth century ... Andrewes was allowed to expound upon his sacramentalist leanings (as were other like-minded preachers) at times when James was under attack for not reforming the Church sufficiently or for attempting to bring the Kirk into conformity.[6]

The picture which now emerges is of an astute monarch, with a clear idea of his divine call to kingship, and a far-sighted statesman who knew how and when to promote his cause through his preachers.

Second, the older studies operated with a clear division between the two nations, dealing with either England or Scotland; in addition, those studies treating England used the unhelpful Anglican/Puritan terminology, as though one was quite separate and opposed to the other.

As regards the separate, hermetically sealed treatments of England and Scotland, James was a monarch with an ambition to unite his two nations and churches.[7] That the latter was not an impossible goal has been made clearer by the acceptance that many, if not the majority, of clergy south of the border were 'Calvinist', or, more accurately, Reformed in their theology, and shared much with their Scottish brethren of what has been termed 'International Calvinism'.[8] We are not talking here of a 'pure' school of John Calvin, but the broad dissemination of ideas from the various Continental Reformers such as Bullinger, Vermigli, Ursinus and Beza, absorbed and adapted to the English and Scottish contexts. This 'International Calvinism' was not simplistic or monolithic, and as David Como argues in the context of the understanding of predestination, was often a 'negative consensus' – knowing what was unacceptable, pernicious and heterodox, but not necessarily always having a positive consensus.[9] While sharing a broad common theology, the sharpening differences in polity which Anthony Milton so carefully documented in the writings of the English clergy, which was at variance with the polity of many of the leading Scottish clergy headed by Andrew Melville and his successors, together with a different liturgical ethos, combined to make James's goal one which was fraught with difficulties.[10]

As regards the Anglican/Puritan terminology, the work of Patrick Collinson, Nicholas Tyacke, Kenneth Fincham and Peter Lake have rendered this, if not untenable, certainly undesirable and inaccurate.[11] The word 'puritan' emerged as a term of abuse and was used quite indiscriminately by those who were content with the status quo against any who espoused further reform, or tighter discipline.[12] It is true that some, such as William Bradshaw in England and Samuel Rutherford in Scotland, gloried in the term. However, Ferrell noted that at the beginning of James's reign some preachers regarded 'puritan' as those who advocated separatism, and 'moderation' meant royal and episcopal toleration of adiaphoric nonconformity, later sermons used the term against any who did not endorse full conformity with the liturgy, rubrics and canons of the Church of England. Those formerly 'moderate' were reclassified as 'puritan'.[13] As for the term 'Anglican', it is difficult to give this any precise definition prior to the Restoration Settlement of 1662. Most of those labelled 'puritan' in England prior to 1662 were members of the Church of

England, either remaining part of it, or never leaving it voluntarily.[14] David Mullan's recent book, *Scottish Puritanism 1590–1638*, which is otherwise excellent, is not altogether helpful in the present debate, particularly as he deals with the piety of Samuel Rutherford and John Forbes of Corse all under this one title. Stephen Foster's and Tom Webster's choice of 'godly' and 'godly clergy', and David Stevenson's 'Radical party' in the Kirk, in place of puritan, are a more helpful way of defining these churchmen.[15] In this study I have tried to avoid the term 'puritan', and have preferred 'godly', with further qualifications such as nonconformist Calvinists and conformist Calvinists, and Patristic Reformed churchmen.

In the light of these factors, my present narrative attempts to look at both sides of Hadrian's Wall, and to view the Stuart divines working within the parameters of a broadly common Reformed theology, transcended and aggravated by mutual national mistrust, different polities and different liturgical practices. James attempted to bring the two churches into some sort of uniformity by a one-sided ecclesiastical osmosis. His son Charles's attempt to impose conformity without consensus resulted in the reversal of the osmotic process, and led to the abolition of episcopacy in England and the development of the National Covenant to become the Solemn League and Covenant, binding the two nations and churches. The two churches were, for the period, tied together in their destiny.[16]

On either side of the border, there were disputes over ceremonies. At first sight this seems to be merely about things adiaphora, and of little consequence. But underneath there emerges unresolved questions about sacramental theology and the appropriate accompanying ceremonial. The Stuart divines of England and Scotland rejected the Roman Catholic doctrines of *ex opere operato* sacraments, transubstantiation and that the eucharist was a propitiatory sacrifice. They also rejected the Lutheran teaching on sacraments, and the 'bare signs' associated with Zwingli. They all agreed that sacraments are signs and seals which exhibit. But behind the common terminology there emerged a tension over whether a sacrament is in some sense an instrument which causes the *res* itself. There is a divergence over the place of regeneration and the rite of baptism, and whether the elements of the sacraments are seals of grace given, or instruments which convey grace. All agreed that the eucharist was a commemoration or representation of the one sacrifice; but a widening divergence emerges between those who view it as a manward representation, focused in the fraction of the bread and the libation of wine; and those who regarded it also as a Godward action, re-presented in the whole action and prayers of the rite. This divergence intensified as certain divines placed more weight on patristic authority than upon the magisterial Reformers, and attempted to reintroduce observances which had fallen into disuse at the Reformation.

The method used in this study is by way of narrating the circumstances of the ceremonial and liturgical controversies alongside the teaching of certain selected divines, presented as a series of cameos or vignettes within the narrative. This inevitably falls under what David Hall has identified as a 'seminary history', but it does so unashamedly and without repentance.[17] As far as it is possible, it is a chronological narrative, though certain works treated were reprinted throughout the period and beyond, and some works, though representative of their time, were posthumously published.

The work is in certain respects a sequel to my earlier book, *Two Faces of Elizabeth Anglican Theology. Sacraments and Salvation in the Thought of William Perkins and Richard Hooker* (Lanham and London, 1999). In that book it was possible to treat the theologies of the sacraments against a broader systematic theology or *Ordo Salutis* presented in the many works of those two divines. In this work, consideration of an individual's broader theological position is not possible, both on account of space, and also because many of the divines wrote only occasional writings. In that respect, the study is partial, and cannot present the sacramental discussion within the wider interlocking theology of the divines discussed.

In the introduction to my earlier work, I suggested that some of the portraits of the ancestors of Anglicanism have been removed and hidden away – one being William Perkins. This study presents the teachings – and in some cases the portraits too – of some of those 'hidden' seventeenth-century divines; it also introduces some of the less familiar but no less important Scottish faces. Thus, *Sacraments, Ceremonies and the Stuart Divines*.

New Haven
Feast of the Purification, 2001

Notes

1 Dugmore, 1942; Holifield, 1974; Stevenson, 1994; 1997.
2 Cuming, 1983; Donaldson, 1954.
3 Patterson, 1997.
4 Ibid., p.342.
5 McCullough, 1998; Ferrell, 1998.
6 Ferrell, 1998, p.171.
7 See Galloway, 1986; Lee, 1990; Morrill, 1994, pp.209–237; Russell, 1994, pp.238–56.
8 Tyacke, 1987; Fincham, 1993. The qualification by White, 1992 needs to be taken into account. For justification of the term 'International Calvinism' see Prestwich, 1985. See also Mullan, 1995.
9 Como, 2000, pp.64–87.
10 Milton, 1995; MacDonald, 1998.
11 Collinson, 1967; Tyacke, 1973; Fincham, 1990; Lake, 1988a.
12 See, for example, Morgan, 1986; Lake, 1993.
13 Ferrell, 1998; see also Fincham, 2000.
14 John Cotton and other New Englanders hoped that the (Congregational) Churches of New England would be an example to show what the Church of England really should be, and they did not regard themselves as disloyal to the 'Anglicanism' they envisaged.
15 Foster, 1978; Webster, 1997; Stevenson, 1974b.
16 See Hirst, 1999, for an overview.
17 Hall, 1987, pp.195, 198.

Chapter 1

The Sacramental Legacy of the Sixteenth-Century Reformation

Continental Reformers: Divergent Sacramental Theologies and Nuanced Terminologies

In urging William Bedell, Bishop of Kilmore, to accept the view that in the sacraments God 'doth offer and exhibit the grace it signifieth', Dr Samuel Ward, the Master of Sidney Sussex College, Cambridge, buttressed his argument thus:

> For as Mr.Beza saith in Col.Mompel. 'Obsignari non potest quod non habetur'. Ursin. Cat.Edit.Cant. 'Sacramentum est opus Dei erga nos, in quo dat aliquid scilicet signa et res signatas, et in quo testatur et se nobis offerre ac dare sua beneficia', et mox 'Baptismus ac coena Domini sunt sacramenta, quia sunt opus Dei qui aliquid ni iis nobis dat et se dare testatur'. – Vid. etiam Calvin.Instit.[1]

Ward, writing in the late 1620s, felt it necessary to anchor his views in the teaching of sixteenth-century Reformed authorities, and cited three authorities whose views he believed confirmed his own. Ward's appeal is a reminder that the seventeenth-century divines of both the English and Scottish churches were heirs to the six-teenth-century Reformation, and received and built upon that heritage. However, this heritage included divergent views on sacramental theology. The differences between Reformers who were otherwise thought to be in agreement – differences which included different understandings and uses of the same terminology – were reproduced by the sixteenth-century English and Scottish divines, and their seventeenth century successors.

The Lutheran/Reformed Divide

In *The Babylonian Captivity of the Church* (1520), Luther had attacked the status of seven church rites as sacraments, and insisted that there were in fact only three rites which qualified for this status – baptism, the mass and confession. For something to be called a sacrament, it needed divine warrant, institution or mandate. It was a word with a promise attached. In this work, and subsequent writings, he attacked the *ex opere operato* concept of sacraments, and the Aristotelian conceptual framework within which the doctrine of transubstantiation was expounded. However, against the fanatics such as Carlstadt, he insisted on an objectivity in the sacraments. Baptism gave remission of sin – original sin, which included original guilt – and although faith was important, faith was ultimately a gift of God, and the efficacy of baptism rested solely on the promise of God.[2] The mass was not a

1

sacrifice offered to God, but a gift which God offers the church, and which the church receives. Nevertheless, even though rejecting transubstantiation, Luther insisted that the bread and wine, by virtue of God's promise – and God does not lie – become the body and blood of Christ. The Risen Christ's body, by virtue of the divinity, is not restricted in one place, and thus can be present where God so chooses. Christ is therefore present bodily in the bread and wine. 'This is my Body' is to be taken at face value.

The Wittenberg reformer found himself battling on two sacramental fronts: against the Roman view of *ex opere operato* grace, and transubstantiation on the one hand; and against the 'spiritualising' of those he called the 'Schwärmer' on the other. Amongst the latter was the Zurich reformer, Ulrich Zwingli, who gradually articulated a very different sacramental theology to Luther. The word *sacramentum*, so Zwingli argued in 1523, is derived from the Latin word for an oath, and he was reluctant to use the word.[3] A sacrament is a sure sign or seal. Sacraments, according to Zwingli, were best understood as badges, or tokens of Christian profession, rather like the livery worn by a soldier. Furthermore, if the word is to be applied to ecclesiastical rites, there are but two: baptism and the Lord's Supper. He thus wrote: 'a sacrament is nothing else than an initiatory ceremony or a pledging. For just as those who were about to enter upon litigation deposited a certain amount of money, which could not be taken away except by the winner, so those who are initiated by sacraments bind and pledge themselves, and, as it were, seal a contract not to draw back.'[4]

Zwingli was heavily indebted to Neoplatonism, and drove a sharp dualism between sign and that which is signified (*res*) in the sacraments. For Zwingli, original sin was to be understood as a disease or condition by which humans are prone to sin, but they do not inherit original guilt. Baptism was less about removing sin than entering the church. After wavering on the question of infant baptism, he launched an attack on the Anabaptists of Zurich, and defended infant baptism on analogy with circumcision in the Old Testament. Baptism was into the covenant, and infants were baptised because their parents were already in the covenant. But salvation came not through baptism, but through faith and the Holy Spirit. On the question of the Lord's Supper, Zwingli had been influenced by the Dutchman, Cornelius Hoen, who argued that in the statement 'This is my Body', the force of the Latin *est* should be taken as 'signifies' or 'stands for'. Zwingli was adamant that earthly elements – be it the water used in baptism, or the bread and wine of the Lord's Supper – cannot carry the spiritual or divine. The bread and wine of the Lord's Supper contained no divine presence, but were to provoke faith. The Supper was a 'memorial', as well as an occasion 'so that we may testify to all men that we are one body and one brotherhood'.[5] Thus a clear rift opened up between the Wittenbergers, for whom sacraments, be they three or two, conveyed and gave something by virtue of the promise attached; and the Zurichers (and Oecolampadius at Basel) for whom sacraments, even though mandated, were the church's obedient response to God to inspire faith and to testify that we pledge ourselves to Christ. For Zwingli, sacraments are not channels of the Spirit to give grace, for the Spirit needs no channel. At very best, sacraments are only signs of grace already given.

These two sharply differing approaches to sacraments – rooted in concepts of God and Christology – were brought together in dialogue at the Colloquy of

Marburg in 1529, where it was hoped that Luther and Zwingli in face-to-face discussion might work out some compromise. In the event, the differences on baptism were not explored, and the focal point was whether and in what manner Christ was present in the elements of bread and wine at the Lord's Supper. Zwingli argued from John 6 that a figurative interpretation was to be given to the words 'This is my Body', whereas Luther held firm that these words were to be taken at face value, and were non-negotiable. Thus there emerged one of what would become many differences between the Wittenbergers, or Lutherans, and the Swiss, or Reformed.

Whether Zwingli's Neoplatonist doctrine, usefully termed 'symbolic memorialism' by Brian Gerrish, might have developed to overcome the sharp dualism he created was rendered an unanswerable question by his death at Cappel in 1531.[6] However, others whose theology was either unconsciously or consciously Reformed rather than Lutheran, found Zwingli's sacramental theology (shared by Oecolampadius at Basel and Guillaume Farel of Bern, Neuchâtel and Geneva), an inadequate one. Some of these sought to develop a mediating position between Zwingli and Luther. As they did so, we find a number of terms and descriptions pressed into use, though different Reformers seem to have meant different things by them. In this development, as well as nuanced differences between Reformers, there emerged a distinct difference between the Genevan approach, represented by John Calvin, and the Zurich approach, represented by Zwingli's successor, Heinrich Bullinger. These have been usefully characterised by Gerrish by the terms 'symbolic instrumentalism' and 'symbolic parallelism' respectively.[7] Gerrish himself noted that these were not exclusive categories, and some divines and documents combine them with different degrees of success and emphasis. Nevertheless, though not water-tight definitions, his categories serve as useful benchmarks.

Martin Bucer: Developing Theologies and Mediation

The Strasbourg reformer Martin Bucer was a Dominican priest, and initially aligned himself with Wittenberg, for which he was excommunicated by the Bishop of Speyer. He came to Strasbourg in 1524, and remained there until the Interim of 1548. Bucer accepted the invitation of Archbishop Thomas Cranmer to come to England, and from 1549 until his death in 1551, he was Regius Professor of Divinity at Cambridge. Through his reputation, even in this short time, he exerted considerable theological influence upon many English adherents of Reformation doctrine.

Although initially 'Lutheran', by 1524 Bucer had adopted the sacramental dualism of Zwingli and Oecolampadius. However, he was an ardent ecumenist, and his experience as an observer at Marburg seems to have inspired him to find a compromise position between Luther and Zwingli. Thus both Peter Stephens and René Bornert posit two periods of sacramental thinking for Bucer: the period 1523–30, characterised by a dualism in which the interior working of the Spirit is sharply divided from the exterior sacramental rite; and 1530–51, when the inward and outward are brought closer together and integrated.[8] Thus in his *Commentary on Matthew* in 1527, Bucer argued that it is the Lord who accomplishes inwardly by the Spirit what is signified by the sign. In his *Commentary on Ephesians* he stated that it is not the sacraments which are the seal of Christians, but the Holy Spirit. In his *Grund und Ursach* (1524), Bucer denied that God binds grace to water in baptism, and in the *Commentary on Matthew* rejected the idea that 'the word of the person baptizing is a vehicle of the Holy Spirit, by which he is conveyed into the water, which is then not water, but is really the Holy Spirit, which at once purges the baptized infant of all sin, giving faith and everything.' [9] In *Grund und Ursach* he said of the Supper: 'The Lord commanded the bread to be eaten and the cup to be drunk, and directed and commanded [to go] at once from the bodily to the spirit, to remember him … The Lord has given nothing bodily in holy communion except eating and drinking, and that for the sake of the spiritual, that is, his remembrance.' [10] And in the *Apologia* (1526), Bucer stated that Christ was able by means of bread and wine to give his body and blood to his own truly and yet spiritually, without any real change of the bread and wine.[11] Bucer seems to wish to say more than Zwingli in terms of the necessity of the sacraments, but like the Zurich Reformer, cleaves sign and thing signified wide apart. The physical cannot mediate the spiritual. The two may be parallel, but are quite different and distinct.

However, after Marburg, Bucer seems to have attempted to draw together sign and signified, as a result of his own further thinking, and in an attempt to bring together the divided Protestant camps. Over the course of time he would introduce a variety of terms to attempt to draw together sign and signified. Bornert comments: 'The sacraments, he says, are not only external signs, but also instruments, channels, organs of the reality of the signs. They present (*praesentare, zustellen*), they offer (*offere, anbieten*), they give (*dare, reichen, darreichen, dargeben, schenken*), they communicate (*communicare, übergehen*) the spiritual gift which the faithful receive (*recipere, empfangen*) by faith.' [12]

Already in 1527, Bucer had started to use the term *exhibere/furtragen*, which becomes a key term. David Wright has noted that in the context in which it is used it can only mean 'confer', 'impart', 'bestow', and from the mid-1530s Bucer instinctively attributed to the rite of baptism itself what a decade earlier he had reserved for the baptism of Christ or the Spirit. Indeed, Wright notes that for Bucer, baptism both signifies and exhibits to adults, but because infants lack consciousness of the rite, to them it exhibits only.[13] There is a certain objectivity here which is new. In the *Catechism* (1534) he wrote:

T.   Why are they called sacraments?
C.   Because in and with these visible signs, God gives and delivers his invisible and hidden grace and the redemption of Christ.
T.   How can water and the outward word, with which baptism is given, regenerate people, renew them with the Holy Spirit, incorporate them in Christ, clothe them with him, and make them participators in his death?
C.   Our Lord Jesus, our high priest and saviour, acts and accomplishes all this through his Holy Spirit. He uses for it the ministry of the church, in outward words and signs. Therefore they are called sacraments and *mysteria*, that is holy secrets – that while one thing happens inwardly through the power of Christ, one sees another outwardly in the ministry of the church … .
T.   He acts in the sacraments. Therefore they are called sacraments of Christ, not of his minister.[14]

In the *Gospels* 1536 he wrote: 'the sacraments, which are as it were visible gospels, instituted by Christ the Lord, so that he may communicate his redemption to us through them. Thus it is quite clear that they are in a certain way instruments and channels of the Spirit and his grace.'[15] Bucer believed that his views accorded with the Lutheran view as he interpreted it, and in the same year he endorsed the Wittenberg Concordat. Concerning its statements on the eucharist he explained: 'the body and blood of Christ himself are truly present, not just *effective*, powerfully, effectively, spiritually, but *vere, substantialiter, essentialiter*, essentially, and truly, and are given and received with bread and wine.'[16]

However, unlike Luther, for Bucer 'with' was not interchangeable with 'under' and 'in'. Indeed, rather than reconciling Wittenberg and Zurich, Bucer had created another distinct theology of sacraments. Furthermore, although Bucer claimed that his later writing only made clear what he had always attempted to say, others have perceived a definite change of mind, or development in his theology. Thus anyone who had read the early Bucer, but not the later Bucer, might well conclude that the Strasbourg Reformer was at one with the Zurichers.

French Mediation Between Wittenberg and Zurich: John Calvin's Symbolic Instrumentalism

In his celebrated *Institutes of the Christian Religion* of 1536, begun at Angoulême and completed at Basel, the young French reformer John Calvin outlined a theology of sacraments which was inspired by Augustine, was respectful to Luther, and a little suspicious of the Zurich approach.[17] In this first edition, Calvin offered two definitions of a sacrament: an outward sign by which God represents and attests his good will towards us; and a testimony of God's grace declared by an outward sign. A sacrament never lacks a preceding promise, and is attached to the promise to confirm and seal it.[18] Against those who say that sacraments add nothing to the word, Calvin explained: 'the seals attached to government documents and other public acts are nothing taken by themselves, for they would be attached in vain if the parchment had nothing written on it. Yet, added to the writing, they do not on that account fail to confirm and seal what is written.'[19] But he also refuted the idea that a sacrament was an oath like that taken by a soldier.[20] Here Calvin seems to take the Lutheran idea of promise, and also the Zurich stress on outward sign, and seal and confirmation, but he distances himself from Zwingli's idea of oath and also, when discussing baptism, a badge. In baptism, sins are washed and we are made righteous by imputation. Ministers are ministers of the outward rite, but Christ is the minister of inward grace. In the Lord's Supper, or eucharist, we are spiritually fed by the Lord's goodness, and give thanks for his kindness. The body and blood of the Lord are 'represented under bread and wine'.[21] However, the chief function of the elements is not to exhibit to us the body of Christ, but as the seal to confirm the promise. Having paid respect to Luther's idea of promise, Calvin here took issue with the idea of ubiquity of the risen body of Christ, and rejected as 'subtle' (with the understanding of seriously mistaken) those who speak of Christ being 'really' or 'substantially' present.

In the same year as the publication of the 1536 *Institutes*, Calvin was persuaded by Farel to stay in Geneva and assist the reformation there. Farel's influence may therefore account for the fact that Calvin's writings between 1537 and 1539 show an increased tendency to distinguish between the outward and the inward – as in the earlier Bucer, and as in Farel's own sacramental teaching.[22] In the 1539 edition of the *Institutes*, we find infant baptism defended on the same grounds as in Zurich, namely covenant and circumcision.

However, in 1538, Farel and Calvin were expelled from Geneva, and Calvin accepted the call as pastor to the French congregation at Strasbourg, and here he seems to have come under the influence of Bucer. Not only did the later Calvin adopt the terminology of Bucer; he also gave the teaching far greater precision and clarity than Bucer was able to do. This is illustrated not only in his 1541 *Short Treatise on the Lord's Supper*, but also in the definitive 1559 edition of the *Institutes*. In the *Short Treatise*, Calvin works with a clear christological basis, the Chalcedonian rule, that humanity and divinity are neither separate, nor confused. Thus he accused Luther of not being clear about local presence, and he accused the Swiss of being far too negative. Important for Calvin was the implication of '*sursum corda*' in the old Mass preface; whereas the schoolmen and Luther seemed to wish to call Christ down from heaven to the elements (*katabasis*), Calvin believed that the Holy Spirit used sacraments so that we might be lifted to heaven where Christ is (*anabasis*). Using the terminology, but not the implications of Aquinas, Calvin could assert that sacraments are 'as instruments' by which the body and blood of Christ are distributed to us.[23] He explained this further in *Institute* 4.14.12:

> God uses the means and instruments which he sees to be expedient, in order that all things may be subservient to his glory, he being the Lord and disposer of all. Therefore, as by bread and other aliment he feeds our bodies, as by the sun he illumines, and by fire gives warmth to the world, and yet bread, sun, and fire are nothing, save inasmuch as they are instruments under which he dispenses his blessings to us; so in like manner he spiritually nourishes our faith by means of the sacraments, whose only office is to make his promises visible to our eye, or rather, to be pledges of his promises.[24]

The sacramental signs are instruments which themselves do not cause anything, but which God uses to give us the reality he promises. They are instruments through which God works as he pleases.[25] The *Genevan Catechism* taught:

> M: Then you judge the power and efficacy of a sacrament not to lie in the external element, but wholly to emanate from the Spirit of God?
> C: I think so: that it pleased God to exercise his virtue through his instruments, for to this end he destined them. And this indeed he does, so as in no way to detract from the virtue of his Spirit'.[26]

But they are thus instruments of grace. Christopher Elwood rightly says:

> In the notion that the sacraments are instruments of God's grace we have the real hallmark of the Calvinist doctrine. Calvin invokes instrumentality as a way of distinguishing sacramental signs from the communicative power that proceeds from and is the exclusive prerogative of God. The signs are efficacious not because of an inherent capacity but in the sense that they are instruments God has chosen to attest to the genuine operation of the Spirit's power to unite believers with the body of Christ.[27]

For Calvin, what is promised is also offered or exhibited.[28] Calvin uses various forms of '*exhibere*' no less than seventeen times in Book 4, chapter 17 of the 1559 *Institutes*. Thus, for example, he asserted that the Supper consists of two things: 'the corporeal signs, which, presented to the eye, represent invisible things in a manner adapted to our weak capacity, and the spiritual truth, which is at once figured and exhibited by the signs ... I say then, that in the mystery of the Supper, by the symbols of bread and wine, Christ, his body and blood, are truly exhibited to us...'[29]

Joseph Tylenda commented:

> [*Exhibere*] is a favorite word of his, and since he uses it so frequently it indicates its importance to him. It is not always easy to translate, and one has to struggle to be sure that Calvin's underlying meaning is properly expressed. Calvin certainly does not use it as a synonym for *adesse*, to be present, because this word indicates a real, physical presence. *Exhibere* does not bring about a presence but presupposes a presence and manifests it. Therefore, the bread and wine of the Supper are *signa*, not *signa repraesentativa*, signs representing something absent, but *signa exhibitiva*, signs manifesting something present.[30]

According to Calvin, whatever God truly exhibits, that he also performs.[31] Although the body of Christ is in heaven, the Holy Spirit acts as a channel and overcomes the barrier of space, and causes the communion of the faithful with the body and blood of Christ.[32] Indeed, Calvin could speak of 'a true and substantial communication of the body and blood of the Lord'.[33] At the Colloquy of Regensburg, he and Melanchthon had signed an emended version of the Augsburg Confession, the so-called *Augustana variata*, with Article 10 reading 'the body and blood of Christ are truly exhibited with the bread and wine to those who eat in the Supper of the Lord.'[34] But the important purpose of both baptism and the Supper was participation or union with the Divine.[35]

Calvin's mature doctrine is represented in summary in the *Confessio Fidei Gallicana* (1559). Article XXXIV teaches:

> We believe that the sacraments are added to the Word for more ample confirmation, that they may be to us pledges and seals of the grace of God, and by this means aid and comfort our faith, because of the infirmity which is in us, and that they are outward signs through which God operates by his Spirit, so that he may not signify any thing to us in vain. Yet we hold that their substance and truth is in Jesus Christ, and that of themselves they are only smoke and shadow.[36]

Article XXXV asserted that in baptism we are grafted into Christ, and Article XXXVI, that the Supper is a witness to the union we have with Christ. By the secret and incomprehensible power of his Spirit he feeds and strengthens us with the substance (*de la substance*) of his body and his blood. And thus Article XXXVII explained:

> We believe, as has been said, that in the Lord's Supper, as well as in baptism, God gives us really and in fact that which he there sets forth to us; and that consequently with these signs is given the true possession and enjoyment of that which they present to us. And thus all who bring a pure faith, like a vessel, to the sacred table of Christ, receive truly

that of which it is a sign; for the body and blood of Jesus Christ give food and drink to the soul, no less than bread and wine nourish the body.[37]

Heinrich Bullinger's Symbolic Parallelism, and the Calvin of the Consensus Tigurinus

Bullinger was born near Zurich in 1504, the son of a priest (!). He was educated at Cologne University, where he mastered scholastic theology.[38] He first met Zwingli in 1524, though he himself already espoused a Reformation stance by that date. He claimed to have arrived at his own Reformed understanding of sacraments by reading Augustine and the Waldensians. Whereas Zwingli stressed the church as the subject of sacraments, Bullinger was adamant that Christ was the subject. However, like Zwingli, he held a symbolic view of sacraments, and sharply divided the sign and the signified. God was not bound by sacraments, and they do not convey grace. Sacraments are God's way of testifying and confirming the Spirit's work on the heart.

With the death of Zwingli in 1531, Bullinger became the effective spokesperson for the Zurich pastors, even though some of these shared Zwingli's sacramental views rather than Bullinger's more nuanced views. But Bullinger felt the need to defend Zwingli's memory, and thus also his sacramental theology. In his reply to Luther's 1544 polemic against Zwingli and other Schwärmer, Bullinger's *True Confession* (1545) emphasised that in the Supper, action brought forth remembrance. The same year he wrote his *Absoluta de Christi Domini et Catholicae eius Ecclesiae Sacramentis*, which prompted dialogue with Calvin in an attempt to reach some *rapprochement* on the sacraments. The *Absoluta* was rewritten and formed the section on sacraments in the *Decades*, published in England in 1551, and later translated into English to become (at least theoretically) required reading for the Elizabethan clergy. In his analysis of these two writings, Paul Rorem has noted how certain material in the former, such as Chapter 11, 'The sacraments do not exhibit that which they signify', were omitted. However, the omission seems to be diplomacy rather than a change of mind. In all his dialogue with Calvin, Bullinger refused to accept that sacraments exhibit anything, and neither would he allow that they are instruments of grace. Writing to Calvin, Bullinger maintained:

> If by 'instrument' you mean 'sign', fine. But if it is something more than sign, you seem to ascribe too much to the sacraments ... It is God who saves and receives us in grace. But this you ascribe to an instrument through which it is worked, some implement or flow-sluice or canal, the very sacraments, through which grace is infused into us ... But we do not believe this ... God alone works our salvation ... God, and no created thing, confers and indeed confers through the Spirit and faith ... The sacraments neither offer (*exhibent*) nor confer, nor are they instruments (*instrumenta*) of offering and conferring, but they signify, testify, and seal.[39]

Given the influence of the *Decades* in England, it is worthwhile looking at the teaching Bullinger gave in *Decades* V, though the genre is supposedly sermons rather than closely argued theological treatise. His discussion on sacraments began with a consideration of the meaning of *signum*, and is concerned to treat Augustine's teaching on signs. As applied to sacraments, the signs are to be understood as things which 'seal up that which they would have certain and sure'.[40] They are given to teach and admonish. Christ is the strength and substance of the sacraments, by whom only they are effectual, and without whom they are of no power, virtue or effect. Denying that sacraments involve a change of substance, Bullinger taught: 'Wax, before it be sealed, is common and usual wax; but when, by the king's will and commandment, that which is engraven in the king's seal is printed in the wax, and is set to evidences and letters patents, by and by it is so esteemed, that whoso shall deface the sealed evidences is attached as guilty of treason.'[41] This, according to Bullinger, is the meaning of consecration – the elements become seals, but do not change in substance: 'so that the body and blood of Christ do abide in their substance and nature, and in their place, I mean, in some certain place of heaven; but the bread and wine are a sign or sacrament, a witness or sealing, and a lively memory of his body given and his blood shed for us.'[42] The substance remains, but consecration or hallowing means that they are sealed to another use.

He noted that the common sort of priests and monks taught that sacraments were not only signs of grace, but causes of grace, which Bullinger repudiated; sacraments are testimonies of grace given, and seals of the truth of God's promise.[43] They also represent, though Bullinger was careful to define this: 'to represent doth not signify (as some dream) to bring, to give, or make that now again corporally present which sometime was taken away; but to resemble it in likeness and by a certain imitation, and to call it back again to mind, and to set it as it were before our eyes.'[44]

Baptism has as its sign water, and it is a badge or cognisance of the people of God, and an assured token of our purification by Christ. It is a sign, a testimony and sealing of our cleansing, and of ingrafting in the church. Infant baptism was defended on analogy with circumcision and covenant theology, and Bullinger here suggests that salvation comes through the covenant, of which baptism is simply the outward sign. He could write: 'The baptizer giveth visibly the sacrament of regeneration, and a testimony of the remission of sins; but the Lord by his Spirit doth invisibly regenerate, and forgiveth sins, and sealeth the regeneration.'[45] Here the outward sacramental sign and the inward spiritual grace do not necessarily coincide in time.

On the Supper, Bullinger stressed that it was primarily an action, a doing. Christ is not bodily present in the bread and wine, but is joined to our hearts and minds by his Spirit. Rejecting the Lutheran view of presence (though without naming Luther) and transubstantiation, Bullinger appealed to his understanding of Augustine on the words of institution: 'By which words he [Augustine] manifestly declared, that he meant not that Christ in his natural body delivered his natural body to his disciples; but that which the faithful do know, to wit, the sacrament or mystery.'[46] He could speak of the bread and wine becoming 'the sacrament' of Christ's body and blood, and he rejected any concept of offering other than of praise and thanksiving. Also, in passing, he commended sitting as the appropriate posture for communion.[47]

As already noted, the more sensitive areas found in the *Absoluta* were omitted from the *Decades*, but Bullinger had not changed his views. Calvin, with an eye on the worsening political situation, still tried to reach agreement with Bullinger, and the result was the *Consensus Tigurinus* of 1549, published in 1551.[48] The *Consensus* was expanded by the Zurichers from twenty articles by Calvin submitted to

Bern in March 1549. In a useful analysis of the *Consensus*, Timothy George notes that the twenty-six articles can be divided into five sections.[49] The first six articles form a Christological introduction, and here we find the word 'exhibit' used, but with reference to Christ, not sacraments. The next three deal with general doctrine of sacraments. Where Calvin had used the word 'exhibit' with reference to sacraments in his initial Bern articles, now the words had been rephrased to read 'there can be no doubt that God grants within us by his Spirit that which the sacraments figure to our eyes and other senses.'[50] In articles 10–15, which are a defence against sacramental materialism, where Calvin had used his favourite term 'instruments', the Zurichers substituted 'implements' (*organa*).[51] Articles 16–20 deal with the necessity of faith. Article 17 notes that sacraments do not confer grace, and 20 teaches that grace is not tied to the time of administration of the sacraments. Articles 21–26 refute certain errors on the eucharist.

George notes that since the published version of the *Consensus* was endorsed not only in Zurich and Geneva but also by the Reformed churches of Neuchatel, Bienne, Pays de Vaud, the Grisons, Basel, St. Gallen, Schaffhausen, Mulhausen, and after some resistance, at Bern, the document purported to be the agreed theology of the Swiss churches, and representative of Swiss Reformed theology.[52] According to Rorem, the agreement rests on Calvin's willingness to omit certain phrases previously essential in his formulations, and yet always objectionable to Bullinger.[53] Gerrish too argues that it did not say all Calvin liked to say about the sacraments, but only what he was not prepared to omit.[54] Readers of the *Consensus*, without access to some of Calvin's other works, might well interpret it as Calvin's teaching, or at least, all he thought was necessary to say on sacraments, and that he and Bullinger essentially were in agreement. But the Calvin of the *Consensus* was not the Calvin of other writings, and there were significant differences between him and Bullinger.

Bullinger was to give further expression to his sacramental teaching in the *Second Helvetic Confession* of 1566, approved by the General Assembly of the Church of Scotland the same year. In this *Confession*, sacraments are described as mystical symbols, holy rites, or sacred actions ordained by God, consisting of his Word, outward signs, and things signified. God uses them to recall to mind in his Church the great benefits he has given, 'whereby he seals up (*obsignat*) his promises, and outwardly represents, and, as it were, offers unto our sight those things which inwardly he performs unto us'.[55] The substance of sacraments is given by God, and the outward signs by ministers. They are mystical tokens of holy things, and the signs and things signified are sacramentally joined together. However, the sign and the promise are not bound to one another. In baptism 'inwardly we are regenerated, purified, and renewed of God through the Holy Spirit; and outwardly we receive the sealing of most notable gifts by the water, by which also those great benefits are represented, and, as it were, set before our eyes to be looked upon.'[56] And of the Supper,

> Outwardly, bread is offered by the minister, and the words of the Lord are heard: 'Take, eat; this is my body;' and, 'Drink of it, all of you; for this is my blood'. Therefore the faithful do receive that which is given by the ministers of the Lord, and do eat the bread of the Lord, and do drink of the Lord's cup. And at the same time inwardly, by the

working of Christ through the Holy Spirit, they receive also the flesh and blood of the Lord, and do feed on them unto life eternal.[57]

Receiving the sign does not mean necessarily that the thing signified is received. The two may coincide, but need not – hence Gerrish's description of Bullinger's view as 'symbolic parallelism'.

Peter Martyr Vermigli: an Italian Reformed Approach

Less well-known than Bucer, Bullinger and Calvin, their contemporary Peter Martyr Vermigli was highly regarded, and after his flight from Italy in 1542, spent periods of time teaching at Strasbourg, Oxford and Zurich. Leaving Strasbourg before Bucer, Vermigli was a guest of Archbishop Thomas Cranmer, and became Regius Professor of Divinity at Oxford. He certainly discussed sacramental theology with Cranmer, and may have influenced certain ideas in the 1549 *Book of Common Prayer*; one of the exhortations in the 1552 *Book of Common Prayer* came originally from his pen.[58] His journey from Catholicism to first an Evangelicalism influenced by Juan Valdes, and then to Reformed theology, was a process over a number of years, and his views on the sacraments were scattered in commentaries as well as tracts and disputations, and were collected together by others in the *Loci communes*.[59] His views have much in common with both Calvin and Bucer, but do not exactly coincide with either. Vermigli thus represents yet another Reformed approach.

Sacraments are signs, and visible words and also seals of God's promise. Vermigli wrote: 'It may seem sufficient to take that definition which Paul uses here, namely to say that the sacraments are *sphragides*, that is, seals of the righteousness of faith. For they seal the promises by which, if faith is joined to them, we are justified ... The head and sum of their signification we place in this, that they seal unto us the gifts and promises of God.[60]

Three factors are needed for a sacrament: Christ's institution, God's word, and the power of the Holy Spirit. As a result, sacraments are a means of grace. However, in imparting grace, God is not bound to use the sacraments, which do not cause grace, but are the implements (*organa*) of God's grace.[61] Here Vermigli uses Bullinger's term, *organa*, but elsewhere he uses the term *instrumenta*, and seems to use them interchangeably. Like Calvin he can say that sacraments exhibit grace. However, neither grace, nor, in the case of the Lord's Supper, Christ's body, are united 'really' (*realiter*), substantially, bodily or carnally, but sacramentally.[62] While there is certainly a conjunction, or union, there are unions other than physical ones, and in sacraments it is 'sacramentally, this is by signification and representation.'[63] Yet if this sounds very close to Calvin, Vermigli also stresses the difference between the inward and outward. Thus on the Supper he contended: 'By his words and institution they become sacraments, that is, *organa* by which the Holy Spirit excites faith in our minds, so that we may be spiritually yet truly fed and sustained by his body and blood.'[64]

Indeed, he insists on a spiritual presence, and spiritual eating of the Supper through faith. He thus presents both symbolic instrumentalism, and symbolic parallelism at one and the same time. Thus although for Vermigli the Spirit uses the signs, the inward element of sacraments comes about by the Spirit stirring up faith, which is the real instrument by which grace comes. The external and internal are not so conjoined that by merely performing the former, the latter always follows. Thus on baptism he wrote:

> Baptism is a sign of regeneration into Christ, into His death, I say, and His resurrection, which succeeded in place of Circumcision, which consists in the laver of water in the Word, in which in the name of the Father and of the Son and of the Holy Spirit, remission of sins and outpouring of the Holy Spirit is offered, and by a visible sacrament we are grafted into Christ and into His Church and the right into the kingdom of heaven is sealed unto us, and we on our part profess that we will die unto sin and live hereafter in Christ.[65]

Again, 'the sign in sacraments should have an affinity and likeness with the thing signified by it. Wherefore since water washes away the filthiness of the body, makes the earth fruitful, and quenches thirst, it aptly signifies remission of sins and the Holy Spirit, by which good works are made plentiful, and grace which refreshes the anguish of mind.'[66] Elsewhere he wrote:

> We see in baptism also that Christ, the Holy Ghost, grace, forgiveness of sins, our gainbirth which they call regeneration, do longer remain in them that be baptised than they do remain with the waters wherewith the faithful be washed. For the water is an instrument which God vouchsafeth to use that we may be grafted into Christ by baptism and we may be born again by the Holy Ghost.[67]

However, Vermigli denied that the Spirit and grace are in the water of baptism,[68] and was suspicious of linking regeneration too closely with the rite.[69] Regeneration occurs if the rite – sacramental signs – are joined by election and predestination. Thus he wrote:

> But if a man ask whether the outward Word or the visible sign of baptism is wholly necessary, we answer that indeed the inward Word, by which men are moved unto Christ and reformed, is absolutely required, if we speak of them that are of mature age; but in children, neither has the inward Word place, nor is the outward Word the ordinary instrument.[70]

An elect infant has the Holy Spirit who will produce faith. Thus, like Zwingli, Bucer, Calvin and Bullinger, Vermigli appeals to a covenant theology to justify infant baptism. He asserted: 'But by the promise and force of the covenant it is forgiveness – when God works this forgiveness we cannot learn from the testimony of Scripture. In infants it is perhaps forgiven when they are yet in the womb, or when they are born, or right after birth, nor is it likely given to all men at the same time.'[71] What is important in baptism for Vermigli is union with Christ, being ingrafted, and a member of the Church.

On the Lord's Supper, Vermigli of course rejected transubstantiation, and the Lutheran idea of ubiquity. Commenting on the words of institution, he asserted: 'Therefore let the meaning be, I give you bread to eat, while offering my body to be fastened to the cross, so that with faithful memory and attentive mind you may spiritually eat among yourselves; and as with the body you can eat bread so with the mind will you eat my flesh.'[72] This sounds close to the symbolic memorialism of Zwingli, and Vermigli did not think Zwingli was wrong on this, though more needed to be said. Thus Vermigli said that the true body and blood is exhibited, 'because faith does not grasp things imagined, but true'.[73] The elements are important on account of the institution of the Lord, the power of the Holy Spirit, and the clearness of the words. The Holy Spirit sanctifies, but by the implements of both words and sacraments. The bread and wine become 'effective signs'. Those faithful who receive partake of a spiritual communion and participation in the body and blood of Christ. Thus he wrote:

> Further, I affirm that the distance of places does not hinder our union with the body and blood of Christ, because the Lord's Supper is a heavenly matter, and while on earth by the mouth of the body we take bread and wine, sacraments of the body and blood of the Lord, yet by faith and the work of the Holy Spirit our souls, to which this spiritual and heavenly food applies, are carried up to heaven and enjoy the present body and blood of Christ.[74]

By the secret and ineffable working, the Holy Spirit effects this communication and participation in his body which dwells in heaven. We taste and enjoy, and are incorporated in him and he with us, 'so that in this eating, made bone of his bone and flesh of his flesh, we feel lively within us the ransom and salvation he accomplished – a co-ownership of all his wealth.'[75] Furthermore, it is not the bread and wine which are transformed, but the faithful. Christians are united, converted and transformed in Christ by the sacred eating. There is a mystical union.

Vermigli thus presented yet another Reformed variation. He worked with concepts found in Zwingli and Bucer, together with elements from Bullinger and Calvin. But a new emphasis seems to be the use of 'sacramental' as a key word. The elements have a *sacramental* presence, and are instruments, but only effective in so far as the Holy Spirit gives faith, and both instruments and faith have their conjunction in Christ. The parallels of the inward and outward are combined in Christ.

German Reformed Input: Zacharias Ursinus and the Heidelberg Catechism

Zacharias Ursinus was born in Bresslau in 1534, and his earlier studies were with Melanchthon. In 1557 he had attended the conference at Worms, and then proceeded to Heidelberg, Strasbourg, Basel, Lausanne and then Zurich. In 1558 he had accepted a call to teach at the Elizabethan Gymnasium at Bresslau, but being perceived by Gnesio-Lutherans as a Crypto-Calvinist, he moved to Zurich in 1560 where he studied with Peter Martyr Vermigli. In 1561 he received a call to Heidelberg, and with Caspar Olevianus, drew up the Heidelberg (Palatinate) Catechism of 1563. This put Heidelberg, until its Lutheran resettlement in 1576, firmly in the Reformed camp. The catechism was influential in the German and Dutch Reformed Churches. However, it was also popular in England, being a prescribed text at Oxford in 1579, and editions being printed for the University in 1588. It was also printed and widely used in Scotland, where it was known as the Palatinate Catechism.[76]

As well as being a chief author of the catechism, Ursinus also wrote an exposition or explication of its propositions, including what he regarded as its teaching on sacraments.[77] The catechism defined sacraments as 'holy visible signs and seals, appointed of God'. According to Ursinus, they are seals of faith, appended to the Gospel, and signs of the covenant.[78] They are signs which exhibit, and seal in their true use, 'inasmuch as they exhibit the things promised in the gospel to those that believe, and also seal the exhibiting or setting forth of these things'.[79] They are 'instrumental causes' in confirming faith.[80] No change takes place in the elements of the sacraments, nor is there a physical or corporal conjunction. Thus he wrote:

> Yet the water is not changed into the blood or Spirit of Christ, nor is the blood of Christ present in the water, or in the same place with the water. Nor are the bodies of those who are baptized washed with this visibly; nor is the Holy Spirit, by his substance or virtue, more in this water than elsewhere; but he works in the hearts of those who are baptized in the lawful use of baptism, and sprinkles and washes them spiritually by the blood of Christ, whilst he uses this external symbol as a means, and as a visible word or promise to stir up and confirm the faith of those who are baptized.[81]

Ursinus thus rejected both Roman Catholic sacramental teaching, and the Lutheran teaching of 'in, with and under'. However, he asserted that another type of union takes place – a sacramental union, or 'relative', which gives rise to a 'joint-exhibition and reception of the signs and things signified in their proper use'.[82] But faith is necessary, and thus although God offers his benefits in the sacraments, the wicked receive only naked signs.[83]

According to the Heidelberg Catechism, in baptism Christ appointed an external washing with water, adding a promise that the baptised are washed by his blood from all sin.[84] Ursinus explained this as sealing remission of sins, or 'a sealing of the promise of grace, that is, of our justification and regeneration, and a declaration of the will of God, to this effect, that he here grants these gifts to those who are baptized, and that he will for ever grant them.'[85] Regeneration and salvation do not depend upon baptism, but the internal is signified and sealed by that which is external and is always joined with it in the 'proper use' of baptism.[86] The emphasis here on proper use is important to Ursinus, because it includes faith and being amongst the covenant elect, and precludes sacraments conveying anything to unbelievers or the wicked. Thus, for adults, baptism should follow faith, since baptism does not save without it.[87] Infants may be baptised because all the children of believers are included in the covenant, and church of God, unless they exclude themselves. In the proper use of the sacrament, 'the exhibition and reception of the signs, and things signified, are inseparably connected. And hence the Holy Ghost interchanges the terms, attributing what belongs to the thing signified to the sign, and what belongs to the sign to the thing, to teach us what he gives, and to assure us that he does really give it.'[88]

The other sacrament, the Lord's Supper, is also called a eucharist, and also a sacrifice of thanksgiving, because 'it is a solemn commemoration, and celebration of the propitiatory sacrifice of Christ.'[89] Whereas baptism is the sign of the covenant between God and the faithful, the Lord's Supper is the sign of the preservation of the same covenant.[90] It was instituted to confirm faith, and also as proof of our union with Christ. The bread and wine are united with the body and blood – not by change, or physical conjunction, but by sacramental union.[91] Ursinus explained:

The rite, or signs are the bread which is broken and eaten, and the wine which is poured out, and drunk. *The things signified* are the broken body, and shed blood of Christ, which are eaten and drunk, or our union with Christ by faith, by which we are made partakers of Christ and all his benefits, so that we derive from him everlasting life, as the branches draw their life from the vine.[92]

Ursinus is insistent that the fraction, or breaking of the bread as a distinct ceremony at the Lord's Supper is crucial; it is 'a necessary ceremony both on account of its signification, and for the confirmation of our faith, and is to be retained in the celebration of the Supper'.[93] Providing there is 'lawful use' – which seems interchangeable with 'proper use' – then, because of the sacramental union, the bread and wine and body and blood are 'always exhibited and received conjointly' – though not without faith properly viewing and apprehending the things promised and now present in the sacrament.[94]

The influence of Vermigli on Ursinus is reasonably clear. He used the terms 'instrument' or 'instrumental causes', and 'exhibit'. Like Vermigli, he stresses the term 'sacramental union' as the proper means of conveying that the sign and thing do have a close relationship; like his teacher, his terminology attempts to find a path between Calvin and Bullinger. On balance, as with Vermigli, this is closer to symbolic parallelism than to symbolic instrumentalism.

Other Influential Reformed Sacramental Theologies

Amongst other Continental Reformers, three particular names should be mentioned in terms of their influence on English and Scottish divines: Jan Laski (John a Lasco), Wolfgang Musculus and Theodore Beza.

Laski (1499–1560) was a Polish nobleman and Catholic priest who embraced the Reformation, and led the church in East Friesland before moving to England to take charge of the foreign congregations in London. Not only was he consulted by Thomas Cranmer concerning revision of the 1549 *Book of Common Prayer*, but he also had links with John Knox.[95] In his *Epitome Doctrinae Ecclesiarum Phrisiae Orientalis* of 1544, and *Brevis et Dilucida de sacramentis Ecclesiae Christ Tractatio* of 1552, Laski stressed that sacraments are seals, rather like seals appended to a document. When a king grants a donation, it is accompanied by a document with the royal seal, confirming what has been given. Sacraments therefore attest something already established. Thus baptism attests our justification and the divine goodwill towards us. They do not give grace, but reassurance. Performing the sacrament – the action – leads to remembrance. Of the Lord's Supper he wrote that we

> ... truly acknowledge and believe our communion with Christ the Lord in faith, inasmuch as it has long since been offered and received by grace. Thus, the entire Church is sealed and confirmed in the faith of that communion by the use of the Sacraments. Yet, the sealing inherent in this communion does not require, nor can it even admit, any real presence of Christ's physical body and blood, much less a reception of them by a carnal mouth.[96]

He was prepared to use Calvin's favourite term 'exhibit', but with his own meaning: 'We do not therefore exclude from the Sacraments a true and salvific exhibition of Christ's body and blood, although we say that this exhibition does not consist in any real connection with the elements, nor in any work of the minister.'[97] For Laski, it is our being lifted to heaven that constitutes the meaning of 'exhibition'. Much of Laski's teaching puts him closer to Zurich than to Calvin and Geneva, and in support of his own views he frequently cited Oecolampadius and Bullinger. He hovers between symbolic memorialism and parallelism.

Wolfgang Musculus was professor at Bern, and Bern had been critical of Calvin's sacramental theology. Musculus's Catechism of 1545 had already indicated a sharp division between the external signs and the thing signified.[98] His *Common Places of the Christian Religion* were published in England in 1563, and in 1578, and here he attempted to bridge the gulf between the sacramental sign and the reality. According to Musculus, a sacramental sign is made up of two things, one visible and the other invisible. The word of institution, or promise, 'doth consecrate sacraments for the church until the very end of the world'.[99] The sacramental signs are tokens of grace – to those who have faith, and thus already have grace.[100] Furthermore, this increase of grace is not tied to the sacrament. He asserted: 'So that in some sorte, that is to saye, sacramentally, there is joyned grace to the sacramental signes: and yet withal it is not so tyed unto them, that hee can be partaker of it, which dothe receive the sacramente without faith.'[101]

On baptism he wrote:

> Wherefore we shall define baptisme arighte, to be the Sacramente of regeneration, purgation, profession, sanctification, consignment, and incorporation into Christ our Savioure. For all these things be wroughte by the Spirite of Christe in the electe and faithfull, of which Baptisme is the sacramente; so that it may be said aright, that the same is wroughte in it, sacramentally, whiche is done in deede and spiritually, by the Spirit of Christe. And these things be done, at the will of the holye Spirite, of Christ, eyther before or after baptisme, or at the very doing of the baptising, least that any man shoulde suppose, that the Spirite is so bounde unto the outward sacramente that it dothe worke this invisible grace of regeneration, washing, initiation, sanctification, and consigning, either in the heartes of al of them that be baptised, either alwayes in the verye acte of baptism itselfe, spiritually and effectually.[102]

Grace thus works when God determines, and need have no connection with the sacrament.

When discussing the Lord's Supper, Musculus preferred to refer to it as the 'mystical supper'. It contains a memory, a mystery and a rite. There is an earthly sign and and a heavenly thing signified.[103] He accepted that in certain senses it can be called a sacrifice, though it is really a commemoration of the sacrifice.[104] However, this is pinpointed in the actual breaking of bread, and pouring the wine into the mouth.[105] In his more general treatment of sacraments, Musculus had rejected the notion of a natural, local or bodily conjunction between sign and signified, and preferred 'sacramental conjunction', 'whereby the thing signified is annexed unto the sign and the effect of the sacrament unto the sacrament'.[106] In considering the notion of presence, he allowed that 'spiritual', 'figurative' and 'significative' were possible terms, but he preferred 'sacramental'. He explained:

> Wherefore when we doe saye, that Christe is spiritually presente in the supper, we do not meane of the invisible presence of his body, whiche the Papists do appoynt under the

forme of bread, but of that way, that hee is present by the working of his spirite, feeding, and refreshing their mindes whiche doe receive with sincere and true faith, that which he gave at hys Last Supper ... the bread of the Supper is the Lordes body Sacramentally.[107]

Musculus echoes some of the concerns of Vermigli, and though he seems to be prepared to use vocabulary which Bullinger rejected, he nevertheless presents himself as a symbolic parallelist.

Thirdly, and also influential, was Calvin's successor at Geneva, Theodore Beza (1519–1605). Beza, the Gentleman from Vezeley, who studied at Orleans with Melchior Wolmar, eventually fled to Switzerland where he was professor of Greek at Lausanne for ten years from 1548 before taking up an appointment at Geneva. In his study of Beza's sacramental teaching, particularly on the Lord's Supper, Jill Raitt has noted a development over time, particularly relating to concepts.[108]

In his *Confession of Faith* in 1556, Beza argued like Calvin that word and sacraments are instruments of the Spirit. They are channels or conduits used by the Holy Spirit to join us to Christ and increase our union with him. Sacraments are not bare or empty figures. He explained:

> We use the word sign in explaining the sacraments, not to designate something ineffectual, as if a thing were represented to us by a picture or mere memorial or figure, but to declare that the Lord, by his singular goodness, to assist our weakness, uses external and corporal things to represent to our external senses the greatest and most divine things, which he truly communicates to us interiorly through his Spirit: so that he does not give us the signified reality, of which we will speak soon, less truly than he gives us the exterior and corporal signs.[109]

Beza taught that the sacramental signs were not changed in substance, quality or quantity, but were like wax seals: 'The principle is not unlike that which underlies the use of wax which is customarily impressed by the seal of a prince or magistrate to confirm a public document. In this case, the nature or substance of the wax differs not at all from any other wax, but in its use, it is far and away different.'[110] There is no commingling, but to receive the sign is to receive the thing signified. He elaborated his understanding by use of the term *analogia*. He explained this in reference to the Supper in three ways. The fraction of the bread represented the passion or suffering of Christ; the distribution teaches that the benefits are given to us as individuals, and the bread made from many grains and the wine from many grapes expresses the unity of the members of the church.[111]

In his later writings associated with the Colloquy of Poissy (where he was joined by Vermigli), we find Beza hesitant about saying that we receive Christ substantially, preferring instead to say 'sacramentally'. He insists that the body and blood of Christ are present in the eucharist, but not united with the elements. He did concede, however, that it was legitimate to say that Christ was corporally, really, and substantially present in the signified *res*. Like Calvin, he was concerned also to stress the notion of union with Christ through the sacraments. By 1567 he could call the sacraments 'effective causes' due to their nature as analogous signs and as their use as instruments of the Holy Spirit.[112]

In his writings of the 1570s and 80s, Beza uses scholastic terms in his discussion. Sacraments are voluntary signs. They have four causes – the efficient cause is

Christ, the material cause, the thing and the signs, the formal cause are the external action and the Holy Spirit, and the final cause is the giving of Christ and his gifts. In addition to the concept of *analogia*, he also introduced in his later writings the idea of *relata*:

> Therefore in these mysteries neither bread nor wine are proposed simply and properly, insofar as they are substantial things, not in themselves insofar as they nourish our bodies with food and drink, but they must be considered *relatively*, namely insofar as not in their nature, but in the word of sacramental institution, faith looks upon them and is moved by them as signs.'[113]

He also differentiated between 'spiritual', which was the understanding of the *analogia* – faith informing our understanding; and the 'mystical' which was the work of the Spirit in sacraments. In developing this terminology from Aristotle and Thomas Aquinas, Beza is a link between Calvin and the later Protestant scholasticism. However, in his emphasis upon instrumentality, and participation or union, and the reception of the *res* with the sign, Beza stood with Calvin as representing symbolic instrumentalism.

From these sketches of the sacramental views of a number of the influential sixteenth-century Reformed theologians, a number of differences emerge. The later Bucer, and the Calvin of the 1559 *Institutes* and works on the Lord's Supper, together with Beza, stressed that sacraments are instruments of grace, though not the cause of grace. However, what is promised is received by the faithful. The *res*, or thing, is exhibited, or presented, or offered, to the recipient. Over against this, Bullinger, who was concerned to defend Zwingli, would allow – under pressure – that sacraments were implements (*organa*), but would not use the term 'instrument', nor the term 'exhibit' as applied to the sign and *res*. Grace was conveyed quite apart from the sacraments, and thus sacraments might not always give what they promised. Jan Laski and Musculus seem to have shared views similar to Bullinger, maintaining a sharp distinction between the outward sign and the inward *res*. Laski will use the word 'exhibit', but with a different meaning to that of Bucer and Calvin. Vermigli and his student Ursinus use the terms 'instrument' and 'exhibit', but prefer to express the link between sign and *res* as 'sacramental'. All used the word 'spiritual presence' for the Supper. Sometimes this is regarded by modern writers as being less real than the Catholic transubstantiation and the Lutheran local presence. However, the Reformers regarded 'sacramental union', 'sacramental presence' and 'spiritual presence' as a higher and superior understanding to a substantial presence or local bodily presence. Calvin and Beza were prepared to accept that in the Supper the faithful do receive the susbtance of Christ's body and blood, with the elements, but not in or under them. At least in this respect, according to Calvin's thought, the Genevan faithful received exactly the 'what' Catholics claimed their faithful to receive, though for Calvin, the Genevans had a higher and superior understanding of the 'how'.

These differing theologies were received and read in England and Scotland. Divines from both countries rejected the 'papist' and Lutheran understanding of sacraments; they also rejected the 'Zwinglian' idea of 'naked and bare signs'. However, it is not at all clear that they were particularly conscious of the nuanced differences between the German Swiss, French Swiss and German Reformed writers, and if they were, it seems that they did not regard it as problematical for the articulation of their own views.

Sacraments in Sixteenth-Century English and Scottish Theology

English Variety

The writings of the Edwardian Reformers such as Cranmer, Ridley and Hooper show a clear move towards a Reformed position, but although attempts have been made to label their views according to Continental Reformed positions – Zwinglian, or Bucerian – they defy such close categorisation, and themselves illustrate a diversity.[114] The Elizabethan Church regarded these as martyrs, and their writings were treasured and read, but were not regarded as any sense official or representative of the English Church. For sacramental views in the Elizabethan Church of England we may briefly survey the Articles of Religion, Alexander Nowell's Catechism, together with the teaching of Dudley Fenner, William Perkins and Richard Hooker.[115]

The Articles of Religion were set forth in Latin in 1563, and in English and Latin in 1571 were a mild revision of the Forty-Two Articles of 1553. Though a number of theologians and bishops were involved in their drafting, the final forms were the editorial work of Archbishop Thomas Cranmer. Phraseology of some of the articles echoed those found in the Augsburg Confession, but by 1553 Cranmer's sacramental views were certainly not Lutheran. Dairmaid MacCulloch suggested that the stance taken by Cranmer in the *Answer* and *Defence*, written against Gardiner, comes closest to the symbolic parallelism of Bullinger, and would not have been happy with Calvin's idea that sacraments contain or exhibit grace.[116] However, the Articles were not an exact expression of Cranmer's own sacramental doctrine, but were wide enough to embrace a variety of 'evangelical' interpretations. However, Article XXV, 'Of the Sacraments', of 1563, represents a reordering of corresponding Article XXVI of 1553. Although sacraments were defined as badges and tokens (cf. Zwingli), they were also described as 'sure witnesses and effectuall signes of grace and Gods good wyll towardes us'. The Article does not specify what is meant by grace. Article XXVII, 'Of Baptisme', defined this sacrament as a sign of profession and mark of difference between a Christian and non-Christian, but also as a sign of regeneration, or new birth, and, 'whereby as an instrument', results in being grafted into the Church. The reference to 'instrument' was unchanged from 1553, and perhaps shows Cranmer accepting the usage of Vermigli and Bucer. Article XXVIII, 'Of the Lordes Supper', was shorter than the 1553 version, omitting a discussion on the location of Christ's body. The body of Christ is given, taken, and eaten only after a heavenly and spiritual manner, and received by faith. The wicked carnally press with their teeth the sacrament of the body and blood of Christ, but do not partake of Christ. The Articles, by their nature, were less precise than an individual's theological account, and were broad enough to allow a latitude of belief.

The catechism of Alexander Nowell was originally composed to be bound with the Articles of Religion, but failed to gain official status. Nowell rewrote the proposed catechism, and although never gaining official sanction, it became the most widely used catechism in the English Church.[117] It was based upon an earlier English catechism by Bishop John Poynet, and on Calvin's catechism. William Haugaard observed:

> When Nowell borrowed from Calvin, he freely changed vocabulary and sentence struc-
> ture, substituting his own synonyms and distinctive grammatical forms. Nowell not only
> elaborated many of Calvin's expositions, but he tended to group several of Calvin's
> answers together without intervening questions. These longer literary paragraphs lost
> something of the crisp brevity of Calvin's form.[118]

Nowell treated sacraments in the fourth and final part of his catechism. In explaining what a sacrament is, Nowell wrote: 'It is an outward testifying of God's goodwill and bountifulness toward us, through Christ by a visible sign representing an
invisible and spiritual grace, by which the promises of God touching forgiveness of
sins and eternal salvation given through Christ, are, as it were sealed, and the truth
of them is more certainly confirmed in our hearts.'[119] It is an outward sign of an
invisible 'grace', and Nowell frequently applied the word grace to the sacraments.
Ian Green suggested that, given the influence of this catechism, it may have played
the largest part in spreading the association of sacraments with grace in the English
Church.[120] The sacraments, according to Nowell, have efficacy, and represent (exhibit) and convey, though the agency is the Holy Spirit.

When turning to treat baptism, Nowell listed the 'outward' as dipped or sprinkled in the name of the Trinity. The 'secret and spiritual grace' is the forgiveness of
sins and regeneration. It is a figure, but not an empty one; it 'hath the truth of the
things themselves joined and knit unto it', suggesting instrumentality. On the bread
and wine at the Supper, Nowell explained:

> ... the word of God and heavenly grace coming to them, there is such efficacy, that as by
> baptism we are once regenerate in Christ, and are first, as it were, joined and grafted into
> his body; so, when we rightly receive the Lord's Supper, with the very divine nourish-
> ment of his body and blood, most full of health and immortality, given to us by the work
> of the Holy Ghost, and received of us by faith, as the mouth of our soul, we are
> continually fed and sustained to eternal life, growing together in them both into one
> body with Christ.[121]

Although Nowell certainly did not follow Calvin slavishly, his concern that the
sacraments do convey grace, and the implicit view of instrumentality suggest that
Nowell's teaching leaned towards symbolic instrumentalism.

Dudley Fenner (1558?–87) was a fellow commoner at Peterhouse, Cambridge in
the 1570s, and became an assistant to Richard Fletcher at Cranbrooke, Kent. He
was a follower of Thomas Cartwright, and followed the latter to Antwerp. He
returned to England in 1583, but was soon in trouble with Archbishop Whitgift over
matters of conformity. Rather than conform, he left for Middleburgh, where he died
a few years later, still at a relatively young age. His widow was to marry the
Cambridge 'godly' divine, William Whitaker. Fenner's work on the sacraments,
entitled *The Whole doctrine of the Sacramentes, plainlie and fullie set downe and
declared out of the word of God* (Middleburgh, 1588), therefore represents a 'nonconformist godly' approach. In this work Fenner defined a sacrament as follows:

A Sacrament of the eternall covenant, is a publike and faithfull worke of the whole Church, wherein by the Ministers putting apart by the worde and prayer, to an holie use, a visible signe, ordeyned of God in the order prescribed, by his deliverie & their receyving of the same, the holy ghost doeth offer & represent lively unto all, but more surelie applie to the due receyver thereof, the offering and giving of God in three persons, & the Churches receyving of Christ crucified, and the covenant concerning justification, and sanctification unto eternall life, fullie ratified and confirmed in him.[122]

Of note here is the concern to place sacraments firmly within a theology of covenant.[123] Baptism can therefore be described as the 'first sacrament of the covenant', and infant baptism is defended on the grounds of the parents being already in the covenant. But faith is required even in infant baptism – the faith of the minister in the sacrament, the parents' faith in the covenant, the church's faith in prayer, and the child's faith required in maturity.[124] In baptism we are set into the body of Christ, and are washed with the washing of our new birth in him, and 'have an assurance of all priviledges' and 'are sett into the right tytle of possession of them, with the rest of the Churche'.[125] There is the need for the inward working of the Holy Spirit. Fenner also has an interesting understanding of 'instruments'. The eyes, ears, hands and *feeling* are all instruments of the outward man, but are also 'effectuall instrumentes of the holy Ghost to worke withall'.[126] Fenner's concern with feeling, with the experiential, is one which he emphasised throughout the work. The outward elements are also instruments:

The outward matters are the creatures ordeyned of GOD, sanctified by the especiall worde and prayer, and so ordered in outwarde manner, as Water to washe, breade to be broken, wine to bee drunken, as is prescribed: their fruite is to represent to the eye, eare, feeling, &c. Secondlie, to seale up and be an instrument more certainely to applye, for although it doeth applie no more then the word preached doeth, neither by other inwarde giftes then the working of the holy ghost by faith, yet because the instruments are more, and in the worke of God hath sanctified more instrumentes in his creatures to our seeing, feeling, receyving, &c. they do more provoke faith, kindle faith, strengthen faith, to the receyving of Christe.[127]

Thus, both the human senses or faculties, and the sacramental elements become instruments of the Holy Spirit. Of the bread and wine, Fenner taught that by prayer and thanksgiving they are 'put aparte from their common uses, to that which is holy'.[128] Sacramental signs offer, represent and seal up. Christ is present, but not in and with the bread, and neither is the bread turned into his body. Fenner rejected the 'papist' and Lutheran teachings. The bread, argued Fenner, is 'an instrument whereby truly is communicated by the working of the H. Ghost to our faith, the very bodye and blood of Christ: for the wordes, *This is my body*, that is, an instrument which offereth and representeth to all, one body, and sealeth up the true receyving of his very body and blood'.[129] They become 'sacramentally' his body and blood. He dwells in us and we in him 'by the vertue and power of his divine working'.

Fenner was one of the first English theologians to use the simplified Ramist method, and his whole treatment lacks some of the more complex arguments and terminology of the earlier Continental Reformers. It is difficult to know exactly where to place his emphasis. His concern that sacraments do represent (=*exhibere*) an understanding of instruments, suggest that he was close to Calvin, though his teacher, Cartwright, was also influenced by Ursinus. Fenner's concern for 'feeling' was important to the spirituality of the 'godly'.[130]

William Perkins (1558–1602) was educated at Christ's College, Cambridge, and was tutored by Laurance Chaderton. Like Fenner, he was influenced by the Ramist method; unlike Fenner, he remained a conformist divine, though one of the 'godly'. He became the most widely published and translated Elizabethan divine. The sacraments are discussed in a number of his works, though perhaps the most well-known was *A Golden Chaine* (1591), where sacraments are set in an *Ordo Salutis*.[131]

According to Perkins, a sacrament is that 'whereby Christ and his saving graces, are by certaine externall rites, signified, exhibited, and sealed to a Christian man'.[132] They are visible words and promises.[133] He explained: 'The element in the Sacrament is an outward seale or instrument to confirme faith, not as a medicine restores and confirmes health, whether we thinke on it or not, whether we sleepe or wake, and that by His owne inherent vertue: but by reasoning in a syllogisme made by the good conscience: the *medium* thereor beeing the outward signe in the Sacrament.'[134]

The elements are voluntary instruments or moral instruments. They do not themselves convey grace. However, an increase of grace is given for those who rightly believe. Thus, in words suggesting a symbolic parallelism, Perkins wrote: 'The grace and mercy of God is free, and not tyed or bound to the outward elements. *Iohn 3.8. The wind bloweth where it listeth*, that is, God gives grace, and vouchsafeth favour, to whom, where, and when it pleaseth him. And hence it is, they whom hee would not have perish, but come to eternall life, shall be saved, though they be not partakers of this Sacrament.'[135] Thus, when Perkins turns to baptism, it is no more than a seal annexed to the covenant. It may convey grace, but here Perkins gave considerable qualification:

> It conferres grace: because it is a meanes to give and exhibit to the beleeving minde Christ with his benefits; and this it doth by his signification. For it serves as a particular and infallible certificate to assure the partie baptized, of the forgiveness of his sinnes, and of his eternal salvation. And whereas the Minister, in the name of God, applies the promise of mercy to him that is baptised, it is indeed as much as if God should have made a particular promise to him. In this regard, baptisme may be well said to conferre grace, as the Kings letters are said to save the life of the malefactour, when they do but signifie to him and others, that the Kings pleasure is to shew favour. Againe, baptisme may be said to confer grace, because the outward washing of the body is a token or pledge of the grace of God: and by this pledge faith is confirmed, which is an instrument, to apprehend or receive the grace of God … It is not an instrument having the grace of God tyed unto it, or shut up in it: but an instrument to which grace is present by assistance in the right use thereof: because in and with the right use of the sacrament, God conferres grace; and thus is it an instrument, and no otherwise, that is, a morall and not a physicall instrument.[136]

With regard to the Lord's Supper, Perkins argued that there is a four-fold action of taking, giving thanks, breaking and eating. Of the presence of Christ in the sacrament, he wrote:

For the first, we hold and teach that Christs body and blood, are truely present with the bread & wine, being signes in the sacrament: but how? Not in respect of place or coexistence: but by Sacramentall relation on this manner. When a word is uttered, the sound comes to the eare; and at the same instant, the thing signified comes to the minde; and thus by relation the word and the thing spoken of, are both present togither. Even so at the Lords table bread & wine must not be considered barely, as substances and creatures, but as outward signes in relation to the body and blood of Christ.[137]

The emphasis here on the mind raises the question of how far Perkins is also operating with a symbolic memorialism.

Perkins also broached the subject of sacrifice in the Lord's Supper. He rejected the 'papist' interpretation. However, he admitted that there was a sacrificial dimension associated with the Supper, 'because it is a commemoration, and also a representation unto God the Father of the Sacrifice of Christ offered upon the crosse.'[138] It is sacramentally the sacrificing or offering of Christ, which is symbolised in the fraction or breaking of the bread – one of the minister's actions at the Supper.[139]

Perkins uses the language of symbolic instrumentalism, as well as parallelism and memorialism. However, whenever he speaks of the sacraments as instruments of grace, he tends to qualify this in a manner which places him between symbolic parallelism and memorialism. This is particularly so in the manner in which his theology of sacraments is tied into his teaching on predestination, allowing God little room for manoeuvre in sacraments.[140]

The contemporary of Perkins, who in subsequent Anglican historiography enjoys a place which he never did in his own day, was Richard Hooker (1554–1600).[141] Hooker had been educated at Corpus Christi, Oxford, and tutored by John Rainolds, who like Chaderton, was counted amongst the 'godly'. There is some evidence that Hooker at one time was also counted amongst this group, but his theological leanings led him to give his full support to the Elizabethan Settlement, and against those such as Cartwright and Fenner who felt it in need of more serious reform. This was encapsulated in his *Of the Lawes of Ecclesiasticall Politie*. In Book Five of this monumental work, Hooker wrote:

When sacraments are said to be visible signes of invisible grace, wee thereby conceive how grace is indeed the verie ende for which these heavenlie mysteries were instituted, and besides sundrie other properties observed in them the matter whereof they consist is such as signfieth, figureth, and representeth theire ende. But still theire efficacie resteth obscure to our understandinge, except wee search somewhat more distinctly what grace in particular that is whereunto they are referred, and what manner of operation they have towardes it ... Sacraments are the powerfull instrumentes of God to eternall life.[142]

Hooker taught that sacraments were powerful instruments of God in which God may and does give grace. They have a moral, ecclesiastical and a mystical element. For Hooker, baptism was primarily about forgiveness of original sin, and much less about incorporation into the covenant.[143] He is concerned that grace is conveyed not in, but certainly through and with the sacrament. The main purpose of the sacraments, so Hooker maintained, was to allow a mystical union with Christ. He rejected transubstantiation, consubstantiation and the view of the 'sacramentarians'

(Zwingli), and insisted on a personal presence of Christ. The elements are not transmuted, but allow a transmutation to take place in us. The meaning of the words of institution are:

> This hallowed foode, through concurrence of divine power, is in veritie and truth, unto faithfull receivers, instrumentallie a cause of that mysticall participation, whereby as I make my self whollie theires, so I give them in hande an actuall possession of all such saving grace as my sacrificed bodie can yeeld, and as theire soules do presently need, this is 'to them and in them' my bodie.[144]

Hooker's insistence that sacraments are instruments through which God conveys grace, and his emphasis on personal presence and mystical union and participation put him close to a number of aspects of Calvin's teaching; he is a 'High' Calvinist.[145]

Between the Articles of Religion, Nowell's Catechism, Fenner, Perkins and Hooker, we find a wide range of emphases, illustrating a wide approach to the understanding of sacraments. With Fenner and Perkins we find something akin to symbolic parallelism, though closer to Ursinus and Vermigli than to Bullinger. With Nowell and Hooker we see more of a Genevan approach, though in Hooker's case, not the Calvin who could sign the *Consensus Tigurinus*.

Scottish Sacramental Theology

The Scottish Reformation was slower and less complete than in England, and the early Reformers such as John Knox (Figure 1.1) had to contend with a Church which was still in places Catholic and unreformed. Knox wrote on the sacraments, but much of this was of a polemical nature, and while it is possible to glean from his writings his views, it is probably the *Scots Confession* of 1560 which gives a more representative picture.[146] This Confession was drawn up by John Knox, together with John Willock, John Winram, John Spottiswoode, John Row and John Douglas. It was accepted by the Scottish Reformation Parliament in 1560, and by the reconstituted Church of Scotland in 1567. As noted earlier, the *Second Helvetic Confession* also enjoyed a special status in the Church of Scotland, though Calvin's *Catechism* also circulated widely.

Articles XXI–XXIII set forth the Church of Scotland's teaching on sacraments. Article XXI identified two gospel sacraments, corresponding to circumcision and passover. These sacraments, instituted by God for the 'faith of his Children', serve 'to seill in their hearts the assurance of his promise, and of that most blessed conjunction, union and societie' which the elect have with Christ. Any 'bare memorialism' was refuted: 'And this we utterlie damne the vanitie of thay that affirme Sacramentes to be nathing ellis bot naked and baire signes.'[147]

In baptism, the recipient is ingrafted into Christ, made a partaker of his justice (righteousness) by which sins are covered and remitted. In the Supper – rightly used – Christ is joined to us, and he nourishes our souls. The union and conjunction is not transubstantiation; rather it is brought about by the operation of the Holy Spirit. The Spirit is able to overcome the distance between the risen Christ and the communicants. The elements are 'Sacramentall Signes'.

Figure 1.1 John Knox *Dispensing the Sacrament*, unfinished portrait by Sir David Wilkie

Article XXII was concerned with the right administration of the sacraments. A lawful minister – one who preaches – is a requirement, as well as the elements appointed by God. But the Kirk of Scotland flees 'the doctrine of the Papistical Kirk, in participatioun of their sacraments'. In the Supper the words of institution 'sanctifyed bread and wine, to the sacrament of his halie bodie and blude, to the end that the ane suld be eaten', not worshipped. Article XXIII asserted that the Kirk baptised infants, but the Supper is restricted to those who can try and examine themselves.

John Craig (1512–1600), a colleague of Knox at St. Giles, three times moderator of the General Assembly, and Royal Chaplain to James VI, was the prime author of the *King's Confession* or *Negative Confession* of 1581. In the same year Craig also published a catechism, which gives some idea of how sacraments were explained at a more popular teaching level. Sacraments are sensible signs and seals of God's favour offered and given to us, and also effectual instruments of the Spirit.[148] Faith is needed for them to be effective and for the receiver to receive Christ. The sacraments have the similitude with the sign of substance and qualities. The elements signify the very substance of Christ's body, and the spiritual qualities which he gives, though no virtue is enclosed in them. Sacraments are used for the nourishment of our faith, as well as an open protestation of our religion.[149] Baptism signifies remission of sins and regeneration; the similitude is of washing, which results in the putting away of sins and the imputation of justice. But it is not the external sign which accomplishes this, but the Holy Spirit.[150] Children dying without baptism are saved by the promise (of the covenant), and infants are baptised because they are of the seed of the faithful.[151] In the Lord's Supper we are joined with Christ's body in a spiritual manner. We receive his very substantial body and blood by faith and the working of the Holy Spirit.[152] The fraction and the libation of the wine signify his broken body and his blood shed.

Summary

The English and Scottish churches of the late sixteenth century both rejected the Catholic and Lutheran concepts of sacraments, and subscribed to views which were broadly Reformed. The divines of both churches read the works of the leading Reformers, and the Reformed Confessions, and reformulated the ideas and teachings they found there. Yet already in those writings we find different approaches to the sacraments, represented by Bucer, Calvin and Beza on the one hand, and Bullinger, with Laski, on the other. Vermigli and Ursinus attempted a mediating view, but simply produced yet another nuanced Reformed view. Terms such as 'exhibit' and 'instrument' were commonly used, but both the Latin *exhibere* and *instrumenta*, and the English 'exhibit' and 'instrument' had a wide range of meanings, and it is far from clear that divines meant the same thing when using these words. This becomes particularly evident in England with the differences between Fenner, Perkins and Hooker. All three could claim continuity with Reformed teaching, but each developed different aspects and emphases within that tradition.

In England the Elizabethan Settlement imposed by Act of Uniformity a slightly revised version of the 1552 *Book of Common Prayer*. In ethos this retained considerable continuity with the previous Catholic rites, both in its liturgical components, and in the directions for vesture of the ministers and ceremonies. In structure and ceremonial it was quite different from the Agendas and rites drawn up for use in the various Reformed cities abroad. Diversity, however, was common, as evidenced by a manuscript of 1564:

> Some say the service and prayers in the chancel; others in the body of the church. Some say the same in a seat made in the body of the church; some in the pulpit with their faces to the people. Some keep precisely to the order of the book; others intermeddle Psalms in metre. Some say with a surplice; others without a surplice.
> The table standeth in the body of the church in some places; in others it standeth in the chancel.
> Some with surplice and cap; others with surplice alone; others with none. Some with chalice; some with a Communion cup; others with a common cup. Some with unleavened bread, and some with leavened.
> Some receive kneeling, others standing, others sitting.
> Some with a square cap; some with a round cap; some with a button cap; some with a hat; Some in scholars' clothes, some in others.[153]

It fell to bishops to attempt to ensure that the rites and ceremonies were followed as directed by the rubrics of the liturgy, and the Injunctions issued under royal authority.

In Scotland, episcopacy survived the immediate Reformation of 1560, but was phased out to leave a Presbyterian structure. The liturgy which was adopted was the *Book of Common Order*, which was a revision of the 1556 *Form of Prayers* drawn up by Knox, Whittingham and others when in exile in Geneva. This was rather different in ethos from the *Book of Common Prayer*. One major difference was pinpointed in sacramental celebration. In England, the old font was retained for baptisms, and kneeling was the required posture for receiving communion. In Scotland, the old fonts were often destroyed, and replaced by a baptismal bowl attached to the pulpit; sitting around the table was the custom for receiving communion. The differences in sacramental theologies of 'International Calvinism', already bequeathed to both churches, when mixed with different polities, liturgies and ceremonies, would become something of a time-bomb, within each church, and between the two.

Notes

1 Ussher, 1864, vol. 15, p.511.
2 For more detailed discussion on Luther, see Sasse, 1977; Heron, 1983; Trigg, 1994; 1995c.
3 Heron, 1983; Stephens, 1986; 1984.
4 Stephens, 1984, p.158.
5 In Proposal, May 1524, cited by Stephens, 1984, p.156.
6 Gerrish, 1992.
7 Ibid.
8 Stephens, 1970; Bornert, 1981. In fact Stephens posits three periods, 1523–30; 1530–40, and 1540–51, and Bornert has 1523–30, and 1530–50. However, Stephens acknowledges that during the third period Bucer consolidates the shift found in the second period.

9   Cited in Stephens, 1970, p.225.
10 Cited ibid., p.242.
11 Ibid., p.246.
12 Bornert, 1981, p.317.
13 Wright, 1994, p.99.
14 Quoted in Stephens, 1970, pp.230–231.
15 53.B.3, quoted in Stephens, ibid., p.217.
16 Quoted in Stephens, ibid., p.254.
17 For the influences, see Wendel, 1963; Torrance, 1988. On the influence of Augustine, see Evans, 1992; Fitzer, 1992.
18 Calvin, 1986, p.87.
19 Ibid.
20 Ibid., p.90.
21 4:25, Ibid., p.103.
22 Jacobs, 1978.
23 *Corpus Reformationem,* 33:439 'parce que ce sont comme instruments par lesquelz le Seigneur Iesus nous les distribue'.
24 4.14.12.
25 4.14.17.
26 Reid, 1954, pp.131.
27 Elwood, 1999, p.71.
28 4.17.10.
29 4.17.11.
30 Tylenda, 1981, pp.31–2. However, Tylenda's next sentence, that Calvin will never abandon this word, overlooks its omission on the sacrament in the *Consensus Tigurinus*, as discussed below.
31 4.17.10.
32 4.17.12.
33 4.17.19 'veram substantialemque corporis ac sanguinis Domini communicatione'.
34 Sasse, 1977, pp.252–60. Sasse, of course, saw this as a defection from the Lutheran teaching.
35 *Genevan Catechism*, in Reid, 1954, p.136; see Gerrish, 1993.
36 In Schaff, 1998, 3: pp.378–9.
37 Ibid., p.380–81.
38 Old, 1975, pp.191–207.
39 CR35:695, quoted from Rorem, 1989, p.34.
40 Bullinger, 5, 1850, p.229.
41 Ibid., p. 270.
42 Ibid., pp. 253–4.
43 Ibid., p. 296, 315.
44 Ibid., p. 327.
45 Ibid., pp. 367–8.
46 Ibid., p. 439.
47 Ibid., p. 422.
48 Text, Bunting, 1966, pp.45–61.
49 George, 1990, pp. 42–58.
50 Article 8, Bunting, 1966, p.52.
51 Bunting here translates *organa* as instruments, even though noting the change in a footnote. Bullinger consistently refused to use *exhibere* and *instrumenta* with regard to the sacraments.
52 George, 1990, pp.47–8.

53 Rorem, 1989, p.46.
54 Gerrish, 1982, p.124.
55 Leith, 1963, p.161.
56 Ibid., p.168.
57 Ibid., pp.170–171.
58 Spinks, 1990a, pp. 94–102.
59 See particularly McLelland, 1957; Corda, 1975. See also McLelland and Duffield, 1989.
60 *Commentary on Romans*, 4:11, 1558. Quoted in McLelland, 1957, p.133.
61 LC 1008, cited Corda, 1975, p.50.
62 'Neque inter symbola et rem significatam coniuncto est, nisi sacramentalis', *A Defence*, 1559, cited Corda,1975, p.81.
63 *The Oxford Disputation*, in McLelland and Duffield, 1989, p.174.
64 Ibid., p.162.
65 Romans 6:5, cited McLelland, 1957, p.140.
66 Ibid.
67 *Sacrament of Thanksgiving*, fol38v, quoted in Jeanes, 1998, p.159.
68 McLelland and Duffield, 1989, p.290.
69 See McLelland, 1957, p.159.
70 Romans 5:19, McLelland, ibid., p.156.
71 Romans 11:14, cited in McLelland, ibid., p.157.
72 McLelland and Duffield, 1989, p.216.
73 Ibid., p.229.
74 Ibid., p.329.
75 Ibid., p.330.
76 For Oxford, see Dent, 1983, p.91. It was printed in Edinburgh in 1591, and again in 1615 'for use of the Kirke of Edinburgh'.
77 Williard, 1954.
78 Ibid., pp.340, 342. Ursinus played an important role in the development of covenant theology. See Weir, 1990.
79 Ibid, p.342.
80 Ibid., p.340.
81 Ibid., p.372.
82 Ibid., p.348.
83 Ibid., p.351.
84 Question and Answer 69. Ibid., p.356.
85 Ibid., p.358.
86 Ibid., p.361.
87 Ibid., p.362, 364.
88 Ibid., p.365.
89 Ibid., p.378.
90 Ibid., p.380.
91 Ibid., p.386.
92 Ibid., p.378.
93 Ibid., p.385.
94 Ibid., p.386.
95 Rodgers, 1994; Spinks, 1984a.
96 Quoted in Rodgers, 1994, p.119.
97 Ibid., p.121.
98 Gorham, 1857, pp.108–110.
99 Musculus, 1578, p.652.

100   Ibid., p.667.
101   Ibid., p.670.
102   Ibid., p.674.
103   Ibid., p.707.
104   Ibid, p.708.
105   Ibid., p.710.
106   Ibid., p.669.
107   Ibid., pp.730–31
108   Raitt, 1972.
109   Quoted Raitt, ibid., pp.21–2.
110   Ibid., p.24.
111   Ibid., p.28.
112   Ibid., p.41.
113   Ibid., p.64.
114   See Smyth, 1926; Brooks, 1965; Hall, 1993; MacCulloch, 1996; Jeanes, 1998.
115   For wider discussion on these, except Fenner, see Spinks, 1999.
116   MacCulloch, 1996, pp.615–6.
117   See Green, 1996, pp.189ff.
118   Haugaard, 1970, pp. 50–65.
119   Corrie, 1853, p.205.
120   Green, 1996, pp.512–3.
121   Corrie, 1853, p.214.
122   Fenner, 1588, A2–3.
123   This will be discussed further below.
124   Ibid., A3.
125   Ibid., E – no pagination.
126   Ibid., A4, italics mine.
127   Ibid., A5–6, though no pagination.
128   Ibid., section D – no pagination.
129   Ibid., E –no pagination.
130   See Beeke, 1991; Kendall, 1979.
131   For a fuller treatment of Perkins, see Spinks, 1999.
132   Perkins, 1616–18, 1:71.
133   Ibid., 1:611.
134   Ibid., 1:547.
135   Ibid., 2:74.
136   Ibid., 2:260.
137   Ibid., 1:590.
138   Ibid., 2:551.
139   Ibid., 1:593.
140   For further discussion, see Spinks, 1999.
141   See Spinks, 1999; MacCulloch, forthcoming. The recent book, Phillip Secor, *Richard Hooker. Prophet of Anglicanism*, 1999, is typical of the 'Anglican mythology' approach (the author even does look-alike guest appearances!), and some of the commentary in the Folger edition of Hooker's works tends towards this romanticised view.
142   Hooker, Laws Book 5:50.3, 1977–1994.
143   Hooker mentions covenant in relation to baptism in passing, but never develops the concept.
144   Hooker, Laws 5:67:12.

145 In his review of *Two Faces of Elizabethan Anglican Theology*, Egil Grislis seems unwilling to class Hooker as Reformed, and wishes to stress his Thomism, and 'Roman Catholic theological background'. Recent scholarship has been more hesitant on the extent of Thomist influence; Grislis's claim of Roman Catholic influence seems to be wishful thinking; Grislis, 2000, p.908.
146 See Torrance, 1996, for Knox's views.
147 Schaff, 1998, vol. 3, pp.467–8.
148 Craig, 1959, pp.147–8.
149 Ibid., p.155
150 Ibid., p.152.
151 Ibid., p.153.
152 Ibid., p.156.
153 Strype, 1821, vol. 1, p. 302.

Chapter 2

Lex Ritualis, Lex Credendi?
From Hampton Court to the Five Articles
of Perth

The Hampton Court Conference and its Implications and Aftermath

The first session of the Hampton Court Conference took place on 14 January 1604. This conference included eight bishops, seven deans, and two doctors of divinity appointed by James to respond to the concerns of four representatives of the signatories of the Millenary Petition. This latter had been presented to James as he made his way from Scotland to London. Prime movers of this petition were Stephen Egerton and Arthur Hildersham, both known for their vocal discontent with various aspects of the Church of England, and also for their repeated nonconformity in matters of liturgical ceremonial. The Millenary Petition itself reiterated criticisms of the *Book of Common Prayer* and its ceremonial which had been articulated previously in the reign of Elizabeth by such protagonists as Thomas Cartwright, and John Field and Thomas Wilcox in their *An Admonition to the Parliament*.[1] Such things as the use of the surplice, the ring in marriage, the sign of the cross in baptism were amongst the several complaints. In Elizabeth's time, appeal was made to the example of the 'Best Reformed Churches'. The signatories of the Millenary Petition hoped that since James VI was schooled in one of the 'Best Reformed Churches', namely Scotland, he would have some sympathy with those who wished to nudge the Church of England in the same direction. The concept that there should be more similarities between the two churches now under one monarch was one which James did indeed warm to, though unfortunately for the petitioners, as events unfolded, James's vision was to conform the Church of Scotland to that of England rather than *vice versa*.

Neither Egerton nor Hildersham were invited to participate in the Hampton Court Conference. Representing the signatories were Laurance Chaderton of Cambridge, John Rainolds of Oxford, John Knewstubbs, rector of Cockfield, Suffolk and Dr Thomas Sparkes, rector of Bletchley, who were regarded as more moderate than Egerton and Hildersham. Also in attendance was Patrick Galloway, minister of Perth. The account of this conference given by William Barlow has usually been taken to demonstrate that little concession was made to those representing the petitioners' cause. Barlow (d. 1613) who was a graduate of St. John's College, Cambridge, Fellow of Trinity Hall, and by 1604, Dean of Chester, represented the views of the episcopal status quo; a face-value reading of his account was challenged by Mark Curtis, who suggested that the 'Anonymous Account' more accurately recorded the common ground between the King and the 'godly' contingent.

According to Curtis, the king made a number of concessions, but not all of these were carried out by the bishops.[2] This view has itself been reassessed by Fred Shriver, who defended Barlow's account, and this in turn has been qualified by Arnold Hunt on the basis of an unpublished account by Chaderton.[3] Whatever the assessment, it remains true that few of the requests articulated in the Millenary Petition were granted at Hampton Court. The petitioners asked: 'That the cross in baptism, interrogatories ministered to infants, confirmations, as superfluous, may be taken away: baptism not to be ministered by women, and so explained: ... that examination may go before the communion: that it be ministered with a sermon'.[4]

As touching baptism, a new rubric ruled out baptism by midwives and laymen. Hunt correctly observed that 'the consequent alteration of the Prayer Book rubric to forbid lay baptism was of considerable doctrinal significance, since it effectively denied the absolute necessity of baptism as a precondition of salvation.'[5] Other objections were dismissed, and the resulting 1604 *Book of Common Prayer* re-imposed almost intact the Elizabethan *lex orandi*, itself hardly altered from Cranmer's 1552 book. But already by 1604 the liturgical text was slipping behind a developing discussion on sacraments and their liturgical expression.

Dissatisfaction on the part of the 'godly clergy' is evidenced in the continued complaint from ministers of the Lincoln Diocese in 1605, and *A Survey of the Book of Common Prayer* (1606). The former once more raised objections to the sign of the cross in baptism. First, it had popish origins: 'The signe of the crosse also is notoriously knowne to bee abused to superstition and Idolatry by the Papists: for both *Stapleton* & *Bellarmine* doe make the speciall badge of their Idolatrous Religion.'[6] Furthermore, it gave rise to misunderstanding: 'The common people in many parts of the land are known not only to retain the superstitious use of it (blessing themselves, their breasts, their foreheads, and everything they take in hand by it) but also to hold that their children are not rightly baptized without it.'[7]

The compilers were concerned that nothing should detract from the water and the word, which are sufficient for the sacrament, 'Seeing this Crossing doeth only signifie the same graces which bapisme both signifieth and sealeth.'[8] But underneath these ceremonial trivia there lurked deeper questions of the sacraments. Thus citing the words from the liturgy, 'We call upon thee for these infants that they comming to holy Baptism, may receive remission of their sinnes, by spirituall regeneration', *A Survey* asked:

> Quaere. *Whither Baptisme it selfe, or Regeneration by the spirit of God, be meant by these words*, spirituall regeneration.
>
> If the former Quaere, *Whither this tend not to the justifying of Popish doctrine, viz, that Sacraments* give grace ex opere operato.
>
> If the later quaere, *Whither it may not as well be said, that we be justified by works, as that sinnes are forgiven by spiritual regeneration*. Seeing forgivenes of sinnes is only by imputation, Rom.4.7.8.[9]

It also drew attention to the words 'Seeing now dearly beloved brethren, that these children be regenerate, and grafted into the body of Christes congregation, Let us give thankes', asking whether '*in these wordes the Popish error of Sacramentes there giving grace*, ex opere operato, *be not implied*'.[10] It asserted that only the Holy Ghost baptised effectually, and therefore objected to the idea of blessing water.[11] And both the writers of *An Abridgement* and *A Survey* regarded kneeling for communion to be a sign teaching transubstantiation.[12] Thus, underneath what appears to be nothing more than ceremonial disputes, there were deeper questions concerning sacramental theology.

One significant addition made in the 1604 *Book of Common Prayer*, however, was in the catechism, which was extended to include treatment of the sacraments. This addition was the work of John Overall, Dean of St. Paul's, and later Bishop of Coventry and Lichfield, and then of Norwich. This new addition asserted that there were only two sacraments which Christ ordained in his Church 'as generally necessary for salvation', baptism and the Supper of the Lord. Sacrament was defined as 'an outward and visible signe of an inward and spiritual grace, given unto us, ordained by Christ himselfe, as a means whereby we receive the same, and a pledge to assure us thereof'. Each sacrament consists of an outward sign and an inward spiritual grace. The inward spiritual grace of baptism was explained as death unto sin, and a new birth to righteousness, and being made children of grace. Repentance is required, which for infants is given by their sureties. The Lord's Supper was ordained for the continual remembrance of the sacrifice of the death of Christ and the benefits which we receive. The outward sign is bread and wine, but the inward which is signified is 'The body and blood of Christ, which are verily, and indeed taken and received of the faithfull in the Lords supper'. The benefits include strengthening and refreshing of our souls, and what is required is examination, a steadfast purpose to lead a new life, thankfulness for God's mercy, and charity with all. Overall's source, greatly précised, was Alexander Nowell's catechism of 1570/73.

Neither Nowell's catechism, in its 1570 format, nor Overall's 1604 liturgical précis, expressed the developing covenant theology with which many linked the sacraments. Already in Zwingli, Bullinger and Calvin, infant baptism was defended by analogy with circumcision in the Old Testament. Calvin's baptismal rite actually speaks of the covenant of grace. However, developed by the Heidelberg theologians, by the 1570s there was a theological distinction between the covenant of works, made with either Abraham or Adam, and the Covenant of Grace.[13] It became common therefore to speak of the sacraments as seals of the covenant. This language is absent from the *Book of Common Prayer*, and does not seem to have been used by Cranmer.[14] Its development and refinement post-dates Calvin and Poynet, but was utilised by Dudley Fenner, and also by William Perkins. Nowell made no use of it, and neither did Overall. His decision not to allude to it may have been theologically motivated, or it may reflect the need for a basic pedagogical simplicity.[15] Whatever the motive, the sacramental section added in 1604 concealed the developments and discussions which were taking place. Elsewhere I have argued that this can be seen in the differences between William Perkins and Richard Hooker, with Perkins using a developing covenant theology and prefering to speak of seals, and Hooker hardly using the term 'covenant', and preferring to speak of the sacraments not as signs of grace received, but as instruments of grace available.[16]

The common use of the term 'covenant' can be seen in Thomas Roger's (d. 1616) commentary on the 39 Articles of Religion, written in 1585, but with a new edition in 1607 which was reprinted many times.[17] Rogers, who was Bancroft's chaplain, and a staunch conformist who also wrote two tracts defending kneeling for communion, speaks of a sacrament as 'a covenant of God his favour to man-ward, confirmed by some outward signe, or Seale instituted by himselfe' and the two dominical sacraments can be described as 'seales of the covenant'.[18] Richard Rogers (1550–1618), more than once disciplined for nonconformity, in *The Practice of Christianity* (1619), explained that sacraments 'do ratifie and confirme that which the Word doth teach, and do most surely and effectually seale up the covenant made betwixt God and the beleever'.[19] In his Catechism of 1612, John Dod, also one of the 'godly' ministers who drifted in and out of conformity, after asserting that the law and Gospel were otherwise called the covenant of works and the covenant of grace, taught that a sacrament is: 'A more finall, effectual and sensible instrument, then the word alone: whereby Christ with all his benefits is offered to all in the Church, and received only by the faithfull'.[20] Baptism is a seal of our entrance into Christianity, and the Lord's Supper a seal of our growth and continuance in Christianity.[21] In his sermons on the Lord's Supper, Dod liked to speak of the seal or sacrament of the 'eternall covenant'.[22]

Thus amongst some Church of England divines, conformist and nonconformist, there was a growing concern to tie sacraments to a covenant theology, and to speak of them as seals of the covenant, which in turn had certain ecclesiological implications. But not all shared this enthusiasm for developing Reformed theology. Others, inspired perhaps by Hooker, but represented by John Overall and Lancelot Andrewes, preferred to develop a more patristically inspired theology.

The range of views in England may be illustrated with reference to the teaching of representatives of what might be loosely termed the 'nonconformist Calvinists', 'Conformist Calvinists', and, following the terminology of Peter Lake, 'Avantgarde Conformists' respectively.

Nonconformist Calvinists: Stephen Egerton and Arthur Hildersham

Stephen Egerton   Stephen Egerton (1555?–1621?) was one of the main signatories of the Millenary Petition. Educated at Peterhouse, Cambridge, he gained his MA in 1579, and in 1583 was incorporated MA at Oxford. He was associated with the Classis movement which espoused a presbyterian polity, and in 1584 had been suspended. However, he seems to have been reinstated fairly quickly, and in the 1590s was sent by the Bishop of London to try to persuade the Separatist leaders, Henry Barrow and John Greenwood, of their errors. In 1598, he became incumbent of St. Anne's, Blackfriars, London, and remained there until his death, though in his later years he was assisted by William Gouge, another noted 'godly' minister who found conformity difficult. Egerton had written briefly on sacraments in his *A Briefe method of Catechizing* (c.1594), and this work was popular, and in its forty-fourth edition in 1644. Egerton had defined a sacrament as a 'a holy signe and seale ordained of God to assure us of his love to us in Christ, and to testifie and confirme our faith and obedience to him, and our love and fellowship one with another'. Baptism is the sacrament of new and spiritual birth, and infants are baptised 'Because the Covenant and promise of God is made to the faithfull, & to their seed'. The Lord's Supper is the sacrament of spiritual nourishment.[23]

Arthur Hildersham   Arthur Hildersham (1563–1632), another main instigator of the Millenary Petition, graduated from Christ's College, Cambridge, and in 1587 was appointed lecturer at Ashby de la Zouch (Figure 2.1). He was immediately in trouble for preaching before receiving ordination, and his subsequent life was a series of deprivations and reinstatements, and included a brief imprisonment in 1616. He had been silenced by William Chaderton, Bishop of Lincoln in 1605, but licensed by William Overton, Bishop of Coventry and Lichfield; and in 1609 William Barlow, by then Bishop of Lincoln, restored him to Ashby. In 1625 he was licensed to preach in the dioceses of London, Lincoln, Coventry and Lichfield. Hildersham's teachings centre mainly on the Lord's Supper, and are found in his *108 Lectures on the Fourth (Chapter) of John* (1609), *A Briefe Forme of Examination* (1619), *The Doctrine of Communicating Worthily in the Lord's Supper* (1619), and his *152 Lectures on Psalm 51*, preached at Ashby de la Zouch from 1626 to 1629. The fact that these sermons were preached at communion services reflects the fact that regular celebration of the Lord's Supper was encouraged by many of the 'godly' ministers, in contrast to the thrice yearly, or in some cases, single annual celebration found in many Jacobean parishes.[24]

Hildersham defined a sacrament as 'A mysticall signe ordained by God, to represent and seale to the worthy receiver, salvation by Christ Jesus'.[25] They are seals of the covenant of grace.[26] Indeed, their force and efficacy depend on the

Figure 2.1   Arthur Hildersham, 1563–1632

covenant.[27] An ordained minister should preside, because he has the commission to apply the king's seal.[28] They are visible signs of invisible grace, and visible words.[29]

Baptism was defined as 'A mysticall washing with water, in the name of the Father, Sonne, and Holy Ghost'.[30] The water signifies the blood of Christ, the washing that we are freed from the guilt of sin and sanctified by the merits of Christ. Yet there appears to be some tension as Hildersham wrestled with grace through faith and the Holy Spirit, and the sacraments as effective seals. He could on the one hand refute Anabaptists by appealing to original sin, asserting 'First, So soone as they are borne, they have title to the seale of Gods Covenant, and the Church may not deny it unto them.'[31] Again, he wrote:

> The second use of this Doctrine is for instruction; to teach us what great neede there is, that infants should be baptized; for this maketh greatly for the confirmation of the faith, and comfort of their parents for the present, and of their own afterwards, that as they are by nature so filthy and loathsome in the sight of God, so the Lorde hath in the bloud of Jesus Christ (whereof the water in baptisme is a signe and seale) provided a laver to wash and cleanse them in, even the *laver of regeneration*, as the Apostle calleth it, Tit. 3.5. yea, a *fountain opened* (as the prophet calleth it, Zac. 13.1) *for sin, and for uncleannes*, sufficient to cleanse them from all this filthinesse, and corruption of their nature.[32]

However, Hildersham also asserted: 'That is only true and compleate baptisme, wherein God hath baptized the party as well as man, that a true and compleat Communion which God hath administred as well as man; that a true and compleat prayer, when the Spirit of God hath joyned with me, and prayed as well as I.'[33] Furthermore, though he makes an exception for infants, he asserted that sacraments can do us no good unless we come to them and use them with understanding, and they should be administered only after instruction by the ministry of the Word.[34] Though he does not make this explicit, implicit here is that infants are baptised on account of the fact that believing parents are in the covenant. This perhaps explains in part why it is the Lord's Supper which is of more interest to Hildersham, because as a minister of the Word, it was his duty to instruct and give proper understanding and proper preparation. He asserted: 'This is the Supper of the Lord, wherein the Body and Bloud of our blessed Saviour is represented, and exhibited by the elements of Bread and Wine, creatures that God hath given (above all things) to strengthen and make glad the heart of man.'[35]

In explaining why the bread and wine are called the body and blood of Christ, Hildersham listed first, 'to give unto the outward signe, the name of the thing signified thereby'; second, 'to shew how certain and neere that spirituall presence and union is, that by the power of his spirit is made between the signe and the thing signified'; and third 'to lift up our harts from the earthly elements unto the consideration of the heavenlie matter represented by them, then if hee should have called them onelie the signes of his bodie and bloud.'[36]

Hildersham explained that the Lord's Supper has both a divine dimension and a human dimension. The divine is Christ's institution of the sacrament, and the human element is the administration by the Minister of the Word and the congregation.[37] Christ consecrated the elements by thanksgiving and prayer to the Father, and secondly 'by instituting & ordaining these elements and actions in this Sacrament to serve unto this end; not onely using them to himselfe, but commanding his Church to doe so also, and promising unto us his gracious and effectual presence in the use of these elements, according to his ordinance'.[38] He explained his understanding of consecration as requiring a declaration of the institution made by Christ, public thanks to God for the work of redemption, and 'earnest praier unto the Lord, that hee would be present with, & blesse this his owne ordinance, making it effectuall to those ends that himselfe appointed it for'.[39]

The Lord's Supper does, declared Hildersham, have a promise of grace. He explained the promise thus:

> As by Baptisme, wee were taught and assured that through the merit of Christ's passion, and of it onely, we were first received into Gods covenant and favour, united to him and his Church, and so obtained remission of all our sins, and the grace of regeneration; so by this Sacrament wee are taught and assured, that through the merit of Christs passion, and of it onely, we are and shal be kept in this blessed estate, nourished and confirmed in it, revivied and comforted in all tentations.[40]

In the liturgical celebration 'the bread is solemnly in the sight of the congregation broken in sunder, & the wine poured forth; & that by the ordinance and commandment of Christ.'[41] Since one of the complaints of the 'godly' clergy was that there was no provision for a fraction and libation in the Prayer Book rite, we may conjecture that this was one ceremony that ministers like Hildersham added to the English liturgy. This was the representation or commemoration of the sacrifice made once by Christ. Indeed, the body and blood of Christ is offered by the minister in his Name and by his commandment to every receiver,[42] though not all receive this promise of grace: 'Many dreame they have in the Sacrament eaten the body of Christ, and drunke his blood, but when their Conscience shall bee a wakened, they will finde they were but in a Dreame.'[43] This is explained by the fact that Hildersham insists that the force and efficacy of the sacrament depends upon the covenant, and worthiness requires a true justifying faith.[44] Much of his homiletic material is concerned with worthy preparation and instruction, which includes knowledge of the Law, Gospel and the sacrament. Thus on the one hand Hildersham wished to stress the importance of the sacraments, but at the same time was fearful of implying any *ex opere operato* qualities.

Conformist Calvinists: John Downame, John Randall and William Attersoll

John Downame   John Downame (d. 1652) was the son of William Downame, Bishop of Chester, and the brother of George Downame, Bishop of Derry, who was one of the first to support *de jure divino* episcopacy. Like Hildersham, John Downame was a graduate of Christ's College, Cambridge, and was probably taught by William Perkins. In 1599 he was instituted to St. Olave, Jewry, and then exchanged this for St. Margaret Lothbury, both of which were London parishes. He seems to have held no benefice between 1618 and 1630, when he became rector of All Hallows the Great, Thames Street London. He was certainly one of the 'godly'.[45] His views on the sacraments are outlined in *A Guide to Godlynesse or a Treatise of a Christian Life* (1622).

The sacraments, explained Downame, are 'seales annexed to the Covenant of grace, purposely instituted of God to strengthen and confirme our faith in this assurance'.[46] The covenant of grace (a topic upon which his brother was to write at length)[47] was treated in the first part of his work. The 'godly' must be ingrafted into Jesus Christ, and they must be in the covenant of grace 'whereby God hath assured us that he will bee our God, and that we shall be his people; he is our gracious Father, and we his children, whom he will accept in his best beloved.'[48] But the sacraments are not just seals of the covenant, or significant signs; they are also 'infallible seales, annexed purposely by God unto his Covenant, to assure us that he will performe all his promises, and to give unto us (like a bond and coveyance legally signed and sealed) just title and interest unto all those blessings, even before we sensibly have them in possession and fruition'.[49] But he also adds: 'they also serve like instruments and conduit pipes to convey to the worthy receiver, Christ, and all his benefits.'[50] Thus for Downame, sacraments effectively move us to go on in the work of sanctification.[51]

When he turned to baptism, Downame asserted that we are sacramentally ingrafted into the body of Christ and made members of the Church. We are baptised into Christ's death and resurrection, being washed and purged from guilt and punishment and raised to new life, 'The which is not onely sacramentally signified by the outward washing and sprinkling with water, which serveth to cleanse us from our bodily defilements, by our stay ... but also certainly sealed and assured, and powerfully conveyed to the worthy receiver.'[52] (See Figure 2.2.)

Downame then turned to consider regeneration, and here, repeating almost the same words, explained the powerful conveyance as 'by the inward operation of Gods Spirit, which powerfully worketh together with his holy ordinances'.[53] What is received is 'the spiritual life of grace'. However, Downame quickly qualified this. It is received, 'potentially to the elect Infants, as they potentially have faith, and by Gods Decree are ordained to beleeve, and actually to those who by faith apply unto themselves Christ and all his benefits'.[54]

Thus baptism does not itself impart the spiritual life of grace to infants. It does so potentially to 'elect Infants'; behind this is Downame's covenant of grace theology which is anchored in an infralapsarian theology of predestination.[55] Baptism thus signifies what is to come, and this for Downame is true for all, not just infants. The virtue of baptism quickens to new life, but must not

> ... be limitted and restrained to the time past, or to the present act of administration ... but the power and vigour of it continueth and extendeth it selfe to the whole course of our lives; and is an effectuall meanes, being recalled to our minds, and afresh applyed by faith, both to assure us of the pardon of all our sinnes, as it is the seale of the Covenant, whose vertue continueth not onely at the first act of sealing, but as long as the tearme specified in the writing, and therefore must continue in full vertue for ever, to our use, seeing it is a seale affixed to an everlasting Covenant ...'[56]

Downame explained that public baptism was beneficial for the congregation because it is a time when we renew our covenant with God by calling afresh the memories of God; we can call to mind the fruits of baptism, and also pray for the baptisand 'that hee may be truly regenerate, ingrafted into the body of Christ as a lively member, and so made partaker of his death, merits, and all his benefits'.[57]

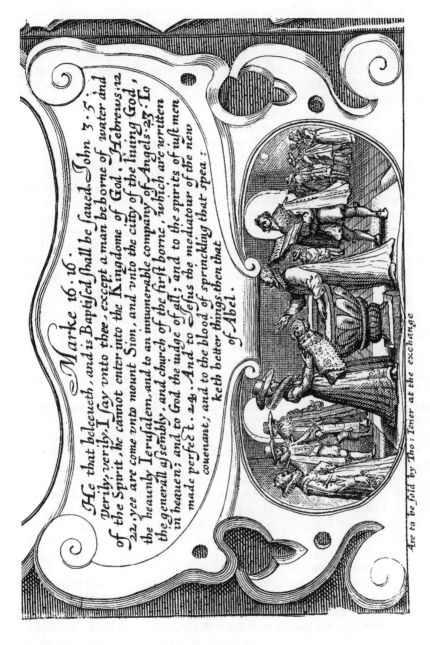

Figure 2.2 Depiction of baptism, England, 1624

For Downame the Lord's Supper 'is a notable meanes of confirming and increasing our faith, being the Lords Seale, wherewith he hath ratified his Covenant of grace and salvation with us'.[58] But it also testifies to our thankfulness to God in Christ for benefits, as well as being a profession of faith, applying all the fruits and benefits, and it is a sacrament of our union with Christ and communion with one another. But Downame, interestingly, denies that it confirms the covenant; rather the elements are seals which enable us to renew the covenant.[59] The Supper enables us to perform Christian duties. God offers and gives, and we take and apply Christ and all his benefits. This is no 'spare meal, and bare commons', but makes us grow in grace and spiritual strength and stature.[60] Downame provided a prayer for before the communion, which in some respects distils his belief. He prays, 'indue us with a true and lively faith, that wee may not onely receive the outward Elements, but also may inwardly feed upon the precious Body and Blood of our Lord and Saviour Jesus Christ, that thereby wee may be inriched with all saving graces, strengthened unto all good duties, and nourished unto everlasting life.' He asks 'Make us partakers of Christs merits, by imputation of his nature and essence by coniunction, and of his power and efficacy by thy holy Spirit.'[61] Downame was more interested in worthy preparation than explaining how the seals convey union. Being trained at Christ's, Cambridge, did he follow Perkins and reserve this for the elect? This is not clear. However, he does seem to move beyond Arthur Hildersham's position, and saw the sacraments as in some way conveying, rather than just signifying, grace.

John Randall   John Randall (1570–1622) had been a student at Trinity College, Oxford and Lincoln College, Oxford, and graduated BD in 1598. He was incumbent and lecturer of St. Andrew Hubbard, Little Eastcheap, London. His series of sermons on the Lord's Supper, which were concerned mainly with worthy reception, were published in 1630, and they contain many allusions to phraseology in the *Book of Common Prayer* communion service. Furthermore, Randall celebrated a monthly communion service, and these sermons promoted the frequency of the sacrament.

Randall taught that the Lord's Supper is above all a banquet and feast of our souls, in which the faithful are nourished to a spiritual and heavenly life.[62] It is the sacrament of the seal of the New Covenant or Testament, and 'an effectuall Pledge and Seale of the whole worke and Covenant of Grace'.[63] It is an effectual bond, pledge and seal of that holy and blessed communion which the faithful have with Christ, and Christ with them.[64] Indeed, 'there is a reall Communion to everie faithfull and spirituall Receiver, for as the Spirit of God works Faith in our Hearts, so Faith causeth us to beleeve that Christ hath made our peace with God, and that we are incorporate into his Body, and made one with him. This is the reall exhibiting of Christ in the Sacrament ...'[65]

The preached word conveys Christ to us 'more largely', the sacrament 'more neerely' but each very powerfully and effectually.[66] The elements are in a sacramental sense the body and blood of Christ.[67] Indeed, 'the same Spirit that was in Christ when he performed the office of our redemption, is in and at the Sacrament, to make Christ really present (yet spiritually) to every faithfull receiver, by the power, merit, and virtue of the body and blood.'[68]

Randall asserted the presence, but never attempted to explain it, though he made a point of rejecting transubstantiation.[69] He was much more concerned with the question of Christ's sacrifice which is figured in the Supper, and particularly in the fraction and pouring out of wine. Thus the Supper is 'a lively commemoration' of his 'sweet smelling Sacrifice'.[70] Randall asserted:

> Our bodily Eyes cannot see so farre, but the Eye of faith sees into Heaven, and beleeves that Christ Jesus sitting at the right Hand of God is here present at the Table, after a spirituall manner, and so doth give and communicate himselfe unto us: The Eye of the Body sees the Bread broken, and the Wine poured out; the Eye of Faith, sees and considers, the breaking of Christs Body, and the shedding of his Blood, for the taking away of our sinnes, and this is that which the Apostle presseth, 1 Cor.11.29 about the discerning of the Lords Body.[71]

The sacrament is a lively remembrance of Christ, and a representation, or shewing forth of the Lord's death.[72] It is 'a fresh and a lively representation and memoriall of his death'.[73] Randall thus had much to say about the sacrificial death of Christ, and the meaning of the elements in relation to the passion: 'I shewed you that the death of Christ must bee meditated upon in the Sacrament of the Lords Supper; here is the eye whereby wee doe discerne Christ crucified in these holy mysteries, even the knowledge of Christ crucified in reference to the Sacrament of the Lords Supper.'[74] Though he denied that communicants were to 'dwell in the grosse and carnall meditation of his wounds and blood-shedding; as the Papists doe', none the less Randall stressed that in the blood of Christ 'there this Treasure lyes', and he stressed the importance of the action of the breaking of the bread and the pouring of the wine.[75] The wine representing the blood of Christ shows the bountifulness of the love of God, the infiniteness of Christ's merit, thankfulness to God, pity for the Jews, and that many shall be saved.[76]

William Attersoll   William Attersoll (d.1640) was a Cambridge graduate, BA Clare Hall in 1582, and MA Peterhouse in 1586. He became incumbent of Isfield around 1600 and remained there until his death in 1640. He was the author of many biblical commentaries and treatises. He also published a lengthy work on sacraments, entitled *The New Covenant, or a Treatise on the Sacraments*, 1614. This book was divided neatly into three parts, or 'books', with the first on sacraments in general, and two further parts on baptism and the Lord's Supper.

Attersoll taught that God had always given sacraments of one sort or another, and cited the tree in the garden of paradise, and the ark given to Noah, as well as circumcision.[77] Sacraments may be defined as 'seales which the Lord alone setteth to his owne letters', and 'instruments which the Holye Ghost useth to this ende, to make us more and more one with Christ'.[78] However, they do not themselves convey grace; 'although God use them as instruments of grace, yet the especiall working and forcible power of them, is not in them, but dependeth on God alone.'[79] They are instruments of the Holy Ghost, 'who worketh by them to the great comfort of the faithfull. Grace is not contained and shut up in them, as water in a vessell, or as a medicine in a boxe.'[80] Word and sacraments are both instruments of the same grace, and both require faith. They cannot give faith; we must bring faith to them.[81] Sacraments are offered to the eyes as well as to the ears, 'so that wee doe ever behold Iesus Christ as it were crucified before us'.[82] A sacrament is '*a visible signe and seale ordained of God, wherby Christ and all his saving graces by certaine outward rites are signified, exhibited, and sealed up unto us*'.[83] It is an instrument to confer and convey Christ;[84] they are means to offer and exhibit to the believer Christ and all his benefits.[85] If any come to the sacraments and leave without grace, the cause is to be found within themselves.[86] Sacraments have four parts to them – the minister, the word of institution, the sign, and the receiver.

Baptism is an outward washing in water in the name of the Trinity, representing an inward cleansing of the soul by the blood of Christ.[87] The latter is the true material cause of the sacrament.[88] The Trinity is always present at baptism, and the Persons of the Trinity 'performe that which is outwardly figured and represented'.[89] Through it a solemn covenant and contract is made.[90] Infants are baptised because they are in the covenant by virtue of their parents. However, it is not essential that their parents are faithful; the Church or some ancestor will suffice: 'for the Church is as it were their mother. Secondly, we must consider, not onely their immediate parents, but their forefathers and ancestors which have led a godly and holy life.'[91] The fact that personal faith is missing for infants was explained by Attersoll thus: 'Baptisme is the Sacrament of repentance and faith, though neither of these be in infancy, yet they are baptized to the repentance and faith to come, which albeit they be not actually formed in them, yet by the fruites afterward they shall appeare to be in them.'[92]

Yet Attersoll did not wish to tie the inward and outward too closely, particularly because faith was necessary. Thus we find a tendency towards symbolic parallelism: 'The fruite or efficacy of the Sacrament is not to be restrained and tyed to the present time of personall receiving, but extendeth it selfe to the whole course of our life afterward.'[93] This is because baptism cannot make a Christian, but is a seal confirming the right to be a Christian.[94]

By far the longest section of Attersoll's work was given over to the Lord's Supper. In the first section on sacraments in general, he had already insisted that sacraments were actions (cf. Bullinger, Peter Martyr Vermigli), not dumb shows. Like Perkins, he taught a four-fold action. At one point Attersoll stated that it was a four-fold action of blessing, breaking and pouring out, and distributing.[95] Later, however, he expounds the same four-fold pattern as Perkins:

> Wherefore the actions and workes of the Minister are foure-fold. First, to take the bread and wine into his hands after the example of Christ ... The second action is blessing and giving of thanks ... to separate the bread and wine so taken from their common use to an holy use ... The third action is breaking the bread & pouring out of the wine, which are necessary rites to be observed, having respect & relation to the unspeakable torments of Christ for us, who was pierced, crucified, & made a curse for us upon the Crosse ... The last action of the Minister is to distribute the bread and wine ...'[96]

He noted that although scripture recorded the words of institution, the evangelists did not record the prayer(s) Jesus uttered at the Last Supper, 'because our corruption and superstition is so great, that if wee had the words, we would ascribe powers & force to the words, sillables, and letters, & therfore the manner of his thanksgiving is pretermitted'.[97] Attersoll was fully aware of the covenant theology, and asserted that scripture teaches a double covenant, one of works and one of grace.[98] The Supper seals up the covenant.

The words of institution, argued Attersoll, are to be interpreted properly, which means in a spiritual and mystical sense. The bread is a sign or sacrament of Christ's true body.[99] Christ is truly exhibited to us, and offered to us, and effectually given to the faithful.[100] But the Lutheran idea that Christ is present in the elements is 'as improbable & impossible as the alchymisticall transmutation' of the Romanists.[101] The words must be understood figuratively.[102] Nevertheless, Attersoll shows his conformist stance by defending kneeling for reception of the elements, and appealed to the writings of Vermigli in support.[103] This is because Christ is truly represented, sealed and exhibited in the sacrament. Attersoll could write: 'For Christ is present among us sundry waies, by his Spirit, by his grace, by his divinity, by faith dwelling in our hearts, he is present in his word, he is present in the ministry of baptisme, he is present in the Sacrament of his body: we onely deny that grosse and fleshly presence which many go about to fasten upon us.'[104] He is present effectually, not fleshly; spiritually, not bodily; sacramentally, not carnally; and mystically, not naturally.[105]

On the question of memorial and sacrifice, Attersoll taught that we offer up ourselves, our souls, our bodies, our alms and our prayers, which are an oblation offered to God. In the sacrament the memorial of his death is repeated; although the cross was once and for all, 'yet to the faithfull in regard of the force, it is still fresh and alwaies present.'[106] Yet like Randall, his main concern is the representation of the cross in the action of the breaking of bread and pouring out of wine, and union with Christ through the sacrament.[107]

Avant-Garde Conformists: Lancelot Andrewes, William Barlow and Christopher Sutton

Lancelot Andrewes   One of the Deans at the Hampton Court Conference was Lancelot Andrewes (1555–1626), then Dean of Westminster but later to be Bishop of Chichester, then Ely, and then Winchester. Though Andrewes seems to have had a 'godly' past, he developed a very different piety and spirituality, as evidenced in his sermons, his few theological writings, and his *Preces Privatae*.[108] He was a favourite preacher at Court, though James had to warn him not to preach on contentious issues such as predestination, where most of his contemporaries detected a drift towards what later would be called Arminianism. He had also caused some upset in his early years by advocating auricular confession.[109] His influence on William Laud and those of the later Caroline divines was considerable, and thus he was very much the prototype for the later 'Patristic Reformed churchmen', or 'Ceremonialists'.[110] In his day, however, he was far from typical of the prevailing English theology and piety.[111]

As a Fellow of Pembroke Hall, Cambridge, one of his duties was to catechise, and at a later date he published a catechism, but there is no treatment of sacraments.[112] Instead we have to rely on his sermons.

As with Hildersham and Downame, Andrewes could use the language of covenant. In a Pentecost Sermon of 1610, speaking of the joy of abiding with Christ in eternity, he said:

Such is this here which Christ promised, and His Father sent this day; and which He will send, if Christ will ask; and Christ will ask if, now we know the covenant and see the condition, we will seal to the deed.

   To a covenant there is nothing more requisite, than to put the seal. And we know the Sacrament is the seal of the new covenant, as it was of the old. Thus, by undertaking the duty He requireth, we are entitled to the comfort which here He promiseth. And 'do this' He would have us, as is plain by His *hoc facite*.'[113]

Baptism was the topic of two of his Pentecost sermons. In that of 1612, he used it to introduce discussion of the Holy Spirit. This is the laver which brings forth new birth in the Spirit and entry into the Kingdom.[114] In the sermon of 1615, Andrewes announced that 'This is the feast of baptism.'[115] At baptism, the whole Trinity is present in person, 'the Son in the water, the Holy Ghost in the dove, the Father in the voice.' Andrewes discussed the text, noting that there are two baptisms – of the people, and of Christ. In his baptism, Christ 'put us on, as we 'put Him on', in ours'.[116] But Andrewes carefully links the baptism in the Jordan with the baptism which Christ had to undergo. He noted that Christ underwent a '*trinam mersionem*' – in Gethsemane, in Gabbatha and in Golgotha. And emphasising the spear with which Christ was pierced, he says:

There, met the two streams of 'water and blood', the true Jordan, the bath or laver, wherein we are purged 'from all our sins'. No sin of so deep a dye but this will command it, and fetch it out. This in Jordan, here now, was but an undertaking of that then; and in virtue of that, doth all our water-baptism work. And therefore are we baptized into it: not into His water-baptism, but into His cross-baptism; not into His baptism, but into His death.[117]

Here Andrewes grounds the sacrament in Christology, as from start to finish, a work of God. In fact, it is by the power of the Holy Spirit, who can be described as a conduit pipe.[118]

   On the eucharist, Andrewes's sermon material can be supplemented by his works against Bellarmine and Perron. Against the former he argued that the eucharist was a commemorative sacrifice; remove transubstantiation 'and there will not long be any strife with us about the sacrifice.'[119] Transubstantiation, he suggested, belonged among the theories of the schools, but not among the articles of the faith. 'We believe no less than you that the presence is real. Concerning the method of the presence, we define nothing rashly, and, I add, we do not anxiously enquire, any more than how the blood of Christ washes in our Baptism, any more than how the human and divine are united in one Person in the Incarnation of Christ.'[120] He can also say of the commemoration of the one sacrifice of the cross: 'And that sacrifice but once actually performed at His death, but ever before represented in figure, from the beginning; and ever since repeated in memory, to the world's end. That only absolute, all else relative to it, representative of it, operative by it.'[121]

   Andrewes was critical of the concern of some 'godly clergy' for a fraction, calling it a 'worshipping of imaginations', and it may be that, like his friend John Overall, he preferred the 1549 canon with the memorial or commemoration articulated in prayer in a Godward direction.[122]

   In his *Preces Privatae* Andrewes had no hesitation in drawing upon the Eastern liturgies of St. Basil and St. John Chrysostom, as a private, and in a sense, parallel to the *Prayer Book* liturgy.[123] One suspects that he found the latter constricting but in the very opposite direction to divines such as Hildersham. Whereas Hildersham agitated for abolition of certain ceremonies, Andrewes witnesses to a concern for extra ceremonies. In his notes on the *Book of Common Prayer*, he gives meticulous details such as washing of the hands immediately before what he calls the 'Prayer of Consecration', and the use of wafer bread and wine in a barrel on a cradle with four feet – which are offered in the name of the whole congregation upon the altar.[124] Here there is a piety which is concerned with the sacraments as works of God, and which must be celebrated with dignity and suitable ceremonial. But the notes also reveal his use of one or two supplemental texts – for example, the offertory sentences. At least in private, therefore, Andrewes was happy to alter the text, and develop new ceremonial, and in one sense was as arbitary with the liturgy and rubrics as were the godly ministers.

A description has survived of the furnishings of Andrewes's chapel at Winchester House in London when he was Bishop of Winchester. The description includes a plan of the chapel, which included an 'altarwise' communion table, on a dias at the east end, with communion rail, and two candlesticks with tapers on the altar. The chalice had engravings, including Christ with a lost sheep on his shoulders, and the chapel had wall hangings depicting Old Testament events, and it was also equipped with a thurible. Clearly here doctrine was given liturgical and ceremonial expression.[125]

William Barlow   Another Dean at the Hampton Court Conference was William Barlow (c.1565–1613), then Dean of Chester, and later to be Bishop of first, Rochester (1605) and then of Lincoln (1608). Barlow had taken part in the Cambridge controversies on predestination in the 1590s, and was no friend of the 'godly'. Barlow's piety was not necessarily aligned to that of Andrewes, though he was a strict conformist churchman, and sided with Overall and Andrewes in the predestinarian debates.[126] Some of his views on sacraments were set forth in his work of 1601 entitled *A defence of the articles of the Protestants religion,* which was an answer to a work accusing protestants of departing from the Creeds. In this work Barlow cites Calvin and the fathers, as well as certain schoolmen, in defence of the protestant faith. Protestants, asserted Barlow, do not reject sacraments. Sacraments are 'a *reall Creede*, acting that which the other [that is, the written Creed] enacteth, performing in deede, which in the *Symbole* we professe in word, and are rather seales'.[127] Baptism ratifies the article of remission of sins, and the eucharist ratifies the article of his death and passion. Baptism is '*the indument of Christ*'.[128] It works a double effect – privately *remissa culpa* in washing us, and positively *data iustitia* in sanctifying us.[129] Nevertheless, 'we ascribe not this power either *ad elementum*, or *momentum*, not to the element of water, as though it had *vim ablutiuam*, as Aquine speaketh, this skouring force; or *regeneratiuam* this renewing power, as Lombard termes it; but unto the bloud of Christ working invisibly by the power of the spirite.'[130]

Barlow went on to unpack his understanding of baptism *vis-à-vis* justification. Appealing to Calvin he asserted that as the king's letters patent under seal confirm a commission, 'So God, having purposed in his eternall counsell to save some, which hee cannot doe before hee have remitted their sinnes, therefore in Baptisme he both conferres this grace, & confirmes it unto them; for which cause the scriptures and fathers speak do call it *sigillum promissionis & remissionis.*[131] This is accomplished derivatively, not originally; effectually, not effectively; as a brook, not a spring. Grace is wrought in baptism as a man writes with a pen: 'powerfully, yet instrumentally, confirmes it visibly, sealing that which concealed'.[132] It is the seal of pre-received grace, since justification by faith is a 'praeaccepted grace'.[133]

On the eucharist Barlow says nothing surprising. He rejects any carnal presence in the elements. There is a *sacramentum* and a *res sacramenti*, the bread and wine, and Christ.[134] Barlow wrote:

> Now his bodie bruised & his bloud poured out can no otherwise be present in the Eucharist, but by a representation therof in the bread broken, & in the wine effused, of the one side; and on the communicantes part, by a grateful recordation of the benefites, a reverent valuation of the sacrifice, a faithfull application of his merites in his whole passion; and therfore his presence must be sacramentall, and our eating spirituall.[135]

In this the operation of the Spirit is crucial, bringing union with God. This is begun in baptism, and continues in faith, hope and charity: 'But if we truely eate the bodie, and drinke the bloud of Christ, then by the power of the holy Ghost, and faith cooperating, this union is strengthened, the vigour and effectes whereof, after a true partipation; we shall feele in our selves more forcible and lively.'[136]

Christopher Sutton   Christopher Sutton (1565–1629) was a graduate of Lincoln College, Oxford, and proceeded to DD in 1608. He had been incumbent of Rainham in Essex, of Caston in Hampshire, and Woodrising in Norfolk. James I liked the style of his preaching, and in 1605 he was installed as a canon of Westminster Abbey, and in 1618 also of Lincoln. His work, *Godly Meditations upon the Most Holy Sacrament of the Lord's Supper* (1601), was a devotional work which was popular and reached its thirteenth edition in 1677. It was also reprinted with an introduction by John Henry Newman, since it was perceived to express an ethos compatible with Tractarianism. The work was in fact a revised and protestantised version of the Italian Jesuit, Luca Pinelli's, *Meditatione brevi del sanctissimo sacramento*. This work was presented for the most part in chapters of 'Teaching', 'Meditation', 'Fruit' and 'Spiritual Soliloquey' or prayer. Though allowance must be made for the fact that Sutton's work was devotional rather than a theological treatise, its ethos is very different from the sermons of Randall, or the treatments by Downame and Attersoll. There are frequent references to John Chrysostom, to Justin Martyr, Irenaeus, Cyprian and Ambrose, as well as to Dionysius the Areopagite, Gerson and Thomas Aquinas, all called upon to support his teaching on the 'Holy Eucharist' (his preferred term), together with prayers which are more akin to those of Andrewes than the long prayers of Downame.

Sutton drew upon Luther's concept of Christ as testator. For Sutton the inheritance is heaven, the legacy is grace, the executor of the will is the Holy Spirit, and the two sacraments of baptism and the eucharist are the seals.[137] In baptism the soul, fallen from the state of innocence, is restored, for God 'hast illuminated it by grace and washed it in the sacred font of Baptism'.[138] The eucharist is figured in the Old Testament – in Melchizadek, the shew bread, the cakes of Elisha, the manna from heaven, and (as in Attersoll) even the ark of Noah.[139] At the Last Supper:

> The visible elements which He took and gave, declare two things; the one, that He would the morrow following make Himself an oblation for the redemption of many upon the altar of the cross; the other, that He would become unto the faithful by this means a divine sustenance for their souls. And thus He provideth for Himself an altar; for His, a table – In both God hath the glory, and man the benefit.[140]

In the eucharist, Christ is both giver and the gift.[141] It can be called a *Viaticum*, since it is a way through, a provision for our souls.[142] Sutton exhorted: 'Consider the Divine Wisdom of the Son of God, who, respecting our weakness, hath conveyed unto us His Body and Blood after a Divine and Spiritual manner, under the forms of Bread and Wine.'[143] What is received is the very body and blood of Christ 'after a most Divine and Heavenly manner'.[144] Sutton was reluctant to discuss the 'how' of the presence of Christ. He rejected transubstantiation, insisting that the fathers do treat and insist on the real presence, but never treated anything like transubstantiation. Sutton explained:

> Truly we give, and that justly, great respect and reverence to the Holy Eucharist; for whereas bread and wine are elements naturally ordained for the sustenance of the body, by the power of Divine Benediction, they do receive a virtue that, being received of the faithful, they become nourishment of the soul, nay, they become means whereby we are sanctified both in body and soul, and are made the members of Christ.[145]

For that reason, so Sutton argues, kneeling is the appropriate posture for reception, and in the celebration of the sacrament, everything is to be done decently and in order: 'To come unto the Holy Table of the Lord in any other behaviour than beseemeth humble suppliants, meekly kneeling upon our knees, being now to receive grace from the Giver of grace, were great indignity offered. To come into such a Presence and to demean ourselves as if we were assembled to sit in commission with God, is sure far from Christian piety.'[146] (See Figure 2.3.) Grace is indeed given, though by God; the sacraments are conduit pipes: 'For we do not celebrate a remembrance only of some thing past, but we are partakers also of grace present; which grace, though not from *ex opere operato*, by that work done, yet by the Sacrament (as water from the fountain by the conduit pipes) is conveyed and derived unto us.'[147] Here Sutton seems prepared to go beyond Andrewes and Calvin, both for whom the Holy Spirit was the conduit pipe. This certainly suggest his position was solidly symbolic instrumentalism. However, like Calvin and Hooker, Sutton emphasised that the goal or object was union with Christ: 'The first and principal effect of the most Holy Sacrament of the Lord's Supper is, as we may so speak, that it deifieth first, that is, it maketh man Divine, or like unto God himself!'[148] Indeed, when the faithful receive the eucharist, 'man doth participate a divine nature immortal and heavenly.'[149]

This concern for participation in the divine pervades Sutton's work, and it was perhaps this which led him to downplay the memorial aspect of the Supper.[150] In the eucharist we honour Christ's passion which is represented in the sacrament. It is 'so solemn a Sacrifice, which doth consecrate man unto God'.[151] Meditation on his

Figure 2.3   Depiction of the Lord's Supper, England, 1624

passion is important, but that is so we are worthy to participate of the Blessed Sacrament.[152] Sutton was not alone in recycling Catholic devotional material, and 'godly' divines did the same. Nevertheless, the genre would place Sutton alongside the piety of Andrewes.

Scotland and Ceremonial Discord

What of north of the border? According to Maurice Lee, in 1603 James's agenda was not a long one. The major task was bringing about the real union of England and Scotland that God, having set him on both thrones, so clearly intended to achieve.[153] But Lee also notes that conformity between the two churches of the two kingdoms had been an element in the calculations of the Scottish government in the days of the regent Morton, and with the succession to the English throne assured, it was a factor in James's decision to restore episcopacy in Scotland in 1600. He suggests that at least one reason for Abbot becoming Archbishop of Canterbury rather than Lancelot Andrewes was because the Scottish Kirk was at one with most of Abbot's 'conformist Calvinist' theology, whereas they would have been alarmed at Andrewes's theology and piety.[154]

How did the Kirk differ from England on liturgy and sacramental theology? The Kirk had adopted the liturgical forms drawn up in Geneva in 1556 by John Knox, William Whittingham, Anthony Gilby, John Foxe and William Cole, though in places the *Book of Common Prayer* seems to have been used.[155] The sign of the cross was not used in baptism, and sitting for reception of the Lord's Supper was the standard practice. The general understanding of the sacraments which circulated in Scotland can be briefly gleaned from the sermons of Robert Bruce, the more popular level catechism of John Davidson, the Latin work on covenant and sacraments by Robert Rollock, and the anti-Romanist work of John Welsh, described by T.F. Torrance as representing the older, evangelical, Scottish divinity.[156]

Divines of the Older Scottish Divinity

Robert Bruce   Robert Bruce (c.1554–1631) was successor to James Lawson and John Knox at St. Giles, Edinburgh. His sermons were first published in 1589, but published in England in 1614 under the title *The Mystery of the Lord's Supper*. Bruce was a popular and successful minister, but fell into disfavour over his hesitancy to accept the royal version of the Gowrie plot, and then subsequent dissension from royal policy. In 1621 he was imprisoned for his defiance of the Five Articles of Perth.

For Bruce, sacraments, together with the word, bring about a conjunction with Jesus Christ.[157] They are signs and seals annexed to the preached word.[158] Thus referring to the Lord's Supper, Bruce wrote:

> I call the Sacrament a holy seal, annexed to the Covenant of grace and mercy in Christ. It is a seal to be administered publicly, according to the holy institution of Christ Jesus, that in its lawful administration the sacramental union between the sign and the thing signified, may take place. In this union Christ Jesus, who is the thing signified, is as truly

delivered to the increase of our spiritual nourishment as the signs are given and delivered to the body for our temporal nourishment.[159]

Bruce could call them 'potent instruments' which deliver and exhibit the things they signify, though they are only effective if the Spirit of God concurs and seals the same truth in the heart.[160] Baptism requires water and the triune formula, and gives remission of sins, mortification and the sealing of our adoption to life everlasting, and regeneration.[161] However, it cannot be given to children of parents who are outside the covenant.[162] The Lord's Supper was appointed to represent our spiritual nourishment; for us to bear witness to the world (badges of our profession); to serve as a comfort and consolation; and an occasion to render thanks to God for benefits received.[163] As we eat and drink with our mouths, so we feed on Christ spiritually in the soul, the elements and our mouths both being instruments of spiritual things. Christ is conjoined with us by the power and virtue of the Holy Spirit.[164] Sanctification of the elements takes place by the institution narrative, an invocation and thanksgiving, and the will of God.[165] And rather like Hildersham, he regarded the fraction as an important ceremony: 'the breaking is an essential ceremony; the pouring out of the wine is also an essential ceremony.'[166] This is because they represent the breaking of the body and the blood of Christ, for in this sacrament we have the fruits of Christ's death, 'the virtue of His sacrifice, the virtue of His passion'.[167]

John Davidson   John Davidson (1549–1604) had studied at St. Andrews, and became an admirer of John Knox. He later studied at Basel. On his return he stayed in England until prohibited from preaching by Bancroft, and developed a dislike of both Scottish royal policies and episcopacy. His catechism of 1602 was structured with long explanations followed by questions and answers. The third section considered sacraments. They are 'holy signes ordayned by Christ in the Newe Testament, to seale up salvation in him, who is signified, represented, and really, though sacramentally, exhibited to them that beleeve'.[168] Baptism in water is the outward sign representing the bloodshed of Christ, and plants us in Christ, and through it we enter the Church. In the Supper the bread and wine set out Christ crucified as the only true food of our souls. It celebrates and keeps fresh in our memories Christ's passion.

In the questions and answers the sacramental signs are said to 'both signifie and truly offer Christ crucified to the receavers for salvation'.[169] Transubstantiation is repudiated, for 'all this communication of Christ by Faith into the Sacraments, is meere spiritual, and supernaturall.'[170] Repudiating a corporal and local presence, Davidson invoked the Reformed *anabasis* concept: 'But contrariwise, by the use of the elements, our hearts are convoyed and carried, to the livelye consideration of his death and resurrection, and from thence to heaven, (where hee sits at the right hand of God) to feed upon him by Faith, to life everlasting, whilk is the verye washing of our sinnes, and true eeting of his body, and drinking of his blude.'[171]

Robert Rollock   Robert Rollock (c.1555–99) was the first Principal of Edinburgh University, and a biblical commentator (Figure 2.4). He taught the Heidelberg Catechism and lectured on Beza's *Quaestiones*, was an early exponent of the

Figure 2.4   Robert Rollock, c. 1555–99

Heidelberg covenant theology, and, like Perkins and Fenner in England, adopted the Ramist approach to knowledge and teaching.[172] Rollock set forth his teaching on sacraments in a Latin treatise entitled *Quaestiones et Responsiones Aliquot de Foedere Die: Deque Sacramento quod Foederis Dei sigillum est* (Edinburgh, 1596).

According to Rollock, both the covenant of works and the covenant of grace were sealed with a sacrament and seal. The sacrament of the covenant of works was the trees of the garden of Eden; those of the covenant of grace, baptism and the Lord's Supper. To the question, 'What is a sacrament?', Rollock answered:

> It is a sign instituted by God, working effectively, visible, by which – with the Word of the Gospel added – the Holy Spirit more completely represents to us those spiritual and heavenly things, and produces more completely the knowledge of them in our minds and the application of them in our hearts, than by the Word of the Gospel alone. When he does this he confirms our faith in the Word of the Covenant and of the Gospel, and brings it about that we believe more and more in it.[173]

Four things are signified in the sacraments: Christ; his cross and passion; its fruits – remission of sins, justification, and the gift of the Holy Spirit, regeneration and eternal life; and its internal applications.[174] By the term 'sacramental sign', Rollock meant not only the sacramental elements but also the rite and external actions. Thus in baptism the sign of Christ is the water, and the pouring of the water is the sign of the cross and passion. In the Lord's Supper, the signs of Christ are the bread and wine, and of his cross and passion, the breaking of bread and the pouring of the wine.[175] The signs of application of baptism is the sprinkling or washing with water, and at the Supper, the distribution of the bread and wine, the taking of the elements by the people, and eating and drinking them.[176] But the signs are certainly not bare signs: 'the signs effectively produce something and are implements and instruments of the holy Spirit.'[177] Rollock further explained of the signs of application: 'And these too are instruments of the holy Spirit, by which he not only produces knowledge – which is the first part of faith – in our minds, but also inwardly produces an application in our hearts : I mean the very thing that they signify, of which knowledge in our minds is produced first.'[178]

They can be called exhibiting signs (*signa exhibentia*) because they are the means by which the Holy Spirit exhibits to us Christ, his cross and his benefits.[179] The causes of the significance of the signs and their operation is two. First, by analogy and proportion between sign and thing signified; and secondly, the spiritual and supernatural relationship between the sign and the thing signified.[180] From this comes the sacramental unity. They are 'related', not confused. Although Rollock speaks of the signs exhibiting Christ, and of the signs as instruments, he is clear that their efficacy rests on the words of institution or mandate of Christ:

> The Lord, precisely by his gratuitous act, has pronounced the words of institution. By these he has settled the use of the external things – for example, of the water that is in Baptism, of the bread and wine that are in the Lord's Supper – so that when it is said at the Supper, 'This is my body', the meaning is, 'This bread is the sign or Sacrament of my body, and now has that use, so that it can represent my body because I so will and institute it'.[181]

Elsewhere Rollock taught that baptism is a seal of the covenant which comes first through preaching: 'except the preaching of the covenant of grace precede, baptism is nothing but an unprofitable ceremony and a dead element.'[182] He dismissed any *ex opere operato* concept of grace:

> Whereof we have to learn, that the power and efficacy of baptism depends neither upon the power of the minister who baptizes, nor upon the force nor power of the words pronounced by the minister in baptism, as if there were any such power or operation in the words, as the Papists falsely attribute unto them; but all the force and efficacy of baptism depends upon the power of God only.[183]

It was only lawful for an ordained minister to baptise, and laymen and women must be prevented from doing so.[184]

Whereas baptism confirms the beginning of faith, the Lord's Supper confirms its continuation.[185] Rollock did not, in *Quaestiones et Responsiones*, give any detailed treatment of the idea of eucharistic presence, since he prefered to speak of the whole range of signs, and explained himself by analogy and relation. The elements are transferred from a common to a holy use – though it is Christ who does this. Elsewhere, however, he attacked the 'Papist' idea of presence and sacrifice. The 'gross and carnal Papists', wrote Rollock, think that they are unable to have joy unless they have the body of Christ bodily and locally present; 'that is, except that with the mouth of the body they eat, devour, and swallow up the very body and flesh of Jesus Christ, and except that after that same manner they drink his blood'.[186] For Rollock, true joy comes neither from a bodily presence nor a bodily absence, but from the effectual presence and operation of the Holy Spirit.[187] Although the breaking of the bread and pouring of the wine represented or signified the passion of Christ, the Supper was in some sense a sacrifice:

> The Lord hath put an end to them all by his death and sacrifice; there is no priesthood committed either to the apostles before, or to ministers now, but that where, by the preaching of the word, they offer the souls of men and women in a sacrifice to the Lord. Away with that devilish sacrifice of the mass, whereby the pope and his clergy deceive the world, making men believe that daily they offer up Christ again, as a propitiatory sacrifice to the Father, for the sins of the quick and the dead. No; there is no propitiatory sacrifice now left to the kirk. That sacrifice which the Lord once offered upon the cross is sufficient and perfect enough to take away the sins of the world.[188]

Rollock's terminology and concerns echo those of Ursinus, and it is no accident that Rollock treats the sacraments with a treatise which was mainly concerned with the Covenant theology which the Heidelberg theologians had developed. Though he can speak of sacraments exhibiting and as being instruments of the Holy Spirit, his concern with application in the mind, and increasing faith puts him close to a type of symbolic memorialism.

Brief mention may be made of Rollock's pupil, Robert Boyd of Trochrig. Boyd (1578–1627) was Principal of Glasgow and then of Edinburgh University. He had taught for five years at the French Protestant academy at Montauban, and then briefly at Saumur. Something of his views on baptism can be gleaned from his vast commentary on Ephesians.

Baptism is not a mere naked sign, simply appointed to represent and seal; it is an 'efficacious seal and instrument' through which Christ, by the Holy Spirit, confers and applies to us the reality of the sacrament, namely our sanctification.[189] Baptism efficaciously seals our union with Christ. He wrote:

> This cleansing of ours is attributed both to the Blood of Christ and to the Holy Spirit, inasmuch as each of these concurs in His own way and order in the work of our sanctification; the Blood of Christ, not only by gaining for us remission of sins, but also the gift of the Holy Spirit who on account of Christ is given to us by the Father, poured into our hearts according to the promise of God the Father. He applies Christ's Blood to our hearts and consciences, first by sealing in us the remission of sins, then by renewing us in Christ's image, both by mortifying the old man in us by the power of Christ's death and Cross, and by vivifying the new man in us by the efficacy of His resurrection and life, or by inspiring us to new life with Christ. Thus without the Blood of Christ we cannot obtain regeneration and without the Spirit of Christ His righteousness is not imputed to us.[190]

Boyd seems to have kept close to the concepts found in Rollock.

John Welsh   John Welsh (c.1570–1622) was a graduate of Edinburgh University, and in 1589 was appointed minister of Selkirk. He attended the prohibited General Assembly of 1605, and was banished by James for life. He served as minister in

France, and then moved to Holland. He was finally permitted to return to London in 1622, and preached a sermon. He died shortly afterwards the same year. In his *Popery Anatomized*, published in Edinburgh in 1602 (Glasgow, 1672), Welsh described sacraments as 'figurs, signs and symbols'.[191] With regard to baptism he wrote:

> As for Baptism, we grant it is a most effectual seal and pledge of our ingrafting in Christ Jesus and of the remission of our sins through his blood, and regeneration through his Spirit; so that either the neglect or the contempt of it (because it is the neglect and contempt of the covenant itself, and of Christ Jesus the foundation of the covenant) is damnable. But that it is so absolutely necessary to infants, that without it they cannot come to heaven; to wit, these whom he hath predestinat, it being neither neglected nor contemned, but death preventing the receving of it; that we all utterly deny as impious, ungodly, and cruel.[192]

Welsh argued that it was impious to teach that God's free grace was bound to the instruments. He attacked transubstantiation, describing it as a 'monstrous exposition', implying that Christ had two bodies, one in the form of a human, and the other in the form of bread. He argued:

> Your interpretation destroys the nature of all Sacraments, and makes the Supper of the Lord no Sacrament; for every Sacrament consists of an outward and visible sign, and of a spiritual thing signified by that sign, the which sign hath a resemblance with the thing signified. The sign is ever earthly, and the thing signified is heavenly, as shall apeear by all the rest of the Sacraments, both of the Old and New Testament.[193]

More positively Welsh wrote of the Lord's Supper: 'This Sacrament of bread and wine, because it not only represents and seals up to us our communion with Christ, but also by it, as by a most effectual instrument, the holy Ghost increases and nowrishes this communion, both with him, and among ourselves: therefore it is called the communion of his body and blood.'[194] He gave a detailed rejection of the concept of the sacrifice of the mass, asserting that the Supper is a commemoration of Christ's one sacrifice once offered upon the cross.[195] And he dismissed ceremonies such as hovering and blowing of the words of institution, and making the sign of the cross, as charms 'after the manner of Sorcerers'.[196]

   The teachings of these divines was not too distinct from those of Hildersham and Downame. However, although the terms 'exhibit' and 'instrument' are used, it is far from clear that each divine meant the same thing by using those terms.[197]

The Five Articles of Perth, Patrick Galloway, and the Liturgical Work of William Cowper

To further the opportunity for conformity between the two churches, in 1610 James had three of the Scottish bishops consecrated by English bishops. Then, with the Church of Ireland adopting Articles in 1615, the monarch turned his attention to engineering liturgical change in Scotland – both in liturgical provision and observance.[198] John Spottiswoode, Archbishop of Glasgow, compiled a list of the King's requirements, which included Articles, a Public Confession of Faith, provision for election of bishops, and revision of rites for baptism, the eucharist and marriage, together with the provision of a rite of Confirmation.[199] This agenda was duly presented to the General Assembly at Aberdeen in 1616. Calderwood recorded that the Assembly appointed Mr Patrick Galloway, Mr Peter Hewat, Mr John Adamsone and Mr William Areskeen 'to revise the booke of Common prayers, contained in the *Psalme book*, and to set down a Common form of Ordinare Service, to be used at all times hereafter'.[200] James visited Scotland in 1617, accompanied by Lancelot Andrewes, whose Holyrood Pentecost sermon had a clear vision of a united British Church.[201] In July of that year, five articles were presented to the synods. These proposed confirmation by bishops, the celebration of holy days, private baptism, private communion, and kneeling to receive communion from the minister's hands. Patrick Galloway, who was a royal chaplain, was asked for his opinion, and dissented from private baptism and kneeling for communion. The General Assembly at St. Andrews did not endorse the articles, but they were introduced by Spottiswoode, by now Primate, at the General Assembly of Perth in August 1618. Though accepted under duress, the Perth Articles were blatantly ignored by many, and their enforcement was impossible. Our concern is with the theological problems raised for some Scottish ministers through these articles, and also the liturgical forms which were authored but never came into use.

A confession of faith was drawn up by the Assembly in 1616, recorded by Calderwood, and apparently expanded from an earlier draft of 1612.[202] In it sacraments were defined as 'certain visible Seales of Gods Eternal Covenant ordained by Christ to represent unto us Christ crucified & to seal up our Communion with him'.[203] They confer grace, not of themselves, but by the powerful operation of the Holy Spirit. In the Lord's Supper, the elements are not changed in substance, but in use. 'We beleeve', said the confession, 'that the body and blood of Christ are truely present in the holy Supper, that they are truely exhibite unto us, and that we in very truth do participat of them, albeit only Spiritually and by Faith, not Carnally or Corporally.'[204] The Supper is a commemoration of the sacrifice of Christ: 'With this one sacrifice, once offered, we are all fully content, neither do we seek any other Expiatorie or Propitiatorie Sacrifice.'[205] That latter is applied to us by faith and wrought in our souls by the Holy Spirit.

Patrick Galloway   Patrick Galloway (1551–1626) was a key player in these events. He had been present as a Scottish observer at the Hampton Court Conference, and had witnessed the move to stop lay baptism and the problem of some English divines over kneeling for communion. He was nominated in 1616 as part of the committee responsible for the revision of the liturgy, and he had theological reservations concerning the Five Articles. Something of his sacramental views are known from the catechism he wrote when in England, in 1588. In this Galloway taught that sacraments were ordained 'To be seales and tokens to confirme our faith more and more in the assurance of Gods promises made in his word'.[206] Their power to confirm is derived from the ordinance if God, to which is joined the effectual working of His Spirit. Baptism is the sacrament of our entry into the Church of God 'wherein by the visible water is represented and offered unto us the spirituall regeneration and washing of our soules'.[207] The spiritual washing results in the 'full and free remission of our sinnes, and purging of our soules from the spirituall filth of sinne by the bloud of

Jesus Christ'.[208] The Lord's Supper is our spiritual nourishment in the Church of God 'in the which be visible elements of Bread and Wine, represented and offered unto us Christes bodie and bloud'.[209] The catechism strongly rejected transubstantiation, and insisted that only the faithful feed on Christ. Nevertheless, grace is offered in the sacrament, though Galloway does not elaborate upon this. There is nothing startling in this, and nothing which would indicate Galloway's reaction against the Five Articles, though his emphasis on baptism as entry into the Church perhaps implied the need for its public celebration.

William Cowper and the draft new liturgical rites   Work on liturgical revision seems to have been set in motion almost immediately in 1616, and three successive drafts have survived.[210] The first was of a Morning Service and prayers only, and seems to have been mainly the work of Peter Howat (Ewat). But at some stage the committee was joined by William Cowper, who became Bishop of Galloway, and he seems to have been responsible for the other two drafts. The first of these is dated by Donaldson 1616–17, and the second 1618–19. Cowper died in February 1619.

In his *Works*, Cowper described both sacraments as seals, and with regard to regeneration, he was able to discuss the topic without any reference to baptism.[211] But sacraments were more than just signs and seals. In the context of Christ's baptism, Cowper wrote:

> That we may the better understand this, wee are to know that the covenant of Grace, whereof Baptisme is a seale, hath two parts in it, to wit, Gods part and mans. Gods part of the covenant containes promises made to us of the remission of our sinnes, and renovation of our nature, comprised in this one word, *I will be your God*. Our part againe contaures promises made to God by us of faith and obedience, comprised in this one word, *We shall be his people*.[212]

The Lord's Supper is a banquet not for our body, but for the soul.[213] Though the elements are signs, they must not be made naked and bare signs, and here Cowper quotes Augustine that they are visible signs of invisible grace.[214] Using the same analogy as Hildersham and Downame, Cowper held that the elements, by God's appointment, change to a 'more excellent use' as wax is stamped with the King's seal: 'so this Bread, though in substance it differ not from other bread, yet concerning the use, it is separate, and much more precious then any other bread in the world; being now appointed by God to be a signe and a seale, and an exhibiting instrument of Christs body, and therefore cannot be profaned nor abused without contempt of Christ Jesus.'[215] The term 'exhibiting instrument' seems a favourite of Cowper, and elsewhere he speaks of the bread and wine being a 'realle and effectual exhibition made of the LORD JESUS to the penitent and beleeving receiver', and as signs representing Christ crucified, seals confirming our faith, and also 'effectual instruments of exhibition'.[216] He argued that there were two chief ends of this sacrament, namely, the commemoration of Christ's death and passion with thanksgiving, and the communication of Christ to his church.[217] Yet like Hildersham, Downame, Attersoll and Bruce, he makes special significance of the fraction, which is 'a lively representation of Christ crucified'.[218]

In the second, more comprehensive, draft liturgy of 1616–17, there are indications of Cowper's theology, but as we have seen, his terminology was shared with other Scottish and English divines.

'The Ordour of Baptisme' began with an expansion of the older 'Knoxian' question to father and godfathers, and baptism is described as 'the seale of the covenant of grace', which is reinforced by a light revision of the older 1556 prayer (derived in turn from Calvin, Farel, and ultimately, the Order of Bern) which itself likens baptism to the covenant of circumcision made with Abraham.[219] The revised prayer asked that the congregation may 'walk before as becommes a people who hes bound up a covenant with the Holie Lord'. It asked: 'And as to these infants we pray thee for Christs saik to ressave them into the number of thy children, wash away their sinnes by the bloode of Jesus Christ, mortifie the powar of sinne unto them, sanctifie them with thy holie Spirit that they may become new creatures.'[220]

The prayer after the baptism carefully allows symbolic parallelism: 'We have in thy name baptised them with water, bot, O Lord, baptise thou them with the holie Spirit that so this baptisme may become to them the laver of regeneration and they, through thy grace renuncing the devil, the world and the flesh, may serve Thee all their daies in holiness of lyfe.'[221] The prayer carefully incorporates some *Book of Common Prayer* phraseology which accompanied the signing of the cross in the English book, though no attempt was made to introduce such a practice in this liturgy.

In the 'Ordour to be observed in Tyme of Holie Communion', petition is made for the communicants to be 'conjoined' with the Lord, as in Bruce and Downame.[222] The Admonition, which is a rubric, required the deacons to set the covered elements on the Table, and notes 'the doctrine of Chryst his death will affect and move the people the more easilie when they see these holie signes which represent Chryst crucefeit unto us.'[223] In a prayer before the sermon, petition is made to illuminate us and transform us so that we may be made Christ-like. After an admonition, God is beseeched 'to joyne thy blessing with thy owne ordinances that these elements may be unto us that which Thou hes appointed them'. And after the taking of the bread and cup a prayer is prayed that asks: 'Lord blesse it that it may be unto us ane effectual exhibiting instrument of the Lord Jesus, for we come here to seeke the Physician of our soules and to celebrat with thanksgeving the remembrance of his death and passion untill his comming againe.'[224]

The third draft of 1618–19 used more phraseology and material from the English 1604 *Book of Common Prayer*, and as a result, in the baptismal rite, the reference to 'the seale of the covenant of grace' disappeared, though in the prayer before the baptism the reference to the congregation as a people 'that have bound up a covenant with the most holy God' was retained.[225] The post-baptismal prayer was rephrased to tone down the symbolic parallelism – 'that as we have in thy name baptized him with water, so thou wilt graciously pleased to [words missing] thy holy Spirit, that so this baptisme may become to him the Laiver of regeneration...' – thus asking God to work the inward simultaneously with the outward.[226] The rite for the Lord's Supper also underwent considerable metamorphosis, with more material from the 1556 *Book of Common Order*, and from the 1604 English *Book of Common Prayer*. However, petition is made that 'this banquet on earth ... shal be perfited and continued for ever in heaven', and although the petition for consecra-

tion is emended, it still retains the distinctive Cowperian phraseology: 'Send doune
o Lord thy blessing upon this Sacrament, that it may be unto us the effectual
exhibitive instrument of the Lord Jesus.'[227]

However, one change which was controversial was that whereas the second draft
mentions the people sitting at the table, the third draft was written after the Five
Articles, and directs that people should kneel for reception of the elements. Cowper
gave his support to the Five Articles. On private baptism, Cowper conceded that
baptism was not necessary for salvation, but he argued that it was a necessary and
profitable help for the parent's faith, and could see no warrant for refusing it. On
the question of kneeling, he noted that different sister churches have different
customs – sitting in Scotland, standing in France, and kneeling in England. And, he
added, 'For to Christ I kneel, praising him when I receive the holy symbols, and
exhibiting instruments of his Body and Bloud.'[228]

To Kneel or to Sit?

The Articles were controversial, particularly as regards kneeling for communion.[229]
Sitting at the table in a succession of sittings was the common Scottish practice. In
England, kneeling was prescribed, but it is clear that in many 'godly' parishes, the
people sat in pews and were communicated. Though not the general Scottish
practice, other divines felt as Cowper did, and could defend the practice. David
Lindsay, a DD of St. Andrews, minister of Dundee and later to become Bishop of
Brechin, argued that sitting was not a necessary gesture to be used at the receiving
of the sacrament, whereas kneeling agrees with the decency of the occasion. He
reasoned:

> But when in the sacrament God openly before his people professeth, that he is a giving
> and delivering to us the greatest benefit that can be given: certainly not onely should
> there bee before and after the gifts received, thanks given, but in the very act of giving
> and receiving, such reverence used, as may sufficiently declare and testifie how highly
> we esteeme of the greatnesse and goodnes of the Giver; and how unworthy we thinke our
> selves to be of his inestimable beneficence, what gesture is meetest to bee used, accord-
> ing to Piety in such a case; whether Sitting, or Kneeling, let them judge that have
> understanding.[230]

In a section entitled 'The Nature of the Sacrament', Lindsay explained that the
Supper is a representation of the sacrifice of Christ, in which the oblation and
sacrifice of himself 'is mystically acted in the breaking of the bread, and taking of
the cup; whereby the breaking of his Body, and sheading of his Bloud is represented, and therefore it may be, and is rightly called a representative sacrifice.'[231]
The words of institution, accompanied by the power of the Spirit, makes a 'reall
and spirituall application of the Propitiatorie Sacrifice'.[232] The bread and wine
become the communion of Christ's body and his blood: 'By the Sacramentall word:
wherein he declareth, that the Bread and the Cup are the instruments of the communication and disposition of his Bodie and Bloud, and the seales whereby he
confirmeth the same'.[233] Lindsay could speak of the 'Sacramental word' which
makes the donation and application of the death of Christ to the believer. Kneeling
was an appropriate gesture, and did not imply transubstantiation.

John Michaelson, minister of Burnt Island, also defended kneeling for communion. He pointed out that in the Gospel accounts, the apostles did not sit 'at an high Table, as wee doe at Dinner or Supper', but reclined.[234] The practice of the Reformed Church in France was to stand, and in England, those ministers who opposed kneeling, advocated sitting in pews, not sitting at table. However, some were so far bent against kneeling, that 'whatsoever is spoken against the idolatrous kneeling of the papistes, they thinke it doeth make against kneeling simplie.'[235] Michaelson explained:

> ... we doe not worship Christ in the bread, nor by the bread: the worship is not relative in this sense, that we worship the bread, because it representeth Christ: neither is it a transient worship, begun in the bread, and from the bread transient to Christ: but immediately we worship Christ in our hearts internally, and externally, by our outward gesture, when wee receive the bread and cup in remembrance of him.[236]

Michaelson also, as part of his argument, outlined the eucharistic actions – which did not include sitting, and therefore the posture was optional: 'The Ministers actions are to take the Bread, to give thankes, to breake it, and to give it: as also to take the Cuppe, and to give it: and the actions of the people are to receive the Cup, and to drinke of it. No Divine ever placed Sitting among the actions and rites necessary, and commanded to be used in the Sacrament.'[237] Kneeling was appropriate and lawful.

Others, however, found problems with the Articles, such as Robert Bruce and David Calderwood. A pamphlet against the Articles printed in Leiden in 1619 seems to have been the work of David Calderwood, who was banished for his continual opposition to episcopacy. In this tract he rejected kneeling for reception of the sacrament on grounds that 'It hath been the uniforme and constant order of this Kirke, since the reformation: that the communicants should receave the sacramentall elements of bread and wine, sitting at the table.'[238] The alteration to the custom of the Kirk was 'unlawfull'. Calderwood proceeded by way of detailed discussion of the Passover seder, contrasting it with what is specific of the Lord's Supper. Kneeling takes away the idea of it being a supper, and the use of the table as a table. The ancients may have called the table an altar, but this is improper speech and dangerous, '& has proven hurtful to the Kirk'.[239] The sacramental supper should resemble a supper, and thus sitting is appropriate. For that reason, he will have no truck with the idea that the supper is a sacrifice other than by analogy and metaphor.[240] But Calderwood also saw kneeling for reception as a breach of the Second Commandment, and he was not impressed by the argument that any spiritual presence requires some outward ceremony of adoration. He denied that it was a custom of the ancient church, and noted that it is not a practice of Reformed churches. He stood fast with the assertion: 'we are not bound to imitate other kirks further then they imitate Christ. Our sitting is not Scottish Genevating, but a commendable imitation of the Apostolicall Churches, and obedience to Christ's institution.'[241]

Calderwood also objected strongly to the permission for private baptism, mainly on ecclesiological grounds. Appealing to the *Book of Common Order*, Calderwood quoted from its opening rubric, namely, 'the sacraments are not ordained of God to be used in private corners, as charmes or sorceries; but left to the Congregation and necessarily annexed to Gods word, as seales of the same.'[242] Calderwood found it useful here to stress the more 'Zwinglian' concept of sacrament as 'a publick action, to be performed publickly, by publick ministers: neither can any necessity or sufficient cause be alledged, wherefore any sacred and publick action, should passe in private.'[243] True, sacraments are not tied to church buildings, but, said Calderwood, 'If therefore the congregation bee in a woode, a house, or a Cave, the sacraments may bee ministred in a house, a woode or a cave. But then the sacraments are ministred, not in private but in publick because they are ministred in the sight of the whole Congregation.'[244] Private baptism breeds a new kind of baptism – one of supposition; it also opens the door to clinical baptisms – which are superstitious, and baptism by women, pagans and even with 'puddly water'.[245]

Calderwood also replied to John Michaelson's work, insisting the kneeling before the sacramental elements was idolatry, and debating on whether Vermigli and Musculus supported such a practice.[246]

Summary

James's English reign began with disputes about ceremonies, and ended with bitterness and division in Scotland over ceremonies. Yet underneath the concerns and disputes there lurked a widening gap over sacramental theology. In addition to being signs, were sacraments also instruments, and conduits of grace? And what did it mean to say that sacraments 'exhibit' and are 'instruments'? Was the commemoration of the sacrifice of Christ concentrated in the ceremony of the fraction and libation, or was it in the whole eucharistic action and prayer? The seeds of ceremonial discord and sacramental divergence continued to interact, and would soon yield a harvest of havoc.

Notes

1   For discussion, see Collinson, 1967.
2   Curtis, 1961, pp.1–16. For the 'Anonymous Account', see Usher, 1910, vol.2, pp.341–54.
3   Shriver, 1982, pp.48–71; Hunt, 1998a, p.224. See also Simpson, 1981; pp.27–41.
4   Cardwell, 1841, pp.131–2.
5   Hunt, 1998.
6   Anon., *An Abridgement of that Booke which the Ministers of Lincolne Diocesse Delivered to his Majestie upon the first of December 1605*, 1617, p.38.
7   Ibid., p.52.
8   Ibid., pp.53–54; Anon., *A Survey of the Book of Common Prayer By way of 197 Quares grounded upon 58 places*, 1610, p.99.
9   Anon., *A Survey*, p.87.
10 Ibid., p.103.
11 Ibid., p.91.
12 Anon., *An Abridgement*, p.40; Anon., *A Survey*, p.73.
13 See Weir, 1990; Muller, 1988.

14 Jeanes, 1998.
15 See for example, Hall, *A Briefe Summary of the Principles of Religion*, 1634, pp.763–4. Hall speaks of sacraments as signs and seals of grace, 'The Old Religion', 1634, p.161. On the other hand, Overall was keen on the 1549 *Book of Common Prayer* communion rite, and it is thought that John Cosin, his librarian, incorporated Overall's views in his first set of Notes on the Prayer Book of 1619. See Cosin, 1843–55, V, p.114. It may be that he deliberately avoided the term.
16 Spinks, 1999, *passim*.
17 Rogers, 1607.The original title was *The English Creed*. See Craig, 1998, pp.154–176.
18 Rogers, 1639, pp.130, 147; 1608.
19 Rogers, 1619, p.262.
20 Dod, 1612, Bb3.
21 Ibid., BB4.
22 Dod, 1611, p.54, 65.
23 Egerton, 1644, pp.13–15.
24 Hunt, 1998b, pp.39–83. However, the cost of protestant celebrations, particularly of the wine, is an important factor in frequency. The Roman Catholic daily or weekly mass with only the priest communicating, and the thrice-yearly communion in one kind only of the laity, was inexpensive compared with the quantities of bread and wine consumed at protestant celebrations.
25 Hildersham, 1619a, p.96.
26 Hildersham, 1619b, p.47.
27 Ibid., p.64.
28 Ibid., p.58.
29 Hildersham, 1609, Lecture 40, p.189; Lecture 27, p.116.
30 Hildersham, 1619a, p.104.
31 Hildersham, 1635, Lecture 55, p.257.
32 Ibid., pp.259–60.
33 Ibid., p.540.
34 Ibid., p.538.
35 Hildersham 1635, p.245.
36 Ibid., pp.43–44.
37 Ibid., p.55.
38 Ibid., pp.55–56.
39 Ibid., pp.56–57.
40 Hildersham, 1619b, p.23.
41 Ibid., p.30.
42 Hildersham 1635, p.584.
43 Ibid., p.105.
44 Hildersham, 1619b, pp.64, 85–6.
45 See Seaver, 1970; Downame, 1622.
46 Downame, 1622, p.492.
47 Downame, 1631.
48 Downame, 1622, pp.8–9.
49 Ibid., p.492
50 Ibid.
51 Ibid., p.493.
52 Ibid., p.494.
53 Ibid., p.495.
54 Ibid.
55 See ibid., pp.7ff; 34–6.

56   Ibid., p.495.
57   Ibid., pp.396–7.
58   Ibid., p.396.
59   Ibid., pp.497–8.
60   Ibid., p.497.
61   Ibid., pp.922–3, reprinted in Appendix. There are echoes of *Prayer Book* language, and are good examples of this type of theology and piety expressed in prayer.
62   Randall, 1630, Sermon 2, p.34.
63   Ibid., Sermon 10, p.199.
64   Ibid., Sermon 4, p.73.
65   Ibid., Sermon 4, p.82.
66   Ibid., Sermon 2, p.37.
67   Ibid., Sermon 4, p.74.
68   Ibid., Sermon 13, p.49. The pagination begins from page 1 again at Sermon 12.
69   Ibid., Sermon 13, pp.47–8.
70   Ibid., Sermon 1, p.15.
71   Ibid., Sermon 2, p.39.
72   Ibid., Sermon 3, p.51; Sermon 4, p.78.
73   Ibid., Sermon 18, p.164.
74   Ibid., Sermon 17, p.151.
75   Ibid., Sermon 12, p.18; Sermon 8, p.158; Sermon 22, pp.280–81.
76   Ibid., Sermon 9, pp.176–81.
77   Attersoll, 1614, p.1.
78   Ibid., p.2.
79   Ibid.
80   Ibid., p.65.
81   Ibid., p.5.
82   Ibid.
83   Ibid., p.14.
84   Ibid., p.15.
85   Ibid., p.25.
86   Ibid., p.23.
87   Ibid., p.152.
88   Ibid., p.254.
89   Ibid., p.165.
90   Ibid., p.194.
91   Ibid., p.219.
92   Ibid., p.236.
93   Ibid., p.260.
94   Ibid., p.269.
95   Ibid., p.51.
96   Ibid., pp.325–6.
97   Ibid., p.53.
98   Ibid., p.290.
99   Ibid., p.340.
100 Ibid., p.345.
101 Ibid., p.350
102 Ibid., p.356.
103 Ibid., pp.405ff; p.425.
104 Ibid., p.456.
105 Ibid., p.473.

106   Ibid., p.455.
107   See also Pemble (1592–1623), Reader in Divinity at Magdalen Hall, Oxford, in his
      An Introduction to the Worthy Receiving the Sacrament of the Lord's Supper, 1628,
      p.8: 'When thou seest the Bread and Wine separated by consecration unto this holy
      use, thinke on Christ ordained and fore-appointed by the Father from everlasting,
      unto the accomplishment of our redemption by his bloud-shedding. When thou seest
      the Bread broken, and the Wine powred forth, thinke on Christ torne and rent in his
      precious body with stripes and wounds, pained even to the the death in his most holy
      soule, full of the wrath of God and indignation of the Almighty, by whom he was
      smitten for thy sinnes, and plagued for thy transgressions.'
108   See Reidy, 1958.
109   Stevenson, 1995, pp.113–17.
110   'Ceremonialists' is the term prefered by Arnoult, 1997. Stevenson has used the term
      'Reformed Patristic Churchmen'in 1994.
111   See Tyacke, 2000, pp.5–33.
112   Andrewes, 1854, VI, 'A Pattern of Catechistical Doctrine'.
113   Ibid., III, Sermon III, p.162.
114   Ibid., III, Sermon V, p.188.
115   Ibid., III, Sermon VIII, p.246.
116   Ibid., p.250.
117   Ibid., p.251.
118   Ibid., Sermon XIV, p.366.
119   Quoted from Stone, Vol.2, 1909, p.265.
120   Ibid.
121   Andrewes, 1854, II, Easter Sermon 1612, pp.304–5.
122   Andrewes, 1874, p.67; *Cosin*, 1843–55, *Works*, V, p.114.
123   After Receiving of the Blessed sacrament he gave this prayer:

> 'We have now, O Christ our God, finished and perfected,
> according to our ability, the mystery of Thy dispensation
> Had the memorial of Thy death;
> Seen the type of thy resurrection;
> For we have   Been filled with Thy endless life;
> Enjoyed Thy never-failing dainties;
> whereof vouchsafe to make us all partakers in the
> world to come.'

124   Andrewes, 1843–55, *Notes*, pp.153, 156.
125   Described by Prynne, 1646. See Tyacke, 2000.
126   See Tyacke, 1987, p.20 for this link.
127   Barlow, 1601, p.103.
128   Ibid., p.142.
129   Ibid.
130   Ibid., pp.142–3.
131   Ibid., p.144.
132   Ibid., p.145.
133   Ibid., p.145.
134   Ibid., p.129
135   Ibid., p.125.
136   Ibid., p.126.
137   Sutton, 1841, p.36.
138   Ibid., p.115.

139   Ibid., p.204ff.
140   Ibid., p.35–6.
141   Ibid., p.45.
142   Ibid., p.63.
143   Ibid., p.54.
144   Ibid., p.237.
145   Ibid., p.283.
146   Ibid., p.162.
147   Ibid., p.70.
148   Ibid., p.60.
149   Ibid., p.56.
150   Ibid., p.84.
151   Ibid., p.103.
152   Ibid., pp.104–5.
153   Lee, 1990, p.105.
154   Ibid., pp.177–9.
155   See Danner, 1999. For the *Book of Common Order*, Maxwell, 1965; Spinks, 1984b.
156   Torrance, 1996. Still of interest is Walker, 1872.
157   Bruce, 1958, p.39.
158   Ibid., p.41.
159   Ibid. p.106.
160   Ibid., pp.44–5, 65.
161   Ibid., p.74.
162   Ibid., p.67.
163   Ibid., p.71.
164   Ibid., pp. 44, 102.
165   Ibid., p.116.
166   Ibid., p.78.
167   Ibid., p.74.
168   In Bonar, 1866, p.339.
169   Ibid., p.341.
170   Ibid.
171   Ibid.
172   See Weir, 1990; Bell, 1985.
173   Rollock, 1596, *Quaestiones et Responsiones*, D2: 'Est signuma Deo institutum, efficaciter operans, visibile, per quod verbo Euangelii additu Spiritus Sanctus magis repraesentat nobis res illas spirituales & coelestes, magifque operatur in mentibus nostris earum cognitionem, in cordibus vero earum applicationem, quam per verbum Euangelii solum: quod dum facit, confirmat fidem nostram in verbum foederis & Euangelii, efficitque ut in ipsum magis ac magis credamus.'
174   Ibid., C3
175   Ibid., C4.
176   Ibid.
177   Ibid., C5: 'sed signa sunt efficaciter aliquid operantia, et Spiritus sancti organa & instrumenta.'
178   Ibid: 'Et haec quoque instrumenta sunt Spiritus sancti, quibus non tantum operatur in mentibus nostris cognitionem, quae est prima pars fidei:sed etiam in cordibus nostris interius applicationem operatur, nempe, illam ipsam quam significant, cuiusque cognitionem in mentibus nostris primum operatur.'
179   Ibid.
180   Ibid., C6.

181 Ibid., C7–C8: 'Dominus iam actis gratiis pronunciavit verba institutionis: quibus explicavit usum rerum externerum. Verbi gratia, illius aquae quae in Baptismo est, panis illius & vini illius que in Coena Domini sunt, ut, cum dicitur in Coena, hoc est corpus meum, sensus est, Panis hic est signum vel Sacramentum Corporis mei, habetque; nunc usum eum ut repraesentet corpus meum quia ego ita volo & institue.'

182 Rollock, 1844, vol.2, p.662 (Fifty-Third Lecture).

183 Ibid.

184 Ibid., p.661.

185 Rollock, 1596, D3.

186 Rollock, 1844 and 1859, vol.2, p.697.

187 Ibid., p.698.

188 Ibid., p.661.

189 Boyd, 1661, p.449.

190 Cited by Torrance, 1958, p.710.

191 Welsh, 1602, p.123.

192 Ibid., pp.87–8.

193 Ibid., p.113.

194 Ibid., p.117.

195 Ibid., p.170.

196 Ibid., p.154. An interesting use of the English language is his treatment of 'How the Mass *crap* in', p.170!

197 As noted above, *Exhibeo* has a wide range of meanings and uses, as did the English 'exhibit', and it is far from clear that divines meant the same thing; that is also true of 'instrument'.

198 For James's ecclesiastical policy in Scotland, see MacDonald, 1998.

199 Sprott, 1871, pp.xv–xvi.

200 Calderwood, 1678, p.663.

201 Stevenson, 1999, pp.455–475.

202 Calderwood, 1678, p.671; Sprott, 1871, p.xix.

203 Ibid., p.671.

204 Ibid., p.672

205 Ibid.

206 Galloway, 1588, Biiii.

207 Ibid., Bv.

208 Ibid.

209 Ibid.

210 Sprott, 1871; Donaldson, 1966.

211 Cowper, London 1629, pp.264, 289, 598.

212 Ibid., p.598.

213 Ibid., p.265.

214 Ibid., pp.261–2.

215 Ibid., p.263.

216 Ibid., pp.264–5.

217 Ibid., p.264.

218 Ibid., p.264.

219 'Knoxian' here refers to the liturgy of the *Book of Common Order* 1561, 1562, and should not be taken to imply sole authorship by Knox.
      The draft liturgy has the following sequence: Address to father and godfather – questions and answers; Prayer before the baptism; Creed; baptism; prayer after the baptism. For the derivation, see Spinks, 1995b.

220 Donaldson, 1996, p.103.

221 Ibid., p.104.
222 The sequence provided was: confession of sins; admonition; confession of sins on the day of the communion; a prayer before coming from the pulpit to the table; an exhortation; prayer; warning to draw near with faith; table prayer; Words of Consecration; delivery of the bread; admonition; delivery of the cup; short admonition; Psalm 103; thanksgiving; blessing.
223 Ibid., p.105.
224 Donaldson, 1996, p.109.
225 Sprott, 1871, p.56.
226 Ibid.
227 Ibid., p.72.
228 Cowper, 1629, pp.9–10.
229 See Ford, 1995, pp.256–77.
230 Lindsay, 1619, pp.71–2.
231 Ibid., pp.84–5.
232 Ibid., p.85.
233 Ibid., p.87.
234 Michaelson, 1620, p.10.
235 Ibid., p.50.
236 Ibid., p.52.
237 Ibid., p.97.
238 Calderwood, 1619, p.33.
239 Ibid., p.39.
240 Ibid., p.57.
241 Ibid., p.62.
242 Ibid., p.96.
243 Ibid.
244 Ibid., p.97.
245 Ibid., p.98.
246 See Calderwood, 1620.

Chapter 3

The Development of Conformist Calvinist and Patristic Reformed 'Sacramentalism', and the Sacramental Rites of the 1637 Scottish *Book of Common Prayer*

The Widening Differences in English Sacramental Discourse

Obsignatory signs: From Nonconforming Ames to Bishop Morton

In his study of the understanding of sacraments amongst those whom he termed puritan, E. Brookes Holifield drew attention to what he called 'puritan sacramentalism', typified by Samuel Ward, Master of Sidney Sussex College, Cambridge, and Cornelius Burges, royal chaplain, and vicar of Watford. Holifield noted that these two divines became less happy with the concept of sacraments as seals confirming grace, and instead wished to stress sacraments as instruments which actually convey grace.[1] It would be more accurate to say, however, that some of those divines schooled in the thought typified by William Perkins, and as maintained by his famous, but nonconforming pupil, William Ames, were becoming more attracted to the type of teaching on sacraments articulated by Richard Hooker; this at least is certainly true of Samuel Ward.

William Ames William Ames (1576–1633) represents a linear development of the type of theology presented by William Perkins in *A Golden Chaine*, 1590, including his use of Ramist charts. Ames was obliged to leave Cambridge because of his constant outspoken criticism of liturgical ceremonies of the *Book of Common Prayer*, and he took refuge in The Netherlands.[2] In his work *The Marrow of Sacred Theology* (1623), published when he was professor at Franeker, Ames defined a sacrament first of all as a sign, and a sign serves three functions – it informs (*notificans*), it reminds (*commonefaciens*) and it seals (*obsignans*).[3] A sacrament of the new covenant is a divine institution in which the blessings of the new covenant are represented, presented and applied through signs perceptible to the senses. However, sacramental signs do not include the spiritual thing they refer to. What they have in common is that they seal the whole covenant of grace to believers. After this initial discussion of what a sacrament is, Ames then turned to ecclesiastical discipline, and the administration of the covenant of grace. Only then did he more briefly treat baptism and the Lord's Supper.[4] In this section Ames states that the two sacraments appointed by Christ are not necessary for salvation, and are only to be celebrated by lawful ministers. Baptism is the sacrament of initiation and

69

regeneration, and although it seals the whole covenant of grace to all believers, it specially represents and confirms our ingrafting into Christ. It stands for adoption in that we are consecrated by it to the Father, Son and Holy Spirit. It is also the seal of sanctification and glorification. Ames gave slightly longer treatment to infant baptism, stressing that the infants of believers are not to be forbidden this sacrament:

> First, because, if they are partakers of any grace, it is by virtue of the covenant of grace and so both the covenant and the first seal of the covenant belong to them. Second, the covenant in which the faithful are now included is clearly the same as the covenant made with Abraham, Rom. 4:11; Gal.3: 7–9 – and this expressly applied to infants. Third, the covenant as now administered to believers brings greater and fuller consolation than it once could, before the coming of Christ. But if it pertained only to them and not to their infants, the grace of God and their consolation would be narrower and more contracted after Christ's appearing than before. Fourth, baptism supplants circumcision, Col. 2:11, 12; it belongs as much to the children of believers as circumcision once did. Fifth, in the very beginning of regeneration, whereof baptism is a seal, man is merely passive. Therefore, no outward action is required of a man when he is baptized or circumcised (unlike other sacraments); but only a passive receiving.[5]

The Supper is the sacrament of nourishment and growth, and must not be given to infants. Transubstantition and consubstantiation are rejected. Spiritual nourishment in the sacrament does not require a physical change, only a change in use. Ames concluded his discussion with some observations of a technical nature on whether 'This is my Body' is a metaphor or metonymy. In many ways, his views, like those of his mentor, William Perkins, approximate to somewhere between Zwingli and Calvin.[6] The influence and popularity of Ames's work amongst English divines was considerable, and may be taken to represent the doctrine of many in the period 1620–40. This seems to be the case, for example, with the simpler catechism of William Twisse (1578–1646) rector of Newington and then Newbury, later to be Prolocutor of the Westminster Assembly.[7]

Archbishop James Ussher　　Archbishop James Ussher of Armagh (1581–1656) seems to have held not dissimilar sacramental views, though he was perhaps closer to Calvin than Ames was. Ussher was educated at Trinity College, Dublin, and later Professor of Divinity. In a sermon to the House of Commons in February 1621, he distinguished between the outward visible *sacramentum*, and the inward and invisible thing, or *res sacramentum*:[8] '... we acknowledge sacraments to be signs; but bare signs we deny them to be; seals they are, as well as signs, of the covenant of grace.'[9] Using the common analogy of the King's seal in wax, Ussher asserted, 'They are not to be accounted barely significative, but truly exhibitive also, of those heavenly things whereto they have relation: as being appointed by God to be a means of conveying the same unto us, and putting us in actual possession thereof.'[10] Ussher's sermon was on the text 1 Corinthians 10:17, and on the subject of the Lord's Supper he stressed the concept of conjunction or union with the divine. He explained:

> If any do further inquire, how it is possible that any such union should be, seeing the body of Christ is in heaven, and we are upon earth: I answer, that if the manner of this

conjunction were carnal and corporal, it would be indeed necessary that the things conjoined should be admitted to be in the same place: but it being altogether spiritual and supernatural, no local presence, no physical nor mathematical continuity or contiguity is any way requisite thereunto. It is sufficient for the making of a real union in this kind, that Christ and we, though never so far distant in place each from other, be knit together by those spiritual ligatures, which are intimated unto us in the words alleged out of the sixth of John: to wit, the quickening Spirit descending downward from the Head, to be in us a fountain of supernatural life; and a lively faith, wrought by the same Spirit, ascending from us upward, to lay fast hold upon him, who 'having by himself purged our sins, sitteth on the right hand of the Majesty on high'.[11]

In *The Principles of Christian Religion with a Brief Method of the Doctrine Thereof*, he wrote:

Q.   What is a sacrament?
A.   A visible sign, ordained by God to be a seal for confirmation of the Gospel, unto those who perform the conditions required in the same.
Q.   How is this done by a sacrament?
A.   By a fit similitude between the sign and the thing signified, the benefit of the Gospel is represented unto the eye, and the assurance of enjoying the same confirmed to such as are within the covenant. Wherefore, as the preaching of the Word is the ordinary means of begetting faith; so both it, and the holy use of the Sacraments, be the instruments of the Holy Ghost to increase and confirm the same ...
Q.   What are the sacraments of this ministry?
A.   The sacrament of admission into the Church is baptism; which sealeth unto us our spiritual birth: the other sacrament of our continual preservation is the Lord's Supper: which sealeth unto us our continual nourishment.[12]

Ussher here certainly calls sacraments 'instruments', but for increasing faith, not grace, and he preferred the term 'seal'.

John Thornborough   John Thornborough (1551–1641), Bishop successively of Limerick, Bristol and Worcester, and who served under Elizabeth, James and Charles, also stressed sacraments as signs and seals of the covenant.[13] He too likened them to a wax seal – 'when wax hath it's printe, and is made a seale, it is no longer common waxe, but hath received another nature.'[14] He asserted that sacraments are 'signes, as doe *exhibite*, & *seale* to us all grace, and promises of Christ'.[15] Like Ussher, he could speak of instruments and taught that 'it pleased God to worke by Sacraments, as by an instrumentall cause'.[16] In the Supper, the bread is to us 'an instrument, and meane for faith'.[17] Thus of the eucharist Thornborough says:

The *Bread* consecrated, and broken, is the visible signe, the memoriall, the figure, the type, the pledge, the image, representing the crucified *Body* of the Sonne of God, exhibiting, and sealing unto our faith, the communion that we have with him: and the *Wine* is the externall signe, putting us in minde of the *Bloud* of *Jesus*, shed for the remission of our sinnes, and assuring us, both of the certainty of the Covenant of grace, & of the continuance thereof.[18]

Grace is granted, says Thornborough, but only to those with faith.[19]

John Preston   John Preston (1587–1628), a Cambridge-trained man whose con-formity was questioned by Lancelot Andrewes, but who was made chaplain to Prince Charles, spoke of the power and virtue which comes from God as the sacrament is received, rather as his power went out to the woman with the issue of blood.[20] In the Supper we renew our covenant with God, and he with us.[21] It is a reminder of the covenant, rather like the rainbow was for Noah.[22]

Jeremiah Dyke   Jeremiah Dyke (1584–1620?) was a Sidney Sussex, Cambridge graduate, incumbent of Epping, Essex, and a reluctant conformist. In his work entitled *A Worthy Communicant*, he describes the Lord's Supper as the seal of the covenant, but it is only for those who are in the covenant of grace.[23] Faith is required to receive the body and blood of Christ, almost as part of a bilateral covenantal agreement; it is as though Christ says, 'According to your preparation with faith, so shall mine Ordinance work, and be effectuall, and empty out it self unto you.'[24] For Dyke it is Christ who is the conduit of grace: 'So here, Christ is the conduit of all grace, and spirituall good, he that would bee filled must come to him. His Ordinances, the Word, and Sacrament they are the cockes of this conduit, so that a man that would be filled, must not only goe to Christ, but to Christ in these Ordinances, must bring his vessell to these cockes.'[25] The bread and wine are sacramental offers, promises and representations. Dyke explained: 'There is in the *Sacrament* a visible remembrance of Christs death, and in the breaking of the bread, and powring out the wine, there is representation of Christs death, and Passion. When I see the wine poured out, it represents unto me the shedding of Christs blood, here I see Christs blood shed on the Crosse.'[26] Indeed, the sacrament of the supper is 'one bason in which this blood is put'.[27]

Stephen Denison   Stephen Denison (d. 1649) was preacher at St. Katherine Cree in London, and a Doctor of Divinity. He wrote against 'Arminianism', and was suspended by Laud when the latter was Bishop of London, though he does not appear to have been in major conflict in the reign of James.[28] In 1634, he published as a work a number of sermons which he had preached on baptism and the Lord's Supper.

Denison taught that preparation for baptism was desirable, citing the example of St. Paul.[29] It should not be postponed, because 'it is the meanes of our admission into the congregation of Saints, as circumcision was unto the Jewes.'[30] It is the badge of a Christian, and a sign and seal of our union with Christ, and of our regeneration, pardon and remission of sins.[31] It is a seal of the covenant, and infants are within the covenant.[32] Baptism must be administered by a lawful minister, though the sacrament does not depend on the minister, 'For blessed bee God for it, the vertue of the Sacrament cleaveth not to the fingers of him that doth administer it, but it is from God.'[33] Presumably with the *Book of Common Prayer* rite of baptism in mind, after explaining that baptism is in the three-fold name, Denison immediately picked up upon the post-baptismal sign of the cross and its military formula: 'And it is very fit that names should bee used in Baptisme, yea that they should be given them: because in baptisme wee professe our selves to become the Souldiers of Christ: and therefore as a Souldier at his first entrance into Warfare gives up his name to his Captaine, even so must we to Christ in our baptisme.'[34] However, Denison gave no discussion of the sign of the cross, suggesting that it was a ceremony that he omitted. The water washes, representing that Christ's blood washes our sins. However, he insisted that baptism did not wash sins *ex opere operato*, for sacraments confirm grace where it is already rather than confer grace where it is wanting.[35] Baptism 'unto the Elect is like our deedes and evidences which wee have shewen for our especiall inheritance, the kingdome of heaven'.[36] Denison exhorted the congregation and readers to remain at baptismal services, and join in the prayer; he also stressed the importance of preaching at baptisms, for the sacrament should not be without the word, for the word is the 'principall', and sacraments 'are the accessory or appendices'.[37]

Denison's practice was of monthly communion, and he warned that the prevailing custom that to receive once or twice a year was insufficient; indeed, such are 'Carnall Gospellers'.[38] Much of his work was taken up with worthy reception, because of a conern that the sacrament was abused.[39] Denison noted that different churches had different traditions regarding the posture of receiving, and that providing all things are done honestly and in due order, this is left to discretion.[40] Like Perkins, Denison notes four actions, though they are related to the bread-taking, giving thanks, breaking and giving.[41] Giving thanks 'was to consecrate the elements, or outward signes unto our holy purpose, to separate them from a common use to a Sacramentall and holy use'.[42] Breaking the bread signifies the bitter passion of Christ upon the cross, and puts us in mind of the crucifying of the body of Christ.[43] Denison gave considerable theological interpretation to the giving of the bread. It represents the action of God the Father delivering the Son to death, and then of offering his merits to the communicant.[44] As regards the presence of Christ, Denison rejected the Lutheran idea that Christ's body may be in many places, and he also repudiated the doctrine of transubstantiation.[45] Interestingly, Denison admits that God could transubstantiate if he so wished, but choses not to do so, for that would overthrow the sacrament *qua* sacrament.[46] The true meaning of Christ's word is 'as though Christ had said, this bread is a lively signe, and this Wine is a lively representation of my body and blood.'[47] He explained further:

> ... the body and blud of Christ are present in [the?] Sacrament vertually. For however his blessed body bee in heaven, yet the vertue and benefits, and merits of the same are really and truly offered unto us in the Sacrament. Whereupon the Bread is termed the Communion of the bodie of Christ, *1 Cor.10.16.* to intimate unto us, though wee partake not of the very flesh of Christ in this holy ordinance, that yet we partake of the benefits thereof.[48]

The words of Christ relating to the New Testament refer to the covenant of grace.[49] However, as noted already, Denison's main concern was with the question of worthiness, and he gave a lengthy discussion on the sin of ignorance. Almost in summary of his work he wrote:

> The Lords Supper was ordained of God to put us in remembrance of Christ his passion, *1.Cor.11.24* to feed our soules to life eternall, *Mat.26.26.* and to confirme our faith, the Sacraments being seales as well as signes, *Rom.4.11.* Therfore we must not repaire unto

this blessed banquet (as some doe) to save our selves from presenting, or for custome, and the like, but wee must come to those very ends, whereunto God hath appoynted this businesse.[50]

Thomas Morton   Last as typifying this broad grouping, are the views of Bishop Thomas Morton (1564–1659). A graduate of St. John's College, Cambridge, Morton rose to become Dean of Gloucester in 1606, Dean of Winchester in 1609, Bishop of Chester in 1616, of Lichfield and Coventry in 1618, and of Durham in 1632. He was no friend of the rising 'Arminian' group, though would be deprived of his see in 1646 with the abolition of episcopacy. Whereas Dyke wrote a devotional work, and Stephen Denison's views are in sermons, Morton's views are known through two works of a polemical nature, against nonconformists on one hand, and against Roman Catholicism on the other.

In a defence of the surplice, the cross in baptism, and kneeling for communion, it is possible to glean something of Morton's views on baptism. He noted that those who object to the sign of the cross in the baptismal rite claim that the ceremony and the accompanying formula signify 'that the child, now baptized, is by baptisme already incorporated into the mysticall body of *Christ*, which is his Church; & therefore is pronounced by the Priest, not in *fieri*, but in *facto esse*, (as the Schools speaketh) to be publikely *Received* into it.'[51]

According to Morton, the ceremony is in fact a token of a duty to be practised afterwards, and to be a sign of the baptism itself. Unlike its use in the Roman rite, he argued, the signing comes after the act of baptism, and not before it.[52] Baptism is a laver of regeneration, and a sacramental sign of new birth.[53] It does not itself confer grace; it is 'a *signe* of Regeneration, that is, *Gratiae collatae*, of *Grace conferred* by the Spirit of God'.[54] Baptism is a dedication, a sacramental stipulation with God, whereas the sign of the cross is a 'Morall representation and protestation unto man'.[55]

In his defence of the posture of kneeling for reception, Morton gave some idea of his understanding of the eucharist. More technical views are also given in his work entitled *Of the Institution of the sacrament of the Blessed Bodie and Blood of Christ* (1631). This was a reply to the work of the Roman Catholic apologist, John Brerely. The eucharist is a mystical sign of the union of the faithful with Christ.[56] The elements are consecrated to a sacramental use, to be seals of the covenant of grace.[57] The mystical object of the sacrament is the body and blood of Christ.[58] They are a sacramental representation.[59] However, Morton insisted that although protestants deny the corporal presence of Christ in the elements, yet they do hold that Christ is present. The bread is 'an *exhibiting Instrument of the Body of Christ*'; communicants '*truly and really participate of the substance of the Body and Blood of Christ*'.[60] There is a '*mysticall Presence*'.[61] In support, Morton cites not only patristic references, but also Calvin, and his statement that communicants do participate of the substance of the body and blood of Christ place him alongside Calvin. Explaining further, Morton wrote that the body of Christ was

Sacramentally represented, and verily exhibited to the *Faithfull* Communicants. There are then three Objects, in all, to be distinguished. The First is *before Consecration*, the *Bread* merely *Naturall*. Secondly, *After Consecration, Bread Sacramentall*. Thirdly,

Christ's owne *Body*, which is the *Spirituall*, and Super-substantiall *Bread*, truly exhibited by this *Sacramentall*, to the nourishment of the soules of the Faithfull.[62]

Indeed, Morton stressed that the 'Spirituall *feeding and* Union with Christ's Body *is more excellent and Reall than the* Corporall Conjunction can be.'[63]

On the question of sacrifice, Morton argued that to call the eucharist a propitiatory sacrifice was improper, since the death is commemoratively shown, not operatively shown.[64] It is a 'Sacrifice Eucharisticall' and a 'sacrifice of worship and veneration'.[65] It is also a sacramental representation, commemoration and application of the one sacrifice.[66] He explained:

> ... although the whole Act of our Celebration, in *Commemoration* of Christ's Death, as proceeding from us, be a *Sacrifice propitious*, as other holy Acts of Devotion, only by God's *Complacency* and *Acceptance*; Yet the object of our *Commemoration* being the *Death and Passion of Christ*, in his *Body* and *Blood*, is to us, by the efficacy thereof, a truly and properly *propitiatory Sacrifice*, and *Satisfaction*, for a perfect remission of all sinnes.[67]

It may be that in this 'dialogue' with Rome, Morton is going as far as he can on this issue of commemoration and sacrifice. In *A Defence*, it is clear that the fraction is an important element in the commemoration: 'There is in the Sacrament a visible remembrance of Christs death, and in the breaking of the bread, and powring out the wine, there is a representation of Christs death, and Passion.'[68]

Conformist Calvinist Sacramentalism: Ward, Burges, Bedford and John Denison

Samuel Ward   Where and how, then, did Samuel Ward differ? Ward (1572–1643) had been a member of Christ's College, and like Ames, a pupil of Perkins (Figure 3.1). He later obtained a fellowship at Emmanuel College, where William Bedell, later to be Bishop of Kilmore, was also a fellow. Ward recorded in his diary the great sense of loss he felt when Perkins died.[69] He recorded his outrage at the attempt to introduce the surplice into Emmanuel College Chapel. When he became Master of Sidney Sussex, he refused to have the chapel consecrated. He was one of the English delegates at the Synod of Dort – where his former friend Ames was a moderator for the Dutch representatives. Logic would suppose that his views on sacraments would have been at one with Perkins and Ames. However, in the late 1620s in his lectures at Cambridge, and in correspondence with Ussher and Bedell, he began to teach a strong sacramental efficacy. In a letter to Ussher he wrote of baptism: 'I know most of our divines do make the principal end and effect of all sacraments to be obsignation, and all sacraments to be merely obsignatory signs; and consequently that ablution of infants from original sin, is only conditional and expective, of which they have no benefit, till they believe and repent; I cannot easily assent hereunto.'[70] Ward posed the question of why bother to baptise infants if the rite itself did nothing. He thus reasoned:

> Though our divines do most-what run upon obsignation, yet often they do expressly hold, that sacraments do offer and exhibit that grace which they signify, and as I conceive must needs offer and exhibit the grace which they signify, before they assure

Figure 3.1   Samuel Ward, 1572–1643

and confirm. For God doth offer and exhibit grace promised in the sacrament; then we exercise our faith in relying upon God, promising, offering, and exhibiting on his part; and so according to the tenure of the covenant, receive the grace promised, and then sacraments in the second place do assure us of the grace received.[71]

Ward thus admitted that most English divines, or at least those of his circle, were content with the concept of sacraments as signs and seals exhibiting what had already been imparted. In contrast, Ward had come to the conclusion that as instruments sacraments actually convey and effect what they signify. Thus he continued:

So that first is a means whereby God doth offer and exhibit on his part the grace signifieth; which we receiving by faith, it then also becometh a pledge, to assure us of the receipt thereof. So the eucharist doth first offer and exhibit 'augmentum gratiae, auctiorem et perfectiorem communionem cum Christi corpore et sanguine, et participationem in beneficiis inde fluentibus;' and then it is a pledge to assure us thereof. And so Ursinus truly saith, 'Baptismus et coena Domini sunt sacramenta, – quia sunt opus Dei, qui aliquid in iis nobis dat, et se dare testatur;' and he hath many speeches to this purpose. So Calvin. So that instrumental conveyance of the grace signified, to the due receiver, is as true an effect or end of a sacrament, when it is duly administered, as obsignation, and is pre-existing in order of nature to obsignation: for obsignation must be that, quod prius datur et exhibetur, as Mr. Beza often saith. Mr. Hooker, in mine opinion, doth truly explicate the nature of sacraments. Nay, it may seem, that obsignation is not so essential as exhibitio rei signatae, for the latter may be without the former, as in the baptism of infants, where no preparation, ex parte suscipientis, but only capacity and not-resistance is sufficient, ad rem signatam recipiendam.[72]

In his lectures he taught that baptism was necessary since it was the ordinary means for the absolution from original sin for infants. Baptism was an instrument which applied the merit of Christ to an infant.[73]

No specific reply from Ussher seems to have survived, but Ward sent a very similar letter to William Bedell, and we have his reply. He appeared not to have read Hooker, and was quite certain that Ward had misinterpreted the Reformers that he had cited. Bedell asserted:

> The grace which the sacraments confer, is of three sorts. The first is, the spiritual things which are proportionable to the outward. The second, the effects of these. The third, the certification of the party in the lawful use of the outward, of the enjoying the two former. As in baptism, 1. the blood and spirit of Christ; 2. the washing of sin, and new birth; 3. the obsignation to the party baptized, that by Christ's blood his sins are cleansed.[74]

Grace, said Bedell, is some special favour in order to salvation promised in the new covenant. The sequence of what God offers or exhibits in sacraments, in his view, was:

1   Offer his covenant, under the condition of faith and repentance, and therein Christ and his benefits.
2   We accept of the covenant according to the tenor of it.
3   God offers to confirm it with sacraments proportional.
4   We receive them, and so are certified of the performance of the covenant, and have the promises thereof conveyed by covenant, and by seal also to us.[75]

Bedell felt that the logic of Ward's teachings on baptism posited two forms of justification, one for infants and one for adults. Of the eucharist he opined:

> It seems to me that God having in the New Testament (confirmed with Christ's blood) offered unto us life under the condition of receiving him, would confirm to as many as receive him that they have life. Therefore he hath instituted bread and wine, the means of natural life, in a certain use, to be seals of spiritual life. We now receiving them, they are pledges unto us, and do certify us of that spiritual life which we have by receiving Christ.[76]

Thus, Ward had shifted to the view of Hooker, which in turn was one logical progression of elements of Calvin's teaching.[77] Bedell stayed with a Perkinsian sacramentalism. The reason for Ward's shift seems to have been from his reading and reflection – a genuine intellectual change.[78]

Cornelius Burges   Cornelius Burges, in 1629, wrote a long book defending the concept of baptismal regeneration as taught in the *Book of Common Prayer*. Though a royal chaplain, Burges, vicar of Watford, Hertfordshire, was to play a key part in the Westminster Assembly of Divines and sided firmly with the presbyterian-minded English divines. However, his views on baptism had been labelled 'Arminian', and so he wrote the treatise to vindicate himself. He differentiated between 'initial' regeneration and 'actual' regeneration. The 'initial' regeneration, rather like a seed, is given in baptism.[79] He likened the process to Elisha stretching himself once, and then again, on the body of the dead child; the first time the flesh grew warm, but the second time the child woke up.[80] Burges wrote:

> It is most agreeable to the Institution of Christ that All Elect Infants that are baptized (unlesse in some extraordinary cases) doe, ordinarily, receive, from Christ, the Spirit in Baptisme, for their first solemne initiation into Christ, and for their future actuall rennovation, in Gods good time, if they live to yeares of discretion, and enjoy the other ordinary means of Grace appointed of God to this end.[81]

Burges made a distinction between regeneration and renovation, and he also – unlike Ward – restricted the conveying of grace to those who were amongst the elect. And he could say towards the end of his lengthy work,

> When I say that, *In the baptisme of Elect infants, Christ doth, ordinarily, bestow his spirit; I adde withall, that, this is not sufficient for the salvation of such as live to years of discretion, but actuall conversion and renovation is to be expected and laboured for, in due and conscionable attendance upon the use of all those further helps and means which God hath sanctified to that purpose.* For so God vouchsafeth to grace all his ordinances, that hee will not have any of them despised nor neglected, by leaving either of them unusefull, through such an efficacy of any that have gone before, as might leave nothing to be done by those that follow after. As he puts his spirit in the hearts of the elect, in their baptisme; so he afterwards puts power into his word effectually to call them home unto himselfe: & then the same spirit workes mightily by that word, and infuseth the *habits* of faith and all sanctifying graces that doe accompany salvation.[82]

Ultimately Burges seems to have expended a vast number of pages to say that infant baptism does something salvific for elect infants, but much more must be done, and will be done by the elect to bring sanctification to fruition.

Thomas Bedford   The development of Ward's views on sacramental efficacy can be seen in the work of his pupil, Thomas Bedford, in his *A Treatise of the Sacraments* (1638). Indeed, apart from his works on sacraments, little is known of his career. Bedford asserted that in the sacraments grace is given to us, not only reported, or proffered, but given and put in our possession.[83] Sacraments are visible representations of grace, and may be compared to 'Chanells, and Conduit pipes, which derive the water from the Spring to the Cistern, for even so do the Sacraments convey Christ with all his benefits to the worthy receiver'.[84] He cited Perkins, but felt the need to modify his words – sacraments are signs to represent, instruments to convey, and seals to confirm the conveyance of Christ with all his benefits.[85] They are 'reall instruments to conferr grace'.[86] Crucial was the fact that they are instituted by Christ, and contain his promise. Hence in the Lord's Supper 'in our Church – Liturgy is the matter whereof the prayer of consecration consisteth. Yet not our formall Recitation of them is that which doth give virtue to the

Element, but the institution of Christ.'[87] Bedford lists the essentials of baptism as the use of water, washing, and the use of the triune name. He also defended the sign of the cross in baptism.[88] He noted the dispute over private and lay baptism, which in his opinion had been settled by King James.[89] Through baptism we are incorporated into Christ. From this flows a two-fold benefit, 'which for distinction sake, we may call the secondary grace of the sacrament, and the more peculiar grace of Baptism, namely, Remission, and Regeneration.'[90] And Bedford quoted from the *Prayer Book* baptismal service to support the work of regeneration.[91] The primary grace of the Lord's Supper is our incorporation into Christ, which, as far as Bedford was concerned, does convey remission of sins.[92]

John Denison   John Denison (d. 1629) would seem also to fit in this category. He was a graduate of Balliol College, Oxford, and a Doctor of Divinity, and is thought to have been related to Stephen Denison. He held benefices in Reading, and in 1610 became rector of Woodmansterne, Surrey. He was chaplain to George Villiers, Duke of Buckingham, and one of James I's chaplains. Though Buckingham was to be associated with the 'Patristic Reformed churchmen', there is no obvious evidence that Denison was associated with them. His work on the Lord's Supper, 'set forth in seven Sermons' was published under the title *The Heavenly Banquet*. Much of what Denison says accords with the position of the 'obsignationists', but his view of sacraments giving grace would seem to set him with Ward and Bedford. His work was bound with a short treatise defending kneeling at Communion.

At the beginning of the work, Denison gave a chart in Ramist fashion, and reminiscent of Perkins, though it is different from the one Perkins gave.[93] The sermons were given titles which reflect a theological and scholastic concern – matter, form, external cause, final cause, for example. Baptism and the Lord's Supper are the 'Evangelicall sacraments' in distinction from the legal sacraments of the Old Testament, and together seal up the covenant of grace.[94] They are military badges 'whereby we publiquely professe our selves to be the souldiers & servants of Jesus Christ, whilst we serve in his Campe, and under his colours.'[95] Just as a seal gives force to a written document, 'so the Sacraments doe confirme to us the Covenant of grace'.[96] But, said Denison, 'The sacraments are as conduit pipes to convey grace into the Cesterns of our hearts: but Christ himselfe is the fountaine, *Of whose fulnesse wee receive grace for grace.*'[97] Denison further elaborated:

> As in humane actions the instrument hath his vertue & activity from the principall agent: so have these sacred ordinances their vertue and efficacy from Christ, the author of the Sacraments. From him proceeds the influence of Grace. We powre on water in Baptisme, but he *baptized with the holy Ghost, and with fire.* In the Lords Supper we deliver the elements, but he it is that gives vertue to the Sacrament. As he did sanctifie himselfe, so I may say hee doth sanctifie the Sacraments for the Churches sake, that she thereby might be sanctified.[98]

What is interesting here is that although the sacramental elements are instruments, nevertheless, Christ uses them to give grace.

Denison's subject was not baptism, though in passing, like his kinsman, he complained that although Christ is the author of baptism, people flock away when it is administered. Denison exhorted: 'But they should knowe, that as they owe their duty of their prayers to the infant, & their silent suffrages for th'incorporating of it into the society of the Saints & so themselves may take occasion, to revive the remembrance of their owne Covenant in Baptisme, and are bound to honour the ordinance of Christ with their presence.'[99]

The sacrament of the Supper is a representation of the passion, and a pledge of unspeakable love.[100] The bread and wine constitute the visible matter. But the invisible is also twofold, namely the body and blood of Christ. Thus, 'in the Sacrament there is offered and exhibited to the worthy communicant corporally bread & wine, but spiritually the body and bloud of Christ. For the Sacraments must bee visible signes of invisible grace.'[101] The bread 'being in especiall manner the instrument of our corporall strength, was fit to set forth our spirituall strengthening by Christ'.[102]

These statements point towards a symbolic instrumentalism, and here Denison is at one with Bedford. Indeed, this finds further confirmation when he turns to deal with the invisible matter in more detail:

> When we say that the body and bloud of Christ is the invisible matter of the Sacrament, we comprehend under them, whole Christ, both soule and body, with all his divine Graces and Merits: Yea the Divinity also in respect of efficacy; yet because the humane nature of Christ is as it were the Conduit pipe, by which the Divinity doth convey grace to us, therefore we mention onely the receiving of that in the Eucharist. But the truth is, that whole Christ, both God and man, is made ours, by the worthy participation of this Sacrament. The elements and author of salvation are both received at one instant, if the heart and hand of the receiver doe their mutuall offices: as the Minister gives the visible signe, so the Spirit of God imparts the invisible Grace.[103]

Denison further explained: 'Now albeit Christ is truly in the Sacrament, yet is hee not locally there, according to the conceit either of Consubtantiation or Transubstantiation. For the body and bloud of Christ are not present in the elements, but to the Communicants.'[104] There is a symbolical and rational union between Christ and the elements, but the spiritual and real union is between Christ and the communicant. Just as the sun gives light, 'So Christ being in heaven, doth by his Spirit in a most inexplicable manner communicate unto his Church on earth, the influence of grace, yea communicates himselfe.'[105] There is a sacramental presence, and Denison states that inward grace is conveyed and confirmed by the outward signs – just as by a charter a King can convey real things.[106] Christ is truly offered and exhibited in the sacrament.[107] In words echoing Christopher Sutton, Denison calls the eucharist 'our Viaticum'.[108]

Like many of his fellow divines, Denison pinpointed the fraction and libation – 'here the Communicants must observe, that when the bread is broken, and the wine powred out, they should then stir up their hearts to meditate upon the paines & Passion of Christ, and apply the same to their soules as a soveraigne cordiall of comfort.'[109] The eucharist is a memorial of our saviour's death, and in it we see the death of Christ.[110] Indeed, the final cause is the remembrance of Christ and showing forth his death.[111] But the eucharist is in no sense an oblation; there is a difference between a sacrament and a sacrifice. Following Luther, Denison insisted that in a sacrament God gives us something, and we do not offer God something.[112]

And the sixth sermon concentrated on worthy reception, and his readers were urged that to communicate once a year is not sufficient.

Patristic Reformed Sacramentalism: The Durham House Churchmen

The Conformist Calvinist sacramentalism typified by Ward and Bedford was not the only development in sacramental theology at this time. Cornelius Burges had written his treatise in part as an apologia addressed to those who called him 'Arminian'. Like the word 'puritan', this was a blanket term of abuse. Because of the theological connotations of 'Arminianism', the emphasis of these divines has been portrayed by some as mainly centering upon disputes over a full-blown Bezean double predestination.[113] Peter White has rightly noted that too much can be made of this doctrine.[114] There were many other characteristics too, perhaps of more importance. For example, these churchmen tended to be more conscious of the Church of England as being quite distinct from Reformed churches, and were in direct lineal descent from the 'Avant-garde' churchmanship of Lancelot Andrewes and John Overall. I have preferred the term 'Patristic Reformed Churchmen', though Sharon Arnoult preferred the term 'Ceremonialists', and Kenneth Steveson has used the term 'Reformed patristic'.[115] Though their piety and theological concerns were not typical of most Jacobean divines, the fine balancing policies of James allowed their growth, and in the reign of Charles they were in the ascendency. The chief proponents of this piety can be identified with those divines who were associated with the patronage of Richard Neile, then Bishop of Durham, and who gathered at his London residence, Durham House. In her doctoral thesis on the Durham House divines, Victoria Raymer aptly summed up their aims and ethos. They: 'sought to make the spirituality prevailing in the Church of England more dependent on sacraments and less on preaching, more involved with worship and less with verbal instruction. They thought the English Church should draw more extensively for models of devotion and conduct from the ancient Church Fathers and less from the Continental Reformers.'[116]

Richard Neile, himself a protégé of Lancelot Andrewes, and who was successively Bishop of Rochester, Lichfield, Lincoln, Durham and Winchester, and finally from 1632 until his death in 1640, Archbishop of York, gathered around himself a group of younger divines who could echo Andrewes in the assertion, 'We as little follow Calvin as we follow the Pope, where either the one or the other departs from the footprints of the Fathers.'[117] Amongst this group were John Buckeridge, John Howson, Matthew Wren, Richard Montagu, John Cosin and William Laud. Their outlook, which has come to be called, somewhat inaccurately perhaps, 'Laudian piety', is perhaps best expressed in an extract from a sermon preached by John Cosin at the consecration of Francis White as Bishop of Carlisle in the chapel at Durham House on 3 December 1626:

> Now to make men observe and do what the Church teaches them is, or should be, in the bishop's hands. We suffer scandal from them of the Church of Rome in many things, in nothing more than this, that we are sent to preach sermons to the people, as men that had some pretty commodities to sell them which, if they liked, they might buy or use; if not, they might let them alone; that we talk of devotion but live like the careless; that we have

a service, but no servants at it; that we have churches, but keep them not like the houses of God; that we have the sacraments, but few to frequent them; Confession, but few to practise it; finally, that we have all religious duties (for they cannot deny it), but seldom observed; all good laws and canons of the Church, but few or none kept; the people are made to do nothing; the old discipline is neglected, and men do what they list. It should be otherwise, and our Church intends it otherwise ...[118]

Here we see the concern with episcopal office, the need to make churches look like churches and have a sense of the sacred through sumptuous furnishing, to celebrate sacraments, and observe the rubrics which those of more Reformed bent frequently ignored. It has been succinctly summed up in the title of an article by Peter Lake: 'The Laudian style: order, uniformity and the pursuit of the beauty of holiness'.[119] One of the trends set in motion by the bishops of this group was the attempt to enforce the permanent placing of the communion table at the east end, and rail it in with communion rails, and, if possible, adorn it. Charles Chauncey, who left his ministry in England for the freedom of New England, complained in 1637:

They will have Priests not Ministers, Altars not Communion Tables, Sacrifices not Sacraments; they will bow, and cringe to and before the Altars, yea, they will not indure any man to enquire after what manner of Christ is in the Sacrament, whether by way of consubstantiation, or transubstantiation, or in a spiritual manner; yea, they will have Tapers, and Books never used, empty Basins and Chalices there, what is this but the Mass itself, for here is all the furniture of it.[120]

Julian Davies has argued that this was not so much 'Laudian' as the royal policy pursued by Charles I, which the bishops felt compelled to carry out, some more enthusiastically than others.[121] More recently Kenneth Fincham has revisited dioc-esan and parish records, and concludes that the central figures in the development were Archbishops Neile and Laud, and not Charles I.[122] Neile led the way, impos-ing the railed altar in the northern province in 1633, and his example was followed, after the hearing of St. Gregory's Church, London in November 1633, by bishops of the southern province. Laud belatedly followed. The policy certainly reflected the sacramental and liturgical interests of the Durham House divines.

This group of churchmen was concerned to rally around and defend the teaching set forth in Richard Montague's *A New Gagg for an old Goose*, 1624, which was regarded by many as espousing an Arminian view of salvation, and attempts were made in Parliament to prosecute him. Those attempts failed, but the implications were debated at the York House Conference in 1626, at the London residence of the Duke of Buckingham. Here Bishop Thomas Morton represented the 'Calvinist Consensus' divines, and debated with Thomas Jackson. In many ways the York House Conference brought to the fore this group of churchmen. However, though sharing common concerns and outlook, these divines were as diverse in their theological views as the 'godly' divines, and this is reflected in their sacramental teaching.

Thomas Jackson   We may begin with Thomas Jackson (1579–1640), who was at one time chaplain to Neile, and was a later successor to John Rainolds as President of Corpus Christi, Oxford. His theological journey seems to have been a move away from a 'godly' Calvinism to one more in keeping with the Durham House group. His life-long work was a series of expositions based on the Apostles' Creed, and it is from these that we can deduce some of his beliefs. In his work on eucharistic theology of this period, C.W. Dugmore noted that 'virtue', in the sense of 'power', was a key word for Jackson, and this is true also for baptism.[123]

Jackson did not assent to the view of Burges that only in elect infants is there the seed of regeneration and grace. He acknowledged that theological opinion was divided on this issue, [124] but his own view was that 'all of us are in baptism thus far sanctified that we are made true members of the visible church, qualified for hearing the word, for receiving the sacrament of Christ's body and blood, and whatsoever benefits of Christ's priestly function are committed to the dispensation of his ministers'.[125] Those who deny that any grace or talent is always given misunderstand baptism. In fact, baptism is 'a mutual covenant or a stipulation between God and us', and in every covenant there is a *ratio dati et accepti* – God gives, we receive.[126] At greater length Jackson explained:

> It is no part of our Church's doctrine or meaning, that the washing or sprinkling infants' bodies with consecrated water should take away sins by its own immediate virtue ... The meaning of our church intends no further than this – that if this sacrament of baptism be duly administered, the blood, or bloody sacrifice, or (which is all one) the influence of his Spirit, doth always accompany, or is concurrent to this solemn act. But whether this influence of his Spirit, or virtual presence of his body and blood, be either immediately or only terminated to the soul and spirit of the party baptized, or have some virtual influence upon the water of baptism, as a mean to convey the grace of regeneration unto the soul of the party baptized, whilst the water is poured upon him, is too nice and curious a question in this age for sober Christians to debate or contend about. It may suffice to believe that this sacramental pledge hath a virtual presence of Christ's blood, or some real influence from his body, concomitant, though not consubstantiated to it, which is prefigured or signified by the washing or sprinkling the body with water.[127]

According to Jackson, 'perennial efficacy or operative virtue of Christ's body and blood' consecrates once and for all the water of baptism and the bread and wine of the eucharist.[128] Thus he rejects both Roman Catholic and Lutheran teaching of presence in the eucharist, but affirms that Christ is really present because he is virtually present.[129] More powerfully than John Preston, he likened this to the Gospel incident of the woman with the issue of blood. Thus:

> We may consecrate the elements of bread and wine, and administer them so consecrated as undoubted pledges of his body and blood, by which the new covenant was sealed, and the general pardon purchased; yet unless he grant some actual influence of his Spirit, and suffer such virtue to go out from his human nature now placed in his sanctuary, as he once did unto the woman that was cured of the issue of blood – unless this virtue do as immediately reach our souls as it did her body – we do not really receive his body and blood with the elements of bread and wine.[130]

But of course, Jackson did believe in this immediacy of 'emission of virtue from his heavenly sanctuary', so that in baptism and the eucharist, we are 'healed by faith relatively or instrumentally'.[131] Jackson thus sees faith as the instrument, but the sacrament conveys the virtue or power of God.

Francis White   Rather different was Francis White (1562–1638), who became Bishop of Carlisle in 1626, and as we have seen, his consecration was the occasion of Cosin's sermon with the Durham House 'manifesto' (Figure 3.2). White was the son of Peter White, vicar of Eaton Socon, near St. Neots, Cambridgeshire. His brother, John (1570–1615) was also a notable divine who had attacked the Roman Church in his work *The Way of the True Church*, in which sacraments are 'like wax of the seal of a covenant'.[132] John did not live to be able to answer the Jesuit Fisher's reply, and so Francis sought to vindicate his brother in *The Orthodox Faith and Way to the Church Explained and Justified* in 1617, and a revised edition in 1624. In this and other works, White was mainly concerned with engaging with the Roman Catholic understanding of the eucharist, and had little to say on baptism, other than to note that this is the occasion when the Church of England uses the ancient sign of the cross.[133] A sacrament can be described as 'a divine instrument and seale authenticall', which in the case of the Lord's Supper really applied the body and blood of Christ to the worthy receiver 'for the remission of sinne, and the impetrating of spirituall and worldly blessings'.[134] The elements are 'conduiets of life, and conveiances of heavenly grace unto us'.[135] White rejected transubstantiation, and the sacrifice of the mass. But the bread and wine become instruments of grace, and the body and blood of Christ are present to the soul.[136] The body and blood are 'now represented, made present, communicated, and received in a mysticall manner, in the lawful use of this Sacrament'.[137] The difference between the Church of England and Rome, asserted White, was not concerning the object, or matter received in and by the sacrament, but touching the manner of presence and the manner of receiving. The manner of receiving is mystical and spiritual, not natural, and the body and blood are eaten and drunk 'by operative faith in the sacrament'.[138] He went on to explain to his readership:

> … the holy Ghost, directly, and in speciall, when the Sacrament is delivered, exhibiteth the Body and Blood of Christ, as a pledge and testimonie of his particular love towards every worthie Receiver; and the lively representation and commemoration of Christ's death and sacrifice, by the mysticall signes and actions, is an instrument of the Divine Spirit, to apply and communicate Christ crucified, and to increase and confirm Faith, Charitie, and pietie of Receivers.[139]

The Supper may also be called a sacrifice of commemoration, praise and thanksgiving, serving to glorify God, in a figurative sense: 'It is a representation and exhibition of the reall sacrifice of Christ once offered upon the Crosse.'[140]

There is nothing here, probably, that Ward could not have said about sacraments, for much of the language can be found in Calvin. However, in the eucharist, we may detect an interest in questions of presence and sacrifice, and the latter was certainly a Durham House concern. White's interest in the 'Laudian piety' is illustrated in a later work of 1636, *A Treatise on the Sabbath-Day*, when he was Bishop of Ely. Here the word 'Altar' is used alongside communion table, while kneeling for receiving the sacrament, bowing the body and uncovering the head are all defended, and the mixed chalice is mentioned. And again we find an interest in the eucharist as sacrifice when White asserts: 'The holy and mysterious Eucharist was celebrate, and the sacrifice of praise and thanksgiving being offered up unto God for his rich grace, represented and exhibited in this Sacrament.'[141]

Figure 3.2   Francis White, 1562–1638

John Buckeridge   Yet another shade of opinion is found in John Buckeridge (1562–1631), who had been closely associated with Lancelot Andrewes (Figure 3.3). It was Buckeridge who served as a link betwen Neile and Andrewes, and who also brought Laud to the attention of Neile. In 1606 he joined Lancelot Andrewes and William Barlow in delivering a series of sermons at Hampton Court addressed to Andrew Melville and certain other Scottish ministers whom James had summoned to London for 're-education'. In his sermon Buckeridge gave them a lesson in church history and obedience to rulers. His views on sacraments were expressed in his published sermon delivered in 1618 on Psalm 95:6, to which was appended a *Discourse concerning Kneeling at Communion*. Like Andrewes and Bedford, Buckeridge describes sacraments as '*canales gratiae*, The Chanels and conduits, wherein Gods mercies and graces doe runne, and are conveyed to us; *Exhibent quod signant*, They exhibit that to us, which they signifie, and represent.'[142]

Sacraments consist of a sign and the thing signified, and grace must be exhibited in, with, or by the sign or it will cease to be a sacrament.[143] They are vessels or instruments of our consecration in which we are offered up to God.[144] In baptism, 'the grace of the Holy Ghost is there signified, and there exhibited. Else he would have said, *ille dabit*, not *ille baptizabit*, and he will give you the holy ghost, which may be given otherwise then by Baptisme.'[145] Baptism is a mutual or reciprocal covenant which regenerates and consecrates us to God.[146] But because sacraments contain or convey grace, they must be reverenced, and so Buckeridge criticized the

Figure 3.3   John Buckeridge, 1562–1631

(Scottish) practice of sitting for reception, and defended kneeling. In his 1618 sermon he urged: 'The sound Physicion kneeled to cure us, and therefore the sicke patients must kneele also when they receive *Calicem Salutaris,* the Cup of blessing, and the Cup of Salvation, the greatest benefit of soule and body, with the greatest humiliation of soule and body: for that is received with Invocation, which should have outward worship with it.'[147] He rejected the idea of impanation or incorporation of the deity in the elements of the Lord's Supper, and he also rejected Jackson's chief category of virtue.[148] The presence is spiritual. However, Buckeridge was keen to defend the concept of sacrifice as applied to the eucharist. Thus the church offers herself as the mystical body, but the eucharist can be called '*sacrificium repraesentatinum,* or *commemoratiuum,* a representative, or commemorative Sacrifice', represented to God, and communicated to us. The Church of England liturgy offers ourselves and souls, which, claimed Buckeridge, exceeds the Roman *canon missae.*[149]

Richard Montagu   According to Victoria Raymer, Richard Montagu (1577–1641) 'was the primary author of the two works in which the theological positions towards which Durham House inclined were first and most exhaustively set forth for the general reading public'.[150] A graduate of King's College, Cambridge, he gained his Doctor of Divinity in 1620. From 1608 to 1616 he was chaplain to James Montague, Bishop of Bath and Wells. In December 1616 he was installed as Dean of Hereford, but exchanged this post for a canonry at Windsor, where John Buckeridge was a canon. Charles I appointed him Bishop of Chichester in 1628, and in 1638 he was translated to Norwich. In Norwich he tried to soften the 'Laudian' discipline of his predecessor, Matthew Wren, but was apparently overruled by Laud on the matter of kneeling at communion rails for reception of the sacrament.[151]

Montagu regarded sacraments as channels through which divine grace flowed to the recipients. They were instituted to confer grace and accomplish what they signify. In *A Gagg*, he defended the baptism of infants on grounds that the faith of the Church, and those who present infants is 'by God reputed their own', and quoted from Richard Hooker to support the view that grace is given in baptism.[152] Life begins with baptism, the Laver of Regeneration, and is confirmed and sustained by the Supper. He repudiated the accusation that for protestants, sacraments are bare figures: 'For it is confessed on either side, that Sacraments, which have their *Beeing* from *institution,* are *signes of Gods love and promise, seales of his covenant and grace, and instruments and conveiances of his mercy.* What they intimate, signifie, and represent, they conveigh unto the soule.'[153]

Though rejecting transubstantiation, and the 'sacramentarian' view which he attributed to Zwingli and Oecolampadius, Montagu stressed that the body and blood of Christ '*is really* participated & communicated; and by means of that *reall participation, life from him and in him conveied into our soules*'.[154] There was certainly a change in the elements – they have a 'Sacramentall Being', and he could cite the epiklesis from the anaphora of St. Basil in support.[155] However, a change in the elements does not logically mean that they are transubstantiated.[156] Citing Thomas Morton, he urged a change in use, to be instruments by faith of grace.[157] The 'how' of the change, so Montagu wrote, cannot be known, for we should not pry into the secret counsels of the Most High.[158] He cited Calvin to assert that the faithful do indeed receive the substance of the body and blood of Christ.[159]

He also defended the use of the term 'Altar' for the Holy Table, and with it the idea that the eucharist is in some sense a sacrifice. It is not a 'proper sacrifice', but only a 'representative, rememorative, and *spiritual* Sacrifice'.[160] Elsewhere he argued that the priest 'offers the merits of Christ to God the father and the Passion; he offers the wounds also and the death, the mediator of God and men by faith on the altar of a heart grateful and contrite and devoted, who, partaking truly, consecrates and devotes to God through Jesus Christ on such an altar everything that pertains to him, soul, body, all.'[161] Montagu may have cited Morton, Hooker and Calvin, but his views are defended and established by reference to Ignatius, Justin Martyr, Cyprian and Ambrose.

The views of Jackson, White, Buckeridge and Montagu are sufficient to illustrate some diversity amongst the 'Patristic Reformed Churchmen'. Nevertheless, this piety emphasised the sacraments and liturgical celebrations as actions where grace was conveyed. This in itself was in harmony with the thinking of Ward, Burges and Bedford. For the Durham House group, there was also interest in the eucharist as in some sense a Godward sacrifice. In addition, these divines thought that such sacramental teaching needed liturgical and ceremonial expression. In the chapel at Durham House, and also at Durham Cathedral itself, some of the ceremonial advocated and developed by Andrewes was further extended. The episcopal members of the Durham House group advocated the table being called an altar, and being in an altar position, with decent furnishing such as tapers and a carpet of silk, and even a cross. Use was made of copes, and ceremonies of bowing and kneeling were emphasised. There is no evidence that Ward or Burges felt such needs, though Paul Micklethwaite, one of Ward's pupils, did. On the whole, however, the ceremonial of the Durham House group was a cause for alarm for conformist Calvinists.[162] Yet although this ceremonial developed and then gave rise to controversy in England, it was in Scotland that such thinking gave rise to new and cataclysmic liturgical revision enshrined in the 1637 proposed *Book of Common Prayer* for Scotland.

Scottish Sacramental Polarisation: The Aftershocks of Perth

James I had kept a rather cynical balance between the various shades of churchmanship in England, but towards the end of his reign, those of the Durham House piety and theology found themselves in the ascendancy, with a shift in the court sermons in the meaning of puritanism. Lori Anne Ferrell detects that, what in 1603 was a moderate conformist position, had, by the end of the reign, become a cypher for anyone who dissented from James's ecclesiastical policies. In England, since those of 'Laudian piety' tended to support *de jure divino* monarchy as well as episcopacy, many gained prominant patronage in the later Jacobean Church and the Caroline Church, with William Laud, Bishop of St. David's, becoming successively Bishop of Bath and Wells in 1626, London in 1628, and Archbishop of Canterbury in 1633.

In Scotland, James's policies were thwarted by continued opposition from Presbyterian divines who objected to having episcopacy foisted on the Church, and who regarded all ceremonial and liturgical enrichment as nothing short of popery. James's plans for a revised liturgy had been shelved, and although the Five Articles had been passed by Parliament, opposition continued, and observance was sporadic. MacKay's study of the minutes of Kirk sessions suggests that the north and east favoured conformity, but the area roughly south of the valleys of the Forth and the Kelvin encouraged resistance.[163] The Perth Article on baptism was seen as encouraging the gross error that children are damned if they die without baptism – that the sacrament does actually have some saving significance – and communion continued in many places to be celebrated with the people seated at long tables covered with linen cloths.[164] MacKay observes that James may have left the Kingdom of Scotland socially, politically and economically more united, peaceful and prosperous than ever before, but he also left a church divided as she had never been before in doctrine, in her conception of discipline, and in her standards of worship; long before 1638 the Kirk in one part of the country showed a very different face from that in another.[165] Charles I was simply unable or unwilling to walk the tightrope which his father had managed to do.

Sacramental thought reflects a similar development to that in England. This may be illustrated on one side by the teaching of Dr John Forbes of Corse and William Forbes, Bishop of Edinburgh, and the 1637 *Book of Common Prayer*; and on the other by George Gillespie, Zacharie Boyd, William Guild and Robert Baillie.

Scottish Patristic Reformed Sacramentalism: John Forbes and William Forbes

John Forbes of Corse   John Forbes of Corse (1593–1648) was the son of Patrick Forbes, who had become Bishop of Aberdeen in 1618 (Figure 3.4). John studied at Aberdeen, Heidelberg, and then with the banished Andrew Melville at Sedan, and was ordained by the Scots Presbytery in Holland in 1619, and in 1620 was appointed to the chair of divinity at Aberdeen. He was one of the famous Aberdeen Doctors who refused to subscribe to the National Covenant, and for that reason he was deprived of his chair in 1641, though the Covenanters had to declare his theology sincere and orthodox.[166] His teaching on sacraments was published in his *Instructiones Historico-Theologicae*, 1645. This is a highly academic work, showing extensive theological knowledge of the fathers, medieval schoolmen, and Reformation thought. It is a long dialogue with many authors, and it is not easy to distinguish Forbe's view from the discussion. He taught that sacraments are ordinances instituted by Christ, and are active efficacious signs. Thus, speaking of the necessity of baptism, he wrote: 'It must be confessed that whether baptism is celebrated with immersion or aspersion, this divine sacrament has a great necessity for the attainment of salvation and eternal life which no one can attain outside the Kingdom of Heaven. It is a means of salvation and an instrument enjoined by Christ.'[167]

Yet at the same time it is not baptism which saves us, but the covenant will of God sealed to us in baptism. Participation in sacraments was a spiritual participation by faith: 'But to this spiritual mode we are stirred and lifted up by the Word and Sacraments, as means and instruments from God instituted to this end, adjusted to our infirmity.'[168]

On the eucharist John Forbes explained that the faithful receive in their hands a sign and memorial of the proper body of Christ:

Figure 3.4   John Forbes of Corse, 1593–1648

That which is the sign, sacrament, symbol, type, figure, image, memorial of the proper body of Christ, although in a certain manner, is called and is that body itself, – that is, significantly, sacramentally, symbolically, typically, figuratively, representatively, and these indeed not vainly; but efficaciously, by divine institution. But that which, in the celebration of the Eucharist, is after the consecration, given to the faithful and by them received with the hand of the body, and taken with the the mouth of the body, is the sign, sacrament, etc., of the proper body of Christ.[169]

In a lengthy passage explaining that sanctification of the elements does not mean a change in their substance, Forbes appealed to the liturgical use of the liturgy of St. Mark, and the place and sense of the epiklesis in that eucharistic prayer. After citing the text of the epiklesis, Forbes explained:

Observe here, 1. That after these words of the Lord, 'This is My body', 'This is My blood', it is still called bread, and that you may know that that bread is understood which is made of flour you perceive the plural number, τοὺς ἄρτους τούτους, these loaves (breads). 2. The Priest still prays that these loaves (this bread) *may be* sanctified, even after the words of the Lord's institution. 3. It indicates that the bread becomes the body of the Lord by the sanctification of the Holy Spirit, and the cup is made His blood, and so becomes to us unto faith, unto soberness, unto healing, etc. The Transubstantiarians reject all these. But from 3. I argue thus: – The bread becomes the body of Christ, not in substance nor properly, as the Transubstantiarians allow, rejecting on that account the expressions which we have shown in Chaper 8: therefore it is the body of Christ improperly and symbolically: it becomes the Sacrament, sign, symbol, image, figure, of the body of Christ. The change, therefore, in the bread is made only in accidentals, remaining the same bread in substance.[170]

Forbes rejected both transusbtantiation and the Lutheran argument from ubiquity. He wrote concerning presence and memorial:

> Observe also this distinction: – Christ who is now intact and glorified, is in the Sacrament symbolically and representitatively: yet he is represented to us in the Sacrament not *as* intact and glorified, but as once broken in body, and with His blood shed, dying for us in His passion. 'This', he says, 'is My body which is broken for you'; 'This is My blood which is shed for you'. And this celebration He enjoined on us in remembrance of Him, that is, according to the interpretation of the Apostle Paul, with mention, or commemoration of His death. Therefore also the symbols of the body and blood are separated, as once in the Passion of Christ the blood was separated from the body by being shed. Hence the Eucharist itself is called a sacrifice, although it is without blood, because it is μνήμη ἀντὶ θυσίας [a memorial in place of a sacrifice], it is ἀνάμνησις θυσίας [a calling to mind of a sacrifice], it is the Sacrament of Remembrance; it is the sacrifice of Christ, not in Himself, but in sacrament, as Eusebius, Chrysostom, and Augustine say, and as Rupert of Duyts calls it the daily obsequies of the Saviour.[171]

Forbes argued that the power of the eucharist lies in it being the memorial of Christ's death, and all the benefits come not from, but through the memorial, from the one sacrifice on the cross. Thus for Forbes, as with so many of his contemporary divines, the fraction was important:

> When the breaking and pouring out of the species alone cannot be propitiatory for us, or merit the remission of sins and eternal salvation, yet that breaking and pouring out of which the Lord speaks in the institution of the Supper may be propitiatory for us, and meritorious of remission of sins and eternal salvation; it is certain that that very breaking and pouring out is understood which was made in that unique oblation in which Christ gave Himself for us to be an offering and sacrifice to God for an odour of sweet smell (Eph.v.2), giving His life for the sheep (John x.15). As therefore the breaking which takes place in the celebration of the Eucharist is the body of Christ dying on the Cross; in the same manner also that which in the Eucharist is called the body of Christ, is that very true body of Christ which was taken of the Virgin Mary, and broken for us on the Cross. Christ Himself, indeed, is immolated in that celebration, yet not in Himself, but in Sacrament.[172]

According to Forbes, in the eucharist we offer the commemoration of that unique immolation of Christ made once, 'suppliantly praying God that, looking on it, He will be propitious to us sinners: *not on account of this our commemoration,* but on account of that bloody, truly and properly sacrificial and propitiatory oblation; which we commemorate and offer to God by an offering not sacrificial but commemorative; not propitiatory and meritorious, but supplicatory and Eucharistic.'[173]

In his *Irenicum* (1629), Forbes had defended the Five Articles of Perth, or, at least, had shown how private baptism and communion, and kneeling for reception, may be allowed. Thus he reasoned:

For, even though the necessity of order and dignity demands that the administration of the Sacraments shall be public and at a public gathering, where such can conveniently be had, yet pastors are not allowed to refuse the Sacraments to the faithful or to their children when so circumstanced that, owing to sickness or to imprisonment, they cannot come to a public place of meeting.[174]

Kneeling before something did not mean that the something was being worshipped, and citing 2 Samuel 7:18, he argued that David in sitting was showing adoration. In communion our King gives himself spiritually to us. Therefore, though no sort of adoration is directed towards the outward minister or sign, we offer it rightly to the one who is both Giver and the Spiritual Gift, namely God and Jesus Christ.[175]

If in the *Instructiones Historico-Theologicae* we have Forbes the professor, and in the *Irenicum*, Forbes the ecumenist and moderate churchman, in his spiritual diary we have Forbes the 'godly' believer. This diary contains spiritual meditations and reflections from 1624 to 1647, and records summaries of sermons he preached, or heard preached, short prayers and self-examination. It also gives an insight into the place which the sacrament of the Supper played in his spiritual life.[176]

Forbes refers in the margin of his diary to 'comfortable communion', which signals his belief in the need for worthy preparation, and his assertion in the *Instructiones* that the wicked do not receive the body and blood of Christ even though they may receive the elements.[177] We find the following entry after the rejection of the 1637 liturgy:

> Upon the 23 day of December 1638, being the Lord's day, I being desyred went & preached in new Aberdene upon Jo.6.26.27 Jesus answered him & said, verily, verily I say unto you, ye seek me not because you saw the miracles, but because ye did eat of the bread & were filled. [labour (or work) *ergazesthe*] not for the meat which perishes, but for that meat which endureth unto everlasting life, which the son of man shall give unto you, for him hath the father sealed. This text I choosed because of the celebration of the h.communion which we did celebrate that day with great comfort, God be praised for this and all his mercies.[178]

In November 1639 Forbes referred to a preparatory sermon on the Saturday, followed by a sermon and the sacrament on the Sunday in New Aberdeen, by Dr William Guild (whose views will be considered later):

> The sermon being ended in the new kirk he did celebrate the h.communion exhorting us all to come to the Lords table worthilie and holilie, when also I did participate of the h:sacrament which was great comfort to my soul, in assurance that I received not only the visible sacrament bodilie, but also the true flesh and blood of Ch: spiritually, according as I prayed to God with many tears to grant me to eat by faith the bodie, & to drink the blood of my Saviour Jesus Ch: so that Ch; might henceforth dwell in me & I in him. and that in him I might find strengths & comforts against all temptations.[179]

On 8 December 1639 he recorded:

> After sermon I went with a vehement desire to the Lords table, & after great abundance of tears I received the h.communion with new increase of unspeakable comfort, & being returned from the table to my ordinarie seat, I did humblie give thanks unto God for his

wonderfull mercies towards me, acknowledging my self to be unworthie of the least of all his mercies, & I besought the Lord to touch my lips with a lyve coal from his altar, & I would receive great comfort, that the Lord had both touched my heart with his h.sp. & made me participant of the sacrifice of the altar, to witt the body and blood of Jes.Ch. who now dwelleth in my heart by faith, & giving now that promised comfort ... to abyde with me for ever. Then I praised the Lord & said, holy, holy, holy, the Lord of hosts, the whole earth is full of glory. I prayed also humblie for my weak sick wife, & for my son, & for all the children of God.[180]

Here we see some insight into Forbes's idea of the eucharist as sacrifice, and an occasion also for intercession of a personal nature.

In a celebration of 26 April 1640, when Dr James Sibbald was the preacher and celebrant, Forbes recorded that when he was sitting at the Lord's Table (any custom of kneeling had been abolished by the 1638 Covenant) and receiving the sacrament, 'the Lord brought into my minde the comfortable saying which the preceding day I had explained, the meek shall eat & be satisfied.'[181] He continued: 'I found a comfortable assurance that I am one of those meek ones & that my heart shall live for ever through the mercies of God in Ch: Jes: forgiving my unmeekness & all my sins, & healing me & vivifying me with the bread of life, and I praised the Lord with exceeding inward spirituall joy, Blessed be the Lord my Sav: for ever and ever amen halleluiah.'[182] Likewise at the 7 June 1640 celebration by Dr Scroggie, Forbes 'did communicate with verie great comfort. The Lord be magnified for ever & ever, for great is his everlasting mercy towards us, & the truth of the Lord endureth for ever amen halleluia.'[183]

After being deprived for his refusal to take the Covenant, Forbes lived for a while abroad, and there he recorded 'comfortable communion' in the French and Dutch churches. With Forbes, therefore, we have a divine of great erudition and learning, who could discourse on the sacraments at a high academic level, and who also recorded his own deep personal devotion to the sacrament.

William Forbes Forbes's namesake, William (1585–1634) defended the Five Articles of Perth.[184] (See Figure 3.5.) Having become Principal of Marishal College, Aberdeen in 1620, he had travelled widely in Europe and was a noted theologian, having studied briefly at Helmstedt University and Heidelberg. His defence of episcopacy made him a target for those committed to the presbyterian polity. Though widely respected in Aberdeen for his breadth of theological learning, his careful assessment of theological questions, and his attempts to find an eirenic position, those of strict presbyterian and predestinarian convictions accused him of Arminianism. In 1621 he was appointed one of the ministers of Edinburgh and, in enforcing kneeling for communion, made a number of enemies. He returned to St. Nicholas, Aberdeen in 1626. In 1633 he was appointed the first Bishop of Edinburgh, but died before the debacle over the 1637 *Book of Common Prayer*. In his posthumous *Considerationes Modestae et Pacificae* Forbes treated the eucharist. This work shows the breadth of his learning, but mainly quotes the views of others as he deals with particular questions, and it is difficult to distinguish between quotations and Forbe's own views. He cited patristic authorities, moderate Roman Catholic writers, as well as Reformed. He was also fond (perhaps too fond for the good of his own reputation) of Lancelot Andrewes, who is cited more than any

Figure 3.5   William Forbes, 1585–1634

other English divine. He rejected the teaching of Zwingli as inadequate, regarding it as locating Christ's presence 'by the contemplation of faith' only, and in which 'sacramental union consists wholly in signification.'[185] Here perhaps he revealed a distaste for the overuse of 'obsignation' or seal which so many divines utilised. He quoted with approval Calvin's assertion that the bread of the eucharist is consecrated to represent and exhibit to us the body of the Lord.[186] He insisted that it is beyond our comprehension how we receive the body and blood of Christ, but rejects a corporeal reception in favour of a means known to God alone:

> The opinion of those Protestants and others seems most safe and most right, who think, nay, who most firmly believe, that the Body and Blood of Christ is truly, really, and substantially present and taken in the Eucharist, but in a way, which is incomprehensible to the human understanding, and much more, beyond the power of man to express; which is known to God alone, and not revealed to us in Scripture; a way, not indeed corporeal, or by oral reception, but not by the mere understanding and simple faith either, but by another way, known (as has been said) to God alone, and to be left to His omnipotence.[187]

Forbes wrote:

> It is most certain, that Christ and His heavenly benefits are exhibited to us by God, and by us received, through the word, baptism, and the other sacraments (concerning which

with God's help we shall speak on another occasion) and most especially through faith on our part, provided it be living. But it is no less certain that by the mystical eating of the Lord's Body and drinking His Blood in the Eucharist, we are much more effectually and fully, more sublimely and augustly, more closely and nearly united and incorporated with the Body and Blood of Christ than through those other means.[188]

Forbes could quote Isaac Casaubon and John Buckeridge, Richard Montagu and Richard Hooker to help refute transubstantiation. Christ is exhibited to us spiritually, not carnally.[189] But this spiritual presence is brought about objectively through the promise of Christ, not subjectively imposed on the elements by our faith.[190] He argued that there was a 'mystic conjunction' brought about by imploring the Holy Spirit in prayer to come upon the elements and consecrate them.[191] He could defend the Perth Article on kneeling thus: 'Enormous is the error of the more rigid Protestants who deny that Christ is to be adored in the Eucharist, save with an internal and mental adoration, but not with any outward rite of worship, as by kneeling or some other similar position of the body.'[192] And as a 'Patristic Reformed' theologian, William Forbes could defend a notion of eucharistic sacrifice:

> The holy Fathers, moreover, say very often that in the Eucharist Christ's Body itself is offered and sacrificed, as appears from almost numberless places, but so, that not all the properties of a sacrifice are properly and really preserved; but by way of commemoration and representation of that which was performed once for all in that one only Sacrifice of the Cross, whereby Christ our high Priest consummated all other sacrifices, and by pious prayer; by which the ministers of the Church most humbly beseech God the Father on account of the perpetual Victim of that one only Sacrifice, Which is seated in heaven on the right hand of the Father, and in an ineffable manner present on the holy table, that He would grant that the virtue and grace of this perpetual Victim may be efficacious and salutary to His Church for all the necessities of body and soul.[193]

However, beyond kneeling for reception, there is no evidence that Forbes openly advocated ceremonies deemed 'popish' by the radicals; when preaching before Charles in the Chapel Royal at Holyrood in 1633, Forbes wore 'his black gown without surplice or rochet'.[194]

The Service Book of 1637

But what of liturgical developments? The story of the making of the 1637 book has been carefully documented by Gordon Donaldson. The main participants were John Maxwell (1591–1647), Bishop of Ross and James Wedderburn (1585–1639), Bishop of Dunblane. The visit of Charles to Scotland in 1633 seems to have been the occasion for reviving the idea of liturgical revision, and John Maxwell seems to have used the English book for services. Charles charged the bishops formally to draw up a new book in 1634, and they were also told to keep in close touch with William Laud. Maxwell made certain proposals in 1634, but different proposals of 1636 were made by Wedderburn. Further changes were made during the printing. Though erroneously referred to as 'Laud's liturgy', it did reflect the Laudian piety, particularly in rubrics about the furnishing of the church and altar. In baptism a petition in the 'Flood Prayer', undermining Luther's original intention in that prayer, asked: 'Sanctify this fountain of baptism, thou which art the Sanctifier of all things'; and in the prayer before the baptism the words were added of the water: 'which we here bless and dedicate in thy Name to this spiritual washing'. In the communion service, the compilers had glanced back to the 1549 *Book of Common Prayer*, perhaps with some help from the writings and practice of John Overall and Lancelot Andrewes. As regards furnishing, a rubric directed: 'The holy Table, having at the Communion time a carpet and a fair white linen cloth upon it, with other decent furniture meet for the high mysteries there to be celebrated, shall stand at the uppermost part of the Chancel or Church, where the Presbyter, standing at the north side or end thereof, shall say the Lord's Prayer with this Collect following for due preparation.'

A rubric directed the preparation of bread and wine with these words: 'And the Presbyter shall then offer up and place the bread and wine prepared for the sacrament upon the Lord's Table, that it may be ready for that service.' The *sursum corda* and preface were linked with the prayer with the words of institution, now called 'The Prayer of Consecration', into which was restored a petition for the word and Holy Spirit modified from the 1549 book. The consecration prayer was followed immediately by the Prayer of Oblation, again suggested from 1549, and the usage of John Overall.[195] Then came the 'Collect of humble access' as a pre-communion preparation. The words of administration were those of 1549, being shorn of the 1552 words, and thus stressing that the sacramental elements were in some way the body and blood of Christ.

William Grisbrooke, though acknowledging that this liturgy was not the work of Laud, nevertheless suggests that it reflected very much the Archbishop's doctrinal views.[196] These may be gleaned from his Conference with the Jesuit, John Fisher, and his defence at his trial before the House of Commons. Laud held that baptism was necessary to the salvation of infants, since it was the ordinary means of entry into the Church, though without binding God to the use and means of that sacrament.[197] Quoting Calvin and Francis White, Laud insisted that 'all sides agree in the faith of the Church of England, That in the most Blessed Sacrament, the worthy receiver is, by his faith, made spiritually partaker of the "true and real Body and Blood of Christ, truly and really", and of all the benefits of His passion.'[198] On the eucharistic sacrifice Laud argued:

> For at and in the Eucharist, we offer up to God three sacrifices: One by the priest only; that is the commemorative sacrifice of Christ's death, represented in bread broken and wine poured out. Another by the priest and the people jointly; and that is, the sacrifice of praise and thanksgiving for all the benefits and graces we receive by the precious death of Christ. The third, by every particular man for himself only; and that is, the sacrifice of every man's body and soul, to serve Him in both all the rest of his life, for this blessing thus bestowed on him. Now, thus far these dissenting Churches agree, that in the Eucharist there is a sacrifice of duty, and a sacrifice of praise, and a sacrifice of commemoration of Christ. Therefore, according to the former rule, (and here in truth too,) it is safest for a man to believe the commemorative, the praising, and the performing sacrifice, and to offer them duly to God, and leave the Church of Rome in this particular to her superstitions, that I may say no more.[199]

When accused of inverting the order of prayers in the English book, and teaching the popish doctrine of sacrifice, Laud replied:

... though I shall not find fault with the order of the prayers, as they stand in the Communion-book of England, (for, God be thanked, 'tis well;) yet, if a comparison must be made, I do think the order of the prayers, as now they stand in the Scottish Liturgy, to be the better, and more agreeable to use in the primitive Church ... I think no man doubts, but that there is, and ought to be offered up to God at the consecration and reception of this sacrament, *sacrificium laudis,* the sacrifice of praise: and that this ought to be expressed in the Liturgy, for the instruction of the people. And these words, 'We entirely desire Thy fatherly goodness, mercifully to accept this our sacrifice of praise, and thanksgiving, &c'. are both in the Book of England, and in that which was prepared for Scotland ... In the meantime there is as little said in the Liturgy for Scotland, which may import an oblation of an unbloody sacrifice, as in the Book of England. As for 'the oblation of the elements', that's fit and proper; and I am sorry, for my part, that it is not in the Book of England.[200]

Forgetting that one of the Scottish practices was to add to the 'Knoxian' liturgy a distinct petition for consecration, the Scottish Commissioners charged that the petition for consecration in the 1637 rite taught the popish doctrine of a corporal presence. Laud commented:

'Tis true, this passage is not in the Prayer of Consecration in the Service-book of England; but I wish with all my heart it were. For though the consecration of the elements may be without it, yet it is much more solemn and full by that invocation ... 'these words', they say, 'intend the corporal presence of Christ in the Sacrament, because the words in the Mass are, *ut fiant nobis,* 'that they may be unto us' the Body and Blood of Christ'. Now for the good of Christendom, I would with all my heart, that these words, *ut fiant nobis,* that these elements might be 'to us', worthy receivers, the blessed Body and Blood of our Saviour, – were the worst error in the Mass ... For if it be only, *ut fiant nobis,* that they may be to us, the Body and Blood of Christ; it implies clearly, that they 'are to us', but are not transubstantiated in themselves, into the Body and Blood of Christ, nor that there is any corporal presence, in, or under the elements. And then nothing can more cross the doctrine of the present Church of Rome, than their own service. For as the elements after the benediction, or consecration, are, and may be called, the Body and Blood of Christ, without any addition, in that real and true sense in which they are so called in Scripture; so, when they are said to become the Body and Blood of Christ, *nobis,* to us that communicate as we ought; there is by this addition, *fiant nobis,* an allay in the proper signification of the body and blood: and the true sense, so well signified and expressed, that the words cannot well be understood otherwise, than to imply not the corporal substance, but the real, and yet the spiritual use of them.[201]

A number of things become clear here. First, Laud, like all the English and Scottish divines, sets the real and spiritual presence over against the Roman corporal presence; the latter is seen not only as erroneous, but also as an inferior understanding, and less real than real presence. Second, Laud appeals to the 'high' elements in Calvin, and thus shows that his Scottish critics didn't know their own tradition. As will be seen, this was in one sense true, as some Scottish divines wanted a more 'pure' Kirk, and deliberately taught that their tradition was other than what it actually had been. However, we also see in Laud that element dear to the Patristic Reformed churchmen, namely the need to understand the eucharist as sacrifice in some sense or other. Last, while Laud was not the author of the 1637 liturgy, it is clear that he found things in it to be 'superior' to the English book which he had preferred them to accept. It was certainly, therefore, a 'Laudian' liturgy, and was a liturgical expression of the Patristic Reformed churchmanship.

Although the bishops attempted to persuade ministers to use the new liturgy, there was widespread rejection of it. In an 'Advertisement' of 6 July 1637 about the book, some prominent ministers listed their objections to the book. Amongst the reasons we find:

> 1. We have had ane forme of publik worship brought in to this land be the mercifull hand of our god, when the darknes of poperie was prevailing, receaved be the whol kingdome, ratified be estaits of parliament, and still since put in practise, quhilk was never yit abolished be any act of generall assemblie (the representative kirk within this Realme) be king and estaits in parliament.
>
> 2. To have the ministers bound to ane service book is to bring in ane reading, and to diminish ane preaching ministrie, and ty them to set words, and prescript formes of worship in morning and evening prayers, ministratione of sacraments, visitatione of sick, all quhilk ane ignorant man not able to preach may dischairge.[202]

In a pamphlet of 1638 it was alleged that 'In the pretended Communion it hath all the substance and essentiall parts of the Masse, and so brings in the most abominable Idolatry.'[203] It complained that the book has 'The oblation of the Bread and Wine before the consecration: It hath the Popish consecration, that the Lord would sanctifie by his Word and by his holy Spirit, these gifts and creatures of Bread and Wine, that they may be unto us the body and blood of his Son', and it advocated kneeling before the consecrated bread and wine. The pamphlet alleged that the 1637 baptismal rite taught that sacraments give grace 'by their work wrought', and a set liturgy quenches the Holy Spirit, 'because he gets no employment'.[204]

Though John Forbes of Corse had no involvement in the 1637 *Book of Common Prayer*, and after his deprivation, seems to have continued to worship with the Presbyterian Kirk, his eirenical approach was not incompatible with the theology of that book, and although William Forbes died before its appearance, his theology was not distant from that of his fellow bishops who were involved with its production. But their views were not the only ones in the Kirk, and the 1637 liturgy was not the only liturgical development in Scotland.

Conventicles and Communion Seasons

The studies of David Stevenson and David Mullan have drawn attention to a development in the Scottish Church which had its origins as a reaction to the Articles of Perth, but which was fuelled by the more aggressive nature of the Caroline episcopate, and developed into a radical group who became fervent Covenanters in 1638, and Protesters in 1651. Their heirs would become the suspended and deprived ministers of the 1660s.[205]

Stevenson notes that some ministers were adamant that the Five Articles of Perth compromised a true church, and refused to assent. Amongst those radicals opposed to royal religious policy were three ministers of the south-west, Robert Blair, John McLellan and John Livingstone. These ministers looked to the leadership of David Dickson, minister of Irvine, and Samuel Rutherford, minister of Anwoth.[206] Robert Blair and John Livingstone, through their opposition to bishops and their dislike of ceremonies, failed to obtain parishes in Scotland, and instead turned to Ulster. There the Irish bishops were pleased to have any protestant ministers, and made concessions to those of tender conscience. Blair and Livingstone made Ulster a base for making forays into Scotland until 1631 when they were suspended, and then in 1634 they were deposed from the ministry.

One important element for these Ulster ministers was worship of a more private nature in smaller groups, and the development of communion seasons, when crowds would come from distant parishes to hear a sermon on the Saturday, and a second sermon on the Sunday before receiving communion. It has been argued that these were an Ulster development, though Stevenson has suggested that in fact they had their origins in Scotland amongst those opposed to episcopacy and the Five Articles, and met clandestinely.[207] However, he notes the direct links with this group and the problems faced by the General Assembly in 1638 and 1639. Ministers such as Alexander Henderson, Henry Guthry and Robert Baillie wished to curb private meetings for worship, whereas the radicals led by Dickson, Rutherford and George Gillespie were happy that these should continue. Furthermore, this group were not only totally opposed to the 1637 liturgy, but sat lightly to the 'Knoxian' forms of worship. They promoted extemporary prayer, and regarded certain common liturgical ceremonies – the recitation of the creed at baptism, the Lord's Prayer, the doxology after the psalm, and the minister kneeling for prayer in the pulpit before preaching – all as dangerous innovations. Indeed, Rutherford asserted: 'Anent read prayers … I could never see precept, promise or practice for them, in God's word. Our church never allowed them, but men took them up at their own choice … it were good if they were out of the service of God.'[208]

The private worship, with prayer from the heart, was now argued as being normative for public worship. Stevenson cites the example of Andrew Cant who had been moved to Aberdeen in 1642. Stevenson notes that Cant 'gave up saying the Lord's Prayer in favour of extemporary prayer, and was copied in this by the other Aberdeen ministers. He also introduced the practice of giving lectures expounding scripture on weekdays in the place of read evening prayers in the kirk; such lectures were becoming increasingly popular among the radicals.'[209]

Robert Bruce wrote of God's 'vocal speeches within me, in the day light, that I heard so sensibly, with great effusion of tears, so far not only by approbation, but to my commendation, that I admire how he should bestow such gracious speeches upon so wretched a creature as I was.'[210] This piety, with an introspective concern for personal assurance, and a covenant theology, were at the heart of the spirituality of the conventicles and the radical party, which could also boast of the 1625 'Stewarton sickness' and the Kirk of Shotts revival in 1630.[211] It found expression in the outdoor mass celebrations of the communion. Leigh Eric Schmidt traced the communion seasons with revivalist preaching back to Robert Bruce, and argues that they were already established in such places as Kirkcudbright, Ayr, Irvine, Lanark and Kilsyth from the 1590s.[212] By the 1630s, communion occasions had clearly been established as important events for the 'godly' in Ulster and the south west of Scotland. Schmidt writes:

What separated the festal communions from earlier sacraments were such characteristics as outdoor preaching, great concourses of people from an extensive region, long vigils of prayer, powerful experiences of conversion and confirmation, a number of popular ministers cooperating for extended services over three days or more, a seasonal focus on summer, and unusually large numbers of communicants at successive tables.[213]

In 1634 Charles I had backed an act to curb these communions. It attacked those

> ... dissobedient people, who ordinarlie, when the communion is ministrat in thair parishes and at all other tymes when thair occasions and their humor serves thame, not onelie leaves thair owne parish kirkes bot runnes to seeke the communion at the hands of suche ministers as they know to be disconforme to all good order, which is the meanes of thair dissobedience to his Majesteis lawes.[214]

Robert Fleming wrote of the 1630 Shotts communion:

> I must ... mention that solemn communion at the Kirk of Shotts, at which time there was so convincing an appearance of God, and downpouring of the Spirit ... which did follow the ordinances, especially on Monday, 21st of June, when there was a strange unusual motion of the hearers, who in a great multitude were there convened of divers ranks. It was known, as I can speak on sure ground, that near five hundred had at that time as discernable change wrought on them, of whom most proved lively Christians afterwards.[215]

Gilbert Burnet, the Scottish minister who became an English bishop in 1689, described such communions as having a new and unusual solemnity:

> On the Wednesday before they held a fast day with prayers and sermons for about eight or ten hours together; on the Saturday they had two or three preparation sermons; and, on the Lord's day, they had so very many that the action continued about twelve hours in some places; and all ended with three or four sermons on Monday for thanksgiving. A great many ministers were brought together from several parts; and high pretenders would have gone forty or fifty miles to a noted communion. The crowds were far beyond the capacity of their churches, or the reach of their voices; so at the same time they had sermons in two or three different places; and all was performed with great shew of zeal. They had stories of many signal conversions that were wrought on these occasions.[216]

Though such occasions had some structure, it is doubtful whether much in the way of written liturgical forms were used, and the occasion and setting called for something very different from the 'Laudian' idea of beauty and set liturgical form. Though these occasions were clearly moving, and for some intensely emotional, with a great regard for the eucharist, they could generate a subjective idea of the sacrament, based on faith and feeling, and intense preparation. Here the sacrament confirmed and sealed grace already given, and tended towards a symbolic memorialism.

'Confessional' Presbyterian Divines

Those ministers and divines associated with the radical party were less enthusiastic than John Forbes of Corse and William Forbes about patristic precedents, and much more concerned for what they took to be a strict Reformed biblical and experiential approach. They held in common a rejection of episcopacy, and strong support for the covenant. Amongst these we may place Zacharie Boyd, John Forbes of Alford and George Gillespie.[217] Though Dickson and Rutherford were within this group, their views will be considered in later chapters.

Zacharie Boyd   Zacharie Boyd (1585?-1653) was a cousin of Robert Boyd of Trochrigg. He studied at the universities of Glasgow and St. Andrews, and then at Saumur where he also taught for a while. He returned to Scotland in 1623, and served as minister of Glasgow's Barony parish, and in various posts at the University of Glasgow. His *A cleare forme of Catechising, before the giving of the Sacrament of the Lord's Supper* (1639), gives some indication of his sacramental teaching and discipline. The catechism was divided up with material for each Sunday. The sacraments cover the Sundays thirty-seven to forty-six.

Having treated the covenant, Boyd predictably began by describing sacraments as seals of the covenant.[218] They serve as confirmation of faith. A sacrament can be defined as 'an outward seal appointed by God, for to certifie us of our Salvation in Christ'.[219] Just as the Jews had two sacraments – circumcision and the paschal lamb – so too are there two gospel sacraments. Baptism is the seal of our entrance into the Church.[220] The elements of water and actions such as sprinkling, dipping and washing constitute the visible sign, but the water represents to us the blood of Jesus Christ and his Spirit.[221] The 'speciall graces sealed up unto us' are our justification and sanctification. The water represents our justification, and dipping the body represents our sanctification.[222] Interestingly, Boyd concentrated on the various actions and what they signify. The dipping signifies mortification of sin; staying beneath the waters, the burial; and coming out, the resurrection, though we have no evidence that Boyd did submerge infants. Baptism, so he argued, is a sacrament which belongs to all the faithful, and their children; children should be baptised 'Because they are entered into the Church, and Baptisme is a seal of their entrance into the same.'[223]

The Supper is a seal of our spiritual nourishment in the Church. The visible signs of bread and wine represent the body and blood of Christ. The breaking of the bread represents 'The breaking of Christs body and soule with unspeakable torments' and the pouring of the wine 'The powring out of Christs blood'.[224] The spiritual grace represented is the nourishment of our souls: 'As the bread eaten feeds the body, and as the wine drunke rejoyceth the heart, so the body and blood of Christ apprehended by a lively faith, like meat strengthneth, and like wine rejoiceth the soule.'[225]

The Supper is not open to children, for it requires understanding, and proper preparation, and part of the catechism is a warning about the perils of not examining oneself before communion. Indeed, we also have two sermons preached by Boyd at one of the great communion gatherings – a fasting sermon the day before, and then the actual pre-communion sermon.[226] The catechism explains that this is because the elements received are not just ordinary bread and wine. The bread of the sacrament is the seal of Christ's body, and one must discern the Lord's body.[227] But as well as self-examination, Boyd exhorted his readers to lift up their hearts to Christ in heaven (the Reformed *sursum corda* of Farel and then Calvin). When the bread is broken, the communicant should remember that the body of Christ was broken on the cross 'with unspeakable dolours for my sinnes'.[228] The body is eaten in a spiritual manner: 'While we believe; that his body was broken for us, we are said to eate his body.'[229] The chief end of the sacrament is 'That the Lords death may thankfully be remembered'.[230] We give thanks by declaring his death until he comes, by praising him in words, and by calling to mind 'all the paines and dolours, which Christ my Saviour suffered from his *Cratch* to the *Crosse*, and praise him for the same'.[231] Boyd certainly valued the sacrament, though his teaching, as far as it was expressed in the catechism, hardly moves beyond symbolic memorialism.

George Gillespie   George Gillespie (1613–48) was associated with the radicals. He was a staunch presbyterian who avoided ordination until the abolition of episcopacy in 1638. He attacked the 1637 liturgy in his book *A Dispute Against the English Popish Ceremonies obtruded on the Church of Scotland* (1637). The title identifies those whom he regarded as opponents and these included from England Richard Hooker and Lancelot Andrewes, and in Scotland, John Forbes. Though not expounding baptism, he objected to the English *Prayer Book* words that baptism is necessary to salvation, and children baptised are undoubtedly saved.[232] He appealed to the professors of Leiden for the condemnation of private baptism as inordinate 'because *baptism is a supplement to public ministry, not to private exhortation.*'[233] Though, in the Lord's Supper a consecration takes place, by word and prayer together, Gillespie was adamant that this does not justify kneeling for reception, and the manner of receiving is not indifferent. It is necessary to follow the example of Christ.[234] In an extended passage, he left no doubts as regards his sentiments about the 1637 communion rite:

> In the pretended communion it has all the substance and essential parts of the Mass, and so brings in the most abominable idolatry that ever was in the world, in worshipping of a breaded God, and makes way to the Antichrist of Rome, to bring this land under the bondage again, as may be seen at large by the particulars of that communion; wherein some things that were put out of the Service book of England for smelling so strong of the Mass, are restored, and many other things that were never in it, are brought in out of the Mass book, though they labor to cover the matter. It has the popish consecration, that the Lord would sanctify by his Word, and by his Holy Spirit, those gifts and creatures of bread and wine, that they may be unto us the body and blood of his Son, and then repeat the words and institutions of God for that purpose. It has an oblation of it again, after it is consecrated, the consummation by the priest, kneeling before the consecrated bread and wine. It takes away the eating and drinking by faith, mentioned in the English Liturgy. It has the patin chalice, two pater nosters in English before the Mass, and several other particulars that would take a long time to rehearse and confute.[235]

John Forbes of Alford   Something of the piety of these divines is to be found in a communion preparation sermon of John Forbes of Alford (1568?–1634). This John Forbes, uncle of John Forbes of Corse, had acted as Moderator at the forbidden Aberdeen General Assembly in 1605 for which he was banished for life. He became minister of the English congregation at Middleburgh from 1611, and then at Delft, and was known not to use any set liturgy. In this sermon of 1629, Forbes took as his text John 6:27, though 1 Cor. 11:28 is given underneath the title, and is certainly treated as well. The communicants were warned not to abuse God's ordinances to perverse ends.[236] Because the Corinthians abused the ordinance, the Lord brought diseases upon them; they had not sought Christ with upright hearts.[237] Indeed, said Forbes, 'it never was the purpose, nor mind of God, since the world beganne, that men should feede on any meat, either corporall, or spirituall, without labour, and pains taking for it.'[238]

We are to labour for the things from above, and this means attaining belief, through hearing the word, participating in the Lord's Supper, and through prayer. Those who seek the bread of heaven shall find the virtue or power of his flesh and blood. The saving virtue of the Deity can only be communicated to mankind through the flesh and blood of Jesus Christ. The sacrament is a seal, and, according to Forbes, it seals five things. First, it seals God's eternal ordination and appointment of Christ as the sole mediator. Second, it seals the power which the father gave to Christ. The third is that Christ has borne our sins. Fourth, God has raised Christ from the dead. Last, he has sealed Christ with the stamp of his divinity. Thus self-examination is necessary,

> for the banquet of the Lords supper, is not a banquet of the flesh of a meere man: but it is of the flesh and blood, of the everlasting King, and Lord, of heaven and earth, even of the eternall God himselfe, and therefore no marvell, that all those, who eating it, & not discerning it so, are counted guiltie of the body and blood of the Lord.[239]

Moderate Presbyterian Divines

William Guild   William Guild (1586–1657), one of the Aberdeen Doctors, was not entirely against episcopacy, and was a royalist, and would be dismissed from his post of Principal of King's College, Aberdeen by Cromwell in 1651 on account of his support for Charles II (Figure 3.6). However, he was persuaded to sign the National Covenant in 1638. Something of his sacramental views were given in his *A Compend of the Controversies of Religion* (1627). Chapter XVII treated baptism. Appealing to Genesis 17:7, Guild taught that 'not onelie are the Parentes within the covenant of grace, but their children also, and their seede after them.'[240] Thus if children of the faithful die unbaptised, they are not deprived of a blessed union with God, and that is true also if they die in the womb.[241] This was backed up by appeal to Exodus 20:5, Acts 2:39, Jeremiah 1:5, and Luke 1:41, amongst other passages. Appealing to Bernard, he argued that the faith of the parent was sufficient for the child. In Chapter XVIII, Guild turned to the Lord's Supper. He first established through scriptural passages that Christ's glorified body was in heaven. Thus Christ cannot be present in the manner of 'Popish' teaching; now he is only spiritually present.[242] Guild therefore asserted that after consecration, the bread and wine remain in substance in the sacrament. It was not the host which was crucified for us: 'That a remembrance is not of a thing present; so neither is Christ's Bodie, after the Popish manner.'[243] Christ is only represented in the sacrament, and is not bodily there.[244] Guild asserted: 'Neither doth the mysticall signes, after sanctification, depart from their owne nature, (sayeth *Theodoret*) for they remaine still in their owne substance, and figure, and shape, and may be handled and touched, as they were before.'[245]

Figure 3.6   William Guild, 1586–1657

Worthy receiving is necessary, and the unworthy do not receive the matter of the sacrament. Thus all faithful Christians are bound to prove and examine themselves before coming to the Supper. Turning to consider the Catholic idea of eucharistic sacrifice, Guild wrote:

> *Note then*, That the Lord's Supper was ordained, that all christians should remember his suffering, and sacrifice on the crosse, and should declare his death, till him-selfe come to judgement againe: but not, that anie should sacrifice Him up againe daylie, as tho hee were alreadie come, and were bodilie present amongst the Priests fingers, daylie to offer up.'[246]

However, he acknowledged that Christians offer up the remembrance of the benefits of the one sacrifice of the cross.[247] Indeed, it is a sacrifice in the sense that it is a representative image of the passion, and because through the sacrament we are made partakers of the fruit of the passion.[248] In a sermon entitled *The Christians Passover*, preached at a communion service before the English congregation in Danzig, Guild asserted that 'the word is not onlie preached that therby (as the apostle saith) *Christ crucified may visiblie* (as it wer) *be set befor our eies*, but the holie Sacrament also of his bodie & blood is institute to be celebrat, *to show forth his death till his againecoming*, or (as the words of my text sayes) to declair unto us, that *Christ our passover is sacrificed for us*.'[249]

In the Supper the saviour must be applied particularly, and fed upon spiritually. What is interesting in this sermon is Guild's discussion of sacrifice. Christ is a sacrifice offered up not only for propitiation, but 'also in the *sacrament* exhibit to man for food & *nutrition*, as the one to *free* us from *deathe*, & as the other to feed us to life'.[250] Christ is prophet, king, and 'a *priest* who hath sacrificed him self for us once upon earth, & interceeds for us still in the heavens'.[251] In the Supper we must implore his mercy.[252] Though not actually stated, the implication seems to be that for Guild, in the Supper we plead the sacrifice of Christ.

Robert Baillie   Though episcopally ordained, Robert Baillie (1599–1662) came to regard episcopacy as unscriptural, and seems to have been outraged by the Laudian piety and the 1637 book.[253] Though compared with Rutherford and Gillespie, he was a moderate, he certainly had no moderate views on the 'Laudian' liturgy. In his *Ladensium autokatakrisis, the Canterburians self-conviction* (1640, enlarged in 1641), he identified in the communion rite 'the Popish Offertorie' with the offering of bread and wine.[254] He objected to the 'Laudian ceremonial', and identified a whole host of English divines, along with William Forbes as being 'Canterburians'. His views are expressed negatively as he reacted against 'the Service Book, Canons, & Episcopacie, which they have pressed upon us with violence'.[255] He believed that the 'Canterburians' and the 1637 book taught a Roman Catholic view of sacraments:

> In the doctrine of the Sacraments, from *Bellarmins* third tombe, they tell us first, that the sacraments of the old testament differ from the new, that the one confers grace, and the other foresigns grace to bee conferred ... They tell us that all baptised infants as well reprobat as elect are in baptisme truely regenerat, sanctified, justified, and put in that state wherein if those who are reprobate and thereafter damned should die, they would be infallibly saved.[256]

They teach that 'the manifold ceremonies of Papists in baptisme and all other sacraments are either to be embraced as pious ancient rites, or so to be stood upon as being only ceremoniall toyes.'[257] The offertory rubric taught propitiatory sacrifice, and the prayer of consecration taught a corporal presence:

> The prayer which stands here in the English booke, drawne from the place wherin it stood of old in the Masse to countenance the transubstantiation of the bread and wine into Christs body and blood, but standing in this place before the consecration it is clear of all such suspicion: Our men are so bold as to transplant it from this good ground to the old wicked soyle at the backe of the consecration where it wont to stand before in the old order of *Sarum*. In the next English prayer we put in the words of the Masse, whereby God is besought by his omnipotent spirit so to sanctifie the oblations of bread and wine, that they may become to us Christs body and bloud, from these words all papists use to draw the truth of their transubstantiation, wherefore the English reformers scraped them out of their Booke, but our men put them fairely in, and good reason have they so to do: for long agoe they professed that about the presence of Christs body and blood in the sacrament after consecration, they are fully agreed with the *Lutherans* and papists in all things that is materiall and needfull ...[258]

Baillie regarded the replacing of the prayer of thanksgiving to follow immediately after the consecration as suggestive of the propitiatory sacrifice of the mass.[259]

Contrasting 1637 with the current English book, he noted in the 1604 edition: 'But our men to returne to the old fashion, command the table to be set at the East end of the Chancell, that in the time of the consecration, the priest may stand so farre removed from the people, as the furthest wall of the church can permit.'[260]

In the 1641 supplement, he took to task William Forbes's teaching, quite wrongly denying that Calvin taught that we received the substance of the body and blood of Christ.[261] Since Forbes had penned the Five Articles of Perth, so Baillie argued, then clearly the ceremony is intended to teach transubstantiation.[262]

In his *A Parallel or Briefe Comparison of the Liturgie with the Masse-Booke* (1641), Baillie showed his detailed knowledge of the medieval liturgical commentators, though he used this knowledge to argue that the 1637 book was an attempt to reimpose the Mass. He objected to the changes made to the English book, arguing as in *Ladensium autokatakrisis*, that the text taught a corporal presence and made the sacrament a sacrifice. And the direction requiring a corporal to be placed over the chalice and paten was 'a Rubrick full of blacke venome'.[263]

Summary

What, then, does this narrative yield? None of these divines move to what was perceived as either a Roman Catholic or Lutheran view of sacraments, even though the opponents of the Patristic Reformed churchmen claimed to detect 'popery'. All these divines, from Ames to Buckeridge and William Forbes, represent developments of aspects already found in sixteenth-century Reformed sacramental theology, and they also contributed to its expanding framework. Amongst some of the conformist Calvinists and many of the Patristic Reformed churchmen we find a shift towards viewing sacraments as instruments. Amongst the latter, this included the sacramental rites themselves. This group also gave equal, if not greater, weight to patristic authority over sixteenth-century Reformed theology, and this gave rise to either a sympathy with, or advocacy for, more elaborate ceremonial and ornamentation, and liturgical enrichment. With a figure like John Forbes of Corse, his views seem to have been based on a genuine scholarly eirenicism and even-handedness. With someone like Buckeridge, it seems to have been policy as well as theological conviction. Whether a revival of the liturgy of 1618 by William Cowper would have proved more acceptable to the Scottish Church than that of 1637 remains a fascinating unanswerable question. But that of 1637 was identified too much with England, and the episcopal power of the 'Patristic Reformed churchmen', and became inseparably intwined with the Five Articles of Perth. The presbyterian party in Scotland found themselves siding with the English nonconformist Calvinists, and the situation slid into crisis. The whole episode resulted in the National Covenant in 1638, and the General Assembly of that year declared the Five Articles to be abjured and removed, and abolished episcopacy, together with the offending liturgy.[264] The National Covenant of Scotland would become the basis of the Solemn League and Covenant of 1643, binding both kingdoms to a second Reformation and anticipating not only a comparable polity, but also a common theology and a common Reformed liturgy.

Notes

1   Holifield, 1974, p.76.
2   See Ames, 1622.
3   Ames, 1997, p.196.
4   Ibid., p.210.
5   Ibid., p.211.
6   See Spinks, 1999.
7   Twisse, 1637.
8   Ussher, 1864, 2, p.427.
9   Ibid., p.428.
10   Ibid., p.429.
11   Ibid., pp.431–2.
12   Ussher, 1864, pp.11, 216 and 219.
13   Not only did Thornborough span three monarchs, but he was successful in preferment despite being a divorced and remarried bishop.
14   Thornborough, 1630, p.19.
15   Ibid.
16   Ibid., p.20.
17   Ibid., p.7.
18   Ibid., p.5.
19   Ibid., p.20.
20   Preston, 1631, p.29. See Morgan, 1957.
21   Preston, 1631, p.51.
22   Ibid., p.53: 'When the Lord hath said it and hath appointed this outward Symboll that thine eyes looke upon, I remember the covenant, and this is a signe betweene us, this shall bind mee to it and him likewise.'
23   Dyke, 1642, p.97.
24   Ibid., p.131.
25   Ibid., p.509.
26   Ibid., pp.525–6.
27   Ibid., p.526.
28   For an analysis of changing ideas on 'conformity' see Lake, 2000, pp.179–205.
29   Denison, 1634, p.13.
30   Ibid., p.16.
31   Ibid., pp.16–17.
32   Ibid., pp.21–2.
33   Ibid., p.38.
34   Ibid., p.47.
35   Ibid., pp.69–70.
36   Ibid., p.71.
37   Ibid., p.81.
38   See ibid., Epistle Dedicatory, and p.148.
39   Ibid., p.88.
40   Ibid., pp.124–5.
41   Ibid., p.155.
42   Ibid., p.162.
43   Ibid., pp.173, 217.
44   Ibid., p.192.
45   Ibid., pp.204–6.
46   Ibid., p.210.

47   Ibid., p.212.
48   Ibid., pp.214–15.
49   Ibid., p.225.
50   Ibid., p.366.
51   Morton, 1618, p.225.
52   Ibid., pp.225, 228.
53   Ibid., p.254.
54   Ibid., p.229.
55   Ibid., p.231.
56   Ibid., p.302.
57   Ibid., p.260.
58   Ibid., p.253.
59   Morton, 1631, p.64.
60   Ibid., p.151.
61   Ibid., p.153.
62   Ibid., p.103.
63   Ibid., p.212.
64   Morton, 1618, p.250.
65   Morton, 1631, p.58, Book 6. The pagination is repeated.
66   Ibid., p.59.
67   Ibid., p.73.
68   Morton, 1618, p.525.
69   Knappen, 1933, p.130.
70   Ussher, 1864, *Works*, 15, p.505. The letter is dated 25 May 1630.
71   Ibid., pp.505–6.
72   Ibid., p.506.
73   In Gataker, 1697–98, vol.2.
74   Ibid., pp.513–14.
75   Ibid., p.514.
76   Ibid., p.515.
77   Spinks, 1999, *passim*.
78   One could speculate that it was connected with the aftermath of the York House
     Conference (see below), though there is no evidence that this was the case.
79   Burges, 1629, p.14.
80   Ibid., p.16
81   Ibid., p.21.
82   Ibid., p.345.
83   Bedford, 1638, p.13. Other works included *Vindiciae Gratiae Sacramentales*, 1650
     and *Some Sacramental Instructions*, 1649.
84   Bedford, 1638, p.70.
85   Ibid., p.72 – though a misprint numbers it p.48.
86   Ibid., p.178.
87   Ibid., p.17.
88   Ibid., p.28
89   Ibid., pp.31–2.
90   Ibid., p.109.
91   Ibid., p.118.
92   Ibid., p.122.
93   See Appendix 3.
94   Denison, 1631, p.23.
95   Ibid., p.25.

96   Ibid., p.26.
97   Ibid., p.27.
98   Ibid., pp.27–8.
99   Ibid., p.40.
100 Ibid., pp.11, 19.
101 Ibid., p.44.
102 Ibid., p.55.
103 Ibid., p.78.
104 Ibid., p.85.
105 Ibid., p.86.
106 Ibid., pp.92–3.
107 Ibid., p.104.
108 Ibid.
109 Ibid., p.128.
110 Ibid., p.195.
111 Ibid., p.189.
112 Ibid., p.134.
113 Tyacke, 1987.
114 White, 1992.
115 Arnoult, 1997; Stevenson, 1994, p.185.
116 Raymer, 1981, p.2.
117 For Neile, Foster, 2000, pp.159–78; Andrewes, 1609, p.309.
118 Cosin, 1843–55, vol.1, p.94.
119 See Fincham, 1993, pp.161–85.
120 Chauncey, 1641, p.6.
121 Davies, 1992.
122 Fincham, 'The Restoration of Altars in the 1630s', forthcoming. I am grateful to Dr
     Fincham for kindly furnishing me with a copy of this article. He is preparing a book
     with Nicholas Tyacke on that subject.
123 Dugmore, 1942, p.52.
124 Jackson, 1844, vol.X, p.336.
125 Ibid., p.337.
126 Ibid., p.339.
127 Ibid., vol.IX, pp.546–7.
128 Ibid., p.603.
129 Ibid., vol.X, p.52.
130 Ibid., vol.IX, p.610.
131 Ibid., p.611.
132 Ibid., p.209.
133 White, 1617, p.29.
134 Ibid., p.157.
135 Ibid., p.161.
136 Ibid., p.158.
137 Ibid., p.161–2.
138 White, 1624, pp.179, 183.
139 Ibid., p.184.
140 White, 1617, p.159.
141 White, 1636, p. 214.
142 Buckeridge, 1618, pp.29–30.
143 Ibid., p.32.
144 Ibid., p.33.

145 Ibid., p.30.
146 Ibid., pp.40, 43.
147 Ibid., p.15.
148 Ibid., p.100.
149 Ibid., p.52.
150 Raymer, 1981, p.209.
151 For a full discussion, see ibid.
152 Montagu, 1624, p.247.
153 Ibid., p.251.
154 Ibid.
155 Montagu, 1625, p.293.
156 Ibid., p.294.
157 Ibid., p.296.
158 Montagu, 1624, p.252.
159 Montagu, 1625, p.290.
160 Ibid., p.287.
161 Montagu, 1640, p.310.
162 Webster, 1997, pp.167ff.; Maltby, 1998.
163 Mackay, 1975–77, p.186; Ford, 1995.
164 Mackay, 1975–77.
165 Ibid., p.200.
166 Low, 1923, p.25.
167 Forbes, 1645, X.4.
168 Ibid., XI.17.
169 Ibid., XI.ix.6; Low, 1923, p.61.
170 Ibid., XI.x.6; cf. Low, 1923, pp.66–7.
171 Ibid., XI.x.44; Low, 1923, pp.76–7.
172 Ibid., XI.xx.12; Low, 1923, p.136.
173 Ibid., XI.xx.25. Low, 1923, p.150.
174 Forbes, 1924, p.120.
175 Ibid., p.81.
176 Forbes, MS 635 Aberdeen University Special Collection. I am indebted to Professor Iain Torrance who not only arranged for me to consult the two manuscript copies, but also kindly allowed me to consult his microfilm of this important diary. It is to be hoped that it will be edited and published.
177 See Low, 1923, p.110.
178 Forbes, Ms Diary, p.167. I have tried to keep the original spelling, though some words are abbreviated. I have left the more obvious abbreviations.
179 Ibid., pp.230–31.
180 Ibid., pp.253–4.
181 Ibid., p.292.
182 Ibid.
183 Ibid., p.319.
184 For a recent treatment of William Forbes, see Martin, 1999. I am grateful to Mrs Martin for kindly furnishing me with the text of her thesis.
185 Forbes, 1850–56, vol.2, p.381.
186 Ibid., p.383.
187 Ibid., p.389.
188 Ibid., p.421
189 Ibid., p.403.
190 Ibid., pp.413, 417.

191   Ibid., pp.423, 531.
192   Ibid., p.545.
193   Ibid., pp.577–9.
194   Spalding, 1850–51, vol.1, pp.39–40.
195   Cosin, 1843–55, *Works*, V, p.114.
196   Grisbrooke, 1958.
197   *A Relation of the Conference between William Laud Late Lord Archbishop of Canter-
        bury and Mr. Fisher the Jesuit*, ed. C.H.Simpkinson, Macmillan, London 1901, p.65.
198   Ibid., pp.338–9, citing White, 1617, and Calvin on 1 Cor. 11:24.
199   Ibid., pp.358–9.
200   Laud, 1847–60, vol.3, pp.344, 358–9.
201   Ibid., pp.354–5.
202   Henderson, 1925–26, p.204.
203   Anon., *Reasons For which the Service Booke, urged upon Scotland ought to bee
        refused*, 1638.
204   Ibid. The pamphlet has four pages, pp.99–114.
205   Stevenson, 1974a; 1974b, pp.135–65; Mullan, 2000.
206   Stevenson, 1974a, p.106.
207   Ibid., p.113.
208   Rutherford, Letters 611, cited by Stevenson, 1974a, p.141.
209   Ibid., p.156.
210   Quoted in Mullan, 2000, p.18.
211   Couper et al., 1995.
212   Schmidt, 1989, p.25.
213   Ibid., p.24.
214   Quoted in ibid., p.31.
215   Fleming, *The Fulfilling of the Scripture*, cited in Couper et al., 1995, p.120.
216   Burnet, 1818, vol.1, p.67.
217   John Cameron (1579–1625), a friend of Andrew Melville, might also perhaps be
        placed in this category, though apart from his brief appointment at Glasgow 1622–3,
        his whole theological academic career was spent in French Reformed academies, and
        his influence in Scotland was minimal. For his sacramental views, see Cameron,
        1642, pp. 502–14.
218   Boyd, 1639, p.66.
219   Ibid., p.67.
220   Ibid., p.68.
221   Ibid.
222   Ibid., p.69.
223   Ibid., p.71.
224   Ibid., p.72.
225   Ibid., p.72.
226   Boyd, 1629. For Boyd's 'watch-word' or exhortation before the communion, see
        Appendix 5.
227   Boyd, 1639, p.80.
228   Ibid.
229   Ibid., p.81.
230   Ibid., p.82.
231   Ibid., p.84.
232   Gillespie, 1993, p.470.
233   Ibid., p.134.
234   Ibid., p.433.

235   Ibid., pp.469–70.
236   Forbes (of Alford), 1632, p.2.
237   Ibid., pp.3, 4.
238   Ibid., p.10.
239   Ibid., pp.66–7.
240   Guild, 1627, p.160.
241   Ibid. One assumes that Guild was less than enthusiastic about the implications of private baptism allowed by the Perth Articles.
242   Ibid., p.166.
243   Ibid., p.171.
244   Ibid., p.172.
245   Ibid., p.172.
246   Ibid., p.180.
247   Ibid., p.189.
248   Ibid., p.190.
249   Guild, 1639, p.A3.
250   Ibid., p.B4.
251   Ibid., p.B1.
252   Ibid., p.B4.
253   See McCoy, 1974.
254   Baillie, 1640, pp.98–9.
255   Baillie, 1641b, p.1.
256   Ibid., p.72.
257   Ibid., p.73.
258   Ibid., pp.107–8.
259   Ibid., p.109.
260   Ibid., p.105.
261   Ibid., 1641 edition, Supplement, p.34.
262   Ibid., pp.42–4.
263   Baillie, 1641a, p.94.
264   *Acts of the General Assemblies of the Church of Scotland 1638–1649*, 1691, p.36.

Chapter 4

From the Long Parliament to the Death of Cromwell

Two Kingdoms United in Covenant and Worship

The debacle of the 1637 *Book of Common Prayer* and the National Covenant of Scotland of 1638 unleashed a train of events which spilled over the border into England, eventually leading to the invasion of England by the Scots army, the calling of the Short and Long Parliaments, and the ensuing power struggle between King and Parliament which escalated to civil war. Amongst the Scottish demands for assisting the English Parliament was closer cooperation between the nations, including a common confession of faith between both Kingdoms.[1] However, during the months of negotiation, the Scottish Covenanters expanded their demands which included a closer union between the kingdoms, religious and civil. The English were reluctant – as Robert Baillie put it, 'The English were for a civill League, we for a religious Covenant.'[2] The two kingdoms entered the Solemn League and Covenant, though the English never interpreted it in the manner that the Scottish Covenanters had envisaged. Though both parties pledged never to agree 'to be divided and withdrawn from this blessed Union and conjunction', it was in many respects a marriage of convenience, with infidelities on both sides, which would in 1660 end in divorce.

Amongst the many grievances on the English Long Parliament's agenda, episcopal power and Laudian piety were prominent. Already in 1640 there were instances of soldiers removing the Laudian communion rails and altars, and in September 1641 the House of Commons passed an ordinance requiring the churchwardens of every parish to remove the communion table from the east end of the church, chapel or chancel, into some other convenient place, and to take away communion rails, and level the chancels, 'as heretofore they were before the late innovations'.[3] Initial proposals for a moderate reform of episcopacy in England gave way to its abolition, and the Long Parliament called an assembly of divines to settle the government and liturgy of the Church of England. The intention of this latter was to clarify the doctrine of the now non-episcopal English Church, and to bring it nearer to the standards of the Church of Scotland and other Reformed churches abroad.[4] Thus the Westminster Assembly of Divines, whose membership included Scottish Commissioners, clerical and lay, convened in the Chapel of King Henry VII on 1st July 1643. Although the Assembly achieved its task, it did so amongst debates which showed sharp disagreements not just over polity, but also over sacraments, soteriology, ecclesiology and liturgy.

The Anabaptists and the Baptismal Controversy

Stephen Marshall and John Tombes   Stephen Marshall (1595–1655), the vicar of Finchingfield, Essex, was one of the most prominent members of the Westminster Assembly, and also a frequent preacher before the Commons and Lords. At one of the appointed Morning Lectures preached to the House of Commons in 1643/4 in Westminster Abbey, Marshall chose as his subject the baptising of infants.[5] The choice was deliberate.

The passing of the Grand Remonstrance in November 1641, with the removal of the Church courts and episcopacy, together with the uncertainties of civil war, resulted in a number of sectarian groups becoming quite open regarding their existence, including the Family of Love and Anabaptists. It was during 1643 that Hanserd Knowles or Knollys, who had already left the Church of England, embroiled the members of Henry Jessey's gathered church in the matter of infant baptism.[6] One beneficed Church of England divine, John Tombes, vicar of Bewdley in Worcestershire, having become convinced of believers' baptism, presented a Latin submission to the Westminster Assembly in 1643, urging the abolition of infant baptism. It was this openness of anabaptism and Tombes' submission that prompted Marshall's sermon defending paedobaptism.

Marshall had been born in Godmanchester, Huntingdonshire, and matriculated at Emmanuel College, Cambridge 1615. After serving as Lecturer at Wethersfield, he was instituted as vicar of the neighbouring parish of Finchingfield in October 1625. He was a reluctant and occasional conformist, but as he witnessed the silencing of a number of his close associates in Essex, he seems to have conformed sufficiently – including the wearing of the surplice – to avoid suspension.[7] But at the outbreak of the political crisis he sided with Parliament and espoused a presbyterian system of government.

In this particular sermon, Marshall took 1 Peter 3:21 as his text, and explained that having on previous occasions treated such issues as the institution of baptism, the minister of the sacrament, and the *res terrena* and *res caelestis*, he would now turn to the issue of who might be baptised. Marshall argued the legitmacy of infant baptism on covenantal grounds, namely that the holiness of infants is a federal holiness. He firmly stated: 'The Lord hath appointed and ordained a Sacrament or *seale of initiation to be administered unto them who enter into Covenant with him, Circumcision* for the time of that administration which was *before* Christs incarnation, *baptisme since* the time of his incarnation; both of them the *same* sacrament for the *spirituall* part, though differing in the outward Elements.'[8]

Marshall's sermon was a catalyst for a whole number of treatises and tracts refuting this open outbreak of anabaptism. Robert Baillie wrote one such treatise, accusing anabaptists of excluding all infants from any interest at all in the covenant of grace, and that many denied original sin. Baptism and circumcision, maintained Baillie, are seals of the same covenant.[9] And Dr Daniel Featley, named to the Assembly, but who obeyed the King's order to withdraw, debated with the anabaptists, arguing that 'All they who are partakers of the grace both signified and exhibited to us in baptisme, may and ought to receive the signe and sacrament thereof.'[10] Since all the children of believers are in the covenant, they should be baptised. Indeed, Featley felt that it was not safe to defer their baptism, not because they would suffer eternal damnation if they died unbaptised, but because it is the ordinary means of salvation and it is commanded by the Lord.[11]

However, John Tombes wrote a lengthy reply to Marshall's sermon, and this reply sparked off an ongoing debate lasting well into the 1650s, with responses from a wide variety of divines, including New England Independents, as well as what were now 'presbyterian Anglicans' (former nonconformist and conformist Calvinists) and 'Royalist Episcopal divines' (Royalist conformist Calvinists and the Patristic Reformed churchmen). All agreed that Tombes's position was erroneous, and they shared a great deal of common ground in defending infant baptism. However, differences over soteriology began to surface.

Tombes's view was that infant baptism was a doubtful practice since it was not testified in Scripture.[12] He did not accept the argument that the covenant with Abraham and the new covenant were one and the same covenant, and thus what applied to circumcision did not necessarily apply to baptism. Appealed to by most divines to prove federal holiness, 1 Corinthians 7:14 was limited by Tombes to matrimonial holiness. Tombes asserted:

> The grace of God is not tied to Sacraments, neither do Sacraments give grace by the work done, and therefore grace is not restrained, though Sacraments be never granted, grace is not denied to an excommunicated person, who is inhibited from the Lord's Supper, the Grace of God is free, whether we understand it of the divine affection, or the effects of it; nor can be made larger or narrower by our act.[13]

In other words, grace is quite independent of sacraments, and so infant baptism is unnecessary. Tombes argued that infant baptism was shown to be deficient by those who used it, since they use godparents, insisted on episcopal confirmation, or instruction and catechesis, or in New England Independency, a Church Covenant was required.[14] The practice had led to false ideas, such as that baptism confers grace, or regenerates, that infants may be saved by their parents' faith, or that some regenerated persons can fall from grace. As far as Tombes saw the matter, there was one end of baptism, namely, 'that it should be a signe that the baptized shews himself a disciple, and confesseth the faith in which he hath been instructed'.[15] Tombes in fact regarded the sacrament of baptism as a duty, or a badge of our profession only. It seals no grace, and its one qualification is confession of faith. Infants cannot be baptised because of their parents' faith.[16] He could thus assert: 'I acknowledge baptisme in its nature to be a seale of the covenant of God, but not a seal actuall, but aptitudinall; that is, all right baptism is in its nature apt to seal … yet … onely to true believers. And God never sealed actually till a person be a beleever.'[17]

Amongst the many responses to Tombes was that of Dr Nathaniel Holmes (1599–1678). Holmes, who seceded from the Parliamentary Church and founded his own congregations, replied asserting that 'A soul may be saved without the use of a seal in some case, but in no case can be saved in the contempt of a seal'; not only did he defend the concept of federal holiness of infants, but was happy to say that 'baptisme gives grace *instrumentally*', though this was different from giving grace absolutely.[18]

John Geree (1601–49) had been deprived of the living of Tewkesbury in the 1620s for nonconformity, but was restored in 1641, and then became rector of

St. Albans, Hertfordshire in 1646. Geree replied to Tombes with this syllogism: 'To whom the Gospel-Covenant is extended in the Churches of Christians, to them the Sacrament of Initiation appointed for that Administration of the Covenant doth belong. To children of beleeving Christians the Gospel-Covenant is extended in the Christian Churches. *Ergo*, To them the Sacrament of Initiation doth belong.'[19] Geree strongly asserted that infants 'are capable of the Grace of the Covenant, of the Circumcision made without hands, Regeneration in the Infusion of the Seeds of Holinesse, Remission of sin, Justification, which consists in imputation'.[20]

Marshall himself replied to Tombes at some length. In the first two parts of *A Defence of Infant Bapism* (1646) he refuted Tombes's patristic citations, and outlined what he regarded as the suspect history of anabaptism. In the third part, Marshall argued that three things must be distinguished: the truth of the thing signified, our interest in that thing, and our obligation.[21] He wrote:

> I say therefore, that in every Sacrament, the truth of the Covenant in it selfe, and all the promises of it are sealed to be Yea, and Amen; Jesus Christ became a Minister of the circumcision, to confirme the promises made unto the Fathers, & so to every one who is admitted to partake of Baptisme, according to the rule which God hath given to his Church, to administer that sacrament, there is *sealed the truth of all the promises of the Gospel*, that they are all true in Christ, and that whoever partakes of Christ, shall partake of all these saving promises; this is sealed absolutely in Baptisme, but as to the second, which is *interesse meum*, or the receivers interest in that spirituall part of the Covenant, that is sealed to no receiver *absolutely*, but *conditionally*; in this particular, all Sacraments are but *signa conditionalia*, conditionall seales, sealing the spirituall part of the Covenant to the receiver, upon condition that hee performe the spirituall condition of the Covenant: ... Now the third thing, *the obligation* which is put upon the receiver, a bond or tie for him to performe, who is admitted to receive the Sacrament, this third I say is also absolute, all Circumcised and Baptized persons did or doe stand absolutely ingaged to performe the conditions required on their part ...[22]

He summarised by saying that in baptism there is first an absolute seal of the truth of the covenant of grace in itself, a conditional seal of the receiver's interest in the covenant, and an absolute obligation to make good the covenant.[23]

However, Reformed internecine sacramental dispute surfaced in the replies to Tombes by Richard Baxter and Thomas Blake.

Richard Baxter and Thomas Blake   Richard Baxter (1615–91), who was self-taught in theology, had been ordained by John Thornborough in 1639, and was assistant curate at Kidderminster. We shall have cause to meet Baxter again later, and are concerned here only with his reply to Tombes. In the opening introduction to his *Plain Scripture Proof of Infants Church-membership and Baptism* (1651), Baxter confessed that in earlier years he had had doubts about infant baptism, but his experience of the Civil War and sectarianism changed his mind. He had met Tombes and had recommended him as curate of Bewdley. Later, however, he publicly disputed with Tombes on the matter of infant baptism, and Baxter took the usual line of arguing that children through their parents entered the covenant, and had a right to baptism. However, in his *Plain Scripture Proof*, Baxter not only attempted to refute Tombes, but also took issue with Cornelius Burges, Samuel

Ward and Thomas Bedford. In the introduction Baxter noted that he had read Burges and Bedford on baptismal regeneration, and found it taught in the *Book of Common Prayer* liturgy, but having read scripture, he decided that the signs can only be signs, and not instruments to impart regeneration.[24] Against Tombes, Baxter asserted that baptism was a divine seal by which God engaged to make good his promises.[25] However, he rejected it as a seal of the Absolute Covenant. He wrote: 'Baptisme was never instituted by God to be a Seal of the Absolute Promise of the first special Grace; but to be the Seal of the Covenant properly so called, wherein the Lord engageth himself conditionally to be our God, to Pardon, Justifie, Adopt and Glorifie us; and we engage our selves to be his People, and so to perform the said Condition.'[26]

For Baxter, it was a seal of the Conditional Covenant. Infants have that faith which is the condition of the covenant in their parents; that faith becomes pardoning and justifying when the conditions of the covenant are fulfilled. He thus rejected the Ward/Bedford view that sacraments are instruments which confer the grace promised.[27] He was prepared to allow – though he himself preferred not to use – the concept of sacraments as moral instruments, but rejected what he perceived to be Bedford's view that they are 'Physical' passive or 'Hyperphysical' instruments.[28] Water cannot either receive grace or convey it, and baptism can give nothing above what was promised in the covenant.[29] The covenant frequently gives full remission without baptism, but baptism never gives remission without the covenant. It is the covenant which is the instrument of donation.[30] It is utterly unknown, asserted Baxter, and unrevealed in the Word, whether God gives infants inherent special grace or not, but if he does, it is more likely to be given before baptism by virtue of the covenant.[31] Baxter decided that it was better to say that all infants of true believers are justified and pardoned (though some fall and perish) than that they are regenerated, or endued with a sincere new nature, and the effectual seed or habit of faith, which he detected to be the position of Burges and Bedford.[32]

At one point in his refutation of Tombes, Burges and Bedford, Baxter denied a distinction between an external and internal covenant.[33] Furthermore, he argued that the principal condition of the promise was saving or justifying faith. It was these points with which Thomas Blake took issue. Blake (1597–1657) was educated at Christ Church Oxford, and held the benefice of Tamworth. He wrote a number of pamphlets and works defending infant baptism.[34] In *The Birth Privilege, or Covenant Holinesse of Beleevers and their Issue* (1644), Blake had attacked Tombes, and defended the right of infant baptism not simply on the grounds of parental faith, but ancestral faith: Scripture, so concluded Blake, points towards the fact that 'Christians have their Birth-right Privilege, that they transmit a Covenant–Holinesse to their Issue, even to their whole posterity.'[35] But Baxter took issue with Blake on this.

Blake's sacramental views, together with what he calls 'digressions' which dispute with Baxter, were set out in *The Covenant Sealed, or A Treatise of the Sacraments* (London, 1655). After surveying various definitions of sacraments, Blake favours 'a sign instituted of God for the use of his people in Covenant, to signifie and seal his Promises upon Terms and Propositions by himself prescribed and appointed',[36] or 'a sign appointed of God, to be received of his Covenant-people, to seal the righteousness of faith unto them'.[37] He listed five possible uses of the word 'seal', and urged that the fifth – for ratification and confirmation – is the correct understanding when applied to sacraments.[38] However, like Baxter he argued that they are not absolute seals, but conditional.[39] There is no saving benefit received in the sacraments longer than the individual keeps the covenant. They seal the righteousness of faith. Blake wrote: '*All that the Sacraments work in the soules of receivers, is by way of sign and seal. They have no immediate effects for the working of any inward graces or priviledges, but as our understanding is exercised by them, as Indicative signes, and our faith, as ratifications and seales of the promises.*'[40] Baptism is 'that door of entrance into the Church of Christ, our matriculation into the society of Saints'.[41] Like Featley, he defended the necessity of baptism on the grounds that it is commanded in Scripture, not because salvation is tied to it.[42] Discussing the teaching of St. Paul, he urged: 'I see no other way of reconciliation, or to make sense of his words, then to understand him that Baptisme saves, as it hath its work on the conscience, as it works upon our understanding, and our faith as a sign and seal, and is no immediate conveyance of happinesse, not any other way of conveyance, then as it hath its work on the conscience of the receivers.'[43]

For this reason, Blake, like Baxter, was critical of Samuel Ward and Thomas Bedford who carried the sacraments 'higher then Scripture hath raised them', and he was alarmed that their error had spread.[44] It was for this reason Blake was critical of the, by now illegal, *Book of Common Prayer* rites: 'And whereas several passages in the *Liturgy* of this Church did seem to favour the opposite opinion, affixing adoption, membership of Christ, and inheritance of the Kingdom of heaven, and regeneration to Baptisme: we know how great offence it gave to many eminently Learned and pious, putting them upon omission of those passages.'[45]

He was also critical of the position taken by Burges, and found Richard Hooker ambivalent on sacramental efficacy, not knowing quite what line he advocated.[46] But for Blake, faith was the instrument of grace, not the sacraments.[47]

Much of this was in total agreement with Baxter. Where, therefore, did they differ? They differed on three particular points relating to baptism and the covenant. First, Baxter insisted that the faith which baptism sealed was 'justifying faith', but Blake argued that a faith which was short of justifying faith was sufficient, that is, a dogmatic faith was sufficient.[48] For Blake, baptism did not seal the act of faith; it sealed the promise of salvation on condition of faith.[49] Second, Baxter made no distinction between an external and internal covenant of grace. Blake, however, did, and claimed that baptism sealed the 'righteousness of faith' which was an objective righteousness won by Christ. Thus infants could be baptised because the external objective covenant, appropriated by parents through the internal covenant, held out a promise to their children. And thirdly, whereas Baxter limited covenant holiness to children of *parents* in the covenant, Blake counted *ancestors*, which could be traced back 'as high as Ancestors have been in Christianity'.[50] Thus beneath the baptismal controversy, in which many rushed to defend infant baptism, there lurked significant differences amongst the paedobaptists regarding covenant and ecclesiology.

A Directory for The Publique Worship of God, throughout the Three Kingdoms

Stephen Marshall's sermon was the catalyst for this baptismal controversy, which rumbled on well into the late 1650s. But Marshall was not only a leading member of the Westminster Assembly of Divines, and favourite preacher for both Houses of Parliament. He was also appointed chair of the sub-committee which was responsible for drawing up *A Directory for the Public Worship*, which was to replace the *Book of Common Prayer*.[51]

The original remit of the Assembly of Divines, which contained some of the finest minds of the Church of England, was to confer on matters of liturgy, discipline and government of the Church of England, though its initial work was a revision of the Thirty-Nine Articles. However, when Parliament accepted the Solemn League and Covenant in September 1643, a new remit was to bring the Church of England into conformity with the Church of Scotland and other Reformed churches, in matters of faith, polity and worship – which would have delighted the compilers of the Millenary Petition. Thus Stephen Marshall, together with Charles Herle, Herbert Palmer and Thomas Young, with four Scottish Commissioners – Robert Baillie, George Gillespie, Samuel Rutherford and Alexander Henderson – and the Independent, Thomas Goodwin (who unofficially co-opted his colleague Philip Nye) constituted the liturgical commission which would author the new liturgy. The *Directory* was completed by 12 November 1644, and by an Ordinance of 17 April 1645, replaced the *Book of Common Prayer*, with use of the latter being made illegal.[52] In fact, the continued use of the *Prayer Book* seems to have been far more widespread than was once thought.[53] Ronald Hutton notes that a sample of churchwardens' accounts for the late 1640s record the retention of the illegal *Prayer Book* in over a third of cases (without proving use), while the *Directory* appeared in less than a quarter.[54] It was not impossible to find closet celebrations of the *Prayer Book* rites, and under Cromwell, clandestine use of the book became more common. The diarist John Evelyn recorded in April 1655 that St. Gregory's was the only London church using the *Prayer Book*, but Paul Seaver found evidence for its use also at St. Peter Paul's Wharf, at St. Benet's, and at St. Mary Magdalen, Milk Street.[55] John Evelyn recorded how a Christmas celebration 1657 which he attended was rudely interrupted:

> I went with my wife &c: to *Lond*: to celebrate *Christmas day*. Mr *Gunning* preaching in *Excester* Chapell on 7: *Micha* 2. Sermon Ended, as he was giving us the holy Sacrament, The Chapell was surrounded with Souldiers: All the Communicants and Assembly surpriz'd & kept Prisoners by them, some in the house, others carried away: It fell to my share to be confin'd to a roome in the house, where yet were permitted to Dine with the master of it, the Countesse of *Dorset, Lady Hatton*, & some others of quality who invited me: In the afternoone came *Collonel Whaly, Goffe* & others from *Whitehall* to examine us one by one, & some they committed to the *Martial*, some to Prison, some Committed: When I came before them they tooke my name & aboad, examind me, why contrarie to an Ordinance made that none should any longer observe the superstitious time of the *Nativity* (so esteem'd by them) I durst offend, & particularly be at *Common prayers*, which they told me was but the *Masse* in *English*, & particularly pray for *Charles stuard*, for which we had no Scripture: I told them we did not pray for *Cha:Steward*, but for all *Christian Kings, Princes & Governors*: The[y] replied, in so doing we praied for the K.

of *Spaine* too, who was their Enemie, & a *Papist*, with other frivolous & insnaring questions, and much threatening, & finding no colour to detaine me longer, with much pitty of my Ignorance, they dismiss'd me: These were men of high flight, and above Ordinances: & spake spiteful things of our B:Lords nativity: so I got home late the next day blessed be God: These wretched miscreants, held their muskets against us as we came up to receive the Sacred Elements, as if they would have shot us at the Altar, but yet suffering us to finish the Office of Communion, as perhaps not in their Instructions what they should do in case they found us in that Action.[56]

In the *Directory*, the English Reformed theologians were able for the first time to give liturgical expression to what they regarded as a consensus on sacramental rites. Any plan to provide a full liturgical text after the manner of the Scottish *Book of Common Order* was ruled out by two factors. First, the English Independents rejected all 'stinted' liturgy. Goodwin and Nye championed their cause, and Charles Herle frequently sided with them in the debates. Second, two of the Scottish Commissioners were of the radical party – Rutherford and Gillespie – and they too were reluctant to accept a written liturgy. Indeed, when Thomas Gataker pointed out to Rutherford that a particular proposal on the table was already to be found in the Knoxian liturgy, Rutherford replied, 'We will not owne this litturgy. Nor are we tyed unto it.'[57] Thus there was little hope that this committee would agree on a set liturgy. Instead, a *Directory* was compiled, giving a suggested structural outline, and the main elements which the various prayers and exhortations might contain.

George Gillespie   The responsibility for the orders for the administration of the sacraments was given over to the Scottish Commissioners. The rather negative views of Gillespie and Baillie on liturgy and ceremonial have been discussed previously. Gillespie's more positive views can be gleaned from his *A Treatise of Miscellanie Questions* (1649). Baptism was intended only for the redeemed in the Lord; it distinguished between those who were the Church, and those who are the world.[58] It is efficacious to all the members of Christ, young and old, by virtue of the word of promise and covenant of grace sealed in that sacrament.[59] On the Lord's Supper, Gillespie was mainly concerned to establish that this 'mystical food' was 'a type and representation of the Everlasting feast and communion with Christ in glory'.[60] If a type of a feast, it should resemble a feast, and communicants should be seated at the table. However, here Gillespie was not attacking kneeling as in the Prayer Book, but receiving in pews which seems to have been the practice of the Independents. Those who receive in pews, said Gillespie, 'shame the poor'.[61]

Samuel Rutherford   Samuel Rutherford (1600?–1661), as noted in a previous chapter, was on the radical wing of the Kirk, had been a frequent Scottish nonconformist, and was eventually removed from his parish of Anwoth and confined to Aberdeen (Figure 4.1). Writing to his parishioners in Anwoth, Rutherford had advised:

> ... that ye should in any sort forbear the receiving the Lord's Supper but after the form that I delivered it to you, according to the example of Christ our Lord; that is, that ye should sit, as banquetters, at one table with our King, and eat and drink, and divide the elements one to another: – the timber and stones of the church walls shall bear witness

Figure 4.1   Samuel Rutherford, 1600?–61

that my soul was refreshed with the comforts of God in that supper: – and that crossing in baptism was unlawful, and against Christ's ordinance.[62]

To one correspondent he wrote that to kneel for reception was idolatry, because religious kneeling, by God's institution, 'doth necessarily import religious and divine adoration'.[63] Though a radical, Rutherford was a leading theologian and political theorist.[64] He set forth his sacramental views in brief in *The Soume of Christian Religion*, which was a catechism (published posthumously), and also in *The Due Right of Presbyteries, or a Peaceable Plea for the Government of the Church of Scotland* (1644), which was a reply to the New England Independents, and other groups which Rutherford viewed as sectarian. Sacraments are pledges of God's grace to strengthen and confirm 'staggering faith'.[65] They are like a king's seal.[66] They are holy signs, religious seals, and instruments by which faith works.[67] But they contain no virtue of themselves; 'the sacrament is bot as the glasse of the physitian that carieth the oyle, bot the oyle and not the glasse cureth the wound.'[68] In a communion sermon, Rutherford asserted that the word and sacraments are 'but empty bottles' unless God fills them with his virtue: 'without this secret virtue we shall set our mouth to an empty bottle, and draw in wind, to the hurt of our souls and stomachs, which shall prove the savour of death unto death, and not the wine of God's refreshing grace.'[69] In word and sacrament Christ takes us into the chariot with himself, and draws our hearts after him.[70] Although not efficient causes of grace, yet they are material causes containing grace.[71] Sacraments as signs 'are objective and morall causes, exciting the mind as the word doth in a morall way, they represent Christ and him crucified ....'[72] They are 'signes exhibitive' and not naked signs.[73] When celebrated rightly, they make some difference to the recipient: 'if a Sacrament make not a thing that was not before, or if God give not, and really produce, conferre and exhibite grace, and a stronger measure of faith, and assurance of remission of sinnes, at the due and right use of the Sacrament, the Sacrament is a naked signe, and not an exhibitive Seale.'[74] But, so Rutherford insisted, they do in fact give grace and pardon in a further degree.

While baptism has a divine warrant (Rutherford cited Genesis 17:10 and Acts 3:25), there is no warrant to bind God's hands so as he could not save by some other means.[75] It is a seal of our incorporation into Christ's visible church, a seal confirming us of our entry in the visible church.[76] However, Rutherford warned: 'The placing of the Font at the *Church doore* as a mysticall signe of our entry in the Church is an Antichristian ceremony of mens devising, which wee disclaime.'[77] Infant baptism was defended in another work, *The Covenant of Life Opened*, where Rutherford painstakingly discussed the relevant scriptural references to show that children were federally holy.[78]

The Lord's Supper seals our growth and union with one another. Change in the elements is a change in usage, not material properties. Explaining the Supper as a seal, Rutherford stressed how sacraments in fact differ from legal seals:

> But God hath given the seale of grace upon condition that wee make use thereof in Faith, else the Sacrament is blanke and null. Therefore if you believe, and not otherwayes, the Sacrament of the Supper sealeth and confirmeth you in this, that *Christ is given already, and is the present given to be nourishment to your soule to life eternall*; and so oft as you eate, the certioration and assurance groweth, and the faith is increased, and a further degree of communion with Christ confirmed; but it is not so in civill seales, though yee repeate and reiterate the same seale of lands, ten thousand times, it never addeth one aker more to the inheritance, because the repetition of a civill seale is not commanded under the promise of addition of new lands, nor is it commanded, as obedience to the owner of the Charter, that hee should make use of the seale; but from the using in faith, the Sacrament, we receive increase of Grace, and a Sacramentall Grace.[79]

On the question as to whether Christ is present, Rutherford asserted: 'Yea, certainlie the Lord doth reallie and truelie, not in imaginatione, give us his bodie and blood, bot after a spirituall manner.'[80]

Coffey urges that Rutherford's was a deeply sacramentalist piety, far removed from Zwinglian memorialism of later Evangelicalism, which may be true.[81] However, his concern for the covenant, and the Spirit in the inward heart meant that although he had great devotion to the Lord's Supper, he tended towards a symbolic memorialist and parallelist understanding of sacraments.

Attention has already been drawn to the fact that Rutherford belonged to that radical presbyterian group which was suspicious of even the inherited *Book of Common Order*. The events of 1638 and the National Covenant allowed Rutherford to return to Anwoth. As some of the Aberdeen ministers now came under suspicion and suspension by the Covenanters, one of Rutherford's group, Andrew Cant, was transferred to Aberdeen in 1642. James Spalding recorded of June that year Cant introduced liturgical innovations of the Covenanter's type: 'He wuld not baptise a bairn, yea albeit at the point of death, but after preaching on Sunday, or any other preaching day in the week … He brought in a lecture-lesson to be used Monday at night, Wednesday, Friday, and Saturday, instead of evening prayers.'[82]

He apparently did not often use the Lord's Prayer in public worship, but 'had prayers extempore long enough', and the other Aberdeen ministers copied his liturgical style.[83] He had originally let it be known that he would not celebrate the eucharist for two years, because the people were ignorant and needed catechising.[84] However, by August, at least, he had changed his mind, for Spalding recorded:

> Upon Sunday the 28th of August, Mr. Andrew Cant and Mr. John Oswald, two of the ordinary ministers of Aberdeen, gave the communion, the first in the old kirk, and the second in the new kirk. They gave the bread to one or two nearest them, then the bason by an elder was set before the people down the board, and ilk man took his communion bread with his own hand out of the bason. The minister thereafter gave the cup to one on ilk side sitting nearest him, and so ilk communicant gave the cup to others, sitting at the table, but not kneeling, as was used before, whereat sundry people murmured and grudged, but could not amend it.[85]

This approach to liturgical forms, and manner of administration of communion, was almost certainly shared by Rutherford and determined his approach to the *Directory* forms.

Alexander Henderson   Alexander Henderson (1583–1646) was minister of Leuchars, and although initially in favour of episcopacy, became convinced that only a presbyterian ministry was validated in scripture. He does not seem to have written on the sacraments, but in a tract of 1641 did give a useful summary of Scottish celebration of the sacraments. Only the minister of the Word has the power and authority to celebrate the sacraments.[86] Baptism should never be administered in private houses, but at public worship. The father of the child is responsible for the baptism:[87]

> After Sermon on the week dayes, and after Sermon in the afternoon, on the Lords day, The Pastor remaining in the same place, where he hath Preached, and having water in a large Basin provided, with a fair Linnen-cloth, in a convenient place, and in a decent manner; The Father, or in his necessary absence, some other man, who is reputed godly, presenteth the child to be Baptized.
> The action is begun with a short and pertinent prayer, next, some words of instruction touching the Author, nature, use, and end of this Sacrament, the duties to be performed, in the one time, of the person to be Baptized, and of the parent or viceparent. Thirdly, he that presenteth the childe, maketh confession of the Faith, into which the childe is to be Baptized, and promiseth to bring up the childe in that Faith, and in the fear of God. Fourthly, the Minister being informed of the name of the childe, Baptizeth the childe so named, by sprinkling with water, *Into the name of the Father, Son, and holy Ghost.* Lastly, the Minister concludeth, as well the publike worship, for that time, as the action, with thanksgiving for the Word, and Sacraments, and with prayer for a blessing, and with such Petitions, as he useth at other times after Sermon, and in end dismisseth, the Congregation with the blessing.[88]

In describing the celebration of the communion, Henderson noted that frequency of celebration varied from parish to parish. Communicants were examined on knowledge of doctrine, and urged to examine themselves, and 'to renew their Covenant made with God in Baptisme, promising to walk as beseemeth Christians'.[89] The ignorant and scandalous were not admitted. The 'Sabbath day' prior to the celebration was the occasion for a warning, and due preparation, with appropriate sermons towards the end of the week:

> Upon the day of the Communion ... a large Table decently covered, is so placed, as that the Communicants may best sit aboute it, and the whole Congregation, may both hear and behold.
>
> The Preface, prayers, and preaching of that day, are all framed to the present matter of the Sacrament, and the duties of the receivers; after Sermon immediately the Pastor useth an exhortation, and debarreth from the Table all ignorant, prophane, and scandalous persons, which being done, he goeth from the Pulpit, and sitteth down with the people at the Table, where the bread standing before him in great Basins, fitly prepared for breaking and distribution, and the wine in large Cups in like manner, he first readeth, and shortly expoundeth the words of Institution, shewing the nature, use, and end of the Sacrament, and the duties of the Communicants; next he useth a prayer, wherein he both giveth thanks, especially for the Inestimable benefit of Redemption, and for the means of the Word and Sacraments, particularly of this Sacrament, and prayeth earnestly to God for his powerfull presence, and effectuall working, to accompany his own Ordinance, to the comfort of his people now to communicate.
>
> The Elements thus being Sanctified by the Word and Prayer, the Minister Sacramentally breaketh the bread, taketh and eateth himself, and delivereth to the people, sitting in decent and reverent manner about the Table, but without difference of degrees, or acceptions of persons; these that are neerest the Minister, having received the bread, do divide it from hand to hand amongst themselves; when the Minister delivereth the bread, according to the commandment and example of Christ, he commandeth the people to take and eat, saying, *Take ye, eat ye; this is the Body of the Lord, which is broken for you: Do it in remembrance of him.* After all at the Table have taken and eaten, the Minister taketh the Cup, and drinking first himself, he giveth it to the neerest, saying, *This Cup is the New Testament, in the Blood of the Lord Jesus, which is shed for many, for the remission of sins; drink ye all of it, for as often as ye do eat this Bread, and drink this Cup, ye do shew the Lords death till he come.* All this time the Elders, in a competent number, and in a grave and reverent manner, do attend about the Table, that all who are admitted to the Table, may have the bread and wine in their own place and order of sitting, the Minister also, continuing in his place, after the giving of the Elements, doth either by his own speech, stir up the Communicants to Spirituall meditations of faith, of the great love of God in Christ, and of the Passion of Christ, and to holy affections of love, joy, godly sorrow, thankfulnesse, and whatsoever may concern them at that time, or causeth be read the history of the Passion, or some other part of the Scripture, which may work the same effect.
>
> After all at the Table have received the Cup, they rise from the Table, and return in a quiet manner, to their places, another company cometh to the Table, and so a third and a fourth, till all have received in the same manner as the first, during which time of removing of the one, and approaching of the other, the whole Congregation singeth some part of a Psalm, touching the Passion, or the love and kindenesse of God to his people, as *Psal.*22, or 103, &c.
>
> After the last company hath received, the Minister rising from the Table, goeth to the Pulpit, where, after a short speech, tending to thanksgiving, he doth againe solemnely

give thankes unto God for so great a mercy, and prayeth as on other Sabbaths; The prayer ended, all joyn in singing a Psalm of praise, sutable to the occasion, and are dismissed with the blessing, before which none are to depart, unlesse in case of necessity.[90]

Henderson's summary account illustrates that, perhaps unlike Rutherford and his circle, ministers such as Henderson kept reasonably close to the 'Knoxian' *Book of Common Order* rites. However, that liturgy did not contain a petition for sanctification, and it seems that, echoing the type of petition formulated by William Cowper, Henderson and many ministers interpolated a petition for God's presence and 'effectuall working' in the sacrament.

Henderson did not express his own sacramental views at any great length, though there are gleanings in his sermons. Preaching a communion sermon on Hebrews 11:28, Henderson, noting the Passover symbolism, explained of sacraments:

> This is ane ordinar thing, to give the name of the sign to the thing signified, as 'Christ our passover is sacrificed for us', 'This is the cup of the new testament in my blood, shed for the remission of the sins of many'. And the reason of this is. 1. Because of the similitude and representation whilk the sign has with the thing signified. Howsoever, indeed, that whilk is natural of it does not make it a sacrament, yet the Lord he has chosen such things as does that to the body, which the thing signified does to the soul. 2. Because it is grounded upon the words of the institution to do so: the Lord he has chosen such a thing for the sign, and therefore it is ascribed to the thing signified. 3.It is so, also, from the use that we have of them. This is all that we should look to in the signs of any sacrament, and no further. Men may call them sacramentaries, who has not a intention of bodily presence, but for these who has it, it is idolatry to say so. And, therefore, as we would wish to be partakers of the thing signified in the sacraments, beware to give any more to the sign than that whilk is right.[91]

In baptism we made a covenant (a synergistic statement!) to be servants and children of God, and to renounce things contrary to his will, and to observe his commandments. In the Lord's Supper we renew our covenant, and 'receave and put to the seal to the covenant'.[92]

It is probably true to say that the Scottish Commissioners shared the broad theology of the sacraments of most of their English counterparts, but not those of the Independents.

Herbert Palmer   One of the English Commissioners, Herbert Palmer, wrote a catechism which explained the Creed, Commandments, Lord's Prayer and the sacraments.[93] According to Palmer, sacraments were appointed – like the Word – 'To confirme and increase our faith and grace'.[94] A sacrament is 'the applying an outward visible creature to our bodies as a signe, seal, and pledge from God of a like inward and spirituall grace to our soules'.[95] Sacraments, though, are not bare signs. In baptism, the outward is washing in the name of the three persons of the Trinity; the inward grace sealed is 'the vertue of Christs blood and of his Spirit, to the washing away of sin; and new birth to the life of grace'.[96] Children are born within the covenant 'and so have right to the seal of it'.[97] The outward of the Lord's Supper is the eating and drinking of bread and wine in remembrance of Christ and his death. The spiritual grace is Christ's body and blood nourishing our souls 'by renewing pardon for sin past, and grace against sinne hereafter'.[98] However, the body and blood are only received by the faithful – as indeed, is the grace of baptism. For Palmer, baptism is efficacious for the faithful, that is, the elect; and only the faithful (elect) receive the body and blood of Christ. Thus self-examination and worthiness are stressed in this catechism.[99]

The order for baptism in the *Directory* began by ruling out private baptism, and lay administration of baptism. In other words, Hampton Court was reaffirmed, and the offending Article of Perth rejected. This caused some debate, with Edmund Calamy and Marshall feeling that this was too restrictive; was the rubric 'Not stricter than the gospell calls for'?, queried Marshall.[100] Rutherford argued that 'It is admission to the church; ergo, it must be in face of the church.'[101] The final order insisted on public baptism by an ordained minister. In order perhaps to make a distinction between Reformed baptism and the Catholic idea of *ex opere operato*, fonts inherited from the pre-Reformation church were no longer to be used. Indeed, Gillespie wanted baptism administered from the pulpit (as described by Henderson) and fonts destroyed because they had 'been so superstitiously abused by Papists and prelates'.[102]

The initial exhortation or 'Instruction' described baptism as a 'Seale of the Covenant of Christ, of our Ingrafting into Christ, and of our Union with him'.[103] It is the seal of remission of sins, regeneration, adoption, and life eternal. The water represents and signifies the blood of Christ and the sanctifying virtue of the Spirit; one removes original and actual sin; the other is virtue against the dominion of sin.[104] Children of Christian parents have the privileges of the covenant and are federally holy before baptism. The phrase 'federal holiness' caused considerable debate in the Westminster Assembly between Goodman, Lazarus Seaman, Stephen Marshall, Richard Vines, Charles Herle, Dr Hoyle, Herbert Palmer, Edmund Calamy, Rutherford and Gillespie. They were anxious to distinguish between federal and real holiness – one which permitted the infant to be baptised, and the other which was a sign and assurance of election and regeneration.[105] The 'Instruction' also noted that the inward grace and virtue of baptism is not tied to the moment of its administration, and that outward baptism is not so necessary that infants dying without it are damned.

Reflecting Reformed practice and the logical conclusion of covenant theology, it is parents who are addressed throughout the rite, and godparents are either suppressed, or become silent witnesses. Parents were exhorted to bring the child up in the knowledge of the grounds of the Christian religion. No credal confession was provided or required, despite the pleas of Baillie and Henderson for use of the Apostles' Creed.[106] At one point certain questions of faith were agreed upon:

Dost thou believe in God the Father, Son and Holy Ghost?
Dost thou hold thyself obliged to observe all that Christ has commanded you? And will you endeavour to do so?
Dost thou desire this child to be baptized into the faith and profession of Jesus Christ?[107]

At a later stage in March, for reasons which are not altogether clear, these were removed from the final text.[108]

Prior to the act of baptism, the rubric instructed, 'Prayer is also to be joyned with the word of Institution, for sanctifying the water to this spirituall use, and the Minister is to pray to this or the like effect.' Here the Augustinian word added to the element so that it becomes a sacrament is the underlying principle.

The suggested prayer stressed the covenant of promise, and asked God to bless his own ordinance (cf. Hildersham) 'That he would join the inward Baptisme of his Spirit with the outward Baptisme of Water'. This provoked some discussion, with Palmer summing up the position with the words, 'We do it in the name of God not only by his command but as his Instruments, he baptizeth, if he doe it he doth it inwardly as well as outwardly.'[109] The traditional trinitarian formula was used, with pouring or sprinkling with no further ceremony (that is, no signing with the cross) to follow. An outline of a thanksgiving prayer concluded the rite.

The rite 'Of the celebration of the Communion, or Sacrament of the Lords Supper' was designed to follow the normal Sunday service, as in the Reformed tradition of Geneva and Scotland, and in places it echoes the *Book of Common Order*. The rubrics suggested frequent celebration of the sacrament, though the Assembly left this to the discretion of the minister. The recommended structure was: exhortation on the benefit of the sacrament, excommunication of the unworthy, and encouragement to those with a sense of sin and repentance; the recital of the Words of Institution; optional explanation of the institution; prayer of thanksgiving or blessing of the elements; fraction and delivery; exhortation; solemn thanksgiving.

After the exhortation the minister was to begin the action by 'sanctifying and blessing' the elements, the term 'consecration' having been rejected by the Assembly.[110] The rubric defined the means of this setting apart or blessing: 'that those elements now set apart and sanctified to this holy use, by the Word of Institution and Prayer'. In this case it was a solemn recital of the narrative, quite separate from the Prayer.

The minutes of the Assembly record that Nye argued for separate prayers over the bread and wine, which was the usual Independent practice, and that this was opposed by George Gillespie, and was a practice criticised by Richard Vines.[111] The Independents had to give way, at least as far as the text of the *Directory* was concerned, though it seems that they simply continued their own practice. The outline of the actual prayer asked God to 'vouchsafe his gracious presence and the effectual working of his Spirit in us and so to sanctifie these Elements both of Bread and Wine, and to blesse his own Ordinance, that we may receive by Faith the Body and Blood of Jesus Christ'. Though sometimes classed as an 'epiklesis', its theology is quite distinct from that articulated in the epikleses of the classical eucharistic prayers.[112]

Two further issues which were hotly debated were the fraction and the posture and place for reception. Discussion on the first centred on whether the minister alone should break the bread, or whether it might be passed around, with every communicant breaking for himself.[113] On the issue of reception, the Scots Commissioners, having rejected kneeling in 1637 and reasserted the practice of communicants seated around the table, were affronted by the Independents who insisted that the elements should be delivered to communicants in their pews. The final rubric, 'the communicants may orderly sit about' the table, 'or at it', was a compromise to allow both uses.

The completed text was carried to Scotland where, in February 1645, the General Assembly endorsed it, though provided always:

> ... that the clause in the Directory of the Administration of the Lord's Supper, which mentioneth the Communicants sitting about the Table, or at it, be not interpreted as if, in the judgment of the Kirk, it were indifferent, and free for any of the Communicants not to come to, and receive at the Table; or as if we did approve the distributing of the Elements by the Minister to each Communicant, and not by the Communicants among themselves. It is also provided, That this shall be no prejudice to the order and practice of this Kirk, in such particulars as are appointed by the Books of Discipline and Acts of General Assemblies, and are not otherwise ordered and appointed in the Directory.[114]

The Assembly went on to express joy 'that these Kingdoms, once at so great a distance in the Form of Worship, are now, by the blessing of God, brought to a nearer uniformity than any other Reformed Kirks.'[115]

James VI and I's vision of his two churches using common worship was, at least in intention, fulfilled, though not in the direction that James, or Charles I, had envisaged. The 'godly' of Hampton Court had been vindicated, albeit temporarily.

The *Directory* was in theory to dovetail with the *Westminster Confession*, and the catechisms which were subsequently compiled. Chapter XXVII of the *Confession* dealt with the sacraments, defined as 'holy signs and seals of the covenant of grace', instituted by Christ, representing Christ and his benefits, and 'to confirm our interest in him; as also to put a visible difference between those that belong unto the church and the rest of the world'. However, 'The grace which is exhibited in or by the sacraments, rightly used, is not conferred by any power in them.'

Indeed, the efficacy resides solely in the work of the Spirit and the word of institution which contains the promise. Chapter XXVIII expounded baptism, which is a sign and seal of the covenant of grace and also of ingrafting into Christ, of regeneration, and remission of sins. Infant baptism was asserted rather than defended: 'Not only those that do actually profess faith in and obedience unto Christ, but also the infants of one or both believing parents are to be baptized.' It is a sin to despise or neglect baptism, but the rite is not so tied to grace and salvation that one cannot be saved without it, or necessarily regenerated by it. And it was explained:

> The efficacy of baptism is not tied to that moment of time wherein it is administered; yet notwithstanding, by the right use of this ordinance, the grace promised is not only offered, but really exhibited and conferred by the Holy Ghost, to such (whether of age or infants) as that grace belongeth unto, according to the counsel of God's own will, in his appointed time.

Chapter XXIX explained that the Lord's Supper sealed benefits and gave spiritual nourishment; it was in manner a sacrifice, but a commemoration of the one offering once for all upon the cross. The institution by Jesus required ministers 'to declare his word of institution to the people, to pray, and bless the elements of bread and wine, and thereby to set them apart from a common to a holy use'. The elements change in use, not substance, and so may not be worshipped. Worthy receivers do receive and feed on Christ crucified in a spiritual or sacramental manner.

The Larger and Shorter Catechisms do not add anything of significance beyond what is contained in the *Confession*, though the Larger Catechism does define a sacrament as a holy ordinance instituted by Christ, ' to signify, seal, and exhibit' benefits and graces to those in the covenant of grace. And the covenant of grace is set in both the *Confession* and Catechisms in the context of the Eternal Decrees and predestination.[116]

In many ways the *Westminster Confession* and Catechisms represent a distillation of one dominant theology found in the English Church at that time, with a concern for double predestination, though infralapsarian, and a covenant theology. The sacramental theology distils the type of teaching that we have encountered in Stuart divines such as Hildersham, Downame, Bruce, Dickson, Bedell and Ussher. It was the theology of seventeenth-century 'International Calvinism'. Such widespread views may be further illustrated by the writings on the Lord's Supper of Anthony Tuckney, Joshua Hoyle, Thomas Gataker and Richard Vines – all members of the Assembly, Richard Gove, and the Exhortation issued for the ministers of the London province in 1650.

Anthony Tuckney   Both the *Westminster Confession* and Catechisms represent the distillation of a broad 'godly' theology, and were the work of committees. One key compiler was Anthony Tuckney (1595–1670), the former fellow of Emmanuel College, Cambridge, and town preacher of Boston, Lincolnshire, who was, from 1653 until the Restoration, Master of St. John's College, Cambridge. Tuckney had already compiled a Catechism when at Emmanuel College, in 1628. Although this brief work is mainly concerned with the two covenants, there is an extended treatment of baptism and regeneration. The sacraments, so Tuckney asserted, were not bare signs but also 'seales and efficacious instruments' which work that which God appointed.[117] They are efficacious in confirming faith and other graces, though this is dependent upon a person being called and having faith. Whatever sacraments may do, it is not because of any power inherent in them. In discussing the question as to whether baptism is an instrumental cause to confer grace, Tuckney answers in the negative. Rather, they profess a promise and are seals of grace which comes through faith. He was prepared to speak of sacraments as efficaciously confirming, sealing and exhibiting instruments, but preferred the term 'instrument of salvation', since they were instruments but not causes of salvation. In infant baptism, regeneration occurs for those who are elected; in the case of adults, they come to baptism already having faith, and are thus regenerated.

Joshua Hoyle   Hoyle was a Yorkshire man, who trained at Oxford and then moved to Ireland where he became a Fellow of Trinity College, Dublin and eventually professor of divinity. He was also vicar of Stepney, and was present there at the outbreak of the Civil War. He was a friend and protégé of Archbishop Ussher. In his *A Rejoynder to Master Malone's Reply Concerning Reall Presence* (1641), he distinguished between a symbolical presence by representation applicable to both baptism and the eucharist, and a spiritual presence which is by virtue of Christ's divinity.[118] Spiritual grace is communicated in us by the Spirit, organically and intrumentally by faith. The Lord's Supper was 'onely a memoriall of that onely and most absolute Sacrifice upon the Crosse'.[119] And rejecting carnal, bodily, substantial and 'Naturall' ideas of eucharistic presence, Hoyle asserted: 'Besides this *Naturall*, there is a *Virtuall* presence by power, and efficacy, (as the Philosopher speakes of a vertuall contact) whereby a thing absent by strong force of operation, workes a present effect: as the Sunne absent in substance, present in heat and light. To this kinde wee referre that *Spirituall* presence of Christ's humane Nature in the Sacrament.'[120]

In this work, in an Irish context, Hoyle was anwering a Jesuit. He not only rejected substantial presence, but also attacked the ceremonies of the Mass. Interestingly, he asked:

> ... is the Altar covered with redde Damaske having a golden Crosse and Armes? Hath it selfe a crosse in the midst? and whether it be of gold, silver, &c. Hath it a thin vaile over it to keepe out the dust? Hath it Candlesticks, Cushions, Palls of all colours, Copes, Girdles &c. Is there a new Masse-Booke? a little bell to give warning when they lift up their God? and gilded Candlesticks to lift him up? a Censer with a silver spoone, a Carpet for the foote?[121]

Here, in condemning Roman ceremonial, Hoyle also condemned much of the Laudian piety; indeed, he was to give evidence against Laud at his trial.

Thomas Gataker   Thomas Gataker (1574–1654) had been a student at St. John's College, Cambridge. In 1599 he was appointed amongst the first fellows of Sidney Sussex College, and was an associate of both Samuel Ward and William Bedell. In 1600 he moved to a tutorship in London, and in 1601 was appointed to the lectureship at Lincoln's Inn. He gained his BD in 1603, but declined to take his DD. In 1611 he was appointed rector of Rotherhithe, Surrey. He supported the reduced episcopacy advocated by Ussher, but served as a member of the Westminster Assembly. He sided with Bedell and Ussher rather than Ward on infant baptism, arguing that infant baptism did not give justification.[122] He had written a work against transubstantiation in 1624, though this work tells us more of what Gataker did not believe than what he did. Thus,

> ... since this *Corporall presence,* such as *the Church of Rome* maintaineth, hath no warrant from *Gods word*, as their owne *Cardinal* [Bellarmine] confesseth; and is besides contrary to *Scripture*, to *nature*, to *sight*, to *sense*, to *reason*, to *religion*, we have little *reason* to receive it, as *a truth of Christ, or a principle of Christianitie*, great *reason* to reject it, as *a figment of a mans braine*, yea as *a doctrine of the divell* [sic], invented to wrong *Christ* and *Christianitie*.[123]

The fraction proved this; although the bread is broken, Christ's corporal body was not broken.[124] Appealing to Augustine, Gataker asserted that signs are one thing, and what they signify is something else: 'But the *Bread* and *Wine* in the *Eucharist* are *Signes of Christs body and blood*, as hath beene before shewed, and the *Auncients* generally avow: And therefore are they not *essentially* either. They *signifie Christs body and blood*: and what they signifie they are not.'[125]

Sacraments, argued Gataker, are seals annexed to God's covenant, like the prince's seal, and are title to and interest in his passion.[126] The bread and wine are Christ's last will and testament.[127] Rejecting the accusation that his view makes the elements bare bread and wine, Gataker insisted that the elements are consecrated by the 'Story of the Institution', and that after consecration they are made symbolically and sacramentally Christ's body and blood.[128] Furthermore, Gataker did concede that the sacrament was in a sense a sacrifice:

> True it is that the *Fathers* tearme the *Lords Supper* oft *a Sacrifice*; (as we also in our *Liturgie*:) partly in regard of the *spirituall Sacrifice of praise* therein offred; and partly because it is a lively *representation and commemoration of Christs Sacrifice once offred on the Crosse;* (as their *Master of the Sentences* himselfe explaineth it;) and partly also because it succeedeth in the roome of the *Passover*, and those other *Sacrifices*, that in the old *Testament* were offred.[129]

However, insisted Gataker, there is no sacrifice separate from praise and representation in the sacrament.

Richard Vines   Richard Vines (1600?–1656), minister of St. Lawrence Jewry after his ejection from the Mastership of Pembroke College, Cambridge for opposing the abolition of the monarchy, preached a series of sermons on the Lord's Supper, which gave a fairly full exposition of the sacrament. For Vines sacraments are '*signacula, symbola,* seals and peldges, or instruments offering, exhibiting and making present to our faith the very benefits they signifie'.[130] They are 'conveying seals', but Vines denied that the elements are instruments in which the very virtue, or grace or benefit is conveyed.[131] Siding with Baxter, he stressed that they are not natural instruments, but moral and voluntary instruments.[132] Vines wrote: 'The middle way holden by the Churches of our Confession, is, That the outward Elements do represent as Signes and exhibit as Seales and morall Instruments to the faith of the receiver, the very Body and Blood of Christ sacrificed, as spirituall repast for our souls.'[133]

Vines listed five different views of eucharistic presence. The first was that Christ is present in the sacrament by efficacy and power to realise and exhibit virtue to and by the ordinance; there was the Lutheran view, the Roman Catholic view, and those who 'know not how'. All of these Vines rejected in favour of the fifth, that the bread and wine are sacramentally Christ's body and blood, or the memorials of them, symbolically representing and exhibiting Christ to believers. The first seems to be the position of Ward, Burges and Bedford.[134]

Richard Gove   Finally we may consider the teaching on the eucharist of Richard Gove (1587–1668). Gove was a graduate of Magdalen College, Oxford, and was incumbent of Hinton St. George in Somerset. He was not *persona grata* with the Westminster Assembly, since he was deprived of his living, and went to reside at East Coker. However, he then 'conformed' to the Assembly standards, and was made minister of St. David's Exeter. At the Restoration he returned to East Coker and became rector. Thus he appears as a sort of Vicar of Bray. His communicants' guide for children published in 1654 thus gives us some insight to catechising by one of those who held the middle ground. His work was divided into six sections.

The first section was a brief catechism, which began with asking which religion the pupil belonged to, and ended with questions on sacraments. Sacraments, together with faithful fervent prayer and the reading of the word are means by which God begins, continues and perfects grace in us.[135] Baptism assures us of the washing of our souls by Christ's blood, and the Lord's Supper is 'a sign, a seale, and pledge' that Christ was given for us and nourishes us and preserves us to eternal life.[136]

As befits such a manual, Gove next proceeded to consider the methods of worthy preparation, stressing that knowledge, faith, repentance, charity and a desire for Christ are necessary.[137] It was ordained by Christ as a thankful remembrance of his death and passion, to assure us of our interest in him, and as a pledge of our union with him and one another.[138] The outward actions are breaking, giving, taking, eating and drinking. The elements are sanctified by the words of institution and blessings by a lawful minister.[139] The inward is the body of Christ crucified and his blood shed for the remission of sins, 'exhibited by God to the faith of the worthy Receiver'.[140] The unworthy receive damnation.[141] To the queston of the gesture of the body, Gove kept an open answer, saying that no specific gesture is prescribed in Scripture, and that one must follow the rule of the Church under which we live, and thus leaves his own options open on whether sitting or kneeling should be followed. Yet, like most of his contemporaries, he stressed the action of the minister in not only sanctifying the elements, but also in breaking the bread and pouring out the wine: 'Hee is then to meditate, that the Body of Christ was as truely crucified, and his bloud shed for the Remission of sinnes, under the sense of Gods wrath due unto them: as hee doth now see the Bread in the Sacrament to be broken, and the wine to be poured out by the Minister.'[142] Christ is apprehended by the hand of faith.

In a third section of this work Gove considered 'Cases of Conscience', considering such things as fasting before communion, or if we have done some wrong to a neighbour, or frequency of reception. A fourth section considered excuses made for not receiving the sacrament. The fifth section was entitled 'Plaine Expressions of sacramentall Truths to Vulgar Capacities', and presents a simple theology of the eucharist. Gove asserted that the sacrament 'doth truely, and really exhibite to the worthy Receiver, the Body and Bloud of Christ, with all the benefits of his Death, and Passion'.[143] Gove explains in length using the analogy of the wax or ink on a parchment, where the power comes not from the material, but from the legal power and authority of the law-giver. Thus:

> So that when we receive this Sacrament after this manner, we may say. Here have I the Body, and Bloud of Christ my Saviour, here have I Remission of all my sinnes; and the Kingdome of Heaven passed over unto mee. And yet that bit of Bread, which I have eaten, hath not the Kingdome of Heaven lying in it, nor the Body of Christ moulded up in it, or converted into it; neither hath the Wine, which I have drunked, the Bloud of Christ within it, or is converted into it.[144]

The power comes from Jesus Christ who has decreed that the elements should be powerful and effectual. They become a seal or sign, and 'an exhibiting instrument of the Body and Bloud of Christ'.[145] Christ is the conduit of all grace, and spiritual good, and anyone who wishes to be filled with grace must come to Christ: 'His Ordinances, the Word, and Sacrament. They are the Cocks of this Conduite.'[146] In his final section, Gove discussed various ignorances touching the Supper, such as receiving infrequently.

Though Gove could describe the eucharist as an exhibiting instrument, he did not discuss the presence of Christ other than as grace coming through the elements as the cocks of the conduit. His view seems to be akin to that of symbolic parallelism merged with instrumentalism, and echoes the type of teaching of Ursinus rather than of Calvin.

An Exhortation to the ministers of the London Province   This work formed part of *A Vindication of the Presbyteriall-Government*, issued to the London Province and published on 2 November 1649. It was signed by George Walker, Moderator, and the two assessors, Arthur Jackson and Edmund Calamy. Though primarily a defence of a presbyterian polity, the Exhortation was addressed to all ministers, and gave an outline of 'sound' teaching, including a section on the Lord's Supper. Here communicants were urged to come with graces to the sacrament, and to labour to stir up gifts in others. The Supper is a love token from Christ, and 'an effectual means to keep his death in perpetual remembrance, that it might be a lively picture of Christ crucified'.[147] The elements of bread and wine are 'Representations, Commemorations, Obsignations, and Exhibitions of Jesus Christ'.[148] Every action has some meaning. When the bread and wine are consecrated, one must remember how Christ was set apart from all eternity to be the redeemer; when the minister breaks the bread, 'You must remember the great sufferings that Jesus Christ endured for Your sins.'[149] This is the bread of heaven, and gives a spiritual union with Christ. But the remembrance must not be just notional, doctrinal and historical, but practical, experimental and applicative.[150] Remembrance is essential if the communicant minister is to find power coming out of 'Christ Sacramental'. With the fraction in mind, the ministers wrote: 'Christ is presented in the sacrament as a *broken Christ*; his bodie broken, and his bloud poured out: And the very breaking of the bread understandingly looked upon, is a forcible argument to break your hearts.'[151]

The sacrament is a commemoration day of the great Benefactor, Jesus Christ.[152] The favourite expression in this document is 'Christ Sacramental'. However, the emphasis is upon mental and emotional remembrance so that the sacrament may be a spiritual food and cordial, a sealing ordinance, and a renewing of the covenant, and a spur to a 'godly' life.

A New Nonconformity: The Royalist Episcopal Divines

If 'International Calvinism' had triumphed as being the official theology as enshrined in the Westminster documents, that type of piety represented by the Durham House divines, or Laudian piety, also had its champions. On the whole these Royalist Episcopal divines refused to cooperate with the Parliamentary Church, and lived as private chaplains, in retirement, imprisonment or exile. Not all were 'Patristic Reformed churchmen', and even less, members of the Durham House circle – for example, Archbishop Ussher refused to cooperate with the non-episcopal Parliamentary Church, and thus counts as Royalist Episcopal, but he was certainly not of the Laudian piety. However, in their opposition to what they regarded as the unlawful usurping of the Church, many of the Royalist Episcopal divines tended to take a theological view which was distinct from those who they now regarded as their opponents. We may take Henry Hammond, John Bramhall, Jeremy Taylor and William Nicholson as representing the more Patristic Reformed spectrum of these divines.

Henry Hammond   Henry Hammond (1605–60) was a staunch defender of the episcopal polity (Figure 4.2). He was educated at Eton, and then Magdalen College, Oxford, where he was a fellow. He was nominated by Parliament to the Westminster Assembly, but never attended. He was given a canonry at Christ Church, Oxford, but after being ejected from his canonry in 1647, he lived in Westwood, Worcestershire. He ridiculed the *Directory*, calling it the 'No-Liturgy'.[153] His own teaching on the sacraments was set out in rather an obscure manner in an expansion of an earlier catechism, entitled *Large additions to the Practical Catechism* (1646). Sacraments were defined as holy rites or ceremonies, or signs and significative rites ordained by Christ himself. They are pledges to assure us, and 'as a means of conveyance, whereby he [Christ] is pleased in a peculiar manner to make over that grace or favour to us'.[154] However, he viewed sacraments as a type of mutual covenant, or a 'mutual confederation' between us and Christ.[155] Baptism signifies getting out of the power, guilt and punishment of sin. It 'secures to the Infant a *non-imputation* of *Adams*

Figure 4.2   Henry Hammond, 1605–60

transgression, seals unto him an assurance of God's not proceeding with him according to the strict *covenant* first made with man'.[156]

In other words, Hammond, like so many of his fellow divines, took for granted the concepts of the covenant of works and the covenant of grace. On the Lord's Supper, Hammond noted that it was not only a sign of the covenant, 'but a seal of it, and an exhibition of it, a real receiving me into the Covenant, and making me partaker of the benefits of it'.[157] Hammond viewed the presence of Christ in the Supper to be 'after a mystical and heavenly manner', and did not elaborate. However, he did believe that the eucharist had sacrificial echoes which were both manward and Godward. He could describe the Supper as a commemoration of the death of Christ, a representation of his passion to God, and the opportunity to offer sacrifices of supplications and praise in the name of the crucified Jesus.[158] The manward/Godward aspects were spelt out: 'That which respecteth or looks towards men, is a professing of our Faith in the death of Christ; that which looks towards God, is our pleading before him that sacrifice of his own Son, and through that humbly and with affiance requiring the benefits thereof, grace and pardon to be bestowed upon us.'[159]

John Bramhall   John Bramhall (1594–1663) was educated at Sidney Sussex, Cambridge, and was ordained in 1616. In 1633 he moved to Ireland as Archdeacon of Meath, and in 1634 became Bishop of Derry. He was a close friend of William Laud, and acted as Laud's clerical agent in Irish affairs. In 1642 he returned to England, and from 1644 lived on the Continent. He attacked the Solemn League and Covenant, but also defended the Church of England against Roman Catholic attacks. He also wrote against Thomas Hobbes, and attacked his view that sacraments were just signs or commemorations; for Bramhall they were also seals that confirm and convey grace.[160] In the period 1644–48, he wrote a defence of infant baptism in the context of those who die without baptism.[161] Here, like Featley, he asserted that there was a difference between the invincible necessity of baptism, and its wilful neglect.[162] Like so many of his contemporaries, he also distinguished between the exterior sacramental ablution, and the grace of the sacrament, which gave interior regeneration. Yet here we have an interesting twist which places him near Ward, Burgess and Bedford, as well as many of the Patristic Reformed churchmen: God is not tied to the sacraments in such a way that he cannot give grace without it, and thus Bramhall does not fret over those who died desiring baptism, or infants who die without it through no fault of their own. However, God does operate with the sacrament; whoever has the sacrament of ablution also has the grace of the sacrament. On the Supper, Bramhall wrote in the context of controversy with Rome, especially in defence of the validity of Anglican ordinations. He argued that transubstantiation is a late doctrine. The Church of England, he argued, held a doctrine of real presence, but was happy to rest with the words of Christ, without enquiring as to how this might be, and he remained reticent in attempting any further explanation.[163] But on the question of sacrifice, he shows himself at one with the Patristic Reformed divines:

We acknowledge an Eucharistical sacrifice of praise and thanksgiving; a commemorative Sacrifice, or a memorial of the Sacrifice of the Cross; a representative Sacrifice, or a representation of the Passion of Christ before the eyes of His heavely Father; an impetrative Sacrifice, or an impetration of the fruits and benefit of His Passion, by way of real prayer; and, lastly, an applicative Sacrifice, or an application of His merits unto our souls.[164]

Jeremy Taylor   Jeremy Taylor (1613–67) was a graduate and Fellow of Gonville and Caius College, Cambridge (Figure 4.3). In 1635, through the patronage of Laud, he moved to a fellowship at All Souls, Oxford. In 1638 he became rector of Uppingham, and in 1642 resigned to become a chaplain to the Royalist forces. He was imprisoned, and then on release in 1645, retired to Wales as a private tutor and chaplain to Lord Carberry at Golden Grove, and worked in close collaboration with William Nicholson. In this enforced leisure, Taylor produced a vast number of works. What is significant is that not only did he write on the theology of baptism and the Lord's Supper, but he also compiled a liturgy in which he articulated his theological views.

Taylor had caused some controversy amongst his fellow divines because of his views on original sin. Although he accepted that humans inherit original sin, he believed that what was lost by the fall was immortality.[165] On the question of

Figure 4.3   Jeremy Taylor, 1613–67

justification, he argued that it is because of the righteousness of Christ that the faith of the believer counts as justification. Faith is seen as a process – it is trust in God and repentance and a turning away from evil. Thus Taylor had no problem with the covenant language in association with baptism. In the *Great Exemplar* he wrote:

> For baptism is the beginning of the new life, and an admission of us into the evangelical covenant, which on our parts consists in a sincere and timely endeavour to glorify God by faith and obedience; and on God's part He will pardon what is past, assist us for the future, and not measure us by grains and scruples, or exact our duties by the measure of an angel, but by the span of a man's hand.[166]

For Taylor, final pardon and complete forgiveness are granted only upon our fulfilment of all the conditions of the covenant, that is, by the obedience of a holy life.[167]

These ideas were articulated in his rite of baptism. His opening exhortation expressed the hope that the child 'may all his life walk in this Covenant of grace and holiness' – the addition of holiness in terms of a process is significant. The prayer after the second exhortation prayed, 'let him … labour and hope for his promises.' The exhortation to the godparents explained, 'it is a Covenant of grace and favour on God's part and of faith and obedience on ours.' The prayer after the baptism asked 'that from his cradle to his grave he may be guided by the Spirit of God in the paths of the divine Commandments.' Faith and holy endeavour are thus held together in justification. The sacrament of baptism is thus not so much a seal of the covenant already made, but a seal of something begun and continuing. The sacrament becomes part of the process.

Like most divines, he defended infant baptism against those such as Tombes with appeal to the circumcision. In his rite Taylor explained that just as circumcision was a seal of the righteousness of faith, so baptism is now the seal of the same faith and the same righteousness, 'our Blessed saviour having made Baptisme as necessary in the New Testament as Circumcision in the Old'.

Taylor had a high view of episcopacy, and a high view of ministry, and like his 'conformist Calvinist' counterparts, rejected baptism by the laity.[168] This theological conviction came out strongly in the signing of the baptised, and in a prayer which sees baptism as part of the power of the keys entrusted to the ordained ministry:

> Our Blessed Lord and saviour Jesus who when he had overcome the sharpness of death did open the kingdom of heaven to all beleevers, and gave unto his Church the keyes of the kingdome, that his ministers might let into it all that come to him, he of his infinite goodness and truth, make good his gracious promises upon this infant, that what we doe on earth according to his will, he may confirme in heaven by his spirit and by his word, to the glory of the blessed and undivided Trinity, God the Father, Son, and Holy Ghost. Amen.

Linked to this rather lofty view of baptism was Taylor's concern that the water used in baptism should be sanctified. In the *Great Exemplar* he wrote: 'The holy Ghost descends upon the waters of baptism, and makes them prolifical, apt to produce children unto God: and therefore St. Leo compares the font of baptism to the womb of the blessed Virgin, when it was replenished with the holy Spirit.'[169] This finds expression in his rite. In the opening exhortation Taylor wrote: 'let us humbly and devoutly pray unto God in the name of our Lord Jesus Christ that he will be pleased to send down his holy Spirit upon these waters of Baptisme; that they may become to this infant [all that shall be washed in them] a laver of regeneration, and a well of water springing up to life eternal.'

Two prayers of blessing were included which were based on the Roman blessing of the font. The second contained the words, 'he blesse and sanctifie by his holy Spirit this water, that it may be instrumental and effective in grace, of pardon and sanctification.' Here, like Bedford, sacraments are instruments of the Spirit through which grace is given.

Taylor wrote at great length on the eucharist in *The Worthy Communicant* and *The Real Presence and Spiritual of Christ in the Blessed Sacrament*, and also devoted considerable space to it in *Clerus Domini* and the *Great Exemplar*. His main concerns seem to have centered on the subjects of eucharistic sacrifice, consecration and presence, and the fruits of communion.

In *Clerus Domini*, Taylor defined how the eucharist may be understood as a sacrifice:

> Now what Christ does always in a proper and most glorious manner, the ministers of the gospel also do in theirs: commemorating the sacrifice upon the cross, 'giving thanks', and celebrating a perpetual eucharist for it, and by 'declaring the death of Christ', and praying to God in the virtue of it, for all the members of the church, and all persons capable; it is *in genre orationis* a sacrifice, and an instrument of propitiation, as holy prayers are in their several proportions.[170]

His favourite terminology scattered throughout his writings is 'representing' or 'commemorating' the death and sacrifice of the cross. But the eucharist is a sacrifice because it is closely related to what Christ does in heaven before the Father. In *The Worthy Communicant* he wrote:

> He became infinitely gracious in the eyes of God, and was admitted to the celestial and eternal priesthood in heaven; where in virtue of the cross he intercedes for us, and represents an eternal sacrifice in the heavens on our behalf ... He hath commanded us to do on earth, that is, to represent His death, to commemorate this sacrifice, by humble prayer and thankful record ... the holy table being a copy of the celestial altar, and the eternal sacrifice of the lamb slain from the beginning of the world being always the same; it bleeds no more after the finishing of it on the cross; but is wonderfully repre- sented in heaven, and graciously represented here; by Christ's action there, by His commandment here.[171]

Henry McAdoo was surely correct when he said that for Taylor there is in the eucharistic action a parallelism which transcends time and space. The Church on earth re-presents to the Father his Son 'as sacrificed' and unites 'the offering' with that one perfect sacrifice which the Offerer himself re-presents and pleads in his heavenly intercession.[172]

In *Real Presence*, Taylor explained his understanding of this: 'This bread is the communication of Christ's body', that is, the exhibition and donation of it; not

Christ's body formally, but virtually and effectively; it makes us communicate with Christ's body in all the effects and benefits.'[173]

'Effectually' present is his favourite term, as is also 'a spiritual real manner', though the bread and wine remained bread and wine:

> The doctrine of the Church of England and generally of the protestants in this article, is, that after the minister of the holy mysteries hath ritely prayed, and blessed or consecrated the bread and wine, the symbols become changed into the body and blood of Christ, after a SACRAMENTAL, that is, in a SPIRITUAL, REAL manner; so that all that worthily communicate do by faith receive Christ really, effectually, to all the purposes of His passion ... The result of which doctrine is this: it is bread, and it is Christ's body: it is bread in substance, Christ in the sacrament; and Christ is as really given to all that are truly disposed, as the symbols are; each as they can; Christ as Christ can be given; the bread and wine as they can ... .[174]

In *Clerus Domini* he stated (as indeed had Calvin) that the Holy Spirit is the consecrator, though he also explained that the consecration or change takes place not in any one instant, but is a divine alteration consequent to the whole ministry – that is, the solemn prayer and invocation.[175]

How did Taylor articulate these concepts in liturgy? His communion rite drew heavily on the liturgy of St. James, with some material from St. Basil and also the *Prayer Book*. He used a *Proskomide* prayer of St. James, but where the Greek prayed for confidence to offer a fearful and unbloody sacrifice, Taylor rephrased it to become 'to represent a holy, venerable and unbloody sacrifice'. In another prayer, before the epistle, again borrowed from the *Proskomide*, where the original Greek requested that we may be made worthy to offer the gifts and sacrifices, Taylor asks that we may finish this service, 'presenting a holy Sacrifice holily unto thee, that thou maist receive it in Heaven, and smell a sweet Odor in the union of the eternal Sacrifice which our Lord perpetually offers'. His understanding of presence is best illustrated by the undertanding of consecration. The Prayer of Consecration begins with an epiklesis for God to send the Holy Spirit to

> bless and sanctifie these gifts.
> *That this Bread may become the Holy Body of Christ.*
> Amen.
> *And this Chalice may become the life-giving Blood of Christ.*
> Amen.

Taylor continued: 'That it may become unto us all that partake of it this day, a Blessed instrument of Union with Christ, of pardon and peace, of health and blessing, of holiness and life Eternal, through Jesus Christ our Lord. *Amen.*'

William Nicholson   William Nicholson (1591–1672) had become rector of Llandilo Vawr in Carmarthenshire in 1629, and then canon of St. David's and archdeacon of Brecknock. He was named to the Westminster Assembly, but never attended, and his posts were sequestered. He taught as a schoolmaster at Newton Hall, with Jeremy Taylor. He would become Bishop of Gloucester at the Restoration. His catechism was published in 1655, and was quite popular.

Sacraments, according to Nicholson, present, exhibit, and seal our redemption.[176] But they are also 'the means instrumental, and ordinary seals' through which God conveys to us the merits of Christ.[177] They are the conditional means by which God imparts grace, not because of any supernatural quality they have, but because God is the Author of the sacraments, and here Nicholson cited with approval a passage from Richard Hooker.[178] The catechism contained a discussion of the meaning of the word 'sacrament' in ancient Latin classical literature, as well as consideration of the matter, essential form and efficient cause of the Christian sacraments. What sacraments do is to represent and set before our eyes under corporal and visible elements what Christ has accomplished for us.[179] They convey grace to the faithful, for they are *'canales gratiae*, "the conduit-pipe of grace"'.[180] Yet at the same time Nicholson asserted that it is faith which is the instrument of grace. Though he used the term 'seals of the covenant', when he treated baptism his emphasis in the Catechism was on remission of sins. He defended the use of sprinkling over dipping as the method, noting that sprinkling or pouring is more symbolic of the sprinkling of Christ's blood for us.[181] Through baptism we are reborn and are made children of grace.[182]

In his section on the Lord's Supper, Nicholson again cited Hooker in support of the view that the manner of the presence of Christ in the sacrament was not crucial. After outlining the various opinions on the presence, he concluded: 'We then believe Christ to be present in the Eucharist divinely after a special manner, spiritually in the hearts of the communicants, sacramentally or relatively in the elements.'[183] Referring back to some possible definitions, he continued: 'And this presence of His is real, in the two former acceptions of real; but not in the last, for He is truly and effectually there present, though not corporally, bodily, casually, locally.'[184]

When answering the question of how this might be, Nicholson spoke of the will and power of Christ, who ordained the elements to be instruments. Thus: 'They remain in substance what they were; but in relation to Him are more. It is spiritual bread and spiritual wine, so called, not so much because spiritually received, but because being so received, it causes us to receive the Spirit, "and by the power of the Spirit a man may be enabled to do all things".'[185]

On eucharistic sacrifice, Nicholson is more concerned with its manward dimension of sacrifice, and shows little interest in the ideas expressed by Bramhall. In words reminiscent of many of the 'godly' divines, Nicholson wrote:

> For here we have Christ crucified before our eyes, represented lively before us as upon the cross: while as the signs of His blessed Body and Blood being sundered the one of them from the other, the one is broken and the other poured out; remembering us how His sacred body was broken with the crown of thorns, the scourges, the nails, the spear; how out of His wounded hands, feet, head, and side, there issued a stream of blood. This He intended by His institution that we should first remember.[186]

This could aptly sum up the fraction and libation that so many of the 'godly' were concerned with. For Nicholson, the merit, force, and virtue of Christ's sacrifice are imparted in the sacrament.[187] Neither on the question of presence nor eucharistic sacrifice does Nicholson show the interests of the Patristic Reformed divines, and certainly on the question of presence, for all his definitions, remains obscure. Perhaps it was for this reason that Dugmore classed him as a Central Churchman.[188]

Summary

In the period when the Church of England was locked in battle over church polity, and was partially reshaped to conform more to the Scottish polity, we find a considerable amount of time and effort also expended on sacramental issues, both theological and liturgical. Though many divines, English and Scottish, presbyterian and episcopalian, united against the views of John Tombes on baptism, they displayed a continued diversity and difference over the relationship of the sacraments to the covenant, justification and grace. The *Westminster Directory* gave expression to what became the dominant stream of conformist Calvinist/presbyterian Anglican belief, and abolished those ceremonies and practices judged contentious by those of tender conscience. The sacramental rites were crafted to harmonise with the other Westminster documents of faith – the *lex orandi* reflected the *lex credendi*. But we also find the views of the Durham House circle or Laudian piety taken further, with a concern that baptism does actually do something, and also a concern that the eucharist has a sacrificial dimension about it. The liturgical freedom of the *Directory* to allow other forms, except the *Book of Common Prayer*, gave Taylor the latitude to experiment with Eastern liturgical material, but with his own nuanced translations allowing the rite to reflect his *lex credendi*. Judith Maltby and, in a different context, Peter White, are probably correct that the unsung majority were content for the continuance of the Prayer Book, or at least, as it was perceived to have been used in the days of James I.[189] Thus Mary Pope, writing in 1647, claimed that for the poor the *Prayer Book* 'was their daily spiritual food, that they feed upon; and in regard of the customs of it, they had gotten it by heart most of it, and found great comfort by it.'[190] Lionel Gatford, in 1654, asserted that 'the Book of *Common-Prayer*, and administration of the Sacraments formerly established and used here in *England* is absolutely the best Form and freest from all just exceptions in all essentiall points and practices of Religion, that ever yet saw light in the Christian world.'[191] However, many of the theologically articulate elite clearly found it an inadequate expression for seventeenth-century sacramental theology, whether that theology was nonconformist/conformist Calvinist, or Patristic Reformed.

Notes

1   See Stevenson, 1997, Study III 'The Early Covenanters and the Federal Union of Britain'.
2   Baillie, 1841–2, vol.2, p.90.
3   *A Declaration of the Commons in Parliament made Septemb.9.1641*, London, 1641, sig.A2v. See Cressy, 2000, p.208.
4   The position of bishops remained ambiguous until around 1645.

5   Marshall, 1644.
6   'Debate on Infant Baptism, 1643' in *Transactions of the Baptist Historical Society*, 1(1908–10), pp.237–45.
7   Webster, 1994.
8   Marshall, 1644, p.26.
9   Baillie, 1646.
10 Featley, 1645, p.50.
11 Ibid., p.40.
12 Tombes, 1646b.
13 Ibid., p.8.
14 Ibid., p.29/30.
15 Ibid., p.33.
16 Ibid., p.155.
17 Tombes, 1646a, p.152.
18 Holmes, 1646, pp.30, 137.
19 Geree, 1646, p.6.
20 Ibid., p.40.
21 Marshall, 1646.
22 Ibid., p.117–18.
23 Ibid., p.118.
24 Baxter, 1651, no pagination in the introduction.
25 Ibid., p.222.
26 Ibid., p.295.
27 Ibid., p.297.
28 Ibid.
29 Ibid., p.298.
30 Ibid., p.326.
31 Ibid., p.301.
32 Ibid., p.316.
33 Ibid., p.109.
34 Blake, 1644; 1645; 1646; 1653; 1655. *Moderate Answer to Two Questions*, 1645 is attributed to Blake, but E.Brooks Holifield argues on theological grounds that T.B. refers to Thomas Bedford, Holifield, 1974, appendix.
35 Blake, 1644, p.13.
36 Blake, 1655, p.8.
37 Ibid., p.36.
38 Ibid., p.327.
39 Ibid., p.333.
40 Ibid., p.352.
41 Ibid., p.66.
42 Ibid., p288.
43 Ibid., p.354.
44 Ibid., p.356.
45 Ibid., p.357.
46 Ibid., pp.374, 410.
47 Ibid., p.410.
48 Ibid., p.96ff.
49 Ibid., p.171.
50 Ibid., p.98.
51 Marshall's main contribution to the *Directory* was the section on preaching. See Spinks, 1995a, pp.91–111.

52   Firth and Rait, 1911, vol.1.pp.755–757.
53   John Morrill, 'The church in England 1642–9', 1982; Spurr, 1991; Maltby, 1998.
54   Hutton, 1985, p.143.
55   Seaver, 1970, p.277; Evelyn, 1959, p.358.
56   Evelyn, 1958, pp.383–4.
57   Westminster Assembly Manuscript Minutes, vol. 2, p.492.
58   Gillespie, 1649, Chapter XVII, p.212.
59   Ibid., p.217.
60   Ibid., pp.227, 223.
61   Ibid., p.228.
62   Bonar, 1850, Letter LXVIII, p.122.
63   Ibid., Letter CLXXIV, p.260.
64   See Coffey, 1997. I gratefully recall conversations on covenant theology with John
     Coffey at the Chapel and Senior Common Room of Churchill College, Cambridge.
65   Rutherford, *The Soume of Christian Religion*, in Mitchell, 1886, p.218.
66   Ibid., p.219.
67   Rutherford, 1644, p.212.
68   Rutherford, *The Soume*, in Mitchell, 1886, p.219.
69   Bonar, 1877, Reprint James A. Dickson, 1986, Sermon 4, p.73.
70   Ibid., Sermon 12, p.279.
71   Rutherford, 1644, p.211.
72   Ibid., p.212.
73   Ibid., p.213.
74   Ibid., p.217.
75   Rutherford, *The Soume*, in Mitchell, 1886, p.221.
76   Rutherford, 1644, pp.214, 215.
77   Ibid., pp.215–16.
78   Rutherford, 1655, pp.73ff.
79   Rutherford, 1644, p.214.
80   Rutherford, *The Soume*, in Mitchell, 1886, p.223.
81   Coffey, 1997, p.87.
82   Spalding, 1830, p.291.
83   Ibid., p.320.
84   Ibid., p.291.
85   Ibid., p.302.
86   Henderson, 1641, p.18.
87   Ibid.
88   Ibid., pp.19–20.
89   Ibid., p.20.
90   Ibid., pp.21–4.
91   Martin, 1867, p.109.
92   Ibid., p.113.
93   Palmer, 1645.
94   Ibid., p.39.
95   Ibid., p.40.
96   Ibid., p.41.
97   Ibid., p.42.
98   Ibid., p.43.
99   Ibid., pp.45–7.
100 Westminster Assembly Manuscript Minutes, vol.2, p.244; Lightfoot, London 1824,
     vol.13, p.297.

101   Lightfoot, Minutes, 1824, vol. 13, p.297.
102   Gillespie, 1846, p.89.
103   Breward, 1980, p.19. See also Baillie, 1959.
104   Ibid.
105   Westminster Assembly Manuscript Minutes 2, pp.255–62.
106   Ibid., 2, p.481.
107   Gillespie, 1846, p.91; Lightfoot, 1824, vol.13, p.326.
108   Baillie, 1959, pp.vi, 29–31 for details.
109   Westminster Assembly Manuscript Minutes 2, p.263.
110   Lightfoot, 1824, p.288.
111   Westminster Assembly Manuscript Minutes 2, pp.103–4; Vines, 1657, p.86.
112   Spinks, 1984a, pp.44–6.
113   Lightfoot, 1824, pp.288–9.
114   Leishman, 1901, p.164.
115   Ibid.
116   Text in *Westminster Confession of Faith*, 1990; Larger Catechism, pp.127ff, Shorter Catechism, pp.285ff.
117   Tuckney, 'A briefe and pithy catechisme', 1628; the manuscript is in poor condition at present. I am grateful to Dr Windeatt, the Librarian, for allowing me access to it.
118   Hoyle, 1641, p.187.
119   Ibid., p.192.
120   Ibid., p.3.
121   Ibid., pp.181–2.
122   Gataker, 1698. This contains Ward's arguments followed by Gataker's rejoinders.
123   Gataker, 1624, p.33.
124   Ibid., p.26.
125   Ibid., p.17.
126   Ibid., pp.21–2.
127   Ibid., p.6.
128   Ibid., pp.13–14.
129   Ibid., pp.112–13.
130   Vines, 1657, p.50.
131   Ibid., p.51, 53.
132   Ibid., p.50.
133   Ibid., p.124.
134   Ibid., pp.110–11.
135   Gove, 1654, p.4.
136   Ibid.
137   Ibid., p.7.
138   Ibid., p.8.
139   Ibid., p.9.
140   Ibid.
141   Ibid., pp.11–12.
142   Ibid., p.14.
143   Ibid., p.43.
144   Ibid., pp.45–6.
145   Ibid., p.48.
146   Ibid., p.61.
147   *A Vindication*, 1650 edition, p.102. My thanks to Professor Iain Torrance for drawing my attention to this in his father's edition.
148   Ibid., p.103.

149 Ibid., p.103.
150 Ibid., p.104.
151 Ibid.
152 Ibid., p.105.
153 Hammond, 1684, vol.1, p.393.
154 Ibid., vol.1, p.114.
155 Ibid., vol.1, p.129.
156 Ibid., *Works* vol.1, p.495.
157 Ibid., vol.1, p.126.
158 Ibid., p.125.
159 Ibid., p.129.
160 *The catching of Leviathan* in Bramhall, 1842–5, vol.4, p.533.
161 *A Short Discourse to Sir Henry De Vic, of Persons Dying without Baptism*, in Bramhall, 1842–5, vol.5.
162 Ibid., p.172.
163 *An Answer to M. De. Millitiere*, in Bramhall, 1842–5, vol.1, p.22.
164 *A Replication to the Bishop of Chalcedon*, in Bramhall, 1842–5, vol.2, p.276; cf. vol.1, p.55.
165 Taylor, 1847–52, vol.7, p.320.
166 Ibid., vol.2, p.237.
167 Allison, 1966, p.75.
168 Taylor, 1847–52, vol.1, p.24.
169 Ibid., vol.2, p.240.
170 Ibid., vol.1, p.33.
171 Ibid., vol.8, pp.37–8.
172 McAdoo, 1988, p.65.
173 Taylor, 1847–52, vol.6, p.53.
174 Ibid., pp.13–14.
175 Ibid., vol.1, pp.48–9.
176 Nicholson, 1842, p.150.
177 Ibid., p.151.
178 Ibid., p.152.
179 Ibid., p.155.
180 Ibid., p.156.
181 Ibid., p.158.
182 Ibid., p.162.
183 Ibid., p.179.
184 Ibid.
185 Ibid., p.188.
186 Ibid., p.176.
187 Ibid., p.188.
188 Dugmore, 1942, p.97.
189 Maltby, 1998; White, 1993, pp.211–30.
190 Pope, 1647, B2. Epistle Dedicatory.
191 Gatford, 1654.

Chapter 5

Kingdoms and Churches Apart:
The Restoration

The Path to the English 1662 *Book of Common Prayer*

South of the border, encouraged by the promise in the Declaration of Breda in 1659 to grant liberty to tender consciences, some of the presbyterian Anglicans presented the monarch-elect with an address and proposals for such liberty, asking him not to restore the *Book of Common Prayer* without modification as regards ceremonies. Charles's reply in *His Majesty's Declaration to all his loving subjects of his kingdom of England and dominion of Wales, concerning ecclesiastical affairs'* was to declare the hitherto outlawed liturgy to be 'the best we have seen',[1] but promised to 'appoint an equal number of learned divines of both persuasions, to review the same, and to make such alterations as shall be thought most necessary'; in the meantime, Charles would still allow a wide latitude on ceremonies. On 25 March 1661, a Royal Warrant set up a commission to review and deliberate on liturgical reform – the Savoy Conference. The Warrant ran for four months. The first meeting took place on 15 April, and deliberations came to an end on 25 July, without much agreement. The Convocation of that November had the task of the official process of revision, and over a period of twenty-two days the text was agreed which was to be, technically at least, the sole lawful liturgy of the Church of England until the 1960s.[2]

The Warrant of March 1661 had appointed twelve divines on each side to deliberate, and each was supported by nine coadjutors. The episcopal Anglican twelve were all bishops, and though these included Archbishop Accepted Frewen of York, it was Gilbert Sheldon, Bishop of London, who presided. Amongst the bishops who recorded their views either on liturgy or sacraments were John Cosin of Durham, George Morley of Worcester, Robert Sanderson of Lincoln, and John Gauden of Exeter. Amongst their coadjutors, Anthony Sparrow had written on the *Prayer Book* liturgy, and Herbert Thorndike wrote on baptism and the eucharist. Notable on the presbyterian Anglican side were Edward Reynolds, newly consecrated Bishop of Norwich, and Richard Baxter, who declined the see of Hereford.

Studies in Comparative Liturgy and the Theology of the Royalist Episcopal Divines

In theory, both the Savoy and the Convocation divines were in a far better position for undertaking liturgical revision than had been their predecessors. We have already observed that divines such as Jeremy Taylor drew on ancient liturgical sources. The seventeenth century witnesses to the interest in collections of liturgical texts, and of a rudimentary comparative liturgy. Cornelius Burges was known for his collection of editions of the *Book of Common Prayer*, and displayed an intricate knowledge of the changes made from 1549 onwards. However, his use of this tended to be mainly concerned with the minutiae of phraseology. For example, he objected to the statement in the baptismal rite that infants 'receive remission of their sins by spiritual regeneration'. He argued that both these are conveyed and sealed in baptism, seminally at least, but remission of sins is not received by spiritual regeneration, but by the blood of Christ.[3] Here a seventeenth-century Reformed doctrinal hermeneutic was applied to the sixteenth-century liturgical text. Both George Gillespie and Robert Baillie also knew the various editions of the Prayer Book; each examined the text to see where it was too close to the Roman Catholic source.[4] Henry Hammond showed his knowledge of Reformed and early liturgy in order to argue that the Westminster *Directory* was not founded on objections to the liturgy of the Church of England, but objections to all and any liturgies.[5]

Hammon L'Estrange   Of particular interest in this area was the work of Hammon L'Estrange, in his *Alliance of Divine Offices*. L'Estrange was a layman, and had at one stage of his life been a keen supporter of strict observance of the Sabbath. However, he was an independent thinker, and in this work had set out the texts of the various *Books of Common Prayer* in parallel, and discussed the texts in relation to the Eastern liturgies of St. Basil, St. John Chrysostom and St. James, as well as the Western sources.[6]

On baptism, L'Estrange noted that it has been given many names, and he gave considerable discussion to the word *sacramentum*. For him, baptism is 'the initiation, the first admission into the gospel-covenant', and a bipartite covenant at that.[7] However, for L'Estrange, this was made for infants by godparents, and had to do with the renunciation of evil, and here he cited Tertullian and Cyprian, together with Gregory the Great.[8] He defended the use of the sign of the cross, and noted that anointings and white vesture had ancient origins.

The Lord's Supper was treated in two sections. For L'Estrange, the 'eucharistic sacrifice' has a fourfold dimension. First we offer the elements, with some left over for charitable use; then 'the consecration of the elements, and presenting them up to God by the prayers of the minister and congregation, whereby they become that Sacrament for which they are set apart and deputed'.[9] Third, praises and prayers are offered to God; and finally, the oblation of ourselves as per Romans 12:1.[10] On the subject of consecration, he wrote: 'Consecration of the elements was made indeed with thanksgiving, not by it; by blessing it was performed, by blessing joined with thanksgiving in one continued form of prayer, or by blessing concomitant with thanksgiving in two distinct forms.'[11]

Of eucharistic presence, which consecration effected, L'Estrange said:

A sacramental verity of Christ's body and blood there cannot be, without the commemoration of His death and passion, because Christ never promised His mysterious (yet real) presence, but in reference to such commemoration. Nor can there be a true commemoration without the body and blood exhibited and participated; because Christ gave not those visible elements, but His body and blood to make that spiritual representation.[12]

He defended kneeling for reception as a ceremony which can be used with edification, noting that sitting was as open to idolatry as any other posture.[13]

Two members of the episcopal team were exponents of this type of basic comparative liturgy – John Cosin and Anthony Sparrow.

John Cosin   John Cosin (1594–1672), now bishop of Durham, was a survivor from Neile's Durham House group of the 1620s, and a proponent of Laudian piety. From 1615, Cosin had been in the employment of John Overall as his librarian, and his first set of notes on the *Prayer Book* may well have been a reworking of Overall's work. After Overall's death in 1619, Cosin became chaplain to Neile. He had been appointed a prebend of Durham in 1624, and there had quickly made enemies of another prebend, Peter Smart, over the ceremonial which he introduced, and the elaborate music of the Cathedral services.[14] He had succeeded Matthew Wren as Master of Peterhouse Cambridge, the chapel of which had been furnished by Wren in full Laudian style. Cosin was later made Dean of Peterborough, but in 1640 his old enemy Peter Smart brought a case against him before the Long Parliament. He went into exile with the Royal Household in France. Cosin continued to reflect upon the liturgical forms of the *Book of Common Prayer*, and he wrote a treatise on eucharistic doctrine. Kenneth Stevenson has rightly observed that 'Cosin's contribution covers many areas: how the liturgy is celebrated, how the devotional life relates to it, how the existing service-book could be changed, as well as how the doctrine of the eucharist should be understood.'[15] His views, as might be predicted, place him amongst the Patristic Reformed churchmen.

Cosin's knowledge of pre-Reformation liturgy had already come to fruition in his *Devotions* of 1627. This was based on the Primers or Books of Hours, and caused consternation amongst the 'godly' who saw it as a throwback to popish monasticism.[16] In that book he included private devotions for the eucharist. In a metrical version of part of Thomas Aquinas' eucharistic hymn, *Lauda Sion*, Cosin wrote:

> True living and life-giving Bread
> Is now to be exhibited

and,

> Christians are by Faith assured
> That by Faith Christ is received
> Flesh and blood most precious.[17]

Another prayer speaks of prayers and supplications, and the remembrance of Christ's passion 'which we now offer up unto thee', in language reminiscent of the canon of the 1549 *Book of Common Prayer*.[18] But what was his understanding of such devotional and liturgical language?

Whether Cosin reworked Overall's notes and made them his own, or whether they are, afterall, his own independent views, we already find in the notes of 1619 a pronounced interest not only in the changes in the succesive prayer books, but also in the concepts of eucharistic sacrifice and presence. This interest was maintained in the Second Series of Notes, and in his work *Historia Transubstantiationis Papalis* (1656), though Cuming noted a change in the view of presence to a more protestant one.[19] All these works display his considerable knowledge of the Fathers, of the Reformation Confessions, and of the classical and Reformation liturgical texts. Cosin rejected transubstantiaion as a recent invention, and maintained a real presence which must 'be understood in a sacramental and mystic sense'.[20] He asserted that the Church of England and all protestants,

> ... know and acknowledge that in the sacrament, by virtue of the words and blessing of Christ, the condition, use, and office, of the bread is wholly changed; that is, of common and ordinary, it becomes our mystical and sacramental food; whereby, as they affirm and believe, the true Body of Christ is not only shadowed and figured, but also given indeed, and by worthy communicants truly received.[21]

He preferred a healthy agnosticism on the manner of presence:

> As to the manner of the presence of the Body and Blood of our Lord in the blessed sacrament, we that are protestant and reformed according to the ancient Catholic Church, do not search into the manner of it with perplexing inquiries; but, after the example of the primitive and purest Church of Christ, we leave it to the power and wisdom of our Lord, yielding a full and unfeigned assent to His words.[22]

But in his 1656 work, he also insisted that the presence was only to the communicants.[23] He defended kneeling for reception as a fitting means to 'testify and express the inward reverence and devotion of our souls towards our blessed Saviour'.[24] However, he was more concerned with the concept of sacrifice, and could speak of Christ's sacrifice 'there represented and commemorated'.[25] He attached considerable importance to the 'prayer of Oblation', and wanted it restored to its 1549 position. Commenting on its text, Cosin wrote: 'the virtue of this sacrifice (which is here in this prayer of oblation commemorated and represented) doth not only extend itself to the living, and those that are present, but likewise to them that are absent, and them that be already departed, or shall in time to come live and die in the faith of Christ.'[26]

Thus the sacrifice is both eucharistical and propitiatory.[27] Cuming aptly notes that Cosin uses the word 'represented' without ever discussing its meaning, observing that there is a slight haziness in his terminology which is only partly concealed by the confidence with which he used it.[28] Cosin wrote little on baptism, other than noting the importance of the renunciation of the devil, and that although the nature and substance of the water remain, it is changed and made the sacrament of regeneration because it is consecrated water.[29]

At some stage, probably in the winter of 1660–61, Cosin seems to have drawn up his own suggestion for revision, entered into a 1619 edition of the *Prayer Book*, and known as the 'Durham Book'.[30] He seems to have drawn upon two documents or drafts he had made at earlier dates, as well as the 1637 Scottish Book, and the *Advices* of Bishop Matthew Wren. Wren (1585–1667), when Bishop of Norwich, had been impeached, and imprisoned in the Tower from 1641 to 1660; with considerable time on his hands, he had written notes for a mild revision of the *Prayer Book*.[31] Amongst his many suggestions was the need for directions for taking the elements and breaking the bread and pouring out the wine.[32] It seems that Cosin had access to this manuscript. The 'Durham Book' itself proposed incorporating the 1637 petition for consecration – 'by ye power of thy holy Word and Spirit vouchsafe so to blesse & sanctifie these thy Gifts & Creatures of Bread & Wine', directions for manual acts in the narrative of institution, and for the prayer of oblation to follow on from the consecration. A suggested phraseology for blessing the water at baptism had been entered and then crossed out.[33]

Anthony Sparrow Anthony Sparrow (1612–85) had been a fellow of Queens', Cambridge, and had been expelled in 1644 for refusing to take the covenant. Now, at the Restoration, he was appointed Archdeacon of Sudbury, and would succeed Reynolds as Bishop of Norwich on the latter's death in 1676. In 1657, Sparrow published *A Rationale upon the Book of Common Prayer of the Church of England*, which was an attempt to show that the *Prayer Book* rites were neither Romish, nor new-fangled. The work took the form of a detailed explanation and justification of rite and ceremony. He cited Chrysostom and Cyril of Jerusalem in support of the use of the Words of Institution for consecration, with added support from Ambrose and Augustine.[34] He defended kneeling for reception as an act of reverence, and advised that any consecrated remains should be 'spent with fear and reverence by the communicants in the Church'.[35] In baptism, he noted that consecration of water was not essential, and although he did not expound a covenant theology, he nevertheless speaks of the priest exacting of the infant 'covenants, contracts, and agreements'.[36] He also gave a vigorous defence of private baptism, with the declaration: 'Nor can I see what can be reasonably objected against this tender and motherly love of the Church to her children.'[37]

Robert Sanderson Robert Sanderson (1587–1663) had managed to survive as a parish minister through the Interregnum, thanks to the admiration he was held in by parishioners.[38] He had at first tried to use the *Book of Common Prayer* without alteration, but some neighbouring ministers began to complain. He therefore used a modified form, learning parts by heart so as to give the impression he was not reading from a book. In his sermons he frequently picked up on the idea of sacrament as an oath, and referred to the signing of the cross in baptism with the words 'manfully to fight under his banner, against sin, the world, and the devil, and continue His faithful soldiers unto our lives end'.[39] Baptism annuls original sin, involves renunciation of the world with its pomps, lusts and vanities, whereby we become members of Christ and are enlightened.[40] For infants who die before the age of reason, baptism saves, since it has sufficient sacramental grace, and God may use extraordinary means to infuse grace.[41] He objected to midwives baptising, and he defended the signing with the cross in baptism.[42] Sanderson, however, was quite prepared to use the term 'covenant' for baptism.[43] It is interesting that in his modified baptismal rite, like Taylor, he introduced this terminology. The opening exhortation describes baptism as 'a Sacrament, ordained by Christ as a seal and pledge of the Covenant of Grace in the New Testament', and that the child may be baptised by water and the Holy Spirit and 'received into the Covenant of Grace'.[44] This may have been a concession to the *Westminster Directory*. Added to the *Prayer Book* prayer immediately prior to the baptism is the request that the candi-

date may remain amongst the number of 'Thy faithful and elect children'.[45] No
mention is made of signing with the cross, and the formula is altered from that of
the *Prayer Book*, though the military imagery of which he seemed fond was
retained.

Sanderson's Office of the Communion begins with an instruction, again being a
nod towards the *Directory*, but otherwise did not depart significantly from the
phraseology of the *Prayer Book* rite.

John Gauden   John Gauden (1605–62) was a graduate of St. John's College,
Cambridge, taking his MA around 1625. He then switched to Oxford, becoming a
commoner at Wadham, and gaining his BD in 1635, and his DD in 1641. He was
one of the Deans of Bocking, a Royal Peculiar, and vicar of Chippenham. He had
openly used the *Book of Common Prayer* for longer than most other loyalists, and
had ghost written *Eikon Basilike*, which promoted Charles I as a martyr king.
However, Gauden had espoused the moderate episcopalian system advocated by
Archbishop Ussher, and tried to steer a compromise during the Interregnum years,
and on account of this was mistrusted by many of his fellow Royalist Episcopa-
lians. Reading the signs of the times, he had attempted to improve his image by
writing a life of Hooker and publishing the unfinished, or unpublished, books of the
Lawes. Much against the wish of Sheldon, he had been made Bishop of Exeter.

In his *Considerations Touching the Liturgy of the Church of England* (1661),
Gauden defended the integrity of the Anglican *Prayer Book* rites, arguing that a set
liturgy defended true doctrine, advanced unity, and was helpful to simpler Christians. He justified the principle of infant baptism on the grounds that all Reformed
agree to 'joyning the Water and Spirit together, and calling *Baptisme the laver of
Regeneration, Tit.3.5.* without *limitations* to any; as *Circumcision* was the seal of
Gods covenant to all the children of *Israel*'.[46] In baptism, original sin is removed,
because regeneration is imputed to the infant, 'when duly consecrated by the Word
and Prayer applyed to the *element*, by an *autoritative* and ordained Minister, and no
hinderance or obstruction to the grace offered and conferred on the Subject fitted
for it'.[47] Gauden argued that passive regeneration by grace is sufficient for removal
of original sin, but after actual sin, it must have active work of regeneration, which
is to 'performe the Evangelical Conditions of actual faith and Repentance'.[48] Like
Burges and Bedford, he could speak of a 'seminal principle' of grace, and reasoned: 'That first little spark & degree of grace, baptismal as fire, will serve to take
tinder which is *dry*, & apt to kindle, but it will not take or continue in grosser
materials, nor on the same tinder, if it be grown more *damp* and *wet*.'[49] Baptismal
grace, asserted Gauden, rests on infants as a Christian honour, and a mark of God's
love and favour.[50] He suggested that the Church of England baptismal rite needed
no change.

In his work, *The Whole Duty of a Communicant*, Gauden defined a sacrament
as a holy seal 'annexed to the Word'.[51] The supper was a renewal of the covenant,
and its object was our mystical union with, and incorporation into Christ.[52] It is 'a
continual Memorial, and Seal of the Covenant of Grace'.[53] Gauden insisted that
in the sacrament there was 'a real and most effectual perception *of the Body and
Blood of Christ*'.[54] Christ has given the elements 'a Sacramental Virtue, and a
supernatural Efficacy'.[55] The sacramental elements are: 'Signs and Seals really

conveying to the believing and prepared soul, by the concurrent Spirit and Power of the Institutor Jesus Christ, that which in their Nature they do fitly represent.'[56] Amusing is Gauden's complaint of irreverence amongst those using the *Directory*:

> I knew one Minister, (and he no small one in the *vulgar esteem*,) would add to his delivery of the elements, such most uncharitable sarcasms as these; *Here, Darest thou take it! To another Take this and love Christ's Ministers better*, so to a *third, Here'take it and leave your lying*; to a *fourth, Take heed the Devil enter not into thee*, and the like: Good God, are these fit decoys of mens *private passions* and *fancies*, to win *Common-people* to the Sacraments ... .[57]

George Morley   George Morley (1597–1684) was educated at Westminster School, and Christ Church, Oxford. Ejected from his living in 1648, he moved to the Continent, and ministered to other exiles, particularly in the Brussels area. In a treatise published in Brussels, he defended private baptism and sick communion. Like Gauden he defined sacraments as 'seals annexed unto the Word'.[58] According to Morley, baptism with water and use of the trinitarian formula *'is all which is essential or absolutely necessary* to Baptism, *or to make the Child so Baptiz'd, partaker of the inward spiritual Grace, signified and exhibited by the Sacrament'*.[59]

Although he wrote against transubstantiation, Morley tended to attack the doctrine on grounds of logic, in that the change did violence to all principles of nature, sense and reason. He did not set out any alternative doctrine, other than to assert a spiritual presence.[60]

Herbert Thorndike   Finally, on the Royalist Episcopal side, we may consider Herbert Thorndike who was one of the coadjutors. Thorndike (1598–1672) was a graduate of Trinity College, Cambridge, becoming a Fellow of the college, and Deputy Orator of the University. He took parochial posts first at Claybrooke, Leicestershire, and then at Barley, near Cambridge. He continued as Bursar of Trinity, and University Lecturer in Hebrew. In 1641, he had written in defence of episcopacy, and it was perhaps inevitable that he should be deprived of his living in 1643, and his fellowship in 1646. He also wrote in defence of ordered worship and a liturgy, and a defence of the Church of England in three books. His breadth of learning was considerable, and he bombarded his opponents with Hebrew, patristic texts, and liturgical texts from antiquity. His style is sometimes obtuse, not unlike John Forbes of Corse, and thus his own views are often indistinguishable from the sources he is citing.

It is clear that for Thorndike the sacraments are not static signs, but rites in which God does something. Though writing a whole book entitled 'of the Covenant of Grace', of which baptism is the condition, covenant theology was not his main defence of infant baptism.[61] Rather, he notes against anabaptists the fact that it is a divine institution which precedes the resurrection of Christ:

> If then our Anabaptists can shew us a new Gospel, to assure us of the gift of the Holy Ghost without baptism, then may they take upon them to assure us of the kingdom of heaven without it. But if the kingdom of heaven depend upon the new birth of the Holy Ghost, and there be no possible means to assure any man of this new birth without the

sacrament of baptism; either infants must be baptized before they go out of the world, or go out of the world without that assurance.[62]

Thorndike grounded infant baptism first of all in the context of original sin. Baptism saves and justifies. Though he appeals to the covenant of Abraham and circumcision, he is more concerned, like the *Book of Common Prayer*, to see infant baptism grounded in the blessing of children in Matthew 19:15.[63] He defended lay baptism in cases of necessity, since 'though it be not necessary, that all infants be baptized, because they are infants; yet will it be necessary, that they be baptized before they go out of the world: and, therefore, while they are infants, rather than they should go out of the world unbaptized.'[64] Thorndike argued that we cannot know if God gives grace to those who die unbaptised, but we can say what benefit baptism is to those who are baptised, which includes regeneration, remission of sins, and the habitual assistance of God's Spirit.[65]

When discussing the eucharist, Thorndike was particularly concerned to discuss the presence of Christ in the sacrament, and the concept of eucharistic sacrifice. He rejected any change of substance in the elements – 'the bodily substance of bread and wine is not abolished nor ceaseth in this sacrament by virtue of the consecration of it.'[66] He speaks of a presence 'mystically and spiritually and sacramentally'.[67] He argued for an approach on analogy with the *communicatio idiomatum* of the two natures of Christ:

> And what shall we then say, when the name of Christ's Body and Blood is attributed to the bread and wine of the eucharist, but that God would have us understand a supernatural conjunction and union between the Body and Blood of Christ and the said bread and wine, whereby they become as truly the instrument of conveying God's Spirit to them who receive as they ought, as the same Spirit was always in His natural Body and Blood?[68]

Thus Thorndike referred to a change 'consisting in the assistance of the Holy Ghost, Which makes the elements, in which It dwells, the Body and Blood of Christ; it is not necessary, that we acknowledge the bodily substance of them to be any way abolished.'[69] This is not incompatible with the petition found in the order of the Lord's Supper in the *Directory* – in fact, it has more support there than in the *Book of Common Prayer*. However, as it becomes apparent elsewhere, Thorndike here had in mind the epiklesis of the Eastern eucharistic prayers, and references to the work of the Spirit in the fathers.[70] Consecration or blessing is by thanksgiving. In a summary of classical anaphoras, he wrote:

> Many are the liturgies (that is, the forms of celebrating the eucharist) in the eastern Churches under Constantinople, Alexandria, and Antiochia, yet extant, which shew the substance of it – (after the deacon had said, 'Lift up your hearts, ' the people answering, 'We lift them up to the Lord'; which evidently pointeth out that which St. Paul calls the 'thanksgiving' or 'blessing', wherein the consecration of the sacrament consisteth, beginning there and ending with the Lord's prayer, in all of them) – to be this: – repeating the creation of all things and the fall of man, to praise God, that He left him not helpless, but called first the fathers, then gave the Law, and when it appeared that all this would not serve to reclaim him to God, sent His only Son to redeem him by His cross, Who instituted this remembrance of it; pray God, therefore, for all this, but especially for the

death and resurrection of Christ; and praying, that the Spirit promised may come upon the elements presently set forth, and make them the Body and Blood of Christ; that they, who receive them with living faith may be filled with the grace of it.[71]

Yet Thorndike refused to be drawn on the exact nature of the change:

But if a man demands further, how I understand the Body and Blood of Christ to be present 'in', or 'with', or 'under', the elements, when I say, they are 'in', and 'with', and 'under', them, as 'in', and 'with', and 'under', a sacrament mystically; I conceive I am excused of any further answer, and am not obliged to declare the manner of that which must be mystical, when I have said what I can say to declare it.[72]

For Thorndike, the presence meant that there was also a sacrificial dimension to the eucharist. It was a commemorative and representative sacrifice, rather like the peace offering of the Old Testament.[73] Thus, he wrote:

... the elements so consecrate are truly the sacrifice of Christ upon the cross, inasmuch as the Body and Blood of Christ crucified are contained in them, not as in a bare sign, which a man may take up at his pleasure, but as in the means by which God hath promised His Spirit; but not properly the sacrifice of Christ upon the cross, because that is a thing that consists in action and motion and succession, and therefore, once done, can never be done again, because it is a contradiction that that which is done should never be undone. It is therefore enough, that the eucharist is the sacrifice of Christ upon the cross, as the sacrifice of Christ upon the cross is represented, renewed, revived, and restored by it, and as every representation is said to be the same thing with that which it representeth; taking 'representing' here, not for barely signifying, but for tendering and exhibiting thereby that which it signifieth.[74]

The presence and representation of the sacrifice together mean that at this 'evangelical banquet' the covenant of grace is renewed.[75]

Presbyterian Anglicans

Edward Reynolds   The only bishop representing the presbyterian Anglican party was Edward Reynolds who had accepted the see of Norwich (Figure 5.1). Educated at Merton College, Oxford, Reynolds (1599–1676) had gained his BA in 1618, and became a Fellow in 1619. He had been a Royal chaplain, vicar of All Saints, Northampton, and preacher at Lincoln's Inn. He was nominated to the Westminster Assembly, and took his seat. From 1645–1662 he was Vicar of St. Lawrence Jewry, London and in 1660 was appointed warden of Merton, and canon of Worcester prior to accepting Norwich. He was acknowledged for his breadth of learning. His views on the eucharist had been set forth in 1638 in his *Meditations on the Holy Sacrament of the Lord's Last Supper*. What is remarkable about these meditations or brief theological treatises is the influence of Richard Hooker on Reynolds, both in approach and understanding. Thus the meditations began with God's freedom, and considered the laws of creation which direct us to God. God gives a covenant and promise and these require a seal or confirmation. Confirmation is given to the soul by the Spirit, and the word preached, and by seal, 'visibly exhibited to the eye, and taste'.[76] The nature of a sacrament is 'to be the representative of a substance,

Figure 5.1   Edward Reynolds, 1599–1676

the signe of a covenant, the seale of a purchase, the figure of a body, the witnesse of our faith, the earnest of our hope, the presence of things distant, the sight of things absent, the taste of things unconceivable, and the knowledge of things, that are past knowledge'.[77]

Like Hooker, Reynolds saw a close analogy between the incarnation and sacramental union: 'Certainly as the Sonne of God did admirably humble himselfe in his *hypostaticall union* unto a visible flesh, so doth he still with equall wonder and lowlinesse humble himselfe in a *sacramentall union* unto visible Elements.[78]

Though Reynolds spoke of sacraments as seals 'to obsignate unto the senses the infallible truth' of the covenants,[79] like Samuel Ward, he seems to have felt that obsignation on its own was inadequate. Thus he could say that the principal end of the Lord's Supper 'is to bee an instrument fitted unto the measure of our present estate for the exhibition or conveyance of Christ with the benefits of his Passion unto the faithfull Soule'.[80] Elsewhere he spoke of the promise being the efficient cause, and the sacrament being the instrumental cause of union with Christ.[81] Like Hooker, this seems to be his main emphasis, and he speaks of 'a *reall* though *mysticall union*',[82] and 'a mysticall and spirituall union'.[83] Reynolds thus wrote:

> ... but as the Author of those mysteries was holy by a fulnesse of grace, the elements holy by his blessing, the tyme holy by his ordination, and the place holy by his presence; so let us by the receiving of them bee transformed as it were into their nature, and bee

holy by that union unto Christ, of which they are as well the instrumentall meanes whereby it is increased, as the seales and pledges whereby it is confirm'd.[84]

On the subject of presence, Reynolds taught 'in this Sacrament wee doe most willingly acknowledge a *Reall*, *True*, and *Perfect Presence* of Christ, not *in*, *with*, or *under* the *Elements* considered absolutely in themselves, but with that relative habitude and respect which they have unto the immediate use whereunto they are consecrated.'[85] Quoting Hooker, Reynolds rejected transubstantiation, and outlined four views of 'divine presence'. He endorsed the fourth, explaining: 'it is a *spirituall Presence, of energie, power, and concomitancy* with the Elements, by which Christ doth appoint that *by* and *with* these mysteries, though not *in* or *from* them, his sacred Body should bee conveyed into the faithfull Soule.'[86]

Reynolds could say that the Supper is the 'mysticall Sacrifice of the Gospel', and that the passion is 'typically and sacramentally shadowed and exhibited in the Bread broken, and the wine powred out';[87] the elements are 'pledges of our Salvation, that wee might at this spirituall Altar see Christ as it were crucified before our eyes, clinge unto his Crosse, and graspe it in our armes, sucke in his Blood, and with it salvation.'[88] Yet in contrast with Cosin and Thorndike, the concept of sacrifice is not one which seems to have interested him; as with Hooker, mystical union was his main focus.

In his work on the Supper, baptism is only mentioned in passing. He distinguished between the union by the grace of the covenant 'effectively', and union by the grace of baptism 'instrumentally', which together unite us to Christ.[89] Baptism is a personal right, which seals and ratifies the covenant.[90] Though not writing on baptism himself, Reynolds did, however, endorse a little work on infant baptism by his close friend, Simon Ford. Ford (1619–99) had been a student at Magdalen Hall, Oxford and was expelled for strong puritan leanings, but restored by the Parliamentary visitation in 1647. He was made a BD in 1649, and DD in 1665, having conformed at the Restoration. When vicar of St. Lawrence, Reading, he had written to defend infant baptism in 1654 and 1656, during the Protectorate when Baptists and Independents were given equal freedom with the presbyterian Anglicans. In 1657 he published a short catechism, which Reynolds commended. In this work Ford taught that because of the covenant, infants had a right and title to baptism even before birth, and that baptism promised the first grace which makes a new heart and works faith and repentance.[91] Though the views of Ford cannot be pressed absolutely on Reynolds, they seem to accord with the brief views expressed in the *Meditations*.

Richard Baxter The Royalist Episcopal bishops at the Savoy Conference declared that they were quite happy with the previous *Book of Common Prayer*, and thus put the onus on the presbyterian Anglicans of demonstrating what was wrong. This was a brilliant tactic by the former, and quite disastrous for the latter, since, like the Millenary Petitioners and the authors of *A Survey*, they had to list each item or phrase, which gave the appearance of being wholly negative and trivial. Entitled *Exceptions against the Book of Common Prayer*, these were divided into General and Particular complaints with detailed amendments. With regard to baptism the 'airy' sign of the cross should go, and more said about solemn covenanting and

Figure 5.2   Richard Baxter, 1615–91

obligations of baptism.[92] Parents should be addressed rather than godparents; the reference to sanctifying the Jordan and all other waters, in the Prayer Book version of Luther's flood prayer, was a doubtful statement; parents should answer in their own name, and not on behalf of the infant; like Burges, they requested a rephrasing of the words 'receive remission of sins by spiritual regeneration', and it was not in conscience possible to assert that 'it hath pleased thee to regenerate this infant by thy Holy Spirit.' Last, there should not be private baptism, unless by an ordained minister and in the presence of a competent number.[93] Here the issues of Hampton Court and the Five Articles of Perth resurfaced.

On the Lord's Supper, the *Exceptions* stated that kneeling for reception should not be compulsory, and in addition to objections to certain collects and rubrics, requested that in the prayer 'We do not presume', there should be theological symmetry between soul/body, body/blood; that the manner of consecrating of the elements be more explicit, together with rubrics directing a fraction; that the words of delivery should be as near to Scripture as possible, and that the Black Rubric explaining kneeling be restored.[94]

However, the *Declaration* had spoken of an alternative form in scriptural phrase, and if the Royalist Episcopal party wished to ignore this, the presbyterian Anglicans did not. A Reformed Liturgy was drawn up, and this was mainly the work of Richard Baxter, whose views defending infant baptism have been considered previously (Figure 5.2). But what of his wider views on baptism, and his views on the eucharist? And how far was his theology reflected in his Reformed Liturgy?

Baxter had apparently read William Ames and had been convinced by his arguments of the unlawfulness of the sign of the cross in the Prayer Book rite of baptism.[95] By the mid-1640s, he had already accepted the Amyraldian view of grace and 'hypothetical universalism'.[96] Baxter taught that in Adam himself the first sin was actual, and thence followed the 'habitual pravity'; Adam's sin is imputed to us through Adam and our parents. However, Baxter differentiated between degrees of sin, and was much more interested in actual sin than original sin.[97] Though Baxter certainly sees baptism linked with justification and forgiveness of sin, it is for him much more a seal of the covenant. In his *Christian Ecclesiastics*, he described the covenant as follows: 'The Christian covenant is a contract between God and man, through the mediation of Jesus Christ, for the return and reconciliation of sinners unto God, and their justification, adoption, sanctification, and glorification by him, to his glory.'[98]

In *The Catechising of Families* Baxter wrote:

Q.7. What is it that God doth as a covenanter with the baptised?
A. You must well understand that two covenanting acts of God are presupposed to baptism, as done before.
I. The first is God's covenant with Jesus Christ, as our Redeemer, by consent, in which God requireth of him the work of man's redemption as on his part, by perfect holiness, righteousness, satisfactory suffering, and the rest: and promiseth him, as a reward, to be Lord of all, and the saving and glorifying of the church, with his own perpetual glory.
II. A promise and conditional covenant, or law of grace, made to lost mankind by the Father and the Son, that whoever truly believeth, that is, becometh a true Christian, shall be saved.
    Now baptism is the bringing of this conditional promise, upon man's consent to be an actual mutual covenant.[99]

This defines how Baxter understood 'covenant of grace' and 'baptismal covenant' as they occur in his liturgy.

Baxter's rite was based upon his own development or interpretation of the Westminster *Directory* rite which he used at Kidderminster.[100] In previous discussion of Baxter, we have noted that infants qualified only if a parent was a believer – not any ancestor. Thus it is little surprise to find that his opening rubric defined which parents qualified for their infant to be baptised. The opening exhortation mentioned the inherited sin of Adam, but that through Christ 'God hath made and offered to the world a covenant of grace.'[101] The covenant is with the Trinity, and results in the washing of original sin. But faith and dedication on the part of the parent(s) is necessary. After confession of faith, renunciation, and promises of duties, a prayer follows, in which comes the statement 'We dedicate and offer this child to thee, to be received into thy covenant and church.' The baptism follows, and then an adaptation of the military formula of the signing (but of course without the sign of the cross) which is now addressed to the congregation, that the child has been received by Christ's appointment into the Church, and solemnly entered into the holy covenant. A prayer asks that the infant may perform the covenant, and finally there is a solemn charge to the parents, and also one to the congregation.

Baxter's eucharistic theology had a trinitarian base, and revolved around the concepts of consecration, commemoration, and communication. It is set out succinctly in a work entitled *A Saint or a Brute:*

> We have here communion with the blessed Trinity, in the three parts of this eucharistical sacrament! As the Father is both our Creator and the offended majesty, and yet he hath sent his Son to be our Redeemer; so in the first part which is the CONSECRATION, we present to our Creator the creatures of bread and wine, acknowledging that from him we receive them and all, and we desire that upon our dedication, by his acceptance they may be made sacramentally and representatively the body and blood of Jesus Christ.
>
> In the second part of the eucharist, which is the COMMEMORATION of the sacrifice offered on the cross, we break and pour forth the wine, to represent the breaking of Christ's body, and shedding of his blood for the sin of man; and we beseech the Father to be reconciled to us on his Son's account, and to accept us in his beloved, and to accept all our sacrifices through him. So that as Christ now in heaven is representing his sacrifice to the Father, which he once offered on the cross for sin, so must the minister of Christ represent and plead to the Father the same sacrifice by way of comemoration, and such intercession as belongeth to his office.
>
> The third part of the eucharist is to OFFER and PARTICIPATION; in which the minister representing Christ, doth by commission deliver his body and blood to the penitent, hungry, believing soul: and with Christ is delivered a sealed pardon of all sin, and a sealed gift of life eternal. All which are received by the true believer.[102]

What is significant here is that although Baxter speaks of consecration,[103] unlike Reynolds, his main preoccupation is not with presence, but with the eucharistic actions and its relation to the one sacrifice of Christ. In this he stands closer to Thorndike, Cosin and Taylor. The eucharist is a commemoration and a representation of the sacrifice. Elsewhere Baxter said:

> The commemoration chiefly (but not only) respecteth God the Son. For he hath ordained, that these consecrated representations should in their manner and measure, supply the room of his bodily presence, while his body is in heaven: and that thus, as it were, in effigy, in representation, he might be still crucified before the church's eyes; and they might be affected, as if they had seen him on the cross. And that by faith and prayer, they might, as it were, offer him up to God; that is, might shew the Father that sacrifice, once made for sin, in which they trust, and for which it is that they expect all the acceptance of their persons with God, and hope for audience when they beg for mercy, and offer up prayer or praise to him.[104]

In this passage Baxter, like Hammond, could speak of the eucharistic celebration as being a pleading of the sacrifice of Christ.

Like his baptismal rite, the Lord's Supper of the Reformed Liturgy seems to be derived from Baxter's interpretation and use of the *Directory*. In his opening explication he could not resist giving a summary of his doctrinal beliefs. The eucharist was instituted 'to be a continued representation and remembrance of his death'. Consecration makes the bread and wine 'sacramentally, or representatively, the body and blood of Christ'; the breaking and the pouring 'represent and commemorate the sacrifice of Christ's body and blood upon the cross once offered up to God for sin'. In his opening exhortation, where according to Travis Du Priest we have 'doctrine without concern for art', [105] Baxter could write: 'see here Christ dying in this holy representation! Behold the sacrificed Lamb of God, that taketh away the sins of the world! It is his will to be thus frequently crucified before our eyes ... Receive now a crucified Christ here represented.'

In addition to these statements, Baxter set out his theology by giving his rite a threefold action. Although he allowed for a shorter form with a single prayer, his ideal was a prayer accompanying each of the actions of consecration, comemoration and communication.

Consecration has a prayer to the Father, with the institution narrative. In the consecration prayer Baxter prayed: 'Sanctify these thy creatures of bread and wine, which according to thy institution and command, we set apart to this holy use, that they may be sacramentally the body and blood of thy son Jesus Christ. Amen.'

The commemoration is achieved by a prayer to Christ, with fraction and libation. The prayer asks Christ through his sacrifice and intercession to reconcile us to the Father. The bread is broken with the words, 'the body of Christ was broken for us, and offered once for all to sanctify us: behold the sacrificed Lamb of God, that taketh away the sins of the world.' And the wine: 'we were redeemed with the precious blood of Christ, as of a Lamb without blemish and without spot.' Here is the pleading of the sacrifice and its representation set out in liturgical action.

Thirdly, the communion is introduced with a prayer to the Holy Spirit, with the words of delivery. Verbose it was, and too full of explication, which, according to Du Priest, instructs the mind, but fails to capture the heart; but it was also highly creative.[106]

A Liturgy With Little Change

The Savoy Conference ended without agreement, and its results were akin to those of Hampton Court. The task of liturgical reform, rubric and text passed to the Convocation which resumed in November. That tale has been told and retold in considerable detail, and no more than a summary is needed here.[107] The key players at this juncture were Cosin, Sanderson, Wren, together with George Morley and William Nicholson, Bishop of Gloucester, with Reynolds and Gauden also making a contribution. But the Cavalier Parliament made it clear that it was content with the previous *Book of Common Prayer*, and Gilbert Sheldon was more concerned with polity than with sacramental theology and liturgical compilation. Baxter's forms were never seriously considered; the Durham Book proposals had been laboriously collated by William Sancroft into the Fair Copy, and he also copied the final proposals into the Convocation Book. Though there were a total of some six hundred changes from the previous book, and Reynolds and Sanderson would compose additional new material, little change was made in the sacramental rites. In baptism, provision was made for the blessing of the water in the prayer immediately prior to the act of baptism – 'sanctifie this Water to the mysticall washing away of sin.' In the Lord's Supper, a rubric directed the place for taking the bread and wine; manual acts were restored to the prayer with the institution narrative, now entitled 'The Prayer of Consecration', and a fraction of sorts incorporated within the manual acts. Provision was made for consecrating additional bread and wine, and any remaining consecrated elements were to be veiled, and then consumed; finally the Black Rubric was restored, though in place of the repudiation of any 'reall and essential presence' of the 1552 version, that of 1661/2 was to repudiate a 'corporal' presence. The sign of the cross in baptism, the provision for private baptism, and kneeling for reception remained. Colin Buchanan is correct to note that the rubrical changes now gave the communion rite two high points – consecration and reception.[108] But William Sancroft's marginal note on the place of the Prayer of Oblation spoke for all partries who sought major change: 'My LL. The BB. At Elie house Orderes all in the old Method'.[109] John Evelyn was to record in his diary for 17 August 1662:

> Being the *Sonday* when the Common-prayer-booke reformed, was ordered to be used for the future, was appointed to be read: & the *Solemn League & Covenant* to be abjured by all Incumbents of England, under penalties of loosing their Livings &c: our *Viccar*, accordingly read it this morning, and then preachd an excellent Sermon on I *Pet*: 2.13. pressing the necessity of obedience to *Christian Magistrates*, & especialy *Kings*:There were strong Guards in the Citty this day, apprehending some Tumult, many of the *Presbyterian* Ministers, not conforming.[110]

Scotland and the Westminster Standards

After the execution of Charles I, the Scots had hailed Charles Stuart as Charles II in 1649, and after he had taken both the National Covenant and the Solemn League and Covenant, he had been duly enthroned at Scone in January 1651. The need to defend the new King with an army had caused a rift in the Kirk between the Resolutionists who supported this, and the Protesters who did not. But in the event, the Scottish army was decisively defeated at Worcester, and the Rump Parliament in 1652 pressed the Tender of Union, bringing English law to Scotland. Not until 1660 was Charles II able to exert authority in his Northern Kingdom. The Act Recissory and the Act Concerning Religion and the Church Government in theory restored the *Book of Common Order* and the Scots Confession as standards, as well as the Five Articles of Perth.[111] In practice, the restoration of episcopacy was such a delicate issue that no liturgical or ceremonial restorations were forced.[112] The more extreme Covenanters had found the objections of the English Independents to set liturgies attractive, and in practice most ministers used forms based on the *Westminster Directory*, though some used the *Book of Common Prayer* as a resource. In baptism, the *Directory* form was frequently supplemented with the creed, and the custom of godparents continued. According to Gilbert Burnet, Archbishop Robert Leighton laboured 'to bring the worship of that church out of their extempore methods into more order; and so to prepare them for a more regular way of worship, which he thought was of much more importance than a form of government'– but in vain.[113] In many places, the Lord's Supper became infrequent. Duncan McCulloch of Glenurquhart passed his whole ministry there without a single celebration of the Supper.[114] Archbishop Leighton's short catechism alludes to the sacraments being visible seals to confirm faith and convey the grace of it, but as befitted a short catechism, gave little of theological depth.[115] The *Westminster Confession* and Catechisms remained in use as a theological norm – illustrating that these represented a distillation of seventeenth-century English-speaking 'International Calvinism'. They also represent an irony in that the Church of Scotland adopted forms authored in the most part by Church of England divines.

David Dickson   Perhaps more representative of many Scottish ministers were the views set forth by David Dickson (1583–1663). Dickson had opposed the Five Articles of Perth, and disliked episcopacy, and in 1637 had been chosen to represent the Covenanters in the initial moves towards the National Covenant. He held chairs of theology at Glasgow and then Edinburgh until his ejection at the Restoration. Echoing Alexander Henderson, Dickson taught that 'It is usuall for Scripture, speaking of Sacramentes, to give the name of the thing signified, to the Signe; because the Signe is the memoriall of the thing signified'.[116] In his work *The summe of Saving knowledge*, Dickson wrote that 'By the *Sacraments* God will have the Covenant sealed for confirming the bargain on the foresaid condition.'[117] The condition referred back to election and the covenant. The covenant was given full treatment in his work *Therapeutica Sacra*, which is concerned with regeneration. Dickson had espoused the triple covenantal scheme – a covenant of redemption between the Father and the Son in addition to the covenants with humanity, the covenant of works and the covenant of grace. In that considerably lengthy work, baptism is mentioned only briefly in passing, when Dickson emphasised that baptism is the sealing of the engagement only, and not of the good things covenanted.[118] This is because for Dickson, baptism may be an expression of election, but does not itself elect and justify. This is explained further in his work *Truths Victory over Error*. This takes the form of questions, which are actually formulated as theological positions, to which an answer is given, either yes or no. If no, then Dickson gives a longer explanation of the reasons, based on scriptural texts. Thus he defined sacraments as holy signs and seals of the covenant of grace, which put a visible difference between those who belong to the Church and those who do not.[119] Grace which is indeed exhibited in or by the sacraments is not conferred by any power in them, because – and this is quite important – faith is the only instrumental cause of justification.[120] Here then, Dickson allows the term 'exhibiting', but not instrumental as regards the sacraments. Sacraments 'are but' signs and seals.[121] To the question '*Are Grace and Salvation so inseparably annexed unto Baptism, as that no person can be regenerated, or saved without it?*', he gives a resounding 'No'.[122] The reason, as shown in the *Therapeutica Sacra*, is that not all baptised are regenerated, because this has to do with election and faith. He also rejected the right of laity and women to administer sacraments, asserting that 'it is unlawful for any man, to affix the Kings seal to a charter, or Letters-patent, unless he be a person authorized, and deputed by the King for that use.'[123] He attacked anabaptism using the covenant argument, yet he also attacked Quakers on the grounds that baptism was mandated.

In his commentary on Matthew, Dickson defended the practice of sitting at the table: '...the Sacrament began, as *They were eating*, that is, sitting still at table, and the Supper not closed ... the first Supper ... is our pattern ... It is requisite also, that the Minister of the Gospel and his flock, so many of them as may communicate together at one Table at once, be assembled together, and joyntly sit down together... .'[124] He rejected any concept of offering or sacrifice, and any change in the elements. There is a spiritual presence, which, Dickson insisted, 'is a true and real presence; because, it comes and flowes from true and real causes, namely from *Faith*, and the *Holy Spirit*.'[125] Christ is spiritually present to the faith of believers.[126] Thus it can be seen that Dickson and those of like mind would have no truck with blessing water or asking for its sanctification, nor would they wish for any idea of offering, or operation of the Spirit on the elements, as suggested by the texts of 1637. According to Dickson, the broken bread 'doth signifie, exhibit and seal up by Christs appointment'.[127] The words 'This bread is Christ's body' are not to be understood physically or miraculously, but judicially – truly and really in divine law.[128] The elements are instruments of security:

> So this bread by Divine Ordinance, doth signifie, exhibit, and confirme the Beleevers right and title unto Christs body, as suffering for the beleevers redemption, more certainly and surely, then if Christs body suffering were physically imbraced by him in his armes, if it were possible: and therefore, as the instrumental elements of civill infeoffment, in the termes of humane ordinance, and institution, are rightly called by the name of the lands disponed, so the sacramentall element of bread is rightly called *Christs body*, disponed in the termes of Divine Ordinance and institution, which appointeth hereby right to be given unto us unto Christs body, as suffering for our redemption.[129]

The Cup reminds us that there is a covenant of redemption made between the Father and the Son whereby Christ was to shed his blood for us.[130] Indeed, 'As Moses celebrated the Passover, in assurance, that the Destroying Angell should not touch the People of Israell, so may everie Believer bee certified, by using the Sacrament: That the Grace promised and sealed in the Sacrament, shall bee bestowed.'[131] The sacramental wine is a sign and pledge of our spiritual and new communion in life and joy in the Kingdom of Heaven.[132]

Robert Craghead   Similar teaching on the Lord's Supper was taught by Robert Craghead, a Scottish minister in Ireland. His devotional manual was published in Edinburgh in 1695, and though after the Restoration era, reflects the theology of the immediate prior decades. Most of the work was concerned with the right disposition and preparation for the sacrament, but the initial chapter gave a brief summation of a more doctrinal nature. According to Craghead, Christ instituted the sacrament as a memorial of his love, 'requiring this his death to be shewed forth until he come again, and allowing his people such Communion with himselfe in this Ordinance, as shal be to them a Seal for their eternal Enjoyment of him, when he cometh again to receive them to himselfe'.[133] Craghead attached considerable significance to the Cup of 1 Cor 10:16, which he regarded as signifying wine, as Christ's blood shed for our redemption, spiritual benefits and communion one with another. Practically no attention was given to the question of presence *vis-à-vis* the elements. Rather, Craghead was concerned with the visible breaking of bread and pouring of wine: 'The breaking of Christs precious Body being thereby signified, Christ requireth this discerning of his Body, *broken saying, this is my body which is broken for you,* 1 Cor.11:24: and the breaking of the bread must be Sacramentally, and publickly performed in sight of the Communicants, for their instruction, as in the first Celebration.'[134]

The sincere believer, in eating the bread according to Christ's institution, will receive Christ: 'If we do not believe, that he really died, then we can have no

Communion of his Body and Blood.'[135] Craghead was at great pains in the rest of his work to discuss exactly what the believer needed to believe, as this affected one's worthiness to receive: 'The transaction betwixt Christ, and partakers of the Lords Supper, is of the greatest importance for a mans soul, for either he shal be guilty of the Body and Blood of the Lord, by unworthy receiving, or be blessed with the Seal of God for his eternal happiness; if he truly receive Christ: Therefore, previous examination is most necessary.'[136]

The Supper is one of the seals of the covenant, and if we are to receive Christ in the sacrament, we must embrace him according to the terms of the covenant.[137] Christ is to be discerned spiritually and believingly.[138] Yet elsewhere Craghead implied that in the Supper we set a seal as a ratification and confirmation of our 'Interest' in Christ.[139] But although Craghead's views, like Dickson's, hover close to a symbolic memorialism, he clearly highly valued the Lord's Supper, and stressed the union between the believer and Christ in the sacrament.[140]

John Blackader Though there was no further liturgical provision beyond the *Westminster Directory*, those who refused to accept episcopacy and renounce the covenant were also likely to trust more in the Holy Spirit than a directory for worship. One die-hard Covenanter was John Blackader, who recorded in his diary accounts of illicit gatherings for the Lord's Supper, around Tieviotdale and East Nisbet in the 1670s, but continuing the practice of the earlier decades of the century. At East Nisbet the multitude 'sat in the Haugh, the Communion Tables set in the midst, and a Large greater multitude on the face of the brae from the bottom to the Top'.[141] Blackader continued:

> This Ordinance of preaching & Administration of his Last Supper, that Love Tocken Left for a memorial of him till his coming again, was so signally Countenanced, backed with power, and refreshing Influences from heaven, that It might be said Thou O God dist send out a plentifull rain whereby thou confirmed thine Inheritance when it was weary. The Table of the Lord was covered avowedly in the open fields in presence of the raging Enemies ... .[142]

Here we find echoes of Psalm 23 applied to the open-air communion. Blackader made reference to solemn thanksgiving and cheerful thanksgiving – as types of prayer offered by certain ministers at this large gathering: 'At this occasion there was two Long Tables [with seats on every side of each Table, and a Shorter Table] at the head, as use to be: At every Table was supposed to sit about 100 persons. Fifteen or 16 Tables in all were served that Day.'[143] At the communion at Irongray, 'There were 2 Long Tables, Longer than at East Nisbet, and more communicants, all the rest of the ministers exhorted to several Tables.'[144] Sitting was the posture for reception; and though a liturgical structure remained, the rite was entirely bereft of a standard liturgical form of prayer. With the abolition of episcopacy in Scotland in 1689, the Scottish ceremonies differed from those in England even more than had been the case in 1603.

Summary

The Restoration broke asunder the brief union of the Church of England and that of Scotland. On the whole, the English liturgists and theologians were ignored, and the 1662 *Book of Common Prayer*, even though altered from that of 1604, represented little change, and left the Church of England with a mid-sixteenth century liturgy, the language of the sacramental rites of which was quite out of tune with most seventeenth-century divinity. Scotland was forced once more to adopt episcopacy, but there was so much opposition to this institution that no attempt was made to reintroduce any liturgy. In the minds of many Scottish divines, episcopacy, ceremonies and liturgy were synonymous, and all should be resisted and removed. In this atmosphere there seems to have been little new theological discourse on sacraments. In England, the theologians and scholars were ignored in the interests of, or under the guise of, seeking a compromise; in Scotland the whole atmosphere was too delicate for such matters to be contemplated. The two churches continued to grow apart, in polity, in liturgy, and in ceremonial.

Notes

1   Cardwell, 1841, p.294.
2   Cuming, 1969, pp.159ff.
3   Burges, 1660, p.30.
4   Gillespie, 1641.
5   Hammond, 1684, vol.1.
6   L'Estrange, 1846; for a full discussion, Marshall, 1993.
7   L'Estrange, 1846, p.361.
8   Ibid., pp.363–4.
9   Ibid., p.271
10 Ibid.
11 Ibid., p.307.
12 Ibid., pp.323–4.
13 Ibid., p.323.
14 See the essays in Johnson, 1997.
15 Stevenson, 1994, p.97.
16 Spinks, 2000.
17 Cosin, 1681, p.262.
18 Ibid., p.265.
19 Cuming, essay on Cosin, 1983.
20 Cosin, 1843–55, vol.4, p.156.
21 Ibid., vol.4, p.172.
22 Ibid., vol.4, p.156.
23 Ibid., vol.4, p.174.
24 Ibid., vol.5, p.345.
25 Ibid., vol.4, p.281; cf.279.
26 Ibid., vol.5, p.352.
27 Ibid., vol.5, p.120.
28 Cuming, 1983, p.134.
29 Cosin, 1843–55, vol.1, p.129; vol.5, p.483.

30   Cuming, 1961.
31   Jacobson, 1874.
32   Ibid., pp.81–2.
33   Cuming, 1983, p.196.
34   Sparrow, 1839 edition, pp.217–9.
35   Ibid., p.225.
36   Ibid., p.233.
37   Ibid., p.242.
38   See Lake, 1988b.
39   Sanderson, 1854, vol.1, Sermon 2 (1632), pp.37–8; Sermon 3 (1633), p.75; Sermon 4 (1636), p.110; vol.3, Sermon 7 (1632), p.314.
40   Ibid. vol.1, Sermon 7, p.186; Sermon 15, p.378; Sermon 15, p.382.
41   Ibid., vol.5, Pax Ecclesiae, p.269.
42   Ibid., vol.3, Sermon 4 (1621) p.141; vol.5, p.227.
43   Ibid., vol.1, Sermon 3, p.75; vol.4, p.100.
44   Jacobson, 1874, p.31.
45   Ibid., p.34.
46   Gauden, 1661, p.13.
47   Ibid.
48   Ibid., pp.14, 16.
49   Ibid., p.14.
50   Ibid., p.16.
51   Gauden, 1688 edition, p.2.
52   Ibid., p.3.
53   Ibid., p.9.
54   Ibid., p.13.
55   Ibid., p.17.
56   Ibid., cf. p.20: 'not by transmutation of their Nature, but by a similitude of virtues, and proportionable effects by a Sacramental Union and Relation depending upon the Truth, Authority and Divine Power of the Institutor, *Jesus Christ*.'
57   Ibid., p.21.
58   Morley, 1683b, Preface pp.x–xi.
59   Ibid.
60   *A Vindication of the Argument drawn from Sense, against Transubstantiation*, in Morley, 1683a, p.10.
61   Thorndike, 1844–56, vol.3, part 1, p.17.
62   Ibid., vol.4, part 1, p.153.
63   Ibid., pp.158, part 162.
64   Ibid., pp.163, 170.
65   Ibid., p.180.
66   Ibid., vol.4, part 1, Of the Laws of the Church, p.6.
67   Ibid., p.98.
68   Ibid., p.25.
69   Ibid., p.34.
70   Ibid., pp.57ff.
71   Ibid., vol.4, part 2, pp.545–6.
72   Ibid., p.35.
73   Ibid., p.104.
74   Ibid., pp.112–3.
75   Ibid., p.116.
76   Reynolds, 1638, p.5.

77   Ibid., p.9.
78   Ibid., p.7.
79   Ibid., p.18.
80   Ibid., p.85.
81   'The Sinfulness of Sin', in Reynolds, 1679, p.132.
82   Reynolds, 1638, p.61.
83   Ibid., p.28.
84   Ibid., p.32.
85   Ibid., p.87.
86   Ibid., p.96.
87   Ibid., pp.61, 47.
88   Ibid., p.111.
89   Ibid., pp.99–100.
90   Ibid., p.98.
91   Ford, 1657, pp.1, 13.
92   Cardwell, 1841, p.310.
93   Ibid., pp.323–5.
94   Ibid., pp.310, 320–23.
95   Baxter, 1649, pp.417ff.
96   Toon, 1967, pp.22–6.
97   Baxter, 1675, pp.74–7.
98   Baxter, 1830, vol.5, p.39.
99   Ibid., vol.19, pp.262–3.
100 Spinks, 1991.
101 For Baxter's Reformed liturgy, see Baxter, 1830.
102 Baxter, 1830, vol.10, pp.317–18.
103 See ibid., vol.4, p.316: 'As Christ himself was incarnate and true Christ, before he
     was sacrificed to God, and was sacrificed to God before that sacrifice be communi-
     cated for life and nourishment to souls; so in the sacrament, consecration must first
     make the creature to be the flesh and blood of Christ representative; and then the
     sacrificing of that flesh and blood must be represented and commemorated; and then
     the sacrifices flesh and blood communicated to the receivers for their spiritual life.'
104 Ibid., vol.4, p.316.
105 Du Priest, 1972, p.134.
106 Ibid., p.223, comparing Baxter with Jeremy Taylor: 'Baxter hopes that the mind will
     instruct and excite the soul; Taylor that the heart will surprise and move the mind.'
107 Cuming, 1983, pp.153–167; Jasper, 1989.
108 Buchanan, 1976.
109 Cuming, 1961, p.180.
110 Evelyn, 1959, p.442.
111 Buckroyd, 1980; Cheyne, 1999, chapter 3.
112 See Hyman, 1995, pp.49–74.
113 Burnet, 1818, vol.1, p.153.
114 Burnet, 1960, p.125.
115 Leighton, 1816, vol.3, p.417.
116 Dickson, 1635, p.272 (on Hebrews 9:28).
117 Dickson, Head 3, 1671 edition.
118 Dickson, 1664, p.96.
119 Dickson, 1685, p.263.
120 Ibid., p.265.
121 Ibid., p.266.

122 Ibid., p.280.
123 Ibid., p.270.
124 Dickson, 1651, p.308.
125 Dickson, 1685, p.302.
126 Ibid., p.293.
127 Dickson, 1651, pp.308–9.
128 Ibid., p.309.
129 Ibid.
130 Ibid., p.310.
131 Dickson, 1635, p.272.
132 Dickson, 1651, p.312.
133 Craghead, 1695, p.1.
134 Ibid., p.5.
135 Ibid., p.8.
136 Ibid., p.15.
137 Ibid., p.26.
138 Ibid., p.27.
139 Ibid., p.73.
140 Cf. ibid., p.62, where communion with Christ is linked to his offices of prophet, priest and king.
141 Blackader, fol.80. I am grateful to the National Library for supplying photocopies of fols 68–100 of this manuscript.
142 Ibid., fol.81.
143 Ibid., fol.83.
144 Ibid., fol.90.

Chapter 6

After-Thoughts

What observations may be drawn from this narrative of ceremonial discord and these cameos on sacramental teachings?

Stuart divines north and south of Hadrian's Wall did their sacramental theology – as indeed, all their theology – within the broad parameters of 'International Calvinism'; they almost all explicitly rejected both the Roman Catholic *and* the Lutheran sacramental views. Many – such as Hildersham, Downame, Ames and Bruce – simply saw their task as reiterating and qualifying what they understood to be the general Reformed consensus on sacraments. But the consensus which they perceived was in fact a chimera, and concealed many unresolved tensions which were found not only between the different sixteenth-century Reformers, but also even within their individual writings on the subject. These unresolved tensions, giving rise to divergences, can already be seen in the treatment of sacraments by William Perkins and Richard Hooker, each developing certain strands of the Reformed tradition.[1] Perkins, like Fenner, was more at ease with the sacramental language of the symbolic memorialism and symbolic parallelism typified by Bullinger, whereas Hooker pursued the symbolic instrumentalist language of Calvin. With the rise in common theological parlance of the covenant of grace, this raised issues for the meaning of baptism. With the Lord's Supper, it raised questions about presence. Furthermore, while all the Stuart divines rejected what they understood to be the Tridentine concept of the sacrifice of the mass, and agreed that the one sacrifice of the cross was commemorated, they differed on whether this was a manward commemoration, ideally concentrated in visual form in the fraction and libation; or a Godward commemoration articulated in prayer and the eucharistic celebration itself.

Those divines who regarded the Patristic writers as equally (John Forbes of Corse), or even more authoritative than the magisterial Reformers (the Durham House circle), tended to put an emphasis on sacraments as instruments of Christ's virtue or grace. Conformist Calvinists such as Ward and Bedford also took this line without appeal to the fathers, but simply on the grounds that there was little point in celebrating sacraments if they did nothing. Yet neither Forbes, nor these latter divines shared the quest of the Patristic Reformed churchmen for increased ceremonial in the sacramental rites. All, however, represent developments of the inherited Reformed sacramental theology with its unresolved tensions and nuanced differences of meaning of identical terminology. What was perceived as a consensus, the Stuart divines, I suggest, burst asunder. Many of the English divines, 'godly' and 'Patristic Reformed', felt frustrated that the *lex orandi* of the *Book of Common Prayer* seemed to be at odds with their developing theology. Attempts to harmonise the *lex orandi* with the *lex credendi* included ceremonial reform, either by abolition or enrichment; and by revised liturgical texts, such as 1618, or 1637.

With the *Westminster Directory* and its accompanying confession and catechisms, we find theology and liturgical rite reflecting one another, though these were an expression of the English nonconformist and conformist Calvinist theology, shared also by the Scottish Covenanters. Other expressions of theology in liturgical rites are found in the work of Jeremy Taylor and Richard Baxter, as well as the liturgical musings of Hammon L'Estrange, Anthony Sparrow, Matthew Wren and John Cosin. Yet all this sacramental and liturgical diversity came to very little in England, for the 1662 *Book of Common Prayer* conceded little to any of the prevailing theologies or proposed rites.

At one level, the reason in England was the Cavalier Parliament, which neither needed, nor felt inclined, to gratify any party held responsible for the events from 1637 to 1659. The great architect of the Restoration, Gilbert Sheldon, had little interest in matters liturgical, or even, apparently, theological. Gilbert Burnet wrote of him: '[he] was esteemed a learned man before the wars: but he was then engaged so deep in the politics, that scarce any prints of what he had been remained.'[2] Lawful authority and church polity were the determining factors. But the failure of the theological parties to agree on some consensus was also an important factor.

In England, a moderately revised Cranmerian text was reimposed, which, with minor exceptions, textually ignored the contemporary theological debate. Post-Restoration commentators and theologians such as Simon Patrick, George Bull and Daniel Brevint would have to read into the language of the text what they thought it ought, or would like it to mean. And thanks to the disastrous attempt to prioritize ceremonial in Scotland, even the *Book of Common Order* was overthrown, leaving Scotland with only the *Directory* – a liturgy tailored to suit the concerns of the English Independents. It was hardly the *lex orandi* of Cowper's draft, which, for all its clumsiness, was representative of the Scottish sacramental divinity. Even the *Directory* was discarded. The story is one of the beginning of sacramental *lex orandi* and *lex credendi* walking in separate directions, or existing in different worlds. So much theology, and so much liturgical knowledge and creativity, yielded such barren practical results. Yet this narrative does raise some questions and comments which relate to the contemporary Church and current theological debate.

Anglicanism

Though a study of sacramental teaching yields only a small piece of the wider, complex seventeenth-century theological jigsaw, it becomes clear from recent studies that the Avant-garde and Patristic Reformed churchmen were a minority view within the broader Calvinist consensus. The selection of divines for the Library of Anglo-Catholic Theology has greatly assisted this distortion. Polity and ecclesiastical legality apart, a great many English divines of the seventeenth century would have found most of the *Westminster Confession* an acceptable contemporary summary of their faith. The confession and catechisms were accepted by the General Assembly of the Church of Scotland, but had been authored mainly by English divines. The *Westminster Confession* must be regarded as an expression of theology representative of many divines in the Church of England in the seventeenth century, regardless of its legal status. It was a theology which was marginalised at the Restoration, though not entirely. It becomes increasingly difficult to speak of 'Anglican' theology prior to 1662, at least in the way it is expounded, for example, in J. Booty and S. Sykes, *The Study of Anglicanism* or many of the writings of Henry McAdoo.[3] Prior to 1662 there were many strands of theology in the English Church, and much of it shared with the Scottish Church. The implications for ecumenism are that present-day Anglicanism has hidden away in its tradition an approach to many issues which was at one time akin to the Reformed tradition. That heritage can be drawn upon in dialogue today, with such figures as Downame, Ussher, Ward and the Denisons being given a hearing alongside Andrewes and Taylor. Anything less is a distortion of the larger historical narrative, and unnecessarily narrows the Church of England and Anglican theological traditions.

Aristotelian Constraints?

John Calvin's theology is not identical with 'International Calvinism', but he was a key figure in Reformed theology. T.F. Torrance has observed that Calvin operated with a dynamic view of space, composed of waves of tensions and dissonances rather than constituting a static container or product.[4] By virtue of his concentration on God and the activity of God in Christ – on things invisible and unlocatable except in the transformed self – he was naturally suspicious of what is visible and externally locatable. Hence he was critical of Luther's apparent Aristotelian receptacle concept of space, and for that reason rejected the Wittenberg reformer's Christology and his understanding of the presence of Christ in the eucharist. Indeed, his Augustinian preference encouraged a Neoplatonist hermeneutic. But Calvin also appreciated the force of Luther's trust in the divine promise, and insisted that in the Lord's Supper Christ's body and blood are truly present, and rejected Zwingli's dualism of Neoplatonism. For Calvin the Holy Spirit is the conduit of grace, and because of the divine promise, sacramental signs are not bare signs, but convey 'a true and substantial communication' of God.[5] As has been noted in the introductory chapter, at times he seems to suggest what Brian Gerrish has called sacramental parallelism, but at others sacramental instrumentalism.[6] Furthermore, his emphasis differed depending on occasion and time of writing.[7] However, he seemed to hold these together in tension, affirming the superiority of the spiritual over the corporeal, but recognising that God can use the imperfect sensible world through the Holy Spirit to convey his substantial spiritual reality.

Though impossible to demonstrate conclusively, it may be that the English and Scottish divines were less well equipped educationally to be able to hold these together easily, and this in part may account for the tendency towards a polarisation, with divines either tending towards a symbolic memorialism, or appearing to concede too much to Rome. This was perhaps because they still operated with a broad Aristotelian concept of space. The syllabus for the BA at both Oxford and Cambridge, and for the MA at the four Scottish universities, was until the late seventeenth century heavily Aristotelian.[8] This already caused some intellectual tensions when such ideas as transubstantiation had to be rejected. If most English and Scottish divines worked with Aristotelian concepts of space, then sacraments had either to be defined as seals of grace given, or instruments and conduit pipes which conveyed grace, in both instances sacraments being *conceived as containers*. On the one hand, for symbolic memorialists and parallelists, the containers were defined by what they could not and must not contain; for the more patristically minded symbolic instrumentalists, they were defined by what they might contain. With Richard Hooker and Edward Reynolds, we encounter divines who seem to be aware of the problem, and hence their very careful preference for sacraments as instrumental causes of 'mystical union'. The term 'sacramental union' seems to be a term used to convey the fact that no normal, rational, or metaphysical account could be given for what were divine mysteries.

Transubstantiation Versus Real Presence?

Amongst the group of writings currently styled 'Radical Orthodoxy' – though perhaps better termed 'Postmodern Romanticism' – there is a tendency to elevate the pre-modern cult with its social cohesion centered on the mass and as romanticised by John Bossy, over the rationalism of modernism, which is traced back though the Enlightenment to the Reformation, and beyond that to Duns Scotus.[9] The sweeping generalisations and tendentious reading of sources which have been detected in some of the 'Radical Orthodox' writings is far beyond the scope of this study. However, in a number of places, Catherine Pickstock has defended 'transubstantiation', using a combination of J.L. Austin's speech-act theories, and an interesting ahistorical, reader-response approach to the Roman mass and particularly the words of institution with the old *canon missae*, and in reference to the teaching of Thomas Aquinas.[10] In one essay she has thus asserted:

> The Institution Narrative, a monologic delineation culminating in Christ's words given in direct speech, is not illocutionary so much as dislocutionary ... The doctrine of transubstantiation enables us to see Christ's words at the Last Supper as simultaneously analytic and synthetic. The statement 'This is my body ...' is on the one hand definitive, and on the other, transformatory. The words dislocate the natural laws connecting substances and their accidents. With these few words, the substance perishes while its accidents (colour, shape, and flavour) survive the annihilation of their former identities. These words transform the inanimate into the animate, the dead into the beatifying. But even saying that these words are simultaneously analytic and synthetic betrays the stuttering of human speech, for in God's terms they are not synthetic at all. For God these four words merely disclose what the bread always was, atemporally and acontextually. God can construct a state merely by declaring it to exist. God's language, then, is the optimum fiat.[11]

Herbert McCabe pointed out some years ago that actually Aquinas did *not* argue that the substance of the elements was changed into the substance of Christ's body and blood; rather, recognising the limitation of the Aristotelian terminology, he introduced Neoplatonic terms of being and linked transubstantiation with creation *ex nihilo* – both of which would have been nonsensical to Aristotle. The consecrated elements are disclosed as the being of Christ.[12] In a subsequent paper,

Pickstock acknowledged this, but still defends the idea of metaphysical change, seemingly contrasting it with the Port-Royal Grammarians' characterisation of Calvinist belief as a 'metaphorical understanding'.[13] But she also notes that Aquinas repeatedly observes that it is actually *desire* for the Body which ensures discernment of the presence of the Body.

Nicholas Wolterstorff has also used J.L. Austin's speech-act theory to elucidate the meaning of the eucharist, but in his case, for John Calvin. Wolterstorff amusingly noted that the theory would be alien to Calvin, who (like Aquinas, for that matter) did not enjoy prescience. Nevertheless, Wolterstorff argues that Austin's categories are helpful in clarifying Calvin. Following Luther, the promise of the words of institution are crucial for Calvin:

> In short, the perlocutionary effect of the sacrament, if we may call it that, is not produced simply by the uttering of the sacramental actions – any more than the perlocutionary effect in speech is produced simply by the sound or the look of the words. It occurs only when the recipients discern the illocutionary acts performed – only when they discern that God is assuring them that the promise made in Jesus Christ remains in effect for them.[14]

Wolterstorff argues, rightly in my view, that whereas Aquinas used sign-activity language, and places causal power in the elements, Calvin used God-activity language and appropriation of the promise.

This raises the question of whether Pickstock really means 'transubstantiation', or whether she should be understood to really mean 'real presence'? The English and Scottish divines discussed above, for all their differences, were united in rejecting what they understood to be the Roman Catholic teaching on sacramental *ex opere operato*, and transubstantiation. They did not regard the logic of the latter as teaching real presence. Rather, they saw its logic as teaching a metaphysical contradiction, resulting in a carnal or corporeal presence – physical and earthly. In contrast, many divines asserted a 'real' or 'spiritual' or 'mystical', or 'sacramental' presence. The elements were instruments of God, and the words of institution, words of divine promise, and the Holy Spirit able to give what was promised without either crass, or sophisticated (Aquinas), ideas of metaphysical change. If the words of institution were metaphorical, then so much the better, for the metaphor was *God the Word's metaphor*.[15] The promise of the words of the Word were sufficient for God to realise what they promised without resorting to what some of the divines termed 'alchemy'.[16] Faithful trust was required that God would disclose the bread and wine as an invisible depth of Body and Blood. These divines believed that their concept of 'real presence' was far more real than transubstantiation. Any discussion, such as Pickstock's, which does not grasp this, distorts and caricatures the complexity of Reformed teaching on this matter.

Presence and Sacrifice in the Lord's Supper

It has been noted that nearly all divines agreed that the presence in the eucharist could best be described as 'sacramental' and 'exhibited'. Though the latter term is clumsy, one wonders why the word 'sacrament' or 'sacramental' was not utilised in the revised liturgies to express the concept of presence. Richard Baxter had used the term in the Savoy liturgy. To my knowledge, not until the 1979 *Book of Common Prayer* of the Episcopal Church of the United States of America was it used. Eucharistic Prayer B in Rite II, the epiklesis prays 'send your Holy Spirit upon these gifts that they may be the sacrament of the Body of Christ and his Blood of the new Covenant.' During the revision stage of the new eucharistic prayers in the Church of England's *Common Worship* (2000), evangelical sensibilities led to the modification of an epiklesis that originally read 'send your Holy Spirit on us and these gifts that broken bread and wine poured may be for us the body and blood of your dear Son.' There was a coordinated campaign to get the reference to 'these gifts' removed; apparently some more conservative evangelicals read transubstantiation into these words. However, the addition of 'sacramentally' or the 'sacrament of the body and blood', which would have had precedent in all sides in the seventeenth century, could, in theory at least, have allowed 'these gifts' to stand, and could have been used by all shades of English churchmanship with good conscience.[17] The failure of the Revision Committee to utilize this phraseology which is so deep in the theological tradition, in *Common Worship*, was a lost opportunity, and has resulted in an unnecessarily weak epiklesis.

On the question of eucharistic sacrifice, Hammond and Baxter could agree that in the eucharist the Church 'pleads' the sacrifice of Christ, and this is also the thought in William Guild's sermon *The Christians Passover*; but no concession was made to this in either the *Directory* or 1662. Its inclusion in prayer in the 1662 text, together with a more deliberately framed fraction and libation, could have gone someway to uniting divines on the commemorative aspect of sacrifice. The Church of Scotland would recapture that phraseology in its 1940 *Book of Common Order*, with the words 'wherefore, having in remembrance the work and passion of our Saviour Christ, and pleading His eternal sacrifice, we Thy servants do set forth this memorial, which He hath commanded us to make.' Here the term 'eternal' reproduces Calvin's comments on Hebrews that 'the blood of Christ is continually being shed before the face of the Father to spread over heaven and earth', and his catechism which speaks of 'le sacrifice unique et perpetuel'. Calvin saw the sacrifice as eternal in the sense of being eternally efficacious; being in heaven (or 'in eternity'); and being part of the covenant of redemption, and seen by God from all eternity.[18] Though thoroughly biblical and Reformed, sensibilities of some Church of England evangelicals (absurdly trying to be more 'biblical' than Calvin), precluded the use of the word 'eternal'.[19] However, the terminology used by Hammond and Baxter, pleading the sacrifice, does occur in two of the Eucharistic Prayers in *Common Worship*, 2000. All Anglicans fully aware of their fuller tradition should be able to use this in good conscience, and it is an articulation of eucharistic sacrifice shared with the Church of Scotland.

Eucharistic Shape and Action

In modern Anglican liturgical history, Gregory Dix is famed for his discovery of a four-action shape of the eucharist – taking, giving thanks, breaking and communion – and many modern Anglican rites have been constructed around these four actions.[20] Dix's book was, in its day, a liturgical landmark, but although now hopelessly out of date, it is still in print, and still recommended to divinity students. This is akin to recommending Darwin's *On the Origin of Species* as the latest thing on evolution. Interestingly, Darwin, like Dix, borrowed other people's theories and made them his own!

Already in my *Two Faces of Elizabethan Anglican Theology*, I noted that as early as 1590 William Perkins outlined this four-action shape, and as noted in this study, several other divines also call attention to these actions. The theory is not Dix's, but is embedded in several sixteenth- and seventeenth-century English sacramental writings, and the time has come to halt giving all the credit to Dix. English it may, but original to Dix, it was not.[21] Furthermore, the idea that these actions were incompatible with the *Book of Common Prayer* rite, as Dix urged, did not occur to the seventeenth century writers. The manual acts placed in the 1662 *Book of Common Prayer* institution narrative were one quite legitimate expression of the eucharistic action. As Colin Buchanan rightly maintains, the 'taking' is not the offertory or preparation of the bread and wine, which is a necessary utilitarian action prior to 'taking'.[22] An older English and a Scottish tradition was to unveil and take the previously prepared elements during the narrative, and there is no reason other than 'Dixian' fundamentalism for that not to be an option in current Anglican and Reformed eucharistic celebration. There is cause for concern that the 'fraction' is usually limited to the bread, and provision should be made for pouring out of the wine from a flagon into chalices, with appropriate words, at the same time as the breaking of the bread.[23] Divines discussed above, English and Scottish, illustrate that time and time again.

Baptismal Covenant?

Many of the divines discussed baptism in the context of covenant and covenant theology. As noted, this had been developed in a more systematic manner by the Heidelberg theologians, and the terminology passed into common parlence. However, it was never given *liturgical* expression, or even used in a technical sense in the rite of baptism in the *Book of Common Prayer*. It was given expression in the *Directory*, and in Baxter's liturgy; the terminology was used by Taylor and Sanderson in their liturgies. As it is discussed in some of the divines, and particularly the Scottish 'Radicals', it suggested a semi-pelagian or synergistic contract with God, even if that was not what they intended.[24] This theology was jettisoned as too synergistic in the Church of Scotland *Common Order* of 1994.[25] However, the terminology was adopted in the 1979 American *Book of Common Prayer*, and urged upon the Church of England in some of the appendices of the *Christian Initiation – a Policy for the Church of England* in 1991. Though not using the term, the baptismal rite in the 1980 *Alternative Service Book* does outline a mini-contract with parents *before* the baptism of an infant. There is an irony that the Church of Scotland recognised the synergism when applied to baptism just at a time when Anglicanism decided to adopt it. In the Scottish *Common Order*, the only question to parents before the act of baptism is whether they believe in the faith as summed up in the Apostles' Creed. Before the baptism, drawing on the French Reformed rite, the minister says:

N—for you Jesus Christ came into the world:
for you he lived and showed God's love;
for you he suffered the darkness of Calvary
and cried at the last, 'It is accomplished';
for you he triumphed over death
and rose in newness of life;
for you he ascended to reign at God's right hand.
All this he did for you, N—,
though you do not know it yet.
And so the word of Scripture is fulfilled:
'We love because God loved us first'.[26]

At least in the *A New Zealand Prayer Book* (1989), and the rites in *Common Worship* (2000), we have examples of more recent Anglican rites where this liturgical synergism developed from Reformed baptismal covenant theology has been toned down and filtered out.

Ceremonial and Liturgical Forms and Vesture

Today, though not common, the alb and stole are not altogether unknown in the Church of Scotland; and communion in pews (à la English Independents) has replaced sitting at tables. Though no liturgy is mandatory, successive Books of *Common Order* provide a liturgical standard. Amongst Anglicans, kneeling is the usual posture for communion, but it is not uncommon to find standing for reception. Furthermore, in spite of canonical oaths, a good number of Church of England Evangelical clergy have abandoned official liturgical forms, and the surplice. True, the latter is abandoned now, not for the Genevan gown, but for either Burton's off-the-peg suit, or the smart casual look from Next, but as in the seventeenth century, it is technically 'nonconformity'. Likewise, many of the younger Scottish ministers prefer an informal approach to worship, and have abandoned the Genevan gown. Yet these new Avant-garde nonconformists in both churches seem oblivious to the recent sociological and anthropological studies which emphasise that symbolism has a profound meaning as humans experience the transcendent and the Divine in worship.[27]

Notes

1   Spinks, 1999.
2   Burnet, 1897, vol.1, p.313.
3   See for example the very different range of authors cited by Kenneth Stevenson as compared with the narrow approach of Henry McAdoo in McAdoo and Stevenson, 1995.
4   Torrance, 1969. See Jammer, 1970 edition; Lindberg, 1992; Cushing, 1998.
5   Calvin, 1986, 4.17.19.
6   Gerrish, 1992, pp.245–58.
7   Rigg, 1985.

8   See Curtis, 1959; Jardine, 1974; Fletcher, 1986; Forbes, 1983; Russell, 1974.
9   See particularly Milbank, 1997; Pickstock, 1997; Ward, 1997; Milbank, et al., 1998. See also Hemming, 2000.
10 Pickstock, 1993; 1997; 1999.
11 Pickstock, 1993, p.131.
12 Macabe, 1987; 1999, pp.131–41.
13 Pickstock, 1999.
14 Wolterstorff, 1996, pp.103–22.
15 For the power of metaphor see Soskice, 1987.
16 See Lindberg, 1992, for the Aristotelian theory of accidents and substances as the basis for the hopes of the alchemists.
17 I say 'in theory' because some clergy have neither knowledge of, nor interest in their tradition, and are happy to move goal posts to narrow the precedents of history to exclude all but their own particular views. For the problem over the epiklesis, see Read, 2000, pp.259–68. Many of us must seem like John Forbes – trying to find an eirenicism for those who wish for no such thing.
18 Spinks, 1990b, pp.185–201.
19 For a recent objection, directed at Nugent Hicks's concept, see Buchanan, 2000. Misuse by Hicks should not be an excuse for evangelicals ignoring Calvin and orthodox Reformed usage.
20 Dix, 1945.
21 It seems that the presbyterian scholar, Richard Davidson, had taught the four-action shape a few years earlier than Dix's publication. Harding, 1996.
22 Buchanan, 1976.
23 Regrettably the International Anglican Liturgical Consultation report, *Renewing the Anglican Eucharist* (1995), oblivious to its seventeenth-century tradition, focused on preparing the table at the Dixian offertory, and the breaking of the bread only receives attention. See Holeton, 1996.
24 *Pace* David Mullan, *Scottish Puritanism*, where although rightly identifying the weakness in the arguments of James B. Torrance, he fails to see the (almost certainly unintended) synergism in Federal Theology.
25 Spinks, 1996, pp.218–42.
26 *Common Order* (1996 revised edition), pp.89–90. Though the language is a little awkward, the theology is impeccable.
27 Grisbrooke, 1991, pp.136–54.

APPENDICES

Appendix 1

Communion Chalices,
England and Scotland

**Figure A1.1 Chalice, Holy Trinity,
Kensington Gore, 1629**

**Figure A1.2 Chalice with paten-
cover, St. Botolph's,
Aldgate, 1635**

**Figure A1.3   Chalices from Fyvie, 1617–19, Cambuslang, 1617–19 and
              Blantyre, 1613–44**

Appendix 2

Communion Prayers from John Downame's *A Guide to Godlynesse*, 1622

A Prayer before receiving the sacrament of the Lords Supper

O Lord our God, who art infinite in goodnesse, grace, and mercy; most true in all thy promises, and most just and powerfull in performance; thou hast, when we were strangers and enemies, subject to the curse of the Law, and liable to thy wrath, by reason of our manifold and grievous sinnes, and utterly unable to free our selves out of the state of death and condemnation, given unto us thine onely and deare Sonne, to worke the great worke of our Redemption, by his perfect satisfaction, death, and obedience. By whom, thy Justice being fully satisfied, and thy wrath appeased, thou hast made with us in him thy Covenant of grace, wherein thou hast promised the free pardon of our sinnes, and the salvation of our soules, grace in this life, and glory and happinesse in the life to come, upon the alone condition of faith, laying hold upon Christ and his righteousnesse, and bringing forth the fruits thereof in hearty repentance and amendment of life. The which, though it be in it selfe of most infallible truth, yet having respect to our weaknesse, doubting, and infidelity, thou hast beene graciously pleased to confirme it unto us, by adding thereunto thy Seales, the Sacraments. So that nothing hath beene wanting on thy part, either for the perfecting the great worke of our Redemption, or the effectuall applying of it unto us for our use and benefit. But (O Lord) wee humbly confesse, that as wee have shamefully broken the Covenant of workes, by fayling in the condition of perfect obedience; and have made voyd thy promises of life and happinesse, by our grievous and innumerable sinnes, both originall and actuall; so also, as much as in us lyeth, wee have deprived our selves of the benefits which thou offerest unto us in the new Covenant of grace in Jesus Christ, by our manifold faylings, wants, and imperfections in performing our promises made unto thee, if thou shouldest looke to the perfection of our graces and outward actions, and not unto the inward truth and sincerity of our hearts. For wee have not thorowly acquainted our selves with the knowledge of thy saving truth, concerning this great mystery of our salvation, not searched and examined these spirituall Evidences, for the cleere understanding of them; and much lesse for the bringing of them home to our hearts and consciences, that in them we might have found peace and comfort in the assurance of thy love and our owne salvation. Our faith hath beene exceeding weake in apprehending and applying Christ and thy gracious promises made in him; and wee too too negligent in using those blessed meanes which thou hast graciously affoorded us, for the strengthening of it. For we have not onely beene exceeding negligent in hearing, reading, and meditating in thy Word, the great Charter of our peace, which containeth in it all our spirituall and heavenly priviledges; but also in making right use of thy Seales, the Sacraments, annexed unto it, especially this of our Lords Supper, which thou hast ordained for the spirituall food of our soules, to nourish them unto everlasting life. Wee have not highly esteemed of this holy banquet, but have often pretended excuses, and absented our selves, when as thou hast graciously invited us unto it. Wee have not hungred and thirsted after this heavenly Manna and waters of life; but with cloyed appetites have carelesly neglected them, when as they have been set before us. And when we have presented our selves at this holy feast, we have come to thy Table, after a cold, carelesse and formall manner, without all due preparation, and have performed this holy action with prophane and unwashen hands, more for custome then for conscience sake. Wee have come in much ignorance of thee and thy truth, thy gracious Covenant, and the Seales annexed unto it; and that little knowledge wee have had, hath beene more in our heads, then in our hearts and affections, in idle speculation, then in use and practice. Wee have not rightly discerned the body of our Lord, nor put that difference which wee ought, betweene these elements consecrated to this holy service, and those which are for common use. We have not duly considered, as became us, the relation betweene the signes and the things signified, but have too much stucke in the outward elements and actions, not looking to the spirituall graces signified and sealed by them. We have not approoved our selves as worthy ghests, by renewing carefully and conscionably our faith and repentance, but have presented our selves before thee with much infidelity and great impenitencie; though, since our last comming to thine holy Table, we have often renewed our sinnes; neither have we brought foorth such plentifull fruits of charity towards our brethren for thy sake; as thou requirest, and as it becommeth the true members of Jesus Christ, either by liberall giving unto those that want, or free forgiving those who have offended us. Wee have not shewed our Saviours death in this holy action, nor thankefully remembred the great worke of our Redemption, by his precious death and blood-shed. And though wee have professed our selves thy servants by wearing thy livery, yet wee have not indevoured to walke worthy this high calling, by gloryfying thee our Lord and Master. O Lord our God, shame and confusion covereth our faces, not onely in the sight and sense of our manifold and grievous sinnes, both originall and actuall; but also of our great imperfections and corruptions, which wee shew in the best duties of thy worship and service. Wee confesse, holy Father, that if thou shouldest enter into judgement with us, and deale with us according to our deserts, thou mightest justly make voyd thy Covenant with us, deprive us of these meanes of our salvation, or else make them uneffectuall and of no use unto us whilest wee injoy them. But seeing wee are heartily sorry for our sinnes, and not onely unfainedly bewaile our imperfections, but also desire and labour after more perfection, promising for the time to come, that wee will more carefully use all good meanes, whereby we may bee inabled to performe all duties of thy service in a more perfect manner; Good Lord, wee most humbly beseech thee, for Jesus Christ his sake, to pardon graciously all our wantes and weaknesses, to accept, according to thy gracious promises, our will, for the deed, our poore indevours, for perfect performance, and to cover all our imperfections, with Christs perfect righteousnesse and obedience, and to wash away all our corruptions in his most precious Blood. And seeing wee doe now againe intend to performe the holy duties of thy service, in hearing thy Word, Prayer, and receiving of the Sacrament of the Lords Supper: Good Lord, wee earnestly beseech thee, for thy Sonnes sake, to assist us so with thy grace and holy Spirit, as that wee may performe these actions of thy service, in some good and acceptable manner, for the advancement of thy glory, the comfort of our soules, and the furthering and assuring of our owne salvation. More especially, wee intreate thee to inable us with thy grace, that wee may bee duely prepared, and come as worthy ghests to thy Table. Give us a lively sight and sense of our sinnes and imperfections, wants and weaknesses, and let us hunger and thirst after Christ and his righteousnesse; and after the spirituall food of his Body and Blood, for the nourishment of our soules unto eternall life. Let us not coldly and formally performe this high and holy dutie, but bend all the powers of our soules to the doing of it, in some such manner as may bee acceptable in thy sight. Inlighten our mindes more and more with the saving knowledge of thee and thy truth, and especially of the great worke of our Redemption, and thine infinite love shining in it, of the Covenant of grace, and Seales annexed unto it; and let not this knowledge reside onely in our understandings, but let it also descend into our hearts, that it may bee profitable for their sanctification. Inable us rightly to discerne our Lords Body, and feelingly to understand the relation betweene the Signes and the things signified, applying both unto our selves in their right use. To this end indue us with a true and lively faith, that wee may not onely receive the outward Elements, but also may inwardly feed upon the precious Body and Blood of our Lord and Saviour Jesus Christ, that thereby wee may be inriched with all saving graces, strengthened unto all good duties and nourished unto everlasting life. Inable us also to bring foorth the fruits of this faith in unfained repentance, bewayling our sinnes past, hating those corruptions which still hang upon us, and resolving to leave them for the time to come, and to serve thee in holinesse and righteousnesse all the dayes of our lives. And as wee have daily renewed our sinnes, so give us now grace, that wee may renew our faith and repentance, bathing our soules and bodies afresh, even in the Fountaine of Christs precious Blood, and in the teares of unfained sorrow, mourning with bitter griefe, because wee have pierced him with our sinnes, and caused the Lord of life to be putt unto a shamefull death. Inflame our hearts with most fervent love towards thee and our neighbours, yea, even our enemies for thy sake, and lincke our hearts together in an holy Communion, as it becommeth the true members of Jesus Christ. Let us also approove our love to bee sound and sincere, by the fruits of it, and especially, by forgiving and forgetting all our wrongs and injuries, as heartily as wee desire to bee forgiven of thee, and by performing all workes of mercy and Christian charity, towards all those who neede our helpe; not onely by comforting and refreshing their bodies, but also by per-forming all Christian duties for the eternall salvation of their soules. And being thus prepared, let us, when we come to thy Table, performe that dutie of thy service in some good and acceptable manner, with all reverence, faith and inward fervencie and devotion. Let us with the outward signes receive the things signified, Jesus Christ and all his benefits; that being more and more united unto him, we may receive from him the Spirituall life of Grace, and those holy vertues of his divine nature, that we may grow up in him unto a perfect man. Let us bring with us the hand and mouth of faith; and let it be more and more strengthened in the assurance of all thy gracious promises, by these seales of thy covenant communicated unto us. Make us partakers of Christs merits, by imputation of his nature and essence by conjunction, and of his power and efficacy by thy holy Spirit; and let us shew his death till he come, gratefully remembering this great worke of our Redemption by his bloud, that we may be thankfull, and prayse thee the blessed Trinity in unity, all the dayes of our lives. Finally, as we doe by these meanes professe our selves thy servants in taking upon us thy livery and cognizance, so give us grace, that we may contantly strive and indevour to walke worthy this high calling, and to glorifie thee in the duties of holinesse and righteousnesse, whilest we have any breath or beeing. Heare us and helpe us, O God of our salvation, and answer us graciously in these our suits and petitions, for Jesus Christ his sake, to whom with thee and thine holy Spirit, be rendred of us, and thy whole Church, all glory and prayse, power and dominion, both now and evermore. Amen.

A Thanksgiving after the Receiving of the Sacrament of the Lords Supper

O Lord our God, most glorious and most gracious, infinite in bountie and goodnesse unto all thy children and servants in Jesus Christ, we doe here offer unto thee the sacrifice of prayse and thankesgiving, and doe laud and magnifie thy great and glorious Name, for all thy mercies and favours vouchsafed unto us; especially because thou hast loved us with an everlasting love, yea so loved us, that thou hast, of thy meere grace and free good will, even when we were strangers and enemies, given unto us thy Best-beloved and onely Sonne, to worke the great worke of our Redemption, and by his death and precious blood-shed to deliver us out of the hands of all our spirituall enemies, and to free us from everlasting death and condemnation, that we might be heires through him of eternall glory and happinesse in thy Kingdome. We prayse thee also for the free covenant of grace and salvation which thou hast made with us in him, whereby thou hast assured us of the remission of our sinnes, our reconciliation with thee, and of endlesse happinesse in the life to come; and for confirming this covenant unto us, by annexing thereunto the seales thy Sacraments, that thereby our weake faith might be strengthened and increased, and wee more and more freed from doubting and incredulity. We thanke thee (holy Father) for renewing this thy covenant with us this day, and for confirming our union with Jesus Christ our head, and one with another, by giving unto us his precious body and blood, as the Spiritual food of our soules, whereby they are nourished unto everlasting life. O Lord our God, it is thy great mercie, that thou nourishest our mortall bodies with food that perisheth, but how wonderfull is this thy bounty and goodnesse, in that thou feedest our soules with this bread of Life that came downe from heaven, and with this food that endureth to life eternall! If thou shouldest permit us but to gather up the crummes that fall from thy Table, we must needes acknowledge, that it were a favour farre above our deserts; O then how should wee admire and magnifie thy mercie and bountie, in vouchsafing such vile and unworthy wretches, this high and holy priviledge, to be seated at thine owne Table, not with ordinary cheare, but with such spirituall and divine delicacies, even the precious body and blood of thine onely deare Sonne, whereby he becommeth one with us, and we with him, even as thou, holy Father, and he are one, in that holy and happie union. O that our narrow hearts were inlarged, that we might in some measure apprehend this thine infinite and incomprehensible goodnesse! O that being cold in themselves, they were warmed and inflamed with the fire and flame of this divine love; that with the lively sense and feeling of it, wee might be mooved to returne love for love, and expresse it by our fervent zeale and indevour in all things, to please and glorifie thee throughout the whole course of our lives and conversations! Which because it is not in our owne power, O thou the rich fountaine of all grace and goodnesse, inspire and inflame our cold and frozen hearts with the beames of thy love, shed abroad in them by thine holy Spirit, that we may love thee with unfained love, and contemning all things in comparison of thee, may long and labour after nothing so much, as to enjoy thee in this life by grace, and the presence of thy blessed Spirit, and by full and perfect vision and fruition in the life to come. To this end, gracious God, blesse unto us thine holy Ordinances and meanes of our salvation, and by the inward assistance of thy good Spirit, make them powerfull and effectuall to the attayning of those ends, for which thou hast given, and wee received them. Let us finde hereby our union with Christ strengthened and confirmed, by feeling the Spiritual life and sap of grace derived unto us, and increased in us, from this roote of righteousnesse, not onely for our further assurance of our justification, but also for the perfecting of our sanctification, and the strengthening of us unto all Christian duties of a godly life. Let us by this Spirituall food of our soules, finde our selves nourished and inriched with all saving graces, especially let us feele our weake faith confirmed and increased, that wee may, without wavering, be perswaded of all thy gracious promises made unto us, and effectually apply unto our selves Jesus Christ and all his benefits, seeing thou hast not onely offred them in thy Word and covenant of grace, but also sealed, and thereby fully assured them unto us by thy seales the Sacraments. Give us grace, that we may approve this faith to be true and lively, by bringing forth plentifull fruits of it in repentance, and newnesse of life; bewayling our sinnes, because they have pearced our Saviour; and fearing to offend thee for the time to come, seeing thine exact Justice would not suffer them to goe unpunished, when thine onely and deare Sonne did beare them upon his Crosse. Let us not by sinne, hazard our soules againe to death for the wages of worldly vanities, seeing to redeeme us from them, our Saviour and surety payd unto thy Justice the inestimable price of his precious blood; but being freed from sinne, let us become his servants that hath redeemed us, serving him in the duties of holinesse and righteousnesse all the dayes of our lives. And as wee have professed our selves to be of thy Family, by taking upon us and wearing thy liverie, so let us adorne our profession, and glorifie thee our Lord and Master, by having the light of our Christian conversation shining before all men; in all things behaving our selves as it becommeth thy children and servants. Let us have our Lords death in remembrance, untill he come; not onely that it may stirre us up to unfained thankefulnesse unto thee, for giving thy Sonne, and to him, for giving himselfe unto us and for us, but also that it may be as a shield of proofe, to arme us against all our spirituall enemies, thy wrath, the curse of the law, Satan, death, sinne and condemnation, that they may never prevaile against us. Let us also, as wee have in this holy communion professed our selves members of the same body, approve our selves to be indeed so, by performing all duties of love towards one another, both in releeving those that want, and forgiving those who have offended us. Finally, we beseech thee (deare Father) to enable us by thy grace and holy Spirit, that we may performe our vowes and promises which we have made unto thee, especially in the time of preparation before wee came to thy Table; and seeing in the sense and feeling of our wants and weaknesses in thy Spirituall graces, required to the worthy receiving of the Sacrament, as knowledge, faith, repentance and charity, wee were displeased with our selves, and promised that we would indevour to have them increased and strengthened for the time to come; good Lord, we beseech thee, give us grace to performe what we have promised, and to labour carefully and conscionably in the use of all good meanes, for the inriching of our soules with these and all other saving graces of thy sanctifying Spirit, that so also wee may bring forth the fruits of them in our godly and Christian lives, to the glory of thy blessed Name, and the comfort and salvation of our bodies and soules, through Jesus Christ our Lord. Amen.

Appendix 3

Sacramental Rites from the Second Draft Scottish Liturgy by William Cowper, Edinburgh, 1618

THE OLD LEITURGIE OR CHURCH SERVICE USED IN THE CHURCH OF SCOTLAND EXPLAINED AND INLARGED, WHEREIN NO CHANGE IS MAID AS CONCERNING THE SUBSTANCE, ONLIE SOME PRAYERS THAT WER PROPER FOR THEIR TYMES, SUCH AS THESE WHICH WAR USED WHEN THE CHURCH WAS UNDER THE TYRANNIE OF STRANGERS, AR OMITTED, AND OTHERS MEETER FOR THIS TYME PLACED IN THEIR ROWME.

THE ORDOUR OF BAPTISME

The children to be baptised being presented in the public assemblie by the father,
assisted with godfathers, or by the godfather in absence of the father,
the pastor demandis of them this question:
Doe ye present these children desyring that they may be ressaved in the fellowship
of Chryst his mistical bodie which is his Church and that they may be marked with
the mark of Christians which is baptisme, the seale of the covenant of grace? Is not
this your desyre?

Answer

Yea, it is.

Then shall the pastor shortlie delyver the doctrine of baptisme
and thereafter demand agane at these who presents the children:
Doe ye renunce and forsaik the devill and all his workis, together with the world
and wicked lustes of the flesh, and will ye not promise for your self and in name of
the child whom ye present to follow the Lord and serve him in Chryst Jesus?

Answer

I forsaik them all and am resolved to fight against them according to my powar and
to serve the Lord Jesus Christ all my daies. The Lord inable me with grace to
performe it.

Then shall the pastor exhort them to humble themselves
and to seeke grace from the Lord to accompanie this sacrament.

Prayer before Baptisme

O Lord who of thy infinite love hes maid a covenant with us in thy deere sonne, our Blessed Saviour Jesus Chryst, wherein thou hes promised to be our God and the God and father of our children, we beseik thee, good Lord, to performe this thy promise toward us. Give us thy grace that we our selves, who ar baptised in thy name, may walk before as beccommes a people who hes bound up a covenant with the Holie Lord. And as to these infants we pray thee for Christs saik to ressave them into the number of thy children, wash away their sinnes by the bloode of Jesus Christ, mortifie the powar of sinne unto them, sanctefie them with thy holie Spirit that they may become new creatures. And, O Lord, what now we doe in the earth according to thy ordinance ratifie thou it in heaven according to thy promise maid to us in Christ Jesus our Lord and onlie Savior. Amen.

> Then the parents being readie to praesent their children
> the pastor shall speak to them in this manner:

Rehearse the confession of faith wherein ye will promise here before God to bring up these children if the Lord spair their daies and wherein, God willing, I shall baptise them.

Answer

I beleve in God the Father Almightie etc.
> This done the children ar praesented and baptised,
> according to the form sett doune in the service booke.

A Prayer after Baptisme

O Lord, who in thy Gospel commanded to bring the infants to Thee, and pronounced that the kingdome of heaven apperteined to such as they ar, we beseik thee to ressave these infants into the communion of thy saints. We have in thy name baptised them with water, bot, O Lord, baptise thou them with the holie Spirit that so this baptisme may become to them the laver of regeneration and they, through thy grace renuncing the devil, the world and the flesh, may serve Thee all their daies in holiness of lyfe. Blesse them, O Lord, with the remission of their sinnes, defend them from the malice of the devil, arme them aganst his restles tentations, guid Thou them saiflie through all the difficulties of this life and in end bring them to lyfe everlasting, through Jesus Christ, to quhom with thee and Thy holie Spirit be all praise, honor and glorie for ever. Amen.

THE ORDOUR TO BE OBSERVED IN TYME OF
HOLIE COMMUNION

> Before the incomming of the pastor, let the reader begin
> at this confession of sinnes with devotion and reverence.

O Lord our God, and our most mercifull father in Chryst Jesus, it beccommes us at all tymes to be humbled in thy praesence, considering our sinnes, which ar mony and great. Bot, O Lord, when we see thy loving mercies renewed againe towards us, after our great unthankfulnes and manifold rebellions against Thee, what great caus have we to be ashamed of our selves. Thy light has shyned to us bot alace we have not casten away the workis of darknes, thy grace that brings salvation hes appeared to us, and thou hes taught us of a long tyme to deny all ungodlines and worldlie lustes, bot we have not yet learned to live soberlie, righteouslie and godlie as becommes thy saints. We acknowledg, O Lord, that if thou wold deal with us after our sinnes and rewaird us according to our iniquities Thou might most justlie banesh us from Thy presence, Thou might tak us from Thy table which thou hes praepared and covered before us this day, and cast us into utter darknes, where is weeping and gnashing of teeth. Bot, O Lord, mercie is with Thee that Thou may be feared, Thy mercie is above all thyne owne workis, and mekle more above our sinfull deedes. Thou hes commanded one of us to forgive ane other seventie tymes seven tymes in the day. O Lord, sen Thou requyres such compassion in Thy creature, what is there in Thy self? Have mercie, therefore, upon us, O Lord, and according to the multitude of thy compassions putt away our iniquities. Let our soules this day be divorced from our sinnes and conjoyned in a holie communion with the Lord, that Thou may live in us and we may live in Thee and unto Thee and for ever hereafter may be with Thee, through Jesus Chryst. Amen.

Ane admonitioun

Als soone as the pastor enters into the pulpitt, the deacons and such as attend the table sal present the elements covered and sett them upon the samin, for besyde that be the word and prayer they ar sanctefeit and changed to the holie use whereunto God hes appointed them, the doctrine of Chryst his death will affect and move the people the more easilie when they see these holie signes which repraesent Chryst crucefeit unto us.

A confession of sinnes to be used by the pastor
at his first entrie to the pulpitt on the day of Communion.

O Lord our God and most mercifull Father in Jesus Chryst, we ar overcome this day with the multitude of thy compassions. We confesse and cry out with thy servant David, O Lord, what is man that thou art so myndfull of him, or the sonne of man that thou suld so farre regaird him, and what ar we, wormes of the earth, that thou, the God of glorie, suld offer thy self unto us and call us to a communion with thee. We ar not worthie, good Lord, of the least of thy mercies, yet it is thy good pleasure to make us this day pertakers of the greatest, for now the windowes of heaven ar opened, the table of the Lord is covered, his delicats ar praepared, the armes of his mercie ar stretched out and his loving voice calles upon us, Come to me all ye that ar wearie and laden and I will refresh you. Good Lord, as all things ar readie on thy part, so we beseik thee to praepair us, for the truth is, O Lord, if we be not changed from that which we ar in ourselves, we can not have fellowship with thee. What communion can be betwene light and darknes, Chryst and Belial? Change us, therefore, O Lord, and transforme us into thy owne similtude. Illuminat us with thy light that we walk no more in darknes. Delyver us from the servitude of Satan and sinne that we may serve the, Our God, in fredome of spirit and newnes of lyfe. Let us this day againe renew the covenant with thee which on our part we have broken so oft. Let us eat at Thy table the bread of lyfe and drink the water of lyfe that we may recover our strenth, that we may die to sin with our Lord and by the powar of his resurrection we may ryse to holines and newnes of lyfe, that so our communion with Jesus may be sealed up, confirmed and continued, till at lenth it be perfyted to the praise of thy mercie and everlasting comfort of our soules in Chryst Jesus, to whom with the and thy holie Spirit be all praise, honor and glorie for ever. Amen.

After sermone a prayer is used to this or the lyke purpose.

O Lord, as the tyme drawes neere that we suld go to thy holie table, let thy grace draw neere to our soules to sanctifie us for our holie communion with thee. Send out thy light and thy truth that they may lead us. We see thou hes covered a table for us and all things perteining to the mariage banquet ar praepared on thy part. Lord, prepair us also and mak us readie, tak our filthie garments away from us and cover us with the righteousnes of thy Chryst. Looke upon us, O Lord, thy poore servants, in mercie. We come not here to professe that we ar without sin, bot as miserable sinners we come to seeke the Saviour and Phisician of our soules, that we may get lyfe in him, who has none in our selves. Come downe, therefore, O Lord, and salvation under thy wings. O sweet Samaritan pitie us that ar deadlie wounded, powre the oile of thy grace into our soules and cure the deadlie diseases of our sinnes. Raise us up, O Lord, and revive us with that bread of lyfe Christ Jesus, who offered himself unto thee upon the crosse in a sufficient sacrifice for our sinnes and whom now thou offers to us in this sacrament as a foode for our soules, that by the strenth of his grace we may live hereafter unto thee and with thee for ever. Amen.

Before the pastor come out of the pulpit to present himself to the holie table, this or the lyke admonition wold be praemitted.

Dearlie beloved in the Lord, let us now enter in our owne harts and consider with our selves that as the benefit is great which here is offered unto us if with a lyvelie faith and penitent hart we ressave this holie sacrament (for then we spirituallie eat the flesh of Chryst and drink his bloode, then we dwell in Christ and Chryst in us, then we become one with him and he with us), so is the danger great if we ressave the same unworthilie, for then we ar giltie of the bodie and blood of Christ our Saviour, we kindle Gods wraith against us and provokes him to plague us with diverse diseases and sundrie kynds of death. And therefore in the name and authoritie of the eternal God I debarre and seclude from this table all blasphemers of God, all idolaters, murtherers, adulterers, all that bear malice or envy, all disobedient persons to their princes, pastors or parents, all theeves and deceavers of their nighbours and finallie all such as lead a lyfe directlie fighting against the will of God. And yet this I pronounce not to seclude ony penitent person, how greevous soever his sinnes have bene before, so that he feele in his hart a sorow for his sinnes and a resolut purpose to amend his lyfe hereafter, for in our best estait we feele in ourselves much frailtie and weaknes and we have neede dailie to fight aganst the lustes of our flesh, yet for all this we will not through unbelief dispair of Godis mercie, which now most lovinglie he renewes toward us againe, bot sen our harts through his grace ar sorowfull that ever we offended him, and desyres nothing more then to be reconciled with him and maid conformable to his holie will. We will aryse and go to his holie table as to a singular and most comfortable medicine for all seeke and diseased soules.

After the admonition let this or the lyke short prayer be praemitted before the action.

O Lord, who art the light of our mynd, the lyfe of our hart, the joy of our spirit and onlie strenth of our soule, schew thy self this day for Chrysts saik a mercifull God, to us poore miserable sinners. Mak this table of Shiloh, that is of thy Chryst, whom thou hes sent to be a Saviour unto us, better nor these waters of Siloam to these poore creatures that lay round about. There they wer cured of bodilie diseases, bot, O Lord, heale thou the diseases of our soules: there, none wes cured bot he that first stepped downe, bot here it is all alyke, O Lord, who come first or who come last to Thy table, for thou art rich in mercie and able to fulfill the necessities of all thy saints and therefore doe we this day wait upon thee, beseiking the to joyne thy blessing with thy owne ordinances that these elements may be unto us that which Thou hes appointed them, for Jesus Chrysts saik. Amen.

Then shall the minister give this wairning to all the communicants.

Ye that trewlie repents of your sinnes and beleves in the Lord Jesus, ye that ar in love and charitie with your nighbours and intends to live a godlie lyfe hereafter, come your way, draw neere to the holie table with faith, feare and reverence, for now the Lord calleth upon yow. Come to me all ye that ar wearie and laden and I will refresh you.

This done, the minister commes downe from the pulpit and goeth to the table, which being plenished with people and there, having shortlie declared how in the celebration of this sacrament we ar bound to follow the institution of Jesus, he shall tak in his one hand the bread and in the other the cuppe and before the breaking and distributing he shall blesse and give thanks, by this or the lyke prayer, after the example of our Lord.

We praesent not ourselves, O Lord, to this holie table trusting in our owne worthines, bot in thy manifold mercies. We confesse with the centurion we ar not worthie that thou suld come under our rooffe, and with that woman of Canaan we acknowledg that we ar not worthie to eat of the crommes that falles from thy table, far less that thou suld sett us downe lyke thy sonnes and daughters to beginne with thee that banquet upon earth which thou hes said shal be perfyted and continued for ever in heaven. O Lord, we acknowledg that no creature can comprehend the lenth and breadth, the depth and hight of this thy most excellent love which moved thee to shew mercie where none was deserved, to give lyfe where death had gotten the victorie, and to delyver us from that fearfull wraith under which Satan drew mankynd by the meanes of sinne from the bondage whereof neither man not angel wes able to mak us free, bot thou, O Lord, rich in mercie and inifit in goodnes, hes provyded our redemption to stand in thy onlie beloved sonne who wes maid man in all things lyke us, except sin, and in his blessed bodie did beare the punishment of our transgressions. He wes offred to thee on the crosse in a sacrifice for satisfaction of thy justice and is geven to us of thy mercie a food for our soule in this sacrament. Lord blesse it that it may be unto us ane effectuall exhibiting instrument of the Lord Jesus, for we come here to seeke the Phisician of our soules and to celebrat with thanksgeving the remembrance of his death and passion untill his coming againe, to declaire and witnes that by Chryst alone we have ressaved libertie and lyfe and redemption from that fearfull wraith to come, and that by Chryst alone thou acknowledges us thy children and heires, and gives us entrance to thy throne of grace. For these and all other thy inestimable mercies we thy congregation moved with thy holie Spirit randers unto thee all praise and honour and glorie and therewith all we offer unto thee the service of our soules and bodies, craving at thy mercifull handis grace to performe it in Jesus Christ. Amen.

The praier being ended, the minister repeats the words of consecration: The Lord Jesus that same night he wes betraied tooke bread and after he had geven thanks he brak it (which he shall doe in lyke manner) and gave it to his disciples saying etc.
Then delyvering it to these sitting with him shall say, Eat of this bread in remembrance of the bodie of Christ broken for you, and tak it as a pledge that Christ is geven you of the Father who repenting of your sinnes beleves in him.

Admonition
The pastor shall not suddenlie give the bread out of his hand, bot by a discret retention stirre up them who ar neerest him to a devout and reverent ressaving that others may learne reverence by their example, who ressave it immediatlie from the pastors hand.
The bread being delyvered, then with a short speech let him stirre up the affection of the ressavers, this or lyk it:
    Lift up your harts to the Lord etc.

Thereafter he taks the cuppe and having repeated the wordes of institution as of before let him give it to the neerest communicant, these words being spoken before he suffer him to drink:
Drink of this cup in remembrance of the bloode of Jesus, shed for you, and tak it for a pledge that Christ is geven you of the Father who repenting of your sinnes beleves in him.

The cup being also delyvered, let the pastor with a short speach stirre up the affection of the people

Lift up your harts unto the Lord, lay hold by faith upon Jesus, whom God the Father, by his Spirit, offers to you in this holie sacrament that ye may draw virtue from the Lord, to quicken and conserve your soules and bodies unto eternal lyfe.

In the tyme of service while the people ar communicating let the reader read distinctlie the historie of Chrysts passion, begin at the 13 chapter of St John and so goe fordward till the people having communicat begin to ryse from the table and others come in their place. All this time of the removing of the one and incomming of the other let him sing a part of the 103 psalme and the table being neere plenished let him conclude so mekle of the psalme as he hes sung, with Glorie to the Father etc., becaus it is a solemne day of thanksgiving and twyse holie to the Lord.

A short thanksgiving after that all the tables are served

What shall we randre to the, O Lord, for all thy benefits toward us? We confesse to thy glorie, we can not requyt thy loving kyndnes when we have geven to serve thy majestie all that we have, yet shall we remaine thy bound debitors in as mekle more as thy Chryst, Our Lord, is more nor we ar, whom thou gave to the death for us. Bot, O Lord, who accepted the widowes myte, becaus it came from a willing mynd, accept also the sacrifice which now we present unto thee. We desyre no thing more nor that be thy owne grace we may become thyne to serve the who of thy infinit love art become ours to save us and that in the strenth of the bread of lyfe, wherewith thou hes fed us this day, we may walk not fourtie dayes onlie, as Elijah did, bot all our daies in a holie and godlie conversation before thee. Mak us wyse, good Lord, to discerne the deceate of sinne in all tyme to come, mak us strong to resist the tyrannie of Satan. Thou knowes and we feele it that he envies our fellowship with thee, and that thou suld shew mercie upon us, which will never be shewed upon him. Good Lord, arme us with thy grace to resist him when he temptes us and if we fall, Lord, let us not perish, bot put under thy mercifull hand and raise us up againe; when of weaknes we forget thee, Lord remember thou us; continue thy good Spirit with us, keepe us under his good regiment and let no iniquitie have dominion over us. Leave us never to our selves, bot graciouslie perfyt this great work of our salvation which thou hes begun in us and this day hes sealed againe unto us, for which we thy redemed ones randres unto the, O most wise and faithfull creator, O loving and most sweet Saviour, O gracious and kynd comforter, holie, holie, holie, Lord God Almightie, all praise, honor and glorie for ever.

> Then, as our Saviour concluded this action with a psalme, let the people praise God in the first two verses of the 106 psalme. They containe a thanksgiving and a notable prayer.
> Thereafter the blessing is pronounced and the assemblie dismissed.

Appendix 4

Sacrament Chart, from John Denison's
The Heavenly Banquet, 1631

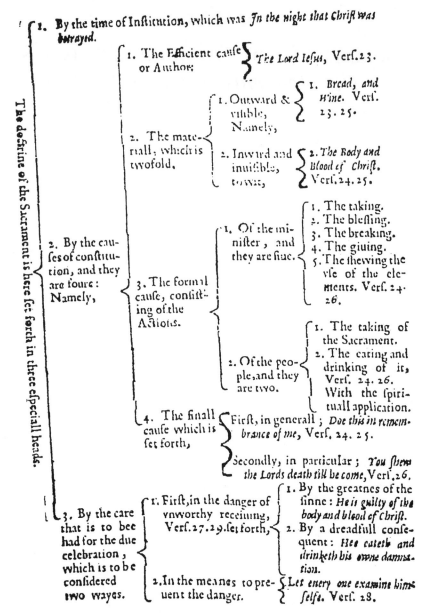

The doctrine of the Sacrament is here set forth in three especiall heads.

1. By the time of Institution, which was *In the night that Christ was betrayed.*

2. By the causes of constitution, and they are foure: Namely,

   1. The Efficient cause or Author: *The Lord Iesus*, Verf. 23.

   2. The materiall, which is twofold.
      1. Outward & visible, Namely,
         1. Bread, and Wine. Verf. 23. 25.
      2. Inward and inuisible, to wit,
         2. *The Body and Blood of Christ.* Verf. 24. 25.

   3. The formal cause, consisting of the Actions.
      1. Of the minister, and they are fiue.
         1. The taking.
         2. The blessing.
         3. The breaking.
         4. The giuing.
         5. The shewing the vse of the elements. Verf. 24. 26.
      2. Of the people, and they are two.
         1. The taking of the Sacrament.
         2. The eating and drinking of it, Verf. 24. 26. With the spirituall application.

   4. The finall cause which is set forth,
      First, in generall; *Doe this in remembrance of me*, Verf. 24. 25.
      Secondly, in particular; *You shew the Lords death till he come,* Verf. 26.

3. By the care that is to bee had for the due celebration, which is to be considered two wayes.

   1. First, in the danger of vnworthy receiuing, Verf. 27. 29. set forth,
      1. By the greatnes of the sinne: *He is guilty of the body and blood of Christ.*
      2. By a dreadfull consequent: *Hee eateth and drinketh his owne damnation.*
   2. In the meanes to preuent the danger. *Let euery one examine himselfe.* Verf. 28.

Place this before Folio 1.

Appendix 5

Zacharie Boyd's Communion
Watch-Word, 1629

Zacharie Boyd. 'A Watch-Word for all communicants, before they come to the supper of the Lord', in *Two Sermons for those who come to the Table of the Lord*, Edinburgh (1629), pp. 65–71.

As for you Brethren and Sisters that are to communicate, to morrow yee shall see *the remembrance* of that, which the Sunne in the Heavens could not behold for doole, viz. *the bloody passion of our LORD.*

This passion was so sore, that the *Sunne, the eye of the world* overclouded himselfe, and as it were *winked*, untill the unspeakable torments of CHRISTS death were past; then were *the Heavens* covered with a *vaile of sacke*; then the *earth* shooke : The stones, the *bones of the earth* were rent at the racking of the *bones of GOD*, the remembrance whereof should make *hearts of stone to cleave asunder.*

To morrow, deare Brethren and Sisters, we are for to *eate with Christ*:

Yea to morrow wee are for to *eate of Christ*, who is both *the feast* and *the Feast-maker*: To morrow wee are all for to sit at his *table*, where he will narrowly behold and clearely consider the faces of our soules, and therefore wee must take care this day that our Soules bee *washen and baptized with the truest teares of repentance.* I read of *Iames* and *Iohn*, while they were *unchristned men*, for to speake so, that is, not *baptized*, they desired the one to sit at CHRISTS right hand, and the other at his left: But the LORD told them, that before such sitting downe, it behoved them to bee *baptized with the baptisme of afflictions*: Hee and hee onely that is partaker of this *Baptisme* to day, shall bee made partaker of *GODS Supper* to morrow. As for these that are *not baptized with teares of griefe* before they sit downe at Table, the LORD hath sworne that they shall not partake of his feast: They may well eate *panem Domini* the LORDS bread, but they shall never taste *panem Dominum*, the LORD bread.

It shall therefore bee our wisdome, that everie one of us bee busie to prepare his owne heart, to decke & trim his soule before hee approach unto this TABLE, for to appeare before his GOD: As *Ioseph was trimmed and powled*, before he would appeare before *Pharaoh*, so must every soule have the *Wedding garment*, before it present it selfe before the LORD at his *Banket.*

Take heede what I say: This day is our preparation day: A day wherein wee must provide that *wherewith wee must come before the LORD* to morrow: If wee doe well, this day must be unto us all a very *painefull day,* even a *day of Battell* against all the pleasures that ever wee had in sinne, since we could discerne good from ill: In this day wee must *trye and search carefully all the secrets of our hearts:* This is the time where in wee must *keepe an Assise* against our selves, both for to *judge and condemne our selves*: In a word, wee must all take such paines *in sifting out all our bypast iniquities*, that the LORD may say of us, as hee said of the woman that broke the Boxe of ointment upon his head, *Shee hath done what shee could*.

Good Brethren and Sisters! What yee can doe, doe: What yee can not doe, pray GOD to doe it, and to pardon you your impossibility: *I beleeve*, (said that poore man with teares, that is all that I can doe;) but I beleeve not as I should, and therefore *LORD helpe thou myne unbeleefe*. Let us all bee earnest to intreat GOD to give us grace to doe what wee *can doe*, and what wee *can not doe* that hee would *pitie us, and pardon us*.

I reade that in the dayes of Hezekiah, a number of the people which had not cleansed themselves, did eate the Passover otherwise then it was written; But what befell them? I pray you: Many of them were *troubled with sore sickenesse*: But how were they cured of these diseases? It is said that Hezekiah prayed for them: *The good LORD*, (said hee) *pardon every one, that prepareth his heart to seeke GOD, the LORD GOD of his Fathers, though hee bee not cleansed, according to the purification of the Sanctuary*. Now what was the fruite of that prayer? This was it, *The LORD hearkned to Hezekiah, and healed the people*.

That which the *Passover* was to them, the *LORDS Supper* is unto us, even *a Sacrament appointed by GOD, for the sealing up of our Salvation*: If wee eate this *supper* otherwise then it is written, let us looke for diverse diseases: *For this cause*, (saith the Apostle,) *Many are weake and sickely amongst you, and many sleepe*, that is, die. Let us therefore, as we would desire our *bodies health, and our soules Salvation*, prepare our selves to *meete the LORD* tomorrow: There is none of us I confesse, that can *prepare* himselfe, *according to the preparation of the Sanctuary*, nor *cleanse* himselfe *according to its purification*, No Soule can bee so well *prepared* and *purified*, as GOD in his Sanctuary requireth. But this I dare be bold to say, that *the good LORD shall pardon every one that prepareth his heart to seeke GOD; though hee bee not so cleansed, as the purification of the Sanctuary requireth*.

GODS word is plaine, that GOD is mercifull: Hee hath sworne by his life, that He *delighteth not in the death of sinners*. He hath sent his word for to tell us, that *If wee will judge our selves, wee shall not bee judged*.

Yea such is his mercy, that while wee are chastised with sicknesse or death for our *carelesse preparation*, he maketh all that to worke to our well, *for when wee are judged, wee are chastened of the Lord; that wee should not bee condemned with the world*.

Now good people, not knowing if ever after this yee shall heare or I teach another *Preparation Sermon* in this place, let me conclude all with that *adew of St.Paul*, said to the elders of Ephesus at Miletum, *I commend you to GOD and to the word of his grace which is able to build you up, and to give you an inheritance amongst all them that are sanctified*.

Passe the rest of this day in a serious meditation of your *owne miserie*, and of the *bloodie agonie* of Iesus our Master, who out of love to us *hang upon a cursed tree* for to purchase unto us the *everlasting blessings of his Father:* To whom with
the Sonne of his love, and with
the Spirit of Comforts, bee
Glory and Majestie,
Dominion, and Power,
now, and ever.
Amen,

Appendix 6

William Guild's Communion Sermon, 'The Christians Passover', 1639

THE CHRISTIANS
PASSOVER

OR

A Sermon preached before the English
congregation in Danzik at their receaveing
of the Holie Communion,

By WILLIAM GUILD D.D.
and Minister at Aberdene.

ANNO M., DC. XXXIX

To the Right Worshipfull, his most worthylie respected, Francis Gordon Esquire,
Agent to his Sacred Majeste of great Britan, & gentilman
of his highnes privie chamber, &c.

Right Worshipfull.

Being *pressed* by sindrie (who with you first heard this sermon) to put it to the *presse*, that therby their memories might be refreshed who heard it, and the more comon benefit therof might extend it self to others who had not that occasion, and I considdering my obligation, what way so ever I may imploy my small talent, to the good of the godlie, & the gaine of soules, not to be defective, or to hide my light (how litle so ever) under a bushell. Therfor I have *suffered* the same to come forth under your *Worship's* patrocinie to a more publik view, whome for many reasons I am bound speciallie to respect, but cheeflie for that true & constant Love you beare to the trueth, as a faithfull servant not onlie to your Royall maister on earthe (whome the lord preserve & *prevent with the blessings of goodnesse)* but to your heavenlie maister, the king of kings & lord of lords who will in his own dew time in mercie reward your service aboundantly, And for my pairt, I beseech god earnestlie, what good soever, any hes receaved by these my poore paines, that the lord would seale it up more & more to their soules confort, and give me a heart to draw the

205

more neerer still to god for his better inableing, to whome *onlie* belongs the glorie of his owne grace, and whose best blessings as I shall wish to your *Worship*, your worthie confort, and hopefull children, and to all that *Worshipfull* and *religious* societie who heard me, so in a speciall manner I shall ever acknowledge my self.[1]

Your Worships *in all Christian and dewtifull observance,* William Guild

The Christian's Passover
I.Cor. 5.7.
For Christ our passover is sacrificed for us.

The *perfection* of the Christians knowledge on *earth*, is (as the apostle showes) *Christ crucified,* & the *perfection* of the Christians happines in *heaven* is lykewise *Christ glorified*, to behold him with the eie of *faith* heer, is the one, crowned with thornes, to behold him *face to face* heerafter, is the other, crowned with glorie. This first knowledge & viewing of Christ, is (like the *Baptist*) a forerinner of the other, & is a speciall act of grace (as the prophet declaireth it) the lord saying, *I will pouure my Spirit on them*, (& then subjoyning.) *and they shall look on him whome they have pierced.* Nather is it onlie theoricall or contemplative, but (as the aspect of the serpent was in the wildernes) it is medicinal & operative, to which therefor we ar so earnestlie exhorted by the apostle, *to look upon Jesus the author & finisher of our faith,* & for which end likewise, the word is not onlie preached that therby (as the apostle saith) *Christ crucified may visiblie* (as it wer) *beset befor our eies*, but the holie Sacrament also of his bodie & blood is institute to be celebrat, *to show forth his deathe till his againecoming*, or (as the words of my text sayes) to declair unto us, that *Christ our passover is sacrificed for us.*[2]

Which words, ar subjoyned by the apostle as a reasone of his former exhortation, as the particle of inference (*for*) does declair, wherin he did exhort the *Corinthians* to purge out the old laven that they might be a new Lump, alludeing so to the old *passover* & ceremonie therof *under the law*, in the time of celebration whereof, it was not lawfull to have any lavened breade within the hous, but to purge it cleane out: even so the apostle would intimat to them, that it was ther dewtie likewise now *under the gospell*, not onlie in like manner, to purge the congregation of such scandalous persons, as the incestuous man was, of whome he spoke before, but also to purge themselves of the laven of all sort of wickednes, and so to mak their whole life (as it wer) a constant celebration of such a festivall, the reason whereof is this, *for Christ our passover is sacrificed for us.*[3]

In these words, then we have to consider I. the dewtie wher unto we ar exhorted, for the performance wherof he subjoynes the reasone, and wich the particle of illation

---

[1] The following scripture references are given in the margin of this paragraph: Psal.22.3.
[2] The following scripture references are given in the margin of this paragraph: I.Cor.2.2; Psal.16.11; Zach.12.10; Heb.12.2; Gal.3.1; I Cor.11.
[3] The following scripture reference is given in the margin of this paragraph: Exod.12.19.

drawes into my text, which is in a word, the purgeing of our selves, a task necessar at all times, but in a speciall manner to be performed at this time, when we should come with the *wedding garment* to sit downe at the table of so great a king, remembring the *prodigalls* foule ragg's wer laid asyd, and he clothed anew, before he was sett at his fathers table to feed on the fatt calf, and as *Joseph* and *Esther* deck't & prepaired themselves fittinglie, before they come to stand in the presence of earthlie princes allanerlie, much more should they doe so, who ar not onlie to stand before, but to banquett with the prince of all princes, & searcher of the hearts, for this holie *shewbreade* must be received by these onlie whose vessells are cleane, this precious *liquour* must be putt into new bottles, this heavenlie *Manna* must have a golden pott to be laid up in, & this so pure a *guest* whose bodie after his deathe was wrapped in fine cleane Linnen, must not, nay, will not be broght now to enter under the roof of an uncleane heart, so that as the *Psalmist* says, *who shall ascend into the hill of the lord, and who shall stand in his holie place? He that hath cleane hands, and a pure heart:* even so I may say who should draw neer now to this table of the lord, & stand in so holie a place as to be pertaker of such heavenlie mysteries? even he onlie that hath cleane hands and a cleane heart in like manner; but seing this is thine owne work, O Saviour, who washed thy disciples feet, therfor with *David* we say, *wash thou us likewise throughlie from our sinnes O lord, creat thou also a cleane heart, & renew a right spirit within us,* & da quod jubes, & jube quod vis.[4]

Next to this dewtie to come to the reasone itself in the words of my text, wherin we have a *sacrifice* spoken of, & therin these things to be considdered, I. *Who is this sacrifice,* or the persone sacrificed. 2. the *act of sacrificeing itself,* and 3. the *persones for whome he was sacrificed.*

First, then, the persone sacrificed is descryved from his name *propperlie,* and next from a title given to him *allegoricallie,* his propper name given to him heer is *Christ,* a greek word, as his other name, *Jesus* is hebrew, insinuating therby this mysterie, that he should be a comon savior both to Jew & gentile who should beleve in him, the partition wall now being broken downe, and (as it was said by peter to Cornelius), *no exception of persones now being with god.*[5]

The signification of which word (*Christ*) is, *anointed,* now, ther wer three sorts of persones anointed (as we find in Scripture) *kings, priests* and *Prophets,* kings to rule, priests to sacrifice, prophets to instruct, and of such, some have bene found to be two of these, as *Melchizedek,* who was king & priest, *David,* who was king & prophet, & *Samuel* who was priest & prophet, but never any was all three but our Savior, who is not onlie the anointed of the lord, but the anointed lord him self, he is then a *king,* both to rule & defend us; a *priest* who hath sacrificed him self for us once upon earth, & interceeds for us still in the heavens, & he is the *Prophet* of his church, instructing us externalie by his word, & internallie by his spirit, a king he is descryved by *Isai.,* of whose dominion ther is no end, a priest for ever by the *Psalmist* after the order of

---

[4] The following scripture references are given in the margin of this paragraph: Matth.22.11; Luc.15.22; Gen.41.14; Esth.51; Psal.24.3; Psal.51.4–11.

[5] The following scripture reference is given in the margin of this paragraph: Act.10.34.

Melchizedek, and a prophet by *Moses* (as it was proclaimed from heaven at his transfiguration), whome all men should heare, to show by these three, that he is all in all, & (as the apostle sayes) that in him all fulnes dwell's. Both *generik,* that is, of all kynd of gifts & graces, fitt for discarge these his three offices. 2. *graduall,* or in the highest degree of eminencie, & 3. *integrall,* or in all the pairts & perfection of everie severall grace, & having dwelling in him a fulnes not onlie of *sufficiencie* (as *Job* speaks) competent to the members of the church militant, & of *affluence* or plenitude, competent to the church triumphant, but also of superaboundance for communication, propper to him onlie who is our heade, & of whose fulnes we receive grace for grace, whence we may observe to our singular comfort.[6]

I. The high advancement of our nature now in the persone of the sonne of god, farre above the *Heavens* to a dignitie of hiest eminencie, *royall, priestly & propheticall,* which before was so low abassed (like *chorazin & bethsaida)* to the lowest *hell's* under the bondage of Satan, the slaverie of sinne, & doome of damnation, through the transgression of the first *Adam.* O then that we had hearts to honour him, who so hes honoured us in the sonne of his Love & hes made us also a royall priesthood to him self heer, & to weare robes & crownes with him self herafter.[7]

2. This unction of our blessed lord & saviour was not for him self only, but for communication to us, so that as that precious ointment that was pouured on *Aarons* heade went downe to the skirts of his garments: even so these graces which wer pouured on him aboundantlie without measure, wer for participation in measure to all his mysticall members, & speciallie that oile of gladnesse wher with he was anointed above his fellowes, is now for all such who mourne in Sion, & comes heer prostrat at his feet with *Marie magdalens* disposition, that (as the prophet sayes) he may give them *beautie for ashes & the oile of gladnes for the spirit of heavines,* for this caus (sayes the spous in the *canticles*) thy *name is as ointment pouured out, therfor the virgens love thee,* to show, that ther is not onlie an *infusion* in him, but an *effusion* of grace upon us from him, as vertue went out of him to cure that poore diseased woman that had the bloodie issue.[8]

Therfor seing to our confort this fulnes is in our blessed saviour for participation, let everie sensible Soule then of their owne defects, have ther recourse now & at all times, to him onlie for furniture & supplie, as to that overflowing fountane of all grace & goodnes, specialie seing he so Loveinglie invites, saying, *Hoe, everie one that thirst's come to the waters,* & so earnestlie calles upon us, saying, *come to me all yee that ar wearie & laden, & I will refresh you.*[9]

---

[6] The following scripture references are given in the margin of this paragraph: I Sam.10.1; Levit.8.12; I King 19.14; Isai.9.6; Psal.110.4; Deut.18.18; Job.20.22; Joh.I.16.

[7] The following scripture references are given in the margin of this paragraph: Rev. 5.20.

[8] The following scripture references are given in the margin of this paragraph: Psal.133.2; Isai. 62.3.

[9] The following scripture references are given in the margin of this paragraph: Isai.55.1; Matth.11.28.

Next to yis propper name which the apostle gives to our Saviour, is that which allegoricallie is ascryved to him, borrowed from that which was given to the Lamb which was the Jewish passover, & transferred for fitnes of speech & fulnes of trueth to Christ him self, the trueth of that type, & substance of that shaddow, long wished & waited for, as that *Salvation to come out of Sion*, to the joy of all people & differenced heer in my text from that passover of the Jews under the law, by calling him *our passover* who ar Christians under the gospell.[10]

The resemblance which causeth this transferring of the name of the one to the other, consists cheeflie in the consideration of these points following I. in the *qualities* of the passover. 2. in the *Preparation* of it, & 3. The *use* & manner of the eating of the Same.

I. First then, as for the Jewish passover & qualities thereof, I. That behoved to be a *Lamb*; even so is Christ styled by the baptist, saying *behold the lamb of god that takes away the sinnes of the world,* & was rightlie prefigured by a lamb, becaus cheeflie of these three qualities, towit as a lamb is harmlesse & *innocent in life, patient in deathe & profitable alwise* both for food & clothing even so was our savior innocent & holie in his life, patient & meek in his deathe therefor (sayes Isai) *as a lamb before his sherar is dumb, so opened he not his mouth.* and 3. profitable is he likewise alway, both for consolation as also imitation, his fleshe also is the food of our soules, & his righteousnes is that robe wherwith we must be clothed, as with our elder brothers garment, if ever we look to have our heavenlie father's blessing.[11]

2. This Lamb was to be taken out of the *flock* to show that Christ was to come of the *race of mankind* so that, as it was said by god to our reproach before, *behold man is become as one of us,* so to our confort may it be said by man concerning Christ now, *Behold god is become lyk one of us,* remaining what he was, & becoming what he was not, *induendo humanitatem, sed non amittendo majestatem.*[12]

3. This lamb behoved to be *without blemish,* to signifie, that he who was to tak away the sinnes of others, behoved to be without sinne him self, actuall or original, for *such a high priest it behoved us to have (sayes* the apostle) *holie, innocet, undefyled, separat from sinners, & made higher then the heavens,* & heerin he differed from the highpriest under the law, who behoved to offer up sacrifice for his owne sinnes, as well as for others.[13]

4. He behoved to be a *male,* prefiguring heerby, not onlie that *Christ* should be man, but also, as the male is the noblest sex to which both *superioritie & strength*

---

[10] The following scripture reference is given in the margin of this paragraph: Psal.53.6.

[11] The following scripture reference is given in the margin of this paragraph: Joh.1.29; Isai.53.7.

[12] The following scripture reference is given in the margin of this paragraph: Gen.3.22.

[13] The following scripture references are given in the margin of this paragraph: Heb.7.26; Heb.9.7.

beyond the female belong's; so is *Christ Jesus* the noblest of mankind, to whome the excellencie both of dignitie & strength above all others pertains, he being heade over all, both of men & angel's, & who like a valiant *Sampson*, by his matchlesse strength hes overcome, & triumphed (even in deathe it self) over all our enemies.

5. He behoved also to be a *yeerold, wich* is a perfect revolution of the mensuration of time, & wherin sufficient experience may be had of the miseries of this naturall life, either by man or beast, denotating, therby, not onlie our saviors perfection every way, but also that he should experimentallie know all the miseries incident to man kynd, being compassed about with all our infirmities sinne onlie excepted, for which he is called by the prophet, *a man full of sorowes,* that so he might be a compassionat highpriest of his fellow brethren.[14]

As these then wer the *qualities* of the Jewish passover, to come next to *the preparation* therof.

I. This lamb behoved to be *killed*, to show that even so behoved our savior to be killed (as *Daniel* prophecied of him,) that so by such a violent sort of deathe, which in the course of justice amongst men is apointed for malefactours it might be seene that he died for sinners, and was reputed as one of such.[15]

2. As the paschal lamb was *killed the fourteneday of the month* or in the *fullmoone,* so heerby was typified, that even so our saviour should suffer deathe in the *fulnes of time,* & when typicall signes & propheticall predictions in his deathe had ther full accomplishment.

3. After the killing of the lamb, the *blood therof was to be sprinkled* upon the dore post's to show, that the effusion of Christs blood, without the particular application therof by faith unto our selves, availes not to salutation, but as the destroying angell passed *onlie* over these houses, whose doreposts wer sprinkled with that blood, even so, the destroying angell of gods wraith passes by *onlie* these soules, whereunto the blood of Christ is applyed by a saveing faith, & whole consciences ar sprinkled with that blood of aspersion.[16]

4. *The flesh was to be rosted* with fire, to denotat therby the dolorous sufferings of our blessed saviour both on the crosse, when rewfully he cryed out, *my god, my god, why hast thou forsaken me?* & abefore in the garden of *Gethsemane*, when (as the prophet speakes in the lamentations) *the lord sent fire from above into his bones,* & when by that bloodie sweat which he endured, his *liver was powred out upon the ground,* with strong cryes and teares praying that, that bitter cup might passe from him, which (alas) the cup of our sinnes had filled, being thus (as *David* said to the prophet) *in a wonderfull strait,* & the physition of our soules drinking

---

[14] The following scripture reference is given in the margin of this paragraph: Isai.53.

[15] The following scripture references are given in the margin of this paragraph: Dan.9.26; Isai.53.12.

[16] The following scripture reference is given in the margin of this paragraph: Lam.1.13.

thus the potion him self wherby we might be purged, & suffering the *phlebotome* wherby we might be cured.[17]

Last of all, as this was the preparation of the Jewish passover, so followes the use & manner of eating the same.

I. *First,* then, the *lamb was to be eaten,* to show that even so must our Saviour *Christ* be applyed particularlie, and fed upon spirituallie, *mente non dente ipsum manducâdo,* so that, he is not like that brasen serpent in the wildernes, onlie to be looked upon seriouslie, but like *manna* which come downe from heaven (as him self tells us) to be fed upon greedylie, therfor (sayes the prophet), eate & let your soule delight it self in fatnes so that he is a *sacrifice* not onlie offered up to god for *propitiation,* but also in the *sacrament* exhibit to man for food & *nutrition,* as the one to *free* us from *deathe,* & as the other to feed us to *life*.[18]

2. He *must be eaten whollie,* heade, feet & purtenance, prefigureing so unto us, that wee must apply *Christ Jesus* whollie to our soules, as god & man both in one persone, relying on the merit of his obedience both active & passive, & acknowledging that ther is nothing in him unprofitable to the soule to be usefullie considdered on, whether his birth, his life, or his deathe his heavenlie speeches, or his holie actions, and what he did as god miraculouslie, or suffered as man meeklie & patientlie.

3. The paschall lamb was to be *eaten with soure herbs* signifieing to the *Jewes,* that they should eate ther lamb with the remembrance ever of that bitter estate of bondage under *Pharao,* from which the lord delivered them by the hand of *Moses,* and we *Christians* should eate our passover in likemanner, with the remembrance of that more bitter estate of a greater and spirituall bondage, wherin we wer under that tyrant *Satan,* and from which the lord hes delivered us by our saviour, the promised *Messias*.[19]

In likemanner, this significed unto us, that with the sauce of true and unfained repentance *deploring* our sinnes, & *imploreing* his mercie, we should participat of the lord *Jesus,* for to such onlie shall he taste sweetest, who feed on him with this bitter sauce, and that soule shall onlie be found to be like *Naomi* or beautifull in his eies, who is first *Marah* or bitter & dejected in it owne ejes, the *countenance of his owne* children (with the spous in the canticles) *being then most comelie, & ther voice sweet,* when ther face is blurred with teares, & ther voice mournfull, and that soule which offer's up to god the sacrifice of a contrit spirit, being most sure to be pertaker of this sacrifice which *Christ* offered on the crosse.[20]

---

[17] The following scripture reference is given in the margin of this paragraph: 2 Sam.24.
[18] The following scripture references are given in the margin of this paragraph: Job.6.50; Isai.55.2.
[19] The following scripture reference is given in the margin of this paragraph: Cant.2.14.
[20] The following scripture reference is given in the margin of this paragraph: v.8.

4. The lamb was also to be *eaten with unlavened breade*, signifieing that we should participat of *Jesus Christ* the true paschall lamb in sinceritie of trueth, sound faith, and charitie, purgeing our soules (as the apostle expones) by repentance of all malice, and so comeing to this holie banquett with the wedding garment.

5. The Jewes did eate of their paschall lamb, with *their loynes girded, their shoes on ther feet, and staves in their hands,* to show unto us who ar Christians, how we should eate of our paschall lamb, towit (as the apostle showes) with our *loynes girded about with trueth our feet shod with the preparation of the gospell of peace,* and like pilgrimes heer (as both the Psalmist and apostle tells us) not setting our affections on earthlie things, but with the patriarch's of old, seeking a better countrie.[21]

6. they *did eate it in half,* now, as two things mak's one to eate in haist, to wit, a hungrie appetit, or an earnest desire to be fordward on ther jorney, so this was to show us, how we should come to eate of our true passover at this time, to wit, with a spirituall appetit of hungring after this heavenlie food, & thirsting (as the prophet tells us) after these waters of life. As also with an earnest desire to be fordward on our jorney more & more (by the grouth of grace) to that heavenlie Canaan, leaving the servitude of sinne, & our carnall pleasures, as the fleshpotts of Egypt.[22]

Last of all it was the law of the passover, that *no stranger nor uncircûcised person might eate thereof*, to signifie that no man who is a stranger to grace and uncircumcised in heart, shall ever be accounted a worthie guest to come this holie table, nor participat of the true paschall lamb Christ Jesus to his salvation, but on the contrair, eating and drinking unworthylie, and so prophaneing this holie mysterie (as the apostle tells us) *he eats and drinks damnation to him self,* & is guiltie of the lords deathe, which thing should mak us like that poore diseased woman with the bloodie issue, as with faith, so with a holie feare to draw neare to this holie sacrament.[23]

Having thus spoken of the persone and his description, who is the sacrifice, followes now to speake of the *act of sacrificing*, which is sett downe as preterit and performed, and therfor (sayes the apostle) *for Christ our passover is sacrificed for us,* showing therby, that he who was said abefore from the beginning of time to be virtuallie sacrificed, was now in the fulness of time actuallie sacrificed, so that what for the salvation of man kynd was by the *wisdome* of the father formerlie *decreed,* was by the *incarnat word* of the father not onlie *declaired,* but also by him as the *power of god* now fullie *accomplished.*[24]

---

[21] The following scripture references are given in the margin of this paragraph: Ephes.6.14; Psal.119.19; I Pet.2.11; Heb.11.16.

[22] The following scripture references are given in the margin of this paragraph: Isai.55.1; Matth.5.6.

[23] The following scripture reference is given in the margin of this paragraph: I Cor.11.29.

[24] The following scripture references are given in the margin of this paragraph: Apoc.5.12; Joh.1.1.

By which sacrificeing of him, is heer signified his passion, which howsoever his whole life was no other thing from the *crib* to the *crosse*, yet by his sufferings on the crosse he is speciallie said heer to be sacrificed, whereon he was both *sacerdos & victima,* or both priest and sacrifice, and suffered not onlie in his bodie at the hands of man, what malice could devyse or rage could inflict, but also in his soule at the hands of god, when he rewfullie cryed out, *my god, my god, why hast thou forsaken me?* as if it had not bene aneugh in the garden to have suffered that bloodie agonie wherin his soule was heavie to the verie deathe, and his bodie in the cold night time lying on the ground swett drops of blood, but after the drinking of that cup that he should yet taste of another, more bitter then that gall and vinager which was offered to him therafter, even this dreadfull derelection, whereof onlie as of his greatest suffering he complained greevouslie, as if all the rest he had despysed & sett to nought in comparison of this, & therfor which most of all he desyres all men to behold & considder, saying, *behold & see if ever the like sorow was like to my sorow, which is done to me, wherwith the lord has afflicted me, in the day of his fierce wraith.*[25]

Thus he suffered upon the crosse not onlie in bodie, but in soule, (which is the verie soule of suffering), 1. as our suretie who had sinned in both, 2. that so he might expiat our sinnes perfectlie, which we had committed both in soule and bodie, & so deliver us from our deserved sufferings in both, which we should other wise have indured eternallie.

3. That he might comfort heerby all these who ar distressed in soule, or troubled in conscience, as having had the proof of a wounded spirit in his owne person and that so he might be a compassionat high priest to his fellow brethren.

But beside this soule sufferings of our saviour on the crosse, he suffered also in his blessed bodie, to wit, *deathe* (as was foreprophecied) which is, *solutio debiti, pretium regni & terminus obedientiae,* or, the payment of our debt or ransome, the purchase of the kingdome to us, & the full extent of our saviours obedience to his father (like *Isaac*) even to the deathe, and not onlie suffered he deathe, but a *bloodie and violent deathe,* for without the effusion of blood ther was no redemption. Nather suffered he onlie a bloodie deathe, but *the deathe of the crosse,* which was a *cruell* and an *accursed* deathe, so to deliver us from the curse of god, the paines of hell, & eternall confusion, and upon which accursed tree he was not only *affixus* but *transfixus,* nailed to it in hands & feet, And thrust through upon it in his blessed heart, & wheron in likemanner his blood was shed not onlie violentlie & universallie, but also frequentlie & aboundlie, *violentlie* to show that he died for malefactours, *universallie,* in hands & feet, heade & heart, because we had sinned in all these & he was perfectlie to purge us from the guilt of all these, *frequentlie,* likewise his blood was shed to clenge us from our frequent transgressions, & *aboundantlie* not in a few dropps, but torrents and streames of blood, to expresse his lairge bountie to us in that which is most precious, the superaboundant *merit* wherof *ascended to heaven* to satisfie gods justice, appease his wraith, procure his

---

[25] The following scripture reference is given in the margin of this paragraph: Lam.1.12.

love, interceed for us continuallie, & to open the heavens (which wer shut before) both to our prayers heer & our persons heerafter. The *merit* of this blood also made *peace* to be on *earthe*, broght downe the gifts of the holie ghost, purges the soule, and calmes the distressed conscience. Yea to deathe, & his strong hold the grave, & hell the same has *descended*, to triumph over the same withall our other spirituall enimies, so that now, *O deathe wher is thy string? & o grave where is thy victorie.*[26]

This blood also hes a threefold confortable qualitie, to wit, it is a *purgeing* blood, a *purchaseing* blood, and a *pleading* blood. *First* then it is not like other blood, polluteing but *purgeing*, therfor called by *Zacharie a fontane opened to the house of David for sinne & for uncleannes*, & compaired to the waters of *Jordan*, cureing & clenging the spirituall leprosie *of Naman*. *Next* this blood is a blood of *purchase*, wherby we ar not onlie delyvered from the destroying angell of gods wraith, & from sinne & the second deathe, but hes gods love procured to us, as a fathers to his children, & ar made pertakers of divine righteousnes and eternall life, so that as by the price of his blood a purchase was made of a little peece of earthe to be a buriall, or resting place for the deade bodies of strangers: So by his precious blood it self is a purchase made of the spacious heavens to be a resting place for ever for the living soules of his elect in glorie.[27]

Thirdlie, or last of all, this blood of Christ, (whose *effusion* was to Satans *confusion*) is not like other blood, a dumb blood, but *hes a voice*, speaking better things then that of *Abell* which craved justice, wheras this cryes for mercie, & therfor is not onlie a *purgeing* blood on *earthe* but a *pleading* blood in *heaven*, on the glistering reednes of which blood when god casts his ejes, ther the guiltnes of that sinner for whome it pleads, is blotted out of his book, and wherby our saviour still acts the second pairt of his priestlie office at the right hand of the father interceeding in heaven, as he acted the first part once for ever by the offering up of him self as a sacrifice heer upon earthe.

Thus then by this sacrificeing of *Christ our passover* was that promise performed made in paradise to our first parents, that the *seed of the woman should tred downe the heade of the serpent,* Thus was that sacrifice typed by *Abells* offered up which found acceptation, and wherin as in *Noah's* the lord smelled a savour of rest or complacencie, thus was the onlie sonne of the father (as *Isaac* was to *Abraham*) offered up on the wood of the crosse, so that as the lord spoke to him, so may we say to god now *lord we know that thou lovest us, seing for our sake thou hes not spaired thy onlie begotten sonne.* Thus was the lamb of god killed, who is heer called, *Christ our passover* sacrificed for us, & Thus was his blood shed that it might be as a reed sea, wherby we might be saved, & wherin all our enimies might perish, & our sinnes like pharao's host sink & be buried, Thus was this true *rock* also stricken (as the apostle calles him) affording aboundantly to all thirstie and wearie sinners the water of refreshment & whose wounded bodie was made like

---

[26] The following scripture references are given in the margin of this paragraph: Isai.53.7; Dan.9.26; Heb.9.22.

[27] The following scripture reference is given in the margin of this paragraph: Zach.13.1.

that *rock full of clifts* (wherof the spous speakes in the canticles,) that therin his wel beloved dove may be secured from her persewing enimies, & delight therin to make her abode. Thus likewise was the *serpent* erected, which by his saveing aspect onlie cureth the fyrie stinging of that old serpent Satan, Thus also was that fontane opened (spoken of by Zacharie) for sinne & for uncleannes, & Thus in like manner was that true *propitiatorie sacrifice* offered up for expiation and atonement, wherein all typicall sacrifices under the Law had ther accomplishment. Thus also was the wine presse trode by our saviour alone, and ther was none of the people with him. And to conclude, thus was that *fatt calf* killed by the loveing father for feasting of his returning prodigall, *Christs* blessed bodie being as a voluminous book, wherin we may reade, *gods justice, Christs love, sinnes merit, & mans confort*, each wound being a letter, his blood the ink, the crosse the presse, justice imprints, mercie dedicats, merit intitulats.[28]

At which passion of his, each creature (alasse) except man, shew as it wer a compastion, the heavens above put on mourning garment, with the glorious creatures of sunne & moone therin, & no marvell, when he died who was the god of heaven, and sunne of righteousnes him self, the earth below also, it trembles, quaking to see dust & earthe so wickedlie to carie against ther creator, the vaile of the temple it rent, as haveing a sympathie with his suffering who was the lord of that temple, and the holie temple of whose bodie (inhabited by the deitie) man was destroying, the rocks they clave asunder, as being moved with that which the hard & rockie heart of man could not be moved withall, and therfor (sayes one) upon that place of *Ezechiel*, wher the lord promises to *tak from man his stonie heart, & to give him a heart of flesh, no, lord* (sayes he) *rather give me a heart of stone, and tak this fleshlie heart from me, for I find that when thy sonne my saviour suffered, the stones did cleave asunder, but the fleshlie heart of man was nowhit moved therby*.[29]

And yet not with standing of all this sensles misreguard, & monstrous ingratitude, this meek lamb who was sacrificed for us, not onlie patientlie indured what Satans rage or mans malice could inflict upon him, but charitablie he prayed for his crucifiers, & lovelinglie on the crosse bowes downe his heade, to kisse (as it wer) everie returning prodigall, obeying therby that suit of his spous in the canticles *let him kisse me with the kisses of his mouth, for his love is better nor wine*, he stretcheth out his armes also to embrace, and opens his heart to receive in the bosome therof everie wearie sinner, sending forth refreshing streames of blood & water aboundantlie to confort all such, & crying from the crosse by the posture of his bodie (as it wer) *hoe everie one that thirsts come to the waters, and, come unto me all yee that ar wearie and loden & I will refresh you*.[30]

---

[28] The following scripture references are given in the margin of this paragraph: Gen.3.15; Gen.4.4; Gen 8.21; Gen.22.12; Exod.12.21; Exod.14.28; I Cor.10.4; Num.11.9; Zach.13.1.
[29] The following scripture reference is given in the margin of this paragraph: Ezech.36.26.
[30] The following scripture references are given in the margin of this paragraph: Cant.1.2; Isai.55.1; Matt.11.28.

Followes now last of all, for whome Christ our passover was sacrificed (*for us*) (sayes the apostle) which words doe include I. the *caus* of his sufferings. 2. *the end, wherfor*, and 3. *the person's* for whome he suffered.

First then he was sacrificed *for us*, that is, for our sinnes, as the prophet Isai. tells us, that he *was wounded for our transgressions, for all we like sheep had gone astray, and the lord laid on him the iniquities of us all,* he might justlie therfor made that challenge which de doth John. 8.46. saying, *who of you can accuse me of sinne?* or inverted that speech of *Davids, I have sinned & done wickedlie but these sheep what have they done?* & said, *these straying sheep of man kynd have sinned & done wickedlie, but I what have I done?* and unto everie one us he might justlie say as *Nathan* said to *David, thou art the man,* and caus of my sufferings, for it is we who have eaten the sowre grapes, & his teeth wer sett on edge, our sinnes wroght his sorowes, our deeds his dolours, & our crymes caused his crucifieing, so that man sinned, and god suffered, we faulted & he was punished.[31]

The sinnes therfor of our soules, made his soule heavie to the deathe, our filling of the cup of iniquitie made him to drink of that bitter cup in his agonie, our hautie ambition caused his so deep dejection, our perverse actions, procured his painfull passions, the pollution of our hearts the piercing of his heart, the sinnefull thoghts of our heads the crowning of his heade with thornes, the straying of our feet in sinne & acting therof with our hands, caused the nailing of his feet & hands to the crosse, our forsakeing of god, his querimonie of being forsaken by him, & our love to sinne his suffering of wraith for sinne, the dint of which blow if he had not stept in & received it in his owne persone *for us,* we had eternallie suffered in easelesse & endlesse torment.

Wherfor let not our thoghts (like Dinah) wander Idlelie elswher, & with our first parents lay the blame on others, who wer but secundarie and subservient instruments, as *Judas* who betrayed him, *Pilat* who condemned him, *the people* that cryed, crucifie him, but reflect upon our selves whose sinnes wer the principall actours and causes of his deathe, & therfor let us mourne for them & mortifie them if ever we look to have the favour of god heer, or expect fellowship with him in glory heerafter.

Secondlie, he was sacrificed *for us,* that is, for our redemption, the end of his sufferings being mans salvation, therfor said the angell before his birth, *and they shall call his name Jesus, for he shall save his people from their sinnes,* and at his birth said the angell likewise, *behold I bring you tydings of great joy which shalbe to all people, for unto you is borne a saviour, which is Christ the lord,* and not onlie a saviour, but who is called also from this glorious work which he hath wrought, *salvation* it self, (as old Simeon styled him, saying *for my ejes have seene thy salvation,* which salvation wherof he is author, the apostle calles a perfect salvation, or εἰς τὸ παντελὲς because he saves both soule & bodie, & not onlie from our

---

[31] The following scripture references are given in the margin of this paragraph: Isai.53.4–5; 2.Sam.24.17.

sinnes (the root of all our miserie,) but also from all our sinnes (as S. John tells us) & all other our spirituall enimies besyds, & not onlie delyvers us from eternall damnation, but procures to us by his deathe eternall life & ever lasting salvation, & so invests us (as our second *Adam*) in a farre better estait then that which we lost by the first, which makes the apostle say, *not as the offence was so is the gift.*[32]

He humbled him self then that we might be exalted, he descended from heaven, that we might ascend, he was poore, that we might be enriched, was emptied, that we might be filled, did sweat that we might be refreshed, was apprehended that (like the scape goate) we might goe free, was bound that we might be loused, condemned that we might be absolved, wounded, that we might be cured, punished, that we might be pardoned, forsaken that we might be accepted, and last he died, that we might Live forever. And in a word as the apostle compryses all his sufferings under these two, *he indured the crosse and despyssed the shame*, the crosse to procure to us a crowne, and the shame to advance us to glorie.[33]

Thirdlie (*for us*) denotats the persones for whome our saviour suffered, these ar we, men by nature, & sinnefull men by the fall of *Adam*, and yet *for us*, and not for the fallen angell's he came into the world & suffered of the world, therfor (sayes the apostle) *he took not upon him the nature of angels, but the seed of Abraham*, to be like unto his brethren in all things, As the *priest and Levit* then passed by the wounded Israelit, so hes our saviour passed by the fallen angels, & onlie (like the Loveing *Samaritan*) hes turned in to us, to powre into our wounds that which was powred out of his owne wounds, and pitieing our miserie, hes bound them up with the hand of his mercie. So that as *Isai* truelie sayes, *unto us is given a sonne,* so no lesse truelie said the angell, *unto you is borne a saviour,* to you, to wit, man kynd that fell, not unto us nor any of our nature, angels that fell, Justlie then with admiration of divine mercie, with the psalmist may we exclame, saying, *what is man that thou should be so myndfull of him, or the sonne of man that thou should visit him?* & more then just cause hes eache one to inquyre with *David, quid rependam?* or *what shall I render unto the lord who hath delt so bountifullie with me?* for he hes delivered our soules from deathe eternall, our ejes from teares and weeping forever, & our feet from falling in the pitt of endlesse perdition. And therfor we should resolve, if we ow our selves fullie unto him for our creation, what can we render furder unto him for our redemption? In the first work he gave us onlie to our selves, but in the second he hes both restored us who wer Lost, and given him self unto us likewise for our restitution, being then first given to our selves, & after our losing being restored, we ow, yea, we twise ow our selves unto him, but what shall we render for him self given both to us & to deathe for us? for altho we should give our selves a thousand times unto him, what ar we in comparison & requytall of our lord. O the abysse then of matchlesse mercie and the deipth of divine bountie! which no soule can sound, no tongue recount, no flesh requyt, the superabundance wherof is that onlie which

---

[32] The following scripture references are given in the margin of this paragraph: Matth.1; Luc.2; Heb.7.25; I Joh.1.9; Rom.5.15.
[33] The following scripture reference is given in the margin of this paragraph: Heb.12.2.

mak's us bankrupt's of our dewtie, that we can never pay the interest. Let be the principall of his Love.[34]

Of all which formerlie spoken, we have these things shortlie to observe, I. the mercie of god, 2. the love of Christ, 3. the merit of sinne, & 4. the dewtie of man.

First then we see the mercie of god towards man, no sooner seing (I should say forseeing) his fall but as soone provyding and decreeing his rysing againe, yea before that with the Israelits we could groane under our bondage, sending the meanes & apoynting the manner of our happie deliverie and, and before that we could resolve to returne with the prodigall sonne, like a most loveing & pitifull father rinning towards us to kisse us with the kisse of peace & embrace us with the armes of compassion, so that it is most true which the psalmist speaketh, *like as a father pitieth his children, so hes the lord pitied us, he hes forgiven all our Iniquities and healed all our diseases, he hes redeemed our life from destruction, & crowned us with loveing kyndnes & tender mercies, & hes not delt with us after our sinnes, nor rewarded us according to our iniquities, Returne then, o my soule, unto thy rest,* may each one of us with the Psalmist say, and let us beseech god that these his mercies may never goe out of our mynd, nor his praises for them out of our mouth.[35]

Secondlie, we see the admirable and matchlesse Love of *Christ, in dieing for his verie enimies,* whose heart for them being first pierced with love, made his heart therafter to be pierced with a lance, and as *Jacob* counted all the yeers of his hard service, which he served for *Rahell,* to be but a few dayes, becaus he loved her: even so that which made all the heavie sufferings of *Christ,* which he endured for man kynd to be but light in his account (as it wer) was the love he carried to us, so that when we look on his sufferings, & how he shed not onlie teares but blood for man, both in his agonie & upon mount *Calvarie,* if the Jewes said when he wep't for *Lazarus, behold how he loved him,* then much more may we say, *behold how he loved us,* and therfor would not onlie content to have his hands & feet pierced, but his heart also (the seat of affection) opened on the crosse, that the piercing lance might be the opening key, and by the lanceing of his bodie might apeare (as throw a lettice) the love of his heart, so that no penitent sinner needs now to doubt of Christ's love, & readie admission to mercie, when he not onlie so kyndlie invites all such to come to him, & needs now to bestow onlie on him one loveing smile but when he sees that his salvation was dearer to him then his verie life, & that he preferred the same before the shedding of his heart blood.[36]

Thirdlie we may see the merit of sinne in Christs suffering for sinne, and how that our saviour undergoing the burden of sinne, behoved to undergoe likewise the

---

[34] The following scripture references are given in the margin of this paragraph: Heb.2.2; Isai.9.6; Luc.2; Psalm.8.4; Pf.116.12.
[35] The following scripture references are given in the margin of this paragraph: Psal.103; Psal.116.7.
[36] The following scripture references are given in the margin of this paragraph: Rom.5.10; Cant.2.9.

burden of wraith, & such bitter sufferings, which wer intollerable for any to beare, but for him onlie who was both god and man, And if this was done to the greene tree, so that he *spaired not his owne sonne,* what may the withered branch expect in that day when gods wraith is kindled in his rage, In what agonizing astonishment shall impenitent sinners be then, greater then that of the *Belthasers,* & (as *David* said,) in what a wonderful strait? Of what a bitter cup shall they then drink, more bitter then wormewood and gall, & what caus shall they then have who forsooke gods precepts to complaine, that they ar not onlie woefullie forsaken of god, but justlie adjudged to eternall torment, which knowes no ease of paine nor end of time, & wher ther is nothing but miserie without measure, sorow without slaking, horrour with out hope, punishment without pitie, and calamitie without côfort. O that men would therfor feare in time to eate the fruit of sinnes forbiddê tree, that so they might escape the dreadfull dint of gods deserved wraith.[37]

Last of all, hence we may considder what is our dewtie, hes Christ loved us with a greater love by farre then *Jonathan* loved *David,* which exceeded the love of wemen, then let us love him againe, & our Christian brother in him, & *totus nobis figatur in corde, qui totus pro nobis fixus fuit in cruce.* And if we love him let us also forbeare sinne which so displeases him, shed his blood, & broght him to deathe, And as the Israelits immediatlie after their eating of the paschall lamb forsooke *Pharaos* bondage, & depairted from *Egypt* to wards ther land of promise, even so, we now having participated of our true lamb *Christ Jesus,* let us in likemanner forsake the slaverie of sinne & bondage of Satan, taking a new course of life now to walk in the path's of pietie, towards our heavenlie countrie, and let us heerby trye if with *Zacheus* salvation this day is come to the house of our soule, or that we have bene worthie pertakers of this blessed Sacrament, and hes receaved saveing grace therby, that as that poore woman who came to our saviour diseased with a bloodie issue, found that she was made whole, after her touching of the hemme of his garment, becaus by that vertue that went out of him her former uncleanes was dryed up therafter, so if we have come hither this day preparedlie sensible of our sicknes, & with faith and feare, as she did, & after participation of this holie mysterie we find in likemanner that the issue of our former uncleannes in sinne be dryed up, & that we find it to decay daylie both in the power and practice therfor, & that we also stryve in the strength of this spirituall food to walk in a new course of life & conversation, offering up our selves (as we ar exhorted) *in a liveing sacrifice* to him who offered him self as a sacrifice to the deathe for us, then we may be sure that we have touched *Christ* by faith, & gotten saveing vertue from him & as he hes honoured us to participat of this his holie table heer, so he will advance us at last to sitt with him at his heavenlie table heerafter, which the lord grant to us, who is *our passover* (sayes the text) & *is sacrificed for us.*[38]

Amen, Amen

---

[37] The following scripture references are given in the margin of this paragraph: Rom.8; Dan.5; 2.Sam.34.

[38] The following scripture reference is given in the margin of this paragraph: Ro.12.1.

Bibliography

A Vindication of the Presbyteriall-Government and An Exhortation to the ministers of the London Province, 1649, 1650.

Acts of the General Assemblies of the Church of Scotland 1638–1649, 1691, Edinburgh.

Allison, C.F., 1966, *The Rise of Moralism: The Proclamation of the Gospel from Hooker to Baxter*, SPCK, London.

Ames, William, 1622, *A Reply to Dr. Mortons generall Defence of three, nocent ceremonies.viz. the surplice, crosse in baptisme, and kneeling of the sacramentall elements of bread and wine*, London.

——, 1997, *The Marrow of Theology*, trans. John Dykstra Eusden, Baker Book edn, Grand Rapids.

Andrewes, Lancelot, 1854, *The Works of Lancelot Andrewes*, Library of Anglo-Catholic Theology, Parker, Oxford.

——, 1874, *Ninety-Six Sermons*, Parker, Oxford.

Anon., 1606 (1610 edn), *A Survey of the Book of Common Prayer By way of 197 Quares grounded upon 58 places*, London.

Anon., 1617, *An Abridgement of that Booke which the Ministers of Lincolne Diocesse Delivered to his Majestie upon the first of December 1605*, London.

Anon., 1638, *Reasons For which the Service Booke, urged upon Scotland ought to bee refused*, Edinburgh.

Arnoult, Sharon Louise, 1997, 'The Face of an English Church: The Book of Common Prayer and English Religious Identity', unpublished PhD dissertation, University of Texas at Austin.

Attersoll, William, 1614, *The New Covenant, or a Treatise of the Sacraments*, London.

Baillie, Robert, 1640, *Ladensium autokatakrisis, the Canterburians self-conviction*, Amsterdam.

——, 1641a, *A Parallel of the liturgie with the masse book*, London.

——, 1641b, *Ladensium autokatakrisis*, 3rd edn with supplement, London.

——, 1646, *Anabaptism, the true Fountaine of Independency, Brownisme, Antinomy, Familisme*, London.

——, 1841–42, *The Letters and Journals of Robert Baillie*, David Lang (ed.), 3 vols, Edinburgh.

Baillie, William, 1959, 'The Rites of Baptism and Admission of Catechumens ("Confirmation") according to the Liturgy and History of the Church of Scotland', PhD thesis, Queen's University Belfast.

Barlow, William, 1601, *A defence of the articles of the protestant religion*, London.

Baxter, Richard, 1649, *Five Disputations on Church Government and Worship*, London.

——, 1651, *Plain Scripture Proof of Infants Church-membership and Baptism*, London.

——, 1675, *Two Disputations of Original Sin*, London.

——, 1830, *The Practical Works of the Rev. Richard Baxter*, W. Orme (ed.), 20 vols, London.

Bedford, Thomas, 1638, *A Treatise of the Sacraments According to the Doctrines of the Church of England, touching the Argument*, London.

Beeke, Joel, 1991, *Assurance of Faith. Calvin, English Puritanism and the Dutch Second Reformation*, Peter Lang, New York.

Bell, M.Charles, 1985, *Calvin and Scottish Theology*, The Handsel Press, Edinburgh.

Blackader, John, n.d., Mr Blacader's Memoirs, Wodrow manuscripts, National Library of Scotland.

Blake, Thomas, 1644, *The Birth Privilege, or Covenant Holinesse of Beleevers and their Issue in the time of the Gospel, Together with the Right of Infants to Baptisme*, London.

——, 1645, *Infants Baptism freed from Antichristianisme*, London.

——, 1646, *An Answer to Mr. Tombes*, London.

——, 1653, *Infant Baptisme maintained in its Latitude*, London.

——, 1655, *The Covenant Sealed, or, a Treatise of the sacraments of both covenants*, London.

Bonar, Andrew A. (ed.), 1850, *Letters of the Rev. Samuel Rutherford*, Carter & Brothers, New York.

Bonar, H., 1866, *Catechisms of the Scottish Reformation*, Nisbet, London.

Bornert, René, 1981, *Le Reforme Protestante du Culte à Strasbourg au XVIe Siècle*, Brill, Leiden.

Boyd, Robert, 1661, *In Epistolam Pauli Apostoli Ad Ephesios Praelectiones*, Geneva.

Boyd, Zacharie, 1639, *A cleare forme of Catechising, before the giving of the Sacrament of the Lords Supper*, Glasgow.

——, 1829, *Two Sermons for those who are to come to the Table of the Lord*, Edinburgh.

Bramhall, John, 1842–45, *The Works of the Most Reverend Father in God, John Bramhall, DD*, Library of Anglo-Catholic Theology, 5 vols, Parker, Oxford.

Bremer, Francis J. (ed.), 1993, *Puritanism: Transatlantic Perspectives on a Seventeenth-century Anglo-American Faith*, Massachusetts Historical Society, Boston.

Breward, I., 1980, *The Westminster Directory*, Grove Liturgical Study 21, Bramcote.

Brookes, P.N., 1965, *Thomas Cranmer's Doctrine of the Eucharist: An Essay in Historical Development*, Seabury Press, New York.

Bruce, Robert, 1958, *The Mystery of the Lord's Supper*, T.F. Torrance (ed.), John Knox Press, Virginia.

Buchanan, Colin, 1976, *What Did Cranmer Think he was Doing?*, Grove Books, Bramcote.

——, 2000, '"Do this in remembrance of me" ... but what do we do?', *Anvil* 17, pp.247–58.

Buckeridge, John, 1618, *A Discourse Concerning Kneeling at the Communion*, London.

Buckroyd, Julia, 1980, *Church and State in Scotland 1660–1681*, John Donald, Edinburgh.

Bullinger, Heinrich, 1850, *Decades*, Parker Society edn, Cambridge University Press, Cambridge.

Bunting, Ian D., 1966, '*Consensus Tigurinus*', *Journal of Presbyterian History* 44, pp.45–61.

Burges, Cornelius, 1629, *Baptismall regeneration of Elect Infants, Professed by the Church of England, according to the Scriptures, the Primitive Church, the present reformed Churches, and many particular Divines apart*, London.

——, 1660, *Reasons shewing the necessity of reformation of the public 1. doctrine, 2. worship, 3. rites and ceremonies, 4. Church-government, and discipline, regarded to be (but indeed, not) established by law*, London.

Burnet, George, 1960. *The Holy Communion in the Reformed Church of Scotland 1560–1960*, Oliver and Boyd, Edinburgh and London.

Burnet, Gilbert, 1897, *History of My Own Times*, Osmund Airy (ed.), 4 vols, Oxford (1818 edn, London).

Calderwood, David, 1619, *Perth Assembly*, Leiden.

——, 1620, *A Defence of our Arguments against kneeling in the acts of receiving the sacramentall elements of bread and wine impugned by Mr. Michelsone*.

——, 1678, *A True History of the Church of Scotland*, Edinburgh.

Calvin, John, 1536, *Institutes of the Christian Religion*, Ford Lewis Battles (ed.), rev. edn, Grand Rapids, 1986.

——, 1559, *Institutes of the Christian Religion*, James Clarke, London, 1962.

——, 1954, *Theological Treatises*, J.K. Reid (ed.), Westminster Press, Philadelphia.

Cameron, John, 1642, *Joannis Cameronis, Scoto-Britanni Theologi*, Geneva.

Cardwell, Edward, 1841, *A History of Conferences and other Proceedings Connected with the Revision of the Book of Common Prayer*, Oxford.

Cheyne, A.C., 1999, *Studies in Scottish Church History*, T & T Clark, Edinburgh.

Coffey, John, 1997, *Politics, Religion and the British Revolutions. The Mind of Samuel Rutherford*, Cambridge University Press, Cambridge.

Collinson, Patrick, 1967, *The Elizabethan Puritan Movement*, Jonathan Cape, London.

Common Order, 1994, rev. edn 1996, St Andrews Press, Edinburgh.

Como, David, 2000, 'Puritans, Predestination and the Construction of Orthodoxy in early Seventeenth-Century England', in Peter Lake and Michael Questier (eds), *Conformity and Orthodoxy in the English Church, c.1560–1660*, Boydell Press, Woodbridge, pp.64–87.

Corda, Salvatore, 1975, *Veritas Sacramenti. Study in Vermigli's Doctrine of the Lord's Supper*, Theologischer Verlag, Zurich.

Corrie, G.E. (ed.), 1853, *A Catechism Written in Latin by Alexander Nowell, Dean of St. Paul's: Together with the same Catechism translated into English by Thomas Norton*, Parker Society, Cambridge University Press, Cambridge 1853.

Cosin, John, 1681, *A Collection of Private Devotions in the Practice of the Ancient Church*, 8th edn, London.

——, 1843–55, *The Works of John Cosin*, Library of Anglo-Catholic Theology, Parker, Oxford.

Couper, W.J. et al., 1995, *Scotland Saw His Glory*, reprint by International Awakening Press, Illinois.

Cowper, William, 1629, *Workes of Mr. William Cowper, Late Bishop of Galloway*, London.

Craghead, Robert, 1695, *Advice to Communicants*, Edinburgh.

Craig, John S., 1959, 'Catechism', in T.F. Torrance (ed.), *The School of Faith*, James Clarke, London.

——, 1998, 'The Cambridge Boies: Thomas Rogers and the "Brethren" in Bury St. Edmunds', in Susan Wabuda and Caroline Litzenberger (eds), *Belief and Practice in Reformation England*, Ashgate, Aldershot.

Cuming, G.J., 1961, *The Durham Book*, Durham University, Oxford University Press, Oxford.

——, 1969, *A History of Anglican Liturgy*, Macmillan, London.

——, 1983, *The Godly Order. Texts and Studies Relating to the Book of Common Prayer*, Alcuin Club/SPCK, London.

Cuming, G.J., 1961, *The Durham Book*, Durham University, Oxford University Press, Oxford.

Curtis, Mark H., 1959, *Oxford and Cambridge in Transition 1558–1642*, Clarendon Press, Oxford.

——, 1961, 'Hampton Court Conference and its aftermath', *History* 46, pp.1–16.

Cushing, James T., 1998, *Philosophical Concepts in Physics*, Cambridge University Press, Cambridge.

Danner, Dan G., 1999, *Pilgrimage to Puritanism. History and Theology of the Marian Exiles at Geneva 1555–1560*, Peter Lang, New York.

'Debate on Infant Baptism, 1643', 1908–10, *Transactions of the Baptist Historical Society* 1, pp.237–45.

Denison, John, 1631, *The Heavenly Banquet; or the Doctrine of the Lords Supper, set forth in seven Sermons*, second impression, London.

Denison, Stephen, 1634, *The Doctrine of both the Sacraments: To wit, Baptisme, and the Supper of the Lord*, London.

Dent, C.M., 1983, *Protestant Reformers in Elizabethan Oxford*, Oxford University Press, Oxford.

Dickson, David, 1635, *A Short Explanation, Of the Epistle of Paul to the Hebrews*, Aberdeen.

——, 1664, *Therapeutica Sacra*, Edinburgh.

——, 1651, *A brief exposition of the evangel of Jesus Christ according to Matthew*, London.

——, 1671, *The summe of saving Knowledge*, Edinburgh.

——, 1685, *Truths Victory over Error*, Edinburgh.

Dix, Gregory, 1945, *The Shape of the Liturgy*, Dacre Press, London.

Dod, John, 1611, *Ten Sermons tending chiefly to thye fitting of men for the worthy receiving of the Lord's Supper*, London.

——, 1612, *The Catechism*, London.

Donaldson, Gordon, 1954, *The Making of the Scottish Prayer Book of 1637*, University Press, Edinburgh.

——, 1966, 'A Scottish Liturgy of the reign of James VI', *Scottish Historical Society Miscellany* 10, pp.87–117.

Downame, George, 1647, *The Covenant of Grace or an exposition upon Luke 1:73.74.75*, London.

Downame, John, 1622, *A Guide to Godlynesse or a Treatise of a Christian Life*, London.

Du Priest, Travis, 1972, 'The Liturgies of Jeremy Taylor and Richard Baxter: A Study of Structure, Language, and Rhythm', unpublished PhD dissertation, Kentucky University.

Dudley, Martin (ed.), 1995, *Like a Two-Edged Sword*, Canterbury Press, Norwich.

Dugmore, C.W., 1942, *Eucharistic Doctrine in England from Hooker to Waterland*, SPCK, London.

Dyke, Jeremiah, 1642, *A Worthy Communicant: A Treatise shewing the Due Order of receiving the Sacrament of the Lords Supper*, London.

Egerton, Stephen, 1644 edn, *A Briefe Method of Catechizing*, London.

Elwood, Christopher, 1999, *The Body Broken. The Calvinist Doctrine of the Eucharist and the Symbolization of Power in Sixteenth-Century France*, Oxford University Press, Oxford.

Evans, G.R., 1992, 'Calvin on Signs: an Augustinian dilemma', in Richard C. Gamble (ed.), *Calvin's Ecclesiology: Sacraments and Deacons*, Garland Publishing, New York and London, pp.153–63.

Evelyn, John, 1959, *The Diary of John Evelyn*, E.S. De Beer (ed.), Oxford University Press, London.

Featley, Daniel, 1645, *The Dippers dipt, or, the Anabaptists Duck'd and Plunged*, London.

Fenner, Dudley, 1588, *The Whole Doctrine of the Sacramentes, plainlie and fullie set downe and declared out of the word of God*, Middleburgh.

Ferrell, Lori Anne, 1998, *Government by Polemic. James I, the King's Preachers, and the Rhetoric of Conformity 1603–1625*, Stanford University Press, Stanford.

Fincham, Kenneth, 1990, *Prelate as Pastor. The Episcopate of James I*, Clarendon Press, Oxford.

—— (ed.), 1993, *The Early Stuart Church 1603–1642*, Stanford University Press, Stanford.

——, 2000, 'Clerical Conformity from Whitgift to Laud', in Peter Lake and Michael Questier (eds), *Conformity and Orthodoxy in the English Church, c.1560–1660*, Boydell Press, Woodbridge, pp.125–58.

——, forthcoming, 'The Restoration of Altars in the 1630s', *History Journal*.

Firth, C.H., and Rait, R.S. (eds), 1911, *Acts and Ordinances of the Interregnum 1642–1659*, 3 vols, H.M. Stationery Office, Wyman & Sons, London.

Fitzer, Joseph, 1992, 'Augustinian Roots of Calvin's Eucharistic Thought', in Richard C. Gamble (ed.), *Calvin's Ecclesiology: Sacraments and Deacons*, Garland Publishing, New York and London.

Fleming, R., 1995, 'The Fulfilling of the Scripture', in J. Couper et al. (eds), *Scotland Saw His Glory*, reprint by International Awakening Press, Illinois.

Fletcher, J.M., 1986, 'The Faculty of Arts', in James McConica (ed.), *The History of the University of Oxford*, Clarendon Press, Oxford.

Forbes, Eric, 1983, 'Philosophy and Science Teaching in the Seventeenth Century', in Gordon Donaldson (ed.), *Four Centuries. Edinburgh University Life*, University of Edinburgh, pp.28–37.

Forbes, John (of Alford), 1642, *A Preparation Sermon to the Lords Table*, Delft.

Forbes, John (of Corse), 1924, *The First Book of the Irenicum*, trans. E.G. Selwyn, Cambridge University Press, Cambridge.

——, Diary, unpublished. MS 635 Aberdeen University Special Collection.

Forbes, William, 1850–56, *Considerationes Modestae et Pacifice*, Library of Anglo-Catholic Theology, 2 vols, Parker, Oxford.

Ford, John D., 1995, 'Conformity in Conscience: The Structure of the Perth Articles Debate in Scotland, 1618–38', *Journal of Ecclesiastical History*, 46, pp.256–77.

Ford, Simon, 1657, *A Short Catechism declaring the practical use of the Covenant-interest, and baptism of the infancy-seed of believers*, London.

Foster, Andrew, 2000, 'Archbishop Richard Neile Revisited', in Peter Lake and Michael Questier (eds), *Conformity and Orthodoxy in the English Church, c.1560–1660*, The Boydell Press, Woodbridge, pp.159–78.

Foster, Stephen, 1978, *Notes from the Caroline Underground*, Archon Books, Hamden CT.

Furcha, E.J. and Pipkin, H.Wayne, 1984, *Prophet Pastor Protestant. The Work of Huldrych Zwingli After Five Hundred Years*, Pickwick Publications, Allison Park.

Galloway, Bruce, 1986, *The Union of England and Scotland 1603–1608*, John Donald Publishers Ltd, Edinburgh.

Galloway, Patrick, 1588, *A catechism: conteyning summarely the chief points of Christian religion*.

Gataker, Thomas, 1624, *A Discussion of the Popish Doctrine of Transubstantiation*, London.

——, 1697–98, *Opera Critica*, 2 vols, Trojecti ad Rhenum.

Gatford, Lionel, 1654, *A Petition for the Vindication of the Publique use of the Book of Common-Prayer*, London.

Gauden, John, 1661, *Considerations Touching the Liturgy of the Church of England*, London.

——, 1688 edn, *The Whole Duty of a Communicant*, London.

George, Timothy, 1990, 'John Calvin and the Agreement of Zurich', in Timothy George (ed.), *John Calvin and the Church*, Westminster/John Knox, Louisville, pp.42–58.

Geree, John, 1646, *Vindicae Paedo-Baptismi: or a Vindication of Infant Baptism, in a full Answer to Mr. Tombes his Twelve Arguments in his Answer to Mr. Marshall's Sermon*, London.

Gerrish, Brian A., 1982, *The Old Protestantism and the New. Essays on the Reformation Heritage*, University of Chicago Press, Chicago.

——, 1992, 'The Lord's Supper in the Reformed Confessions', in Donald K. McKim (ed.), *Major Themes in the Reformed Tradition,* Eerdmans, Grand Rapids, pp.245–58.

——, 1993, *Grace and Gratitude: The Eucharistic Theology of John Calvin*, Fortress Press, Minneapolis.

Gillespie, George, 1649, *A Treatise of Miscellanie Questions*, Edinburgh.

——, 1846, *Notes of Debates and Proceedings of the Assembly of Divines and other Commissioners at Westminster, February 1644 to January 1645*, D. Meek (ed.), Oliver and Boyd, Edinburgh.

——, 1993, *A Dispute Against English Popish Ceremonies*, C. Coldwell (ed.), Naphtali Press, Dallas.

Gorham, G.C., 1857, *Gleanings of a Few Scattered Ears during the Period of the Reformation in England*, London.

Gove, Richard, 1654, *The Communicants Guide*, London.

Green, Ian, 1996, *The Christian's ABC: Catechisms and Catechizing in England c.1530–1740*, Clarendon Press, Oxford.

Grisbrooke, W. Jardine, 1958, *Anglican Liturgies of the Seventeenth and Eighteenth Centuries*, SPCK, London.

Grislis, Egil, 2000, review of *Two Faces of Elizabethan Anglican Theology, Church History* 69.

Guild, William, 1627, *A Compend of the Controversies of Religion*, Aberdeen 1627.

——, 1639, *The Christian Passover*, n.p.

Hall, Basil, 1993, 'Cranmer, the Eucharist and the Foreign Divines', in P. Ayris and D. Selwyn (eds), *Thomas Cranmer: Churchman and Scholar*, The Boydell Press, Woodbridge.

Hall, D.D., 1987, 'On Common Ground: The Coherence of American Puritan Studies', *William and Mary Quarterly* 44, pp.193–229.

Hall, Joseph, 1634, *Works*, London.

Hammond, Henry, 1684, *The Works of Dr. Hammond in Four Volumes*, London.

Harding, Thomas and Bruce, 1996, *Patterns of Worship in the United Church of Canada*, Evensong Publications, Toronto.

Haugaard, William P., 1970, 'John Calvin and the Catechism of Alexander Nowell', *Archiv für Reformationsgeschichte* 61, pp.50–65.

Hemming, Laurence Paul (ed.), 2000, *Radical Orthodoxy? – A Catholic Enquiry*, Ashgate, Aldershot.

Henderson, Alexander, 1641, *The Government and Order of the Church of Scotland*, Edinburgh.

——, 1867, *Sermons, Prayers, and Pulpit Addresses by Alexander Henderson 1638*, Thomas Martin (ed.), John Maclaren, Edinburgh.

Henderson, J.M., 1925-26, 'An "Advertisement" about the Service Book, 1637', *Scottish Historical Review* 23, pp.193–204.

Heron, Alasdair, 1983, *Table and Tradition*, The Handsel Press, Edinburgh.

Hildersham, Arthur, 1609, *108 Lectures on the Fourth (Chapter) of John*, London.

——, 1619a, *A Briefe Forme of Examination*, London.

——, 1619b, *The Doctrine of Communicating Worthily in the Lord's Supper*, London.

——, 1635, *152 Lectures on Psalm 51*, London.

Hirst, Derek, 1999, *England in Conflict 1603–1660*, Oxford University Press (Arnold), New York.

Holifield, E. Brookes, 1974, *The Covenant Sealed: Puritan Sacramental Theology in Old and New England 1570–1720*, Yale University Press, New Haven and London.

Holmes, Nathaniel, 1646, *A Vindication of Baptizing Believers Infants. In some Animadversions upon Mr. Tombes His Exercitations about Infant Baptisme*, London.

Hooker, Richard, 1975–94, *Of the Lawes of Ecclesiasticall Politie*, Folger Library Edition, Cambridge MA.

Hoyle, Joshua, 1641, *A Rejoynder to Master Malone's Reply Concerning Reall Presence*, Dublin.

Hunt, Arnold, 1998a, 'Laurance Chaderton and the Hampton Court Conference', in Susan Wabuda and Caroline Litzenberger (eds), *Belief and Practice in Reformation England*, Ashgate, pp.207–28.

——, 1998b, 'The Lord's Supper in Early Modern England', *Past and Present*, 161, pp.39–83.

Hutton, Ronald, 1985, *The Restoration. A Political and Religious History of England and Wales 1658–1667,* Clarendon Press, Oxford.

Hyman, Elizabeth Hannan, 1995, 'A Church Militant: Scotland, 1661–1690', *Sixteenth Century Journal* 26, pp.49–74.

Jackson, Thomas, 1844, *The Works of Thomas Jackson, DD*, 12 vols, Oxford University Press, Oxford.

Jacobs, Elfriede, 1978, *Die Sakramentslehre Wilhelm Farels*, Theologische Verlag, Zurich.

Jacobson, William (ed.), 1874, *Fragmentary Illustrations of the History of the Book of Common Prayer*, John Murray, London.

Jammer, Max, 1970, *Concepts of Space*, Harvard University Press, Cambridge MA.

Jardine, Lisa, 1974, 'The Place of Dialectic teaching in sixteenth-century Cambridge', *Studies in the Renaissance* 21, pp.31–62.

Jasper, R.C.D., 1989, *The Development of the Anglican Liturgy 1662–1980*, SPCK, London.

Jeanes, G., 1998, 'Signs of God's Promise. Thomas Cranmer's Sacramental Theology and Baptismal Liturgy', unpublished PhD Thesis, University of Wales.

Johnson, Margot (ed.), 1990 *Thomas Cranmer,* Turnstone Ventures, Durham.

—— (ed.), 1997, *John Cosin*, Turnstone Ventures, Durham.

Kendall, R.T., 1979, *Calvin and the English Calvinists to 1649*, Oxford University Press, Oxford.

Knappen, M.M., 1933, *Two Elizabethan Diaries by Richard Rogers and Samuel Ward*, American Society of Church History, Chicago.

L'Estrange, Hammon, 1846, *The Alliance of Divine Offices*, Parker, Oxford.

Lake, Peter, 1988a, *Anglicans and Puritans? Presbyterian and English Conformist Thought from Whitgift to Hooker*, London.

——, 1988b, 'Serving God and the Time: The Calvinist Conformity of Robert Sanderson', *Journal of British Studies* 27 (1988), pp.81–16.

——, 1993, 'Defining Puritanism – again?', in Francis J. Bremer (ed.), *Puritanism: Transatlantic Perspectives on a Seventeenth-Century Anglo-American Faith*, Massachusetts Historical Society, Boston, pp.3–29.

——, 2000, 'Moving the Goal Posts? Modified Subscription and the Construction of Conformity in the Early Stuart Church' in P. Lake and M. Questier (eds), *Conformity and Orthodoxy in the English Church, c.1560–1660*, The Boydell Press, Woodbridge, pp.179–205.

—— and Michael Questier (eds), 2000, *Conformity and Orthodoxy in the English Church, c.1560–1660*, The Boydell Press, Woodbridge.

Laud, William, 1847-60, *Works*, Library of Anglo-Catholic Theology, 7 vols, Parker, Oxford.

——, 1901, *A Relation of the Conference between William Laud Late Archbishop of Canterbury and Mr. Fisher the Jesuit*, C.H. Simpkinson (ed.), Macmillan, London.

Lee, Maurice, 1990, *Great Britain's Solomon: James VI and I in His Three Kingdoms*, University of Illinois Press, Urbana and Chicago.

Leighton, Roberts, 1816, *The Genuine Works of R.T. Leighton, DD*, 4 vols, London.

Leishman, Thomas, 1901, *The Westminster Directory*, Blackwood, Edinburgh.

Leith, John, 1963, *Creeds of the Church*, Aldine Publishing Company, Chicago.

Lightfoot, John, 1824, *The Whole Works of the Rev. John Lightfoot DD*, J.R. Pitman (ed.), London.

Lindberg, David C., 1992, *The Beginnings of Western Science*, University of Chicago Press, Chicago and London.

Lindsay, David, 1619, *The Reasons of a Pastors Resolution, touching the Reverend receiving of the holy Communion*, London.

Low, W.L., 1923, *The True Catholic Doctrine of the Holy Eucharist*, Scottish Chronicle Press, Edinburgh.

McAdoo, H.R., 1988, *The Eucharistic Theology of Jeremy Taylor Today*, Canterbury Press, Norwich.

McAdoo, Henry and Stevenson, Kenneth W., 1995, *The Mystery of the Eucharist in the Anglican Tradition*, Canterbury Press, Norwich.

McCabe, Herbert, 1987, *God Matters*, Chapman, London.

——, 1999, 'The Eucharist as Language', *Modern Churchman* 15, pp.131–41.

McCoy, F.N., 1974, *Robert Baillie and the Second Scots Reformation*, University of California Press, Berkeley and Los Angeles.

MacCulloch, Dairmaid, 1996, *Thomas Cranmer*, Yale University Press, New Haven.

——, 'Hooker's Reputation', forthcoming.

McCullough, Peter E., 1998, *Sermons at Court. Politics and Religion in Elizabethan and Jacobean Preaching*, Cambridge University Press, Cambridge.

MacDonald, Alan R., 1998, *The Jacobean Kirk, 1567–1625. Sovereignty, Polity and Liturgy*, Ashgate Publishing, Aldershot and Brookfield.

Mackay, P.H.R., 1975–77, 'The Reception Given to the Five Articles of Perth', *Records of the Scottish Church History Society* 19, pp.185–201.

McLelland, Joseph C., 1957, *The Visible Words of God*, Oliver and Boyd, Edinburgh.

—— and Duffield, G.E., 1989, *The Life, Early Letters and Eucharistic Writings of Peter Martyr*, Sutton Courtenay Press, Appleford, Abingdon.

Maltby, Judith, 1998, *Prayer Book and People in Elizabethan and Early Stuart England*, Cambridge University Press, Cambridge.

Marshall, Paul V., 1993, *The Voice of a Stranger*, Church Hymnal Corporation, New York.

Marshall, Stephen, 1644, *A Sermon of the Baptizing of Infants preached in the Abbey-Church at Westminster at the Morning Lecture Appointed by the Honorable House of Commons*, London.

——, 1646, *A Defence of Infant Baptism: in answer to two Treatises, and an Appendix to them concerning it*, London.

Martin, Joyce Bradbury, 1999, 'An Irenic Theologian: William Forbes, First Bishop of Edinburgh', unpublished MLitt thesis, University of Oxford.

Maxwell, W.D., 1965, *The Liturgical Portions of the Genevan Service Book*, Faith Press, London.

Michaelson, John, 1620, *The Lawfulnes of Kneeling, in the act of Receiving the Sacrament of the Lordes Supper*, Aberdeen.

Milbank, John, 1997, *The Word Made Strange*, Blackwell, Oxford.

—— , Pickstock, C. and Ward, G. (eds), 1998, *Radical Orthodoxy: A New Theology*, Routledge, London.

Milton, Anthony, 1995, *Catholic and Reformed. The Roman and Protestant Churches in English Protestant Thought, 1600–1640*, Cambridge University Press, Cambridge.

Montagu, Richard, 1624, *A Gagg for the new Gospell? No: A new Gagg for an old Goose*, London.

——, 1625, *Appello Caesarem. A Just Appeale from two unjust informers*, London.

——, 1640, *Theanthropikon: pars posterior*, London.

Morgan, Irvonwy, 1957, *Prince Charles's Puritan Chaplain*, Allen and Unwin, London.

Morgan, John, 1986, *Godly Learning: Puritan Attitudes towards Reason, Learning and Education 1560–1640*, Cambridge University Press, Cambridge.

Morley, George, 1683a, *A Vindication of the Argument drawn from Sense, against Transubstantiation, in Several Treatises*, London.

——, 1683b, *Several Treatises, written upon Several Occasions*, London.

Morrill, John (ed.), 1982, *Reactions to the English Civil War 1642–1649*, London.

——, 1994, 'A British patriarchy? Ecclesiastical imperialism under the early Stuarts', in Anthony Fletcher and Peter Roberts (eds), *Religion, culture and society in early modern Britain*, Cambridge University Press, Cambridge, pp.209–37.

Morton, Thomas, 1618, *A Defence of the Innocencie of the Three ceremonies of the Church of England*, London.

——, 1631, *Of the Institution of the sacrament of the Blessed Bodie and Blood of Christ*, London.

Mullan, David, 1995, 'Theology in the Church of Scotland 1618-c.1640: A Calvinist Consensus?', *Sixteenth Century Journal* 26, pp.595–617.

——, 2000, *Scottish Puritanism 1590–1638*, Clarendon Press, Oxford.

Muller, Richard A., 1988, *Christ and the Decree*, Baker Book House, Grand Rapids.

Musculus, Wolfgang, 1578, *Common Places*, London.

Nicholson, William, 1842, *An Exposition of the Catechism of the Right Reverend Father in God, William Nicholson*, Parker, Oxford.

Old, H.O., 1975, 'Bullinger and the Scholastic Works on Baptism. A Study in the History of Christian Worship', in *Heinrich Bullinger 1504–1575. Gesammelte Aufsätze zum 400. Todestag*, Theologischer Verlag, Zurich.

Palmer, Herbert, 1645, *An Endeavour of Making the Principles of Christian Religion*, London.

Patterson, W.B., 1997, *King James VI and I and the Reunion of Christendom*, Cambridge University Press, Cambridge.

Pemble, William, 1628, *An Introduction to the Worthy Receiving the Sacrament of the Lord's Supper*, London.

Perkins, William, 1616–18, *Works*, 3 vols, J. Legatt and C. Legge, Cambridge.

Pickstock, Catherine, 1993, 'Liturgy and Language: The Sacred Polis', in Paul Bradshaw and Bryan Spinks (eds), *Liturgy in Dialogue*, SPCK, London, pp.115–37.

——, 1997, *After Writing. On the Liturgical Consumation of Philosophy*, Blackwell, Oxford.

——, 1999, 'Thomas Aquinas and the Quest for the Eucharist', *Modern Theology* 15, pp.160–80.

Pope, Mary, 1647, *A Treatise of Magistracy*, London.

Preston, John, 1631, *Three Sermons upon the sacrament of the Lords Supper*, London.

Prestwich, Menna (ed.), 1985, *International Calvinism 1541–1715*, Clarendon Press, Oxford.

Prynne, William, 1646, *Canterburies Doome*, London.

Raitt, Jill, 1972, *The Eucharistic Theology of Theodore Beza*, AAR, Chambersburg.

Randall, John, 1630, *Three and twentie Sermons: or, catechisticall Lectures Shewing the Due Order of Receiving the Lord's Supper*, London.

Raymer, Victoria, 1981, 'Durham House and the Emergence of Laudian Piety', unpublished PhD dissertation, Harvard University, 1981.

Read, Charles, 2000, '"No way to run a railway" – Revising the Eucharist for Common Worship', *Anvil* 17, pp.259–68.

Reidy, Maurice F., 1955, *Bishop Lancelot Andrewes*, Loyola University Press, Chicago.

Reynolds, Edward, 1638, *Meditations on the Sacraments of the Lords Last Supper*, London.

——, 1679, *Works*, London.

Rigg, J.W., 1985, 'The Development of Calvin's Baptismal Theology 1536–1560', unpublished PhD dissertation, University of Notre Dame.

Rodgers, Dirk W., 1994, *John a Lasco in England*, Peter Lang, New York.

Rogers, Richard, 1619, *The Practice of Christianity*, London.

Rogers, Thomas, 1608, *Two Dialogues or Conferences. Concerning Kneeling in the very act of receiving the sacamental bread and wine, in the Supper of the Lord*, London.

——, 1639 edn, *The Faith, doctrine and religion professed and protected in the realm of England*, London.

Rollock, Robert, 1596, *Quaestiones et Responsiones Aliquot et Foedere Die: Deque Sacramento quod Foederis Dei signillum est*, Edinburgh.

——, 1844 and 1849, *Selected Works of Robert Rollock*, 2 vols, The Woodrow Society, Edinburgh.

Rorem, P., 1989, *Calvin and Bullinger on the Lord's Supper*, Alcuin/Grow Liturgical Study 12, Grove Books, Bramcote.

Russell, C. (ed.), 1973, *The Causes of the English Civil War*, Macmillan, London.

Russell, John L., 1974, 'Cosmological Teaching in the Seventeenth-Century Scottish Universities, Part 1', *Journal of the History of Astronomy* 5, pp.122–32.

Rutherford, Samuel, 1644, *The Due Right of Presbyteries, or a Peaceable Plea for the government of the Church of Scotland,* London.

——, 1655, *The Covenant of Life Opened,* Edinburgh.

——, 1877, *Fourteen Communion Sermons by Samuel Rutherford,* A.A. Bonar (ed.), Charles Glass, Glasgow, reprint James A. Dickson, 1986.

——, 1886, *The Soume of Christian Religion,* in A.F. Mitchell (ed.), *Catechisms of the Second Reformation,* James Nisbet, London.

Sanderson, Robert, 1854, *The Works of Robert Sanderson,* 6 vols, William Jacobson (ed.), Oxford University Press, Oxford.

Sasse, Herman, 1977, *This is My Body,* Lutheran Publishing House, Adelaide.

Schaff, P., 1988, *The Creeds of Christendom,* 3 vols, Baker Book House edn, Grand Rapids.

Schmidt, Leigh Eric, 1989, *Holy Fairs. Scottish Communions and American Revivals in the Early Modern Period,* Princeton University Press, Princeton.

Seaver, Paul S., 1970, *The Puritan Lectureships 1560–1662,* Stanford University Press, Stanford.

Secor, Phillip, 1999, *Richard Hooker. Prophet of Anglicanism,* Burns and Oats, Tunbridge Wells.

Shriver, Fred, 1982, 'Hampton Court Re-Visited: James I and the Puritans', *Journal of Ecclesiastical History* 33, pp.48–71.

Simpson, Martin A., 1981, 'The Hampton Court Conference, January 1604', *Scottish Church History Society Records* 21, pp.27–41.

Smythe, C.H., 1926, *Cranmer and the Reformation under Edward VI,* Cambridge University Press, Cambridge.

Soskice, Janet Martin, 1987, *Metaphor and Religious Language,* Clarendon Press, Oxford.

Spalding, James, 1830, *The History of the Troubles and Memorable Transactions in Scotland from 1624–1645,* King, Aberdeen.

Spalding, John, 1850–51, *Memorials of the Troubles in Scotland and in England 1624–1645,* 2 vols, Bennett, Aberdeen.

Sparrow, Anthony, 1839, *A Rationale Upon the Book of Common Prayer of the Church of England,* Parker, Oxford.

Spinks, Bryan D., 1984a, *Freedom or Order? The Eucharistic Liturgy amongst the English Independent or Congregationalist Tradition, 1645–1980,* Pittsburgh Theological Monographs, Pickwick Publications, Alison Park.

——, 1984b, *From the Lord, and 'The Best Reformed Churches',* CLV, Rome.

——, 1990a, '"And with thy Holy Spirite and Worde": Further Thoughts on the Source of Cranmer's Petition for sanctification in the 1549 Communion Service', in Margot Johnson (ed.), *Thomas Cranmer,* Turnstone Ventures, Durham, pp.94–102.

——, 1990b, 'The Ascension and the Vicarious Humanity of Christ: The Christology and Soteriology Behind the Church of Scotland's Anamnesis and Epiklesis', in J. Neil Alexander (ed.), *Time and Community,* Pastoral Press, Washington, pp.185–201.

——, 1991, 'Two Seventeenth-Century Examples of Lex Credendi, Lex Orandi: The Baptismal and Eucharistic Theologies and Liturgies of Jeremy Taylor and Richard Baxter', *Studia Liturgica* 21, pp.165–89.

——, 1995a, 'Briefe and Perspicuous Text: Plain and Pertinent Doctrine: Behind "Of the Preaching of the Word" in the Westminster Directory', in Martin Dudley (ed.), *Like a Two-Edged Sword*, Canterbury Press, Norwich, pp.91–111.

——, 1995b, 'Calvin's Baptismal Theology and the Making of the Strasbourg and Genevan Baptismal Liturgies 1540 and 1542', *Scottish Journal of Theology* 48, pp.55–78.

——, 1995c, 'Luther's Timely Theology of Unilateral Baptism', in *Lutheran Quarterly* 9, pp.23–45.

——, 1996, '"Freely by His Grace": Baptismal Doctrine and the Reform of the Baptismal Liturgy in the Church of Scotland', in Nathan Mitchell and John Baldovin (eds), *Rule of Prayer, Rule of Faith*, Liturgical Press, Collegeville, pp.218–42.

——, 1999, *Two Faces of Elizabethan Anglican Theology. Sacraments and Salvation in the Thought of William Perkins and Richard Hooker*, Drew University Studies in Liturgy 9, Scarecrow Press, Lanham and London.

——, 2000, 'What was wrong with Mr. Cosin's "Couzening" Devotions? Deconstructing an Episode in Seventeenth-Century Anglican "Liturgical Hagiography"', *Worship* 74, pp.308–29.

Sprott, George W., 1871, *Scottish Liturgies of the Reign of James VI. The Book of Common Prayer and Administration of the Sacraments*, Edmonston and Douglas, Edinburgh.

Spurr, John, 1991, *The Restoration Church of England 1646–1689*, Yale University Press, New Haven and London.

Stephens, W.P., 1970, *The Holy Spirit in the Theology of Martin Bucer*, Cambridge University Press, Cambridge.

——, 1984, 'Zwingli's Sacramental Views', in E.J. Furcha and H. Wayne Pipkin (eds) *Prophet, Pastor, Protestant*, Pickwick Publications, Allison Park, pp.155–69.

——, 1986, *The Theology of Huldrych Zwingli*, Clarendon Press, Oxford.

Stevenson, David, 1974a, 'Conventicles in the Kirk, 1619–37. The Emergence of a Radical Party', *Records of the Scottish Church History Society* 18, pp.99–114.

——, 1974b, 'The Radical Party in the Kirk, 1637–1645', *Journal of Ecclesiastical History* 26, pp.59–79.

——, 1997, *Revolution and Religion in 17th-century Scotland*, Variorum Ashgate, Aldershot.

Stevenson, Kenneth W., 1994, *Covenant of Grace Renewed. A Vision of the Eucharist in the Seventeenth Century*, Darton, Longman and Todd, London.

——, 1995, '"Human Nature Honoured": Absolution in Lancelot Andrewes', in M. Dudley (ed.), *Like a Two-Edged Sword*, Canterbury Press, Norwich.

——, 1997, *The Mystery of Baptism in the Anglican Tradition*, The Canterbury Press, Norwich.

——, 1999, 'Lancelot Andrewes at Holyrood: The 1617 Whitsun Sermon in Perspective', *Scottish Journal of Theology* 52, pp.455–75.

Stone, Darwell, 1909, *A History of the Doctrine of the Holy Eucharist*, 2 vols, Longmans, London.

Strype, John, 1821, *The Life and Acts of Matthew Parker*, 1, Clarendon Press, Oxford, p.302.

Sutton, Christopher, 1841 edn, *Godly Meditations upon the Most Holy Sacrament of the Lord's Supper, 1601,* Appleton, New York.

Taylor, Jeremy, 1847–52, *The Works of Jeremy Taylor*, R. Heber and C.P. Eden (eds), 10 vols, Longmans, London.

Thornborough, John, 1630, *The Last Will and Testament of Jesus Christ, touching the blessed sacrament*, London.

Thorndike, Herbert, 1844–56, *The Theological Works of Herbert Thorndike*, 6 vols, Parker, Oxford.

Tombes, John, 1646a, *An Apology or Plea for Two Treatises, and Appendix to them Concerning Infant Baptisme*, London.

——, 1646b, *Two Treatises and an Appendix to Them concerning Infant-Baptisme*, London.

Toon, Peter, 1967, *The Emergence of Hyper-Calvinism in English Nonconformity 1689–1765*, Olive Tree, London.

Torrance, T.F., 1958, Report of the Special Commission on Baptism, *Reports to the General Assembly of the Church of Scotland.*

—— (ed.), *The School of Faith*, James Clarke, London, 1959.

——, 1969, *Space, Time and Incarnation*, Oxford University Press, London and New York.

——, 1988, *The Hermeneutics of John Calvin*, Scottish Academic Press, Edinburgh.

——, 1996, *Scottish Theology. From John Knox to John McLeod Campbell*, T & T Clark, Edinburgh.

Trigg, Jonathan D., 1994, *Baptism in the Theology of Martin Luther*, Brill, Leiden.

Tuckney, Anthony, 1628, 'A briefe and pithy catechism', in MS III.13.I. Emmanuel College Library, Cambridge.

Twisse, William, 1637, *A briefe Catecheticall Exposition of Christian Doctrine*, London.

Tyacke, Nicholas, 1973, 'Puritanism, Arminianism and Counter-reformation', in C. Russell (ed.), *The Origins of the English Civil War,* London.

——, 1987, *Anti-Calvinists. The Rise of English Arminianism c.1590–1640*, Clarendon Press, Oxford.

——, 2000, 'Lancelot Andrewes and the Myth of Anglicanism', in P. Lake and M. Questier (eds), *Conformity and Orthodoxy in the English Church, c.1560–1660*, The Boydell Press, Woodbridge, pp.5–33.

Tylenda, Joseph N., 1981, 'The Ecumenical Intention of Calvin's Early Eucharistic Teaching', in Brian A. Gerrish (ed.), *Reformatio Perennis. Essays on Calvin and the Reformation in honor of Ford Lewis Battles*, Pickwick Press, Pittsburgh, pp.27–47.

Usher, R.G., 1910, *The Reconstruction of the Church of England*, 2 vols, Appleton, New York and London.

Ussher, James, 1864, *The Whole Works of the Most Rev.James Ussher, DD.*, C.R. Erlington (ed.), Hodges and Smith & Co., Dublin 1864.

Vines, Richard, 1657, *A Treatise of the Institution, Right Administration and Receiving of the Sacrament of the Lord's Supper*, London.

Wabuda, Susan and Litzenberger C. (eds), 1998, *Belief and Practice in Reformation England*, Ashgate, Aldershot.

Walker, James, 1872, *The Theology and Theologians of Scotland*, T & T Clark, Edinburgh.

Ward, Graham, 1997, *The Postmodern God*, Blackwell, Oxford.

Webster, Tom, 1994, *Stephen Marshall and Finchingfield*, Essex Records Office, Chelmsford.

——, 1997, *Godly Clergy in early Stuart England. The Caroline Puritan Movement, c.1620–1643*, Cambridge University Press, Cambridge.

Weir, D.A., 1990, *The Origins of the Federal Theology in Sixteenth-century Reformation Thought*, Clarendon Press, Oxford 1990.

Welsby, Paul, 1958, *Lancelot Andrewes 1555–1626*, SPCK, London.

Welsh, John, 1602, *Popery Anatomized*, Edinburgh.

Wendel, F., 1963, *Calvin. The Origins and Development of his Religious Thought*, Collins, London.

Westminster Assembly Ms. Minutes, Dr. Williams's Library, London.

Westminster Confession of Faith, 1990, Free Presbyterian Publications, Glasgow.

White, Francis, 1617, *The Orthodox Faith and way to the Church explained and Justified*, London.

——, 1624, *A Replie to Jesuit Fisher's Answer*, London.

White, Peter, 1992, *Predestination, Policy and Polemic*, Cambridge University Press, Cambridge.

——, 1993, 'The via media in the early Stuart Church', in Kenneth Fincham (ed.), *The Early Stuart Church 1603–1642*, Stanford University, Stanford, pp.211–30.

Williard, G.W., 1954, *The Commentary of Dr. Zacherias Ursinus on the Heidelberg Catechism*, Eerdmans, Grand Rapids.

Wolterstorff, Nicholas, 1996, 'Sacraments as Action, not Presence', D. Brown and A. Loades (eds), *Christ: The Sacramental Word*, SPCK, London, pp.103–22.

Wright, David, 1994, 'Infant Baptism and the Christian Community in Bucer', in David Wright (ed.), *Martin Bucer. Reforming Church and Community*, Cambridge University Press, Cambridge, pp.95–106.

Index

237